THE CAUSE OF ALL NATIONS

THE CAUSE
OF ALL NATIONS

*An International History
of the American Civil War*

DON H. DOYLE

BASIC BOOKS
A Member of the Perseus Books Group
New York

Published by Basic Books,
A Member of the Perseus Books Group

Books published by Basic Books are available at special discounts for bulk purchases in the United States by corporations, institutions, and other organizations. For more information, please contact the Special Markets Department at the Perseus Books Group, 2300 Chestnut Street, Suite 200, Philadelphia, PA 19103, or call (800) 810-4145, ext. 5000, or e-mail special.markets@perseusbooks.com.

Set in 11.5-point Adobe Garamond Pro

A catalog record for this book is available from the Library of Congress.
Library of Congress Control Number: 2014953875
ISBN: 978-0-465-02967-9 (hard cover)
ISBN: 978-0-465-08092-2 (e-book)

10 9 8 7 6 5 4 3 2 1

This one is for
Jackson Doyle DeWitt
Charlie Doyle Baker
Caroline Claire DeWitt
Citizens of a new world, heirs of a vast future

The world is a solidarity, and the cause of America is the cause of Liberty. So long as there shall be across the Atlantic a society of thirty millions of men, living happily and peacefully under a government of their choice, with laws made by themselves, liberty will cast her rays over Europe like an illuminating pharos. America disencumbered of slavery will be the country of all ardent spirits, of all generous hearts. But should liberty become eclipsed in the new world, it would become night in Europe, and we shall see the work of Washington, of the Franklins, of the Hamiltons, spit upon and trampled under foot by the whole school which believes only in violence and in success.

—ÉDOUARD LABOULAYE, PROFESSOR AT THE
COLLÈGE DE FRANCE, PARIS, 1864

CONTENTS

List of Illustrations   *xi*

Time Line of Key Events, 1860–1870   *xiii*

Introduction: American Crisis, Global Struggle   1

PART I
ONLY A CIVIL WAR?

CHAPTER 1   Garibaldi's Question   15

CHAPTER 2   We Are a Nation   27

CHAPTER 3   We Will Wrap the World in Flames   50

PART II
THE AMERICAN QUESTION

CHAPTER 4   The Republican Experiment   85

CHAPTER 5   The Empires Return   106

CHAPTER 6   Foreign Translations   131

CHAPTER 7   Foreign Legions   158

PART III
LIBERTY'S WAR

CHAPTER 8   The Latin Strategy   185

CHAPTER 9   Garibaldi's Answer   210

CHAPTER 10   Union and Liberty   240

CHAPTER 11   The Unspeakable Dilemma   257

CHAPTER 12   Shall Not Perish   281

Coda: Republican Risorgimento   299

Acknowledgments   *315*

Abbreviations   *319*

Notes   *321*

Index   *371*

LIST OF ILLUSTRATIONS

1. *The Triumph*   13
2. Henry Shelton Sanford   18
3. Giuseppe Garibaldi   19
4. Jefferson Davis's inauguration   33
5. Jefferson Davis   34
6. *The Outbreak of the Rebellion in the United States in 1861*   53
7. William Seward and Abraham Lincoln   66
8. Carl Schurz   71
9. John Bigelow   74
10. Thurlow Weed   79
11. *The Pending Conflict*   83
12. Frederick Salomon   93
13. William Howard Russell   101
14. Benito Juárez and Abraham Lincoln   116
15. Cinco de Mayo, 1862   125
16. Matías Romero   128
17. *The Arrival of Maximiliano and Carlota in Veracruz, 1864*   130
18. Agénor de Gasparin   133
19. Mary Louise Booth   136
20. Édouard Laboulaye   139
21. Karl Marx with his wife, Jenny   152
22. Recruitment poster for the Garibaldi Guard   161
23. German recruitment poster   161
24. Irish recruitment poster   162

25. Immigrant recruitment poster 164
26. *The Garibaldi Guard Marching in Review* 172
27. *The American Flag* 183
28. Judah P. Benjamin 189
29. Edwin De Leon 194
30. James Murray Mason 199
31. John Slidell 201
32. Giuseppe Garibaldi with Dr. Nélaton 228
33. Confederate cotton bond prices 259
34. Pope Pius IX and his court 263
35. *Something for Paddy* 268
36. *Britannia Sympathises with Columbia* 293
37. The French medal for Mrs. Lincoln 296
38. *The Execution of Emperor Maximilian of Mexico* 301
39. *La Liberté éclairant le monde* (Liberty enlightening the world) 312

TIME LINE OF KEY EVENTS,
1860–1870

1860

May–September: Giuseppe Garibaldi and the Thousand conquer southern Italy

November 6: Abraham Lincoln elected president of the United States

December 20: South Carolina declares secession; Mississippi, Florida, Alabama, Georgia, Louisiana, and Texas follow by early February

1861

January 11: Mexico's Reform War ends with victory of Benito Juárez and republicans

February 4: Delegates of seceding states meet in Montgomery, Alabama, to create the Confederate States of America (CSA)

February 13: CSA approves foreign commissions to Washington and Europe

February 18: Jefferson Davis inaugurated as provisional CSA president for one year

March 2: US Congress passes Morrill Tariff

March 3: Czar Alexander II emancipates Russia's serfs

March 4: Abraham Lincoln's inaugural address defines secession as rebellion without cause

March 18: President Pedro Santana of Dominican Republic declares reannexation to Spain

April 1: Secretary of State William Henry Seward advises Lincoln to confront Spain and France

April 12: CSA attacks Fort Sumter

April 15: Lincoln calls for troops from all states; Henry Sanford, head of Union secret service, arrives in Europe

April 17: Virginia followed by Arkansas, Tennessee, and North Carolina secede

April 19: Lincoln announces plans to blockade Southern ports

April 29: CSA European Commission—William Yancey, Pierre Rost, and Ambrose Dudley Mann—convenes in London

May 13: Charles Francis Adams, US minister to Britain, arrives in London; Britain declares neutrality, recognizing both sides as belligerents; France, the Netherlands, Spain, Belgium, Portugal, Brazil, and Hawaii follow by August

June: Mary Louis Booth translates Agénor de Gasparin's pro-Union *Uprising of a Great People*

July 19: President Benito Juárez suspends payment on Mexico's foreign debt for two years

July 21: CSA routs Union at First Battle of Bull Run

September 8–9: Henry Sanford meets with Giuseppe Garibaldi at Caprera

September 14: Carl Schurz, US minister to Spain, urges Seward to adopt emancipation; John Bigelow, US consul general, arrives in Paris to promote public diplomacy

October 31: Tripartite Treaty of London: France, Spain, and Britain agree to invade Mexico

November: James Spence's pro-CSA *The American Union* published in Britain

November 6: Jefferson Davis elected to six-year term as CSA president

November 8: CSA envoys John Slidell and James Mason abducted onboard British ship *Trent*

November 24: US special agents Thurlow Weed, Archbishop John Hughes, and Bishop Charles McIlvaine arrive in Europe and help defuse *Trent* crisis

December 4: Member of Parliament (MP) John Bright's speech at Rochdale, England, urges support of Union

December 8: Tripartite Alliance invasion of Mexico begins with landing of Spanish fleet; British and French follow in early January

December 25: Lincoln and cabinet decide to release Slidell and Mason

1862

January: Carl Schurz meets privately with Lincoln to urge emancipation

January 29: Confederate envoys Slidell, Mason, and Henry Hotze arrive in London

February 22: Jefferson Davis inaugurated as CSA president for six-year term

March 17: Judah P. Benjamin appointed CSA secretary of state

April 9: Breakup of Tripartite Alliance in Mexico; British and Spanish withdraw troops

May 1: Hotze launches CSA journal the *Index* in London; New Orleans captured by Union

May 5: Mexican republican army thwarts French army at Puebla

June 29: Edwin De Leon, CSA special agent for public diplomacy, arrives in Europe

July 1: Seven Days Battle ends Union general George McClellan's Virginia campaign

July 16: Slidell meets Napoleon III at Vichy to discuss cotton bribe and alliance

July 18: British Parliament debates motion by William Lindsay to recognize CSA

July 22: Lincoln announces emancipation plan to cabinet, decides to postpone

August: Gasparin's *America Before Europe* published in New York

August 28–29: CSA routs Union at Second Battle of Bull Run and later advances into Maryland

August 29: Garibaldi wounded at Aspromonte during march on Rome

September 1: Theodore Canisius, US consul to Vienna, invites Garibaldi to lead Union army

September 14: British prime minister Palmerston initiates plan to intervene in American war

September 17: Battle of Antietam; CSA retreats from Maryland

September 22: Lincoln unveils Emancipation Proclamation

October 3: Garibaldi's letter "To the English Nation" urges support of Union as Garibaldi demonstrations break out across Europe

October 6: Emancipation Proclamation publicized in Europe

October 7: William Gladstone's Newcastle speech advocates recognition of CSA

October 18: Pope Pius IX issues public letter to US archbishops, calling for peace in America

October 23: Palmerston postpones British intervention plans

1863

January 1: Emancipation Proclamation enacted; public emancipation meetings in Britain follow

January 22: Polish uprising against Russia distracts Europe for months

March 19: CSA cotton bonds begin sales on European stock exchanges

May 19: French forces defeat Mexican republicans at second Battle of Puebla

June 7: French troops enter Mexico City

June 18: Slidell meets with Napoleon III a third time

June 30: MP John Roebuck's motion to recognize CSA defeated in British Parliament

July 3–4: Union victories at Gettysburg and Vicksburg; cotton bond prices begin steep decline

July 10: Mexico's Council of Notables declares Empire of Mexico; crown to be offered to Archduke Maximilian of Austria

August 4: Benjamin instructs Mason to end CSA mission in Britain; Mason withdraws September 28; Benjamin later expels British consuls in Confederacy

September 4: Father John Bannon sent to Ireland as CSA special agent to thwart Union recruitment

September 25: Russian naval fleet welcomed in New York and later in San Francisco

November 16: Edwin De Leon's intercepted letters published, lead to his dismissal

November 19: Lincoln's Gettysburg Address

December 3: Pope Pius IX issues letter to "President" Jefferson Davis

1864

March 3: Bishop Patrick Lynch appointed CSA special envoy to the Vatican

April 4: US Congress passes resolution opposing monarchy in Mexico and refusing recognition of Maximilian and Empire of Mexico

April 10: Maximilian in Trieste accepts crown as emperor of Mexico

April 11–22: Garibaldi's visit to London sets off enormous demonstrations of support

May 21: Emperor Maximilian and his wife, Charlotte, arrive in Mexico

September: Union general William T. Sherman captures Atlanta, later begins March to the Sea

November 8: Abraham Lincoln wins reelection against General George McClellan

December 8: Pope Pius IX issues "Syllabus of Errors," denouncing liberalism and democracy

December 27: Duncan F. Kenner, CSA special agent, sent to Europe to offer emancipation in exchange for French or British support

1865

January 12: Francis P. Blair Sr. meets with Jefferson Davis to propose peace and united invasion of Mexico under Davis's command

January 31: Thirteenth Amendment abolishing slavery passed by US Congress

February 3: Peace conference at Hampton Roads, Virginia, discusses reunion, invasion of Mexico, and future of slavery, but fails to end war

February 17: Sherman's March arrives at Columbia, South Carolina

February 21: Kenner arrives in Europe and later meets with Slidell, Mason, and Mann

March 4: Lincoln's second inaugural address; Slidell proposes emancipation to Napoleon III in exchange for French aid

March 14: James Mason meets with Palmerston in final plea for recognition

March 22: CSA general Camille de Polignac asks Napoleon III for French support of Louisiana

April 2: Jefferson Davis and CSA government abandon Richmond in flames

April 4: Lincoln visits Richmond

April 9: General Robert E. Lee surrenders CSA army at Appomattox

April 14: John Wilkes Booth assassinates Abraham Lincoln

April 26–June: Public demonstrations and letters of sympathy for Lincoln abroad

May: Grant sends General Philip Sheridan to Texas to intimidate French in Mexico

May 10: Jefferson Davis captured in Georgia and imprisoned

July 15: Spanish forces withdraw from Santo Domingo

September 15: Maximilian adopts the infant Agustín Iturbide as his heir to the Mexican throne

October 11: Morant Bay Rebellion, British massacre of blacks in Jamaica

1866

January 22: Napoleon III announces withdrawal of French troops in Mexico

June 14: Austro-Prussian War begins; Austria cedes land to Bismarck's united Germany and cedes Venice to Italy

1867

March 12: French complete withdrawal of troops from Mexico

May: Hyde Park demonstrations pressure British Parliament to pass Reform Act of 1867

June 19: Maximilian executed by Mexican republicans

July 1: British North America Act creates the Dominion of Canada

October 18: Russia transfers Alaska to United States

1868

September 18: Spain's Glorious Revolution begins; Queen Isabella II later deposed by republic

October 10: Cuba's Ten Years' War for independence and emancipation begins

1870

July 4: Spain passes law gradually ending slavery in Cuba and Puerto Rico

July 19: Franco-Prussian War begins

September 2: Napoleon III captured during war, deposed, later flees to England; France proclaims Third Republic

September 20: Rome, abandoned by French, is taken over by Italy; Papal States constricted to Vatican

AMERICAN CRISIS, GLOBAL STRUGGLE

For a time the war was thought to be confined to our own domestic affairs, but it was soon seen that it involved the destinies
of mankind; its principles and causes shook the politics of Europe to the centre, and from Lisbon to Pekin divided the governments of the world.

—George Bancroft, American diplomat
and historian, February 12, 1866

So it seems your Republic is going to pieces?" an unnamed
high officer of the French imperial government snidely remarked to
the American guest attending a concert at Emperor Napoleon III's residence in the Tuileries Palace. It was early March 1861, and the news
coming over by steamship that winter all pointed toward the rupture of
la Grande République. "Oh, no, I hope not yet," the flustered American
answered. "Yes, but it will," the French official replied. "No Republic ever
stood so long, and never will. Self-government is a Utopia, Sir; you must
have a strong Government as the only condition of a long existence."[1]

Four years later in April 1865, thousands of students gathered in Paris's Latin Quarter in defiance of government bans on political demonstrations. They planned to march en masse past the Tuileries Palace and
out the Champs-Élysées to the home of John Bigelow, the US minister

to France. "Malakoff," nom de plume of Dr. William E. Johnston, the *New York Times* correspondent in Paris, described what happened next. Gendarmes poured out of the police station near Pont St. Michel, unsheathed their swords, broke up the crowd, and arrested several students. Some managed to get away and make their way through the back streets of Paris toward Bigelow's house. It was nearly three miles away, and they arrived "tired, heated, excited, and covered with dust," only to find a line of police barricading the front door.

Emboldened by their own defiance, the students broke through the cordon of police and were admitted into the home of the astonished American ambassador. One of the young men stepped forward, pulled a paper from his pocket, and read an address expressing profound sorrow for the death of Abraham Lincoln and undying solidarity with the American republic. In his best French, Bigelow graciously thanked the students, who burst into cheers: *Vive Lincoln! Vive la Grande République américaine!*[2]

During the previous four years, no one had worked harder than John Bigelow to cultivate exactly the kind of sympathy these young men evinced, but he was astonished by their daring demonstration. "I had no idea that Mr. Lincoln had such a hold upon the heart of the young gentlemen of France," he wrote Secretary of State William Seward later that night.[3]

Not long after the students left, a deputation of opposition republicans and liberals arrived in front of Bigelow's home. As Malakoff reported, more than two dozen police rushed forward to stop them and then, seeing who descended from the carriages, stood back. Like the students, the liberal politicians had decided to convert an occasion of bereavement into a political demonstration of solidarity with their friends in America.[4]

"You cannot see, because it is your every day life," Malakoff told American readers, "the magnitude of the events through which you are passing in the light of their influence on the rest of the world." Those who took cruel delight in predicting the breakup of America, he mused, "are naturally vexed to find that the republic is the strong government, and the monarchy the weak one." Far from proving the inherent frailty and failure of the democratic experiment, four years of ferocious rebellion, devastating internecine war, and even assassination left the world with an unexpected lesson in the resilience of self-government.[5]

These two Parisian vignettes at the beginning and end of America's Civil War illustrate much of what this book is about. The smug satisfaction of aristocratic governing classes who thought they were witnessing the demise of the democratic experiment was answered four years later by a resurgence of hope and defiant spirit among its adherents everywhere.

WHILE THE WAR WAS BEING FOUGHT ON THE BATTLEFIELDS OF BULL Run, Antietam, and Gettysburg, another contest was waged overseas. The Confederacy sought international recognition and alliances to secure independence, and the Union was determined not to let that happen. "No battle, not Gettysburg, not the Wilderness," one historian claimed, "was more important than the contest waged in the diplomatic arena and the forum of public opinion." The history of Civil War diplomacy—that is, the formal negotiations among governments and the strategies surrounding them—has been told and told well. This book turns to the less familiar forum of public opinion, which was filled with clamorous debate for four years. It took place in print (in newspapers, pamphlets, and books) as well as oratory (in meeting halls, pubs, lodges, union halls, and parliaments). Wherever free speech was stifled, as it was in France, the debate continued over private dinner tables and at cafés. Whatever one's views, there was general agreement that the American question mattered greatly to the world and to the future.[6]

The term *public diplomacy* did not come into common usage until World War I, but America's Civil War witnessed what were arguably the first deliberate, sustained, state-sponsored programs aimed at influencing the public mind abroad. Diplomats for the North and South understood the enormous power the press had gained, thanks to vast improvements in print technology and the expansion of literacy, which made cheap publications and mass-audience journalism possible. They also grasped the key role that journalists, intellectuals, reformers, dissident political leaders, and other opinion leaders had in influencing popular sentiment. Not since Benjamin Franklin's residence there, US diplomat Henry Sanford wrote to Secretary of State William Seward from Paris in August 1861, had there been such an occasion for attention to cultivating public favor abroad. "We ought to spend money freely in the great centers in forming public opinion."[7]

The Union and Confederacy each hired special agents, who usually operated under cover of some kind. They were typically veteran journalists and political operators whose job it was, as one of them deftly put it, to give "a right direction to public sentiment" and correct "erroneous" reports that favored the other side. Some bribed editors and hired journalists, while others published their own pamphlets, books, and even newspapers. Few were above planting rumors or circulating damaging stories, and some of what they produced can only be described as propaganda and misinformation. But that was only part of the story of what was more often a sophisticated appeal to ideology and values.

Union and Confederate agents alike complained to their home offices that the other side had more funds, more men, and more of the foreign press and government leaders in their pockets. Each side was feeling its way in a new arena of combat, often experimenting without clear evidence as to which tactics were working. One concept the Union seemed to grasp more willingly and adopt more nimbly was the lesson that efforts to "educate" the foreign public on their own usually failed and often backfired. Success in this battle over public opinion seemed to reward those who enlisted native authors and public figures on their side. The most effective of these were not hired pens but volunteers who wrote and spoke with conviction and appealed to the fundamental values, ideals, prejudices, and fears of their people in their own idiom.

In today's parlance the diplomatic duel that took place during America's Civil War can be understood as a contest of smart power, the adroit combination of *hard-power* coercion with *soft-power* appeals to basic values. Hard-power diplomacy typically involves the threat or use of military force, but can also include economic coercion (blockades, embargoes) and inducements (low tariffs, commercial monopolies). The employment of soft power involves persuasion and information, but the underlying strategy is to appeal to the fundamental values and interests of the foreign country, to demonstrate that the two countries in question share common aspirations. Soft power resides in "the power of attraction," not in crude propagandizing.[8]

The Union won and the South lost this diplomatic duel abroad not because the Union possessed an obviously more appealing message. To the contrary, at the outset many foreigners found the South's narrative of valiant rebellion against the North's oppressive central government far more attractive. Slavery had never disqualified a nation from acceptance into the family of nations. The United States and most European powers had at some point sanctioned slavery with no loss of status under international law. Confederate emissaries abroad were nonetheless instructed to avoid discussion of slavery as the motive for secession, and they happily pointed to Lincoln's own promises to protect slavery in the Southern states as proof that this was not the issue. Southern diplomats crafted an appeal that evoked widely admired liberal principles of self-government and free trade. The conflict, they told the world, was one arising naturally between industrial and agrarian societies, not freedom and slavery. The industrial North wanted high protective tariffs, while the agrarian South wanted free trade with Europe. It was a winning argument.

The tariff contention dovetailed perfectly with the main economic thrust of Southern diplomacy, for Europe had become heavily dependent upon the South's cotton. European anxiety over the disruption of the cotton trade went far beyond fear of lost profits, for the prospect of a cotton famine threatened massive unemployment and social unrest, if not revolution. Southern leaders had rehearsed their foreign policy for years, and they began their rebellion fully confident that Europe would bow to "King Cotton." "What would happen if no cotton was furnished for three years?" South Carolina's James Henry Hammond asked in 1858. "England would topple headlong and carry the whole civilized world with her, save the South. No, you dare not make war on cotton. No power on earth dares to make war upon it. Cotton is king."[9]

The South's primary foreign policy objective was to secure international recognition as a legitimate member of the family of nations, and it seemed to be well on the way to winning that prize before any major battles had even taken place. In May 1861 the government of Great Britain recognized "certain States styling themselves the Confederate States of America" to be engaged in what it characterized as a "regular war" between "two contending parties," and it extended "belligerent rights" to both sides. This abruptly nullified the Union position that the conflict was nothing more than a "domestic insurrection" and a "causeless rebellion." France and six other nations quickly followed Britain's lead, and it looked to everyone that the South would win full recognition in due time.

Separatist movements do not always have to win on the field of battle to win independence. Nationalist liberation struggles are frequently decided by third-party intervention, military or diplomatic. Had the South won international recognition, the Confederacy would have been vested with sovereignty under international law and empowered to make commercial treaties, guarantee loans, and form military alliances. Recognition would have meant Southern independence.

At the beginning of the war, Union envoys were forced to answer the South's impassioned appeal to liberal principles of national self-determination with rather tedious legalistic arguments to the effect that the Union was permanent, secession was illegal under the Constitution, and the "so-called Confederacy" (as Union officials insisted on calling it) was nothing more than treasonous rebellion. The United States, Secretary of State Seward explained, was fighting for national self-preservation. This left foreigners to contrast the North's fight for conquest with the South's for independence. It looked as though the North was mimicking the monarchical empires of the Old World, while the South was aligning its cause with liberal nationalist aspirations for liberty and independence. Underscoring this, Seward adopted a classic hard-power strategy by threatening war against any nation that dared to recognize or aid what he insisted was a domestic insurrection within *one* sovereign nation.

The Union also sought to demonstrate that the South's rebellion was without legitimate cause. Toward that end, Lincoln in his first inaugural address affirmed the right of states to preserve slavery. He not only denied the president's constitutional power, but disclaimed any personal intention to interfere with slavery in the states where it already existed. He was extending an olive branch to moderate Southerners, especially in the border states, but this was also intended to assuage foreign powers. Lincoln and Seward, crafting this strategy together, sought to delegitimize in the eyes of the world any claim that the Lincoln government threatened the South with wholesale abolition and racial mayhem. But it cost them dearly, and over the next four years, the Union's greatest challenge overseas would be to retrieve the valuable moral capital that had been sacrificed to this early argument for a causeless rebellion.

Thus, both sides began the war by denying slavery to be at issue. This left foreign observers wondering: Just what were the Americans fighting over? Was this only a civil war, a domestic dispute over territory and tariffs? Just another quarrel within a factious democracy? Or were there, behind the rhetoric and posturing, vital principles at stake that really mattered beyond America's borders?

WHILE UNION AND CONFEDERATE AGENTS SET OUT TO TELL THE world their versions of the cause and purpose of the war, foreigners began answering these questions for themselves. Foreign politicians, journalists, reformers, and intellectuals joined a lively debate on what they called the American question and what it meant to them. Both liberals *and* conservatives began framing the American conflict as part of a much larger social and ideological struggle that went back to the American and French Revolutions. The American contest, in this rendering, was a decisive showdown between the forces of *popular* versus *hereditary* sovereignty, *democracy* versus *aristocracy, free* versus *slave* labor, all rolled into one grand epic battle taking place in the distant American arena. It was the final test of what both sides referred to as the republican experiment.

Among skeptics the term *experiment* carried the inference that democracy and republicanism were unproven. Government by the people, the theory went, was destined, sooner or later, to descend into anarchy or tyranny, especially under the strain of war. America's Great Republic was only the latest in a string of examples of failed republics that went back to ancient Rome. Among democracy's defenders, in contrast, the word *experiment* suggested that the world was awaiting a crucial verdict and that friends of freedom must stand with America in its hour of trial. Both uses of the term also implied momentous change in the future. The American war, many observers came to believe, would decide the destiny of democracy and free labor for generations to come.[10]

It was difficult to deny that between 1776 and 1860, the experiment in government by the people had not fared well around the world. Britain enjoyed freedom of speech and assembly, a constitutional monarchy, and strong parliament, but in continental Europe France and many other nations muzzled the press and drove free speech and public demonstration from the public square. Republicans and radicals met in secret, sometimes in fraternal lodges or at public banquets, and employed symbols and coded language to veil their protests. Journalists and intellectuals learned to make clever, oblique criticisms of autocratic regimes and, even then, did so at great risk. Suddenly, in 1861 the American question created new opportunities for liberals, republicans, and radicals to engage in public debate. In talking about America, they could talk about their own future. America's war became theirs, too.

Before 1860 the United States had offered republicans everywhere a working model of how a free, self-governing people might live in peace and prosperity. It was an imperfect society, flawed not least by slavery, which mocked its claims to equality and liberty. But the Great Republic served as proof that people could govern themselves without a king, aristocracy, or established church and that republicanism was far more than a fantasy entertained by intellectuals in their salons. Following the Napoleonic Wars, a stream of migration began to flow across the Atlantic, and after the famines and failed revolutions of the late 1840s that stream grew to flood tide. The attraction went beyond economic opportunity; America became firmly linked in the European imagination to ideals of liberty, equality, and self-rule.

No wonder so many aristocrats were absolutely gleeful in pronouncing the American debacle as proof that the entire experiment in popular government had failed. European government leaders welcomed the fragmentation of the ascendant American republic. American poet Walt Whitman hardly exaggerated when he wrote in 1864 that "there is certainly not one government in Europe but is now watching the war in this country, with the ardent prayer that the United States may be effectually split, crippled, and dismembered by it. There is not one but would help toward that dismemberment, if it dared."[11]

The American crisis not only heartened the enemies of democracy; it also emboldened them to invade the Western Hemisphere, to topple governments, install European monarchs, and reclaim lost American empires. Suddenly, the Civil War rendered the Monroe Doctrine toothless. Republican regimes in Mexico, the Dominican Republic, Peru, Chile, Uruguay, Paraguay, and, not least, the United States were suddenly vulnerable to imperialist aggression, including nefarious plots to install European princes and recolonize their lands.

The most audacious of European schemes was Napoleon III's Grand Design for a Latin Catholic empire. It began with an allied invasion of Mexico late in 1861 and led to the installation of the Hapsburg archduke Maximilian as emperor of Mexico in 1864. The Grand Design went far beyond Mexico to envision the unification of the "Latin race" in America and Europe, under the auspices of the French, and to reverse the advances of Anglo-Saxon Protestantism and egalitarian democracy in the Western Hemisphere.[12]

As its bid to win support in Britain foundered, some thought due to popular antislavery sentiment, the Confederacy sought to align itself with Napoleon III by adopting a Latin strategy that would make common cause with the French and the Catholic Church against the "Puritan fanatics" of the North. The Confederacy sent emissaries to the Vatican, appealing to Pope Pius IX, the archenemy of republicanism, to bless their "holy war" against the "infidels" of the North. They also contrasted the North's "mobocracy" to the traditions of patrician rule among the South's European-style gentry. Southerners even encouraged Europeans to think the Confederacy might prefer a monarchical form of government, perhaps under a European prince. On several occasions Southern leaders proposed some kind of permanent league with, or protectorate under, France, Britain, or Spain. All this portended far more than mere separation under a new flag.

Southerners also took pains to emphasize they were sympathetic with European designs to restore monarchy and Catholic authority in Latin America. Confederate diplomats were instructed to repudiate the South's earlier imperialist ambitions for a tropical empire in Latin America. They assured Europeans that with an independent South, expansion would no longer be necessary.[13]

The Confederacy's gravitation toward antidemocratic alliances helped sharpen perceptions of the North and South abroad. Learning from the transatlantic dialogue on the American question, Union advocates put aside their legalistic arguments against secession and fashioned an appeal to ideals of human equality and liberty against those of aristocracy and slavery.

Lincoln's Gettysburg Address in late 1863 masterfully summarized the new message the Union broadcast to the world. The war was now defined as a trial of democracy for "this nation, or any nation so conceived." Lincoln promised a "new birth of freedom," and not only for America's slaves, for the Union's survival would mean that "government of the people, by the people, for the people, shall not perish from the earth."[14]

At the end of the war, Eugène Pelletan, a leading French republican, expressed eloquently what the American question had meant to the world: "America is not only America, one place or one race more on the map, it is yet and especially the model school of liberty. If against all possibility it had perished, with it would fall a great experiment."[15]

Some readers may feel such unqualified admiration of America was undeserved. The Union, everyone knows, had been painfully slow to embrace emancipation, and America's deeply ingrained racial prejudice would long outlast slavery. These were only some of the egregious flaws in the nation foreign admirers hailed as the Great Republic.

Yet we miss something vitally important if we view Pelletan and other foreigners who saw America as the vanguard of hope as naive or misguided. Foreign admirers typically regarded the United States not as some exceptional city upon a hill, but as exactly the opposite: an imperfect but viable model of society based on universal principles of natural rights and theories of government that originated in Europe but had thus far failed to succeed there. In the 1860s they were horrified to see government of the people seriously imperiled in the one place it had achieved its most enduring success. Abraham Lincoln was hardly boasting when he referred to America as the "last best hope of earth." His was a forlorn plea to defend America's—and the world's—experiment in popular government.

In the mid-nineteenth century, it appeared to many that the world was moving away from democracy and equality toward repressive government and the expansion of slavery. Far from being pushed off the world's stage by human progress, slavery, aristocratic rule, and imperialism seemed to be finding new life and aggressive new defenders. The Confederate South had no intention of putting slavery on the road to extinction; its very purpose in breaking away was to extend and perpetuate slavery—forever, according to its constitution. Had the Confederacy succeeded, it would have meant a new birth of slavery, rather than freedom, possibly throughout the Americas, and it would have been a serious blow to the experiment in egalitarian democracy throughout the Atlantic world.

Long after the defeat of the Confederacy, enemies of liberal, egalitarian society had every reason to look back on America's Civil War with regret. In 1933, during an after-dinner discussion in Munich, Adolf Hitler bemoaned the South's defeat in chilling terms: "The beginnings of a great new social order based on the principle of slavery and inequality were destroyed by that war, and with them also the embryo of a future truly great America that would not have been ruled by a corrupt caste of tradesmen, but by a real *Herren*-class that would have swept away all the falsities of liberty and equality." Hitler's reading of America's history might have been grotesquely flawed, but his outburst echoed the same refrains against the evils of "extreme democracy" and "fanatical egalitarianism" heard in the 1860s.[16]

AMERICA'S CIVIL WAR LIES AT THE HEART OF THE STORY AMERICANS tell themselves about themselves. A century after the war, one historian complained that it had inspired "some of our worst navel-gazing" and that most historians seemed content to portray the war as "a conflict all our own, as American as apple pie." At its 150th anniversary, the story of "our" Civil War continued to be told within a tightly bound national narrative of fratricidal war, sectional conflict, and a troubled reconciliation that came at the expense of racial justice. Beginning in the 1960s, the Civil War became frequently interpreted as the prelude to the civil rights movement, America's "unfinished revolution," and an important step forward in the nation's painful and reluctant reckoning with race.[17]

This book tells the story of a conflict that mattered greatly to the wider world. At stake were nothing less than the fate of slavery and the survival of the "last best hope" for the embattled experiment in government by the people. America's Civil War shook the Atlantic world, and its reverberations at home and abroad shaped the world we inhabit today. Nothing Lincoln said proved more prescient than his observation that "the struggle of today, is not altogether for today—it is for a vast future also."[18]

PART I

ONLY A CIVIL WAR?

1. *The Triumph,* by Morris Traubel, 1861. A German immigrant artist portrays Liberty leading Humanity, Christianity, Justice, and the founding fathers in triumph over the enslaved realm of a crocodilian King Cotton. (LIBRARY OF CONGRESS)

CHAPTER 1

GARIBALDI'S QUESTION

Tell me, also, if this agitation is regarding the emancipation of
the Negroes or not.
—GIUSEPPE GARIBALDI, ITALIAN GENERAL, JUNE 27, 1861

O N A HOT SEPTEMBER DAY IN 1861, HENRY SHELTON SANFORD,
wearing a suit and small wire-rim spectacles perched on his nose,
walked along a narrow path across a small, windswept island named Caprera, located off the northern tip of Sardinia in the middle of the Mediterranean Sea. He was thirty-eight, a career diplomat, officially serving
as US minister to Belgium, but it was in his unofficial capacity as head
of Union secret service operations in Europe that he had traveled to
Caprera to offer a command in the Union army to the most celebrated
hero of the day.

After walking nearly a mile beneath a relentless sun, he arrived at a
rustic house built like a South American hacienda, with whitewashed
buildings and walls enclosing a rough dirt courtyard full of dogs, chick-
ens, and a donkey. Inside the house Sanford waited amid barrels, saddles,
and crude furnishings. Then he entered: Giuseppe Garibaldi, the "Hero
of Two Worlds."

Garibaldi was among that rare company of global idols—like George
Washington, the Marquis de Lafayette, or more recently John F. Kennedy
and Nelson Mandela—who transcend local fame and come to symbolize

whatever ideals an admiring world attaches to them. In 1861 Garibaldi personified the Italian unification movement known as the Risorgimento (Resurgence), which had fascinated the international press and public for years. During the 1830s Garibaldi had been implicated in a revolutionary plot in Genoa and fled to South America with a price on his head. In southern Brazil he and a band of Italian exiles took up arms in the War of the Farroupilhas (Ragged Ones), a republican rebellion to secede from the slave-based Empire of Brazil. In the 1840s Garibaldi and his Brazilian wife, Anita, moved to Montevideo, Uruguay, where he led his Italian Legion against Argentine dictator Juan Manuel de Rosas. For makeshift uniforms, they donned the red smocks of slaughterhouse workers. The Red Shirt would become the emblem of the Garibaldini.[1]

The 1848 revolutions erupting across Europe called Garibaldi and his men back to Italy. He led the heroic defense of the Republic of Rome against French forces sent by Napoleon III to restore Pope Pius IX to his throne. Rome was forced to surrender, but not before Garibaldi led a desperate retreat across the Italian mountains with the armies of Catholic Europe (France, Austria, Naples, and Spain) in dogged pursuit. Near the Adriatic, Anita, pregnant and ill with malaria, died in his arms as enemy troops closed around them. Garibaldi escaped, fled Italy, and eventually sought asylum in America.

After exile in New York and travels in South America and the Pacific, Garibaldi returned to Italy to make a home on Caprera, and he lived there quietly until 1860. That year he stunned the world by leading a daring invasion of the Bourbon Kingdom of the Two Sicilies. With nothing more than a ragtag army of volunteers known as the Thousand, Garibaldi landed in Marsala, pushed back a royal Bourbon army several times larger, swept across Sicily, marched up the peninsula, and entered Naples to cheering crowds, all within four months. Dozens of international reporters and illustrators followed the Thousand during the campaign. As they moved across the Mezzogiorno, as the Italian South was known, the Garibaldini would raise their arms, point with one finger to signify one Italy, and shout *l'Italia unità!*

No wonder Unionists in America were so enthused about the idea of his coming to raise his sword for *l'America unità*. Everyone in Europe and the Americas knew who Garibaldi was, why he was famous, and what he looked like. His image, with his bright-red shirt and his mesmerizing gaze, was published in a steady stream of books and magazines catering to admiring fans. Women everywhere adored him. The Garibaldi fashion, featuring red blouses with puffed sleeves and short military-style jackets, had become the rage in Europe and America. His visit to London in 1864 would arouse such enormous demonstrations of public affection that conservative leaders feared he might ignite revolutionary unrest. English Protestants revered Garibaldi all the more because he was the nemesis of Pope Pius IX, who denounced him as an enemy of the Catholic Church. Garibaldi, in turn, denounced the pope as the enemy of human freedom, and he promised to make Rome the capital of a united Italy. Garibaldi named his donkey at Caprera Pio Nono in irreverent honor of His Holiness. Though a solitary and private man, Garibaldi, one Union diplomat noted, "is at this moment in and of himself one of the great Powers of the world."[2]

All during the summer of 1861, while America prepared for war, the press at home and abroad had been alive with rumors that the champion of Italian reunification was about to lead the reunification of the United States. "Garibaldi Coming to America!" one headline announced. "Bully for Garibaldi!" "Garibaldi Not Coming," another announced with equal certainty a few days later. Beginning in June and continuing through October, a series of contradictory reports, denials, and stony silence from US and Italian government officials left the world in suspense.

Whether Lincoln, or his secretary of state, William Seward, had given much thought as to how an aging Italian general who did not speak English, was severely crippled by recurring bouts of arthritis (he hobbled on crutches to greet Sanford), and had a proven record for insubordination would actually serve as commander of Union forces is unknown. Still, to have Garibaldi take command of a Union army would have been a brilliant public diplomacy coup. No foreign power would dare take sides with Southern slaveholders against the Hero of Two Worlds.[3]

Only later would it become known that the proposal to invite Garibaldi to lead the Union army had been his idea all along. Most of the rumors coursing through the international press could be traced back to Caprera. Candido Vecchi, the general's secretary, later admitted to planting the idea with Henry Tuckerman, an American journalist who had

2. Henry Shelton Sanford, US minister to Belgium and unofficial head of Union secret service operations in Europe. (MATHEW BRADY PHOTOGRAPH, LIBRARY OF CONGRESS)

written a laudatory article for the *North American Review* on Garibaldi as "the hero of the century." Garibaldi himself wrote to several old friends in America recalling his "happy sojourn in your great country" and lamenting that while Italy was nearly reunited, it pained his heart to see America fragmenting. "If I can aid you in any way," he added in one letter, "my agent in New York . . . is instructed to take and execute your orders." When Garibaldi met that July with George Fogg, a US diplomat, he took the occasion to tell him, "If your war is for freedom, I am with you with 20,000 men." The story flashed through the international press like lightning.[4]

While Garibaldi and his supporters fomented rumors of his coming to America, Seward and the diplomatic corps kept silent lest it appear they were soliciting foreign aid and violating neutrality laws by recruiting on foreign soil. Besides, any offer to such a famous foreign general was sure to stir jealousy among Union officers at home.

3. Giuseppe Garibaldi, known as the Hero of Two Worlds for his exploits in South America and Europe. (LIBRARY OF CONGRESS)

But in June 1861, unbeknownst to any US official, James W. Quiggle, a holdover from President James Buchanan's administration serving in an obscure post as US consul to Antwerp, Belgium, took it upon himself to write to Garibaldi. Quiggle had been following the Garibaldi story all summer, and, according to Henry Sanford, he and his "exceedingly pretty" young wife, Cordelia, decided to reach for glory before Lincoln's new appointee to Antwerp arrived. Quiggle must have met Garibaldi previously and purported to "know him personally." He used this, in any case, as the pretext for his self-appointed diplomatic initiative.[5]

"The papers report that you are going to the United States to join the Army of the North in the conflict of my country," Quiggle wrote Garibaldi on June 8, 1861. "If you do, the name of La Fayette will not surpass yours. There are thousands of Italians and Hungarians who will rush to join your ranks and there are thousands and tens of thousands of Americans who will glory to be under the command of 'the Washington of Italy.'" Quiggle took the occasion to offer his own sword to Garibaldi's campaign in America.[6]

From his island retreat on Caprera, Garibaldi responded warmly, addressing Quiggle as *Mio caro amico* (My dear friend) and gallantly adding, "I kiss devotedly the hand of your lady." "I should be very happy," he told Quiggle, "to be your companion in a war in which I would take part by duty as well as sympathy." The newspaper reports of him coming to America, he confessed to Quiggle, had not been "exact," but he quickly added that if the US government would find his services of "some use, I would go to America, if I do not find myself occupied in the defense of my country."

Garibaldi then posed the question to which Quiggle, Sanford, Seward, and Lincoln could not give satisfactory answer in the summer of 1861: "Tell me, also, if this agitation is regarding the emancipation of the Negroes or not."[7]

Still operating entirely on his own authority, and without bothering to notify Henry Sanford, his superior in Brussels, Quiggle answered Garibaldi on July 4 to explain US policy on the matter of slavery. "You propound the question,—whether the present war in the United States is to emancipate the Negroes from slavery?" To his credit Quiggle explained Union policy honestly and accurately: the government's sole aim was to "maintain its power and dignity . . . and restore to the Government her ancient prowess at home and throughout the world." It would be a "dreadful calamity," he informed Garibaldi, again in harmony with official Union policy, "to throw at once upon that country in looseness, four millions of slaves." "But if this war be prosecuted with the bitterness with which it has commenced," Quiggle presciently added, "I would not be surprised if it result in the extinction of slavery in the United States."[8]

The next day Quiggle sent copies of all the correspondence to Seward in Washington. Mail from Antwerp to Washington usually took about twelve days by steamship. If Quiggle sent the packet on July 4, it should have arrived at the State Department by July 17, but it was not marked "received" until July 27.

These were hellish days for the Lincoln administration, and if correspondence from a minor consulate in Belgium went unnoticed, it was understandable. On July 21 the first major engagement of the war took place outside Washington. The Battle of Bull Run was a humiliating Union defeat marked by inept leadership and a panicked (some said cowardly) retreat back to the capital. Quite apart from its devastating effect on Union military and civilian morale, the international repercussions were ominous. Seward was terrified that Britain and France would use this sensational Rebel victory as a pretext for recognizing the Confederacy. With the enemy at the gates of Washington, it was now the viability of the United States as a nation that was in doubt.[9]

Quiggle's dispatch might have been dismissed as the harebrained scheme of an overreaching minor official, but Bull Run put everything in a new light. On July 27 (the same day Quiggle's dispatch was marked received), after consulting with Lincoln, Seward sent instructions to Henry Sanford, in his role as unofficial head of secret service operations in Europe:

> I wish you to proceed at once and enter into communication with the distinguished Soldier of Freedom. Say to him that this government believes his services in the present contest for the unity and liberty of the American People would be exceedingly useful, and that, therefore they are earnestly desired and invited. Tell him that this government believes he will if possible accept this call, because it is too certain that the fall of the American Union . . . would be a disastrous blow to the cause of Human Freedom equally here, in Europe, and throughout the world.

It was Seward at his best, deftly elevating the Union cause above the mere subjugation of rebellion and cleverly enveloping the slavery issue within the universal cause of "Human Freedom." Seward must have been among the New York dignitaries who met Garibaldi during his American exile more than ten years earlier, for he added, "General Garibaldi will recognize in me, not merely an organ of the government but an old and sincere personal friend."[10]

Sanford had received Seward's instructions on August 10 and for the first time learned what Quiggle had been doing under his very nose. What infuriated Sanford was not just Quiggle's secrecy and insubordination, for enclosed with Seward's instructions he found a gushing letter of commendation from Seward thanking Quiggle on behalf of President Lincoln for his service to his country and promising him a commission in Garibaldi's Union army.

Sanford minced no words in his reply to Seward, characterizing Quiggle as "a low, besotted Pennsylvania politician with a single eye to money making and political capital." When he met with Quiggle a few days later, Sanford impressed upon him the absolute necessity of "profound secrecy and great discretion." Little good it would do. Sanford warned Seward he would probably soon be reading an account of this "with a flaming biography of G's patron, the illustrious Quiggle." They would never hear the end of Quiggle's and Garibaldi's names "joined in euphonious partnership." Sanford, however, was an ambitious, young career diplomat who valued Seward's confidence in him, and he was not about to allow his irritation with Quiggle to spoil what might be his own moment of glory.[11]

SANFORD'S MISSION TO CAPRERA HAD NOT REMAINED SECRET FOR long. On August 11 the *New York Daily Tribune* ran a story (possibly leaked by Seward or someone privy to the plan) that an official offer had already been tendered and accepted. "Garibaldi Coming: He Offers to Fight for the Nation," the headline announced. The same story reached Europe on August 20, just as Sanford arrived in Turin, Italy's capital at the time. There he met with the US minister to Italy, George Perkins Marsh, who brought him up to date on the political winds whirling about Garibaldi in Italy.[12]

Both men were savvy enough to realize that the famed Italian general might be trying to use an American offer to force King Victor Emmanuel II's hand. Garibaldi wanted to complete the Risorgimento by marching on Rome and Venice, still in the hands of the pope and the Austrians. But even if he was bluffing, Garibaldi might have to come to America if only to save face, Sanford reasoned. Concerned with avoiding public embarrassment should Garibaldi turn him down, Sanford and Marsh decided to send a secret messenger ahead to Caprera with careful instructions to float an unofficial offer and learn if the Italian general was inclined to accept.[13]

Giuseppe Artoni, Marsh's personal secretary, an Italian immigrant from Philadelphia. was given clear instructions to deliver a written message that Sanford and Marsh had crafted to dodge any specific offer of rank and avoid committing the Union to emancipation. It invited Garibaldi "to take part in the contest for preserving the unity and liberty of the American people and the institutions of Freedom and Self Government."[14]

Sanford and Marsh had no way of knowing that the irrepressible Quiggle had, in the meantime, taken it upon himself to send a copy of Seward's letter of commendation to Garibaldi. "From this you will see," Quiggle crowed, "that the President has thanked me for my letter to you." He then informed Garibaldi that Sanford was on his way with "an invitation to go to the United States, and offering to you the highest Army Commission which it is in the power of the President to confer." Again, Quiggle assured Garibaldi that "thousands of your countrymen, thousands of Hungarians, and tens of thousands of my countrymen will rush to your arms upon your very landing at New York."[15]

When Artoni arrived at Caprera, no doubt exhausted by his travels, he found himself flustered in the presence of the Italian hero, who peppered him with questions about the military rank on offer and his powers to decree emancipation. Artoni was a mere messenger with no authority to negotiate, but in the presence of Garibaldi's charisma he apparently told him whatever he wanted to hear. Garibaldi, satisfied that all his conditions had been met, sent Artoni back with a message in French, apparently to lend diplomatic gravitas, telling Sanford that he would "be very happy to serve a country for which I have so much affection and of which I am an adoptive citizen." But he added an ambiguous proviso: "Provided that the conditions upon which the American government intends to accept me are those which your representative (*Mandataire*) has verbally indicated to me, you will have me immediately at your disposal."[16]

Garibaldi's letter to Sanford also asked for time to consult King Victor Emmanuel II. Just as Sanford suspected, Garibaldi would try to arouse popular pressure among Italians by threatening to leave for America, what he called his second country, unless the king marched on Rome. King Victor Emmanuel II was irritated by Garibaldi's gambit, particularly by his impertinent demand that the king answer within twenty-four hours. He called Garibaldi's bluff, delayed his answer, told him he was free to go to America, and then turned the tables by urging him to remember that Italy was his *first* country.[17]

Once Sanford learned of the king's reply, he felt confident that Garibaldi would have to accept the American offer. On September 7 he hastened to Genoa to secure passage to Caprera and wrote to Seward that Garibaldi leaving for America would cause an "immense sensation here."

September 7, as it happened, was the first anniversary of Garibaldi's entry into Naples, and Sanford described the amazing scene in Genoa that night: the streets were full of people shouting *Viva Garibaldi!* "and in the principal square a wax figure of him is mounted on a kind of altar surrounded by flags at which people are bringing candles by the hundreds to burn, as you have seen in the churches of patron saints." Using an assumed name, Sanford chartered a small steamboat and sailed into the night to Sardinia, where he arrived the next day, took a small boat to Caprera, and then made his way by foot to Garibaldi's rustic island home.[18]

At last Garibaldi and Sanford were face-to-face, and the two men talked late into the evening as the sun set on Caprera. Garibaldi was dismayed to learn that, despite Quiggle's and Artoni's assurances, he was being invited to serve as major general in command of only one army, not as commander in chief of all Union armed forces. Sanford tried to explain to the Italian general that the president was the sole commander in chief and that a major general would have "the command of a large *corps d'armée* to conduct in his own way within certain limits in the prosecution of the war." Garibaldi was either being stubborn or looking for some face-saving excuse to back away from the American invitation.[19]

The difference over military rank might have arisen from an honest misunderstanding, given the myriad languages involved and the misleading promises of Artoni and Quiggle. But Garibaldi's question about emancipation exposed genuine moral confusion over just what the Union was fighting for. Sanford could only offer feeble official excuses about the legal limits of federal power to interfere with slavery. Garibaldi was incredulous. Could slavery not be abolished? If the war was not being prosecuted to emancipate the slaves, he put it bluntly, the whole conflict was nothing more than an "intestine war" over territory and sovereignty, "like any civil war in which the world at large could have little interest or sympathy."[20]

Sanford went to sleep at Garibaldi's house thinking he might salvage something from his mission to Caprera, for late that night Garibaldi had broached the idea of visiting the United States to view the situation for himself. Sanford felt that the public diplomacy value of a visit from Garibaldi, whose every utterance would be reported to the international press, might prove a great deal less risky than having the headstrong Italian actually command an army.[21]

The next morning Garibaldi backed away from the plan to visit America, explaining that he could not bear to watch his adopted country "engaged in a struggle for the salvation of Republican institutions" without throwing himself into battle. The two men spoke for hours that morning, and Sanford realized he had no satisfactory answers for Garibaldi and the questions the Italian hero was raising about emancipation could only embarrass the Union. Sanford left Caprera at noon to begin the long journey back to Turin to confer with Marsh and then return to his post in Brussels.[22]

It had been nearly a month since Sanford left Brussels. After Caprera he crafted a story that made Garibaldi's insistence on military rank—not slavery—the main point of disagreement. He collaborated with Marsh and Nelson M. Beckwith, an American confidant in Paris who had accompanied him at least as far as Turin. Beckwith, in his role as private citizen, helped spin the story as a dispute over rank. Marsh, for his part, knew better. He wrote Seward a few days later to explain that Garibaldi would not lend his name to the Union cause unless he was convinced that it was fighting to abolish slavery.[23]

Whatever else Garibaldi was bluffing about that summer, he was sincere in his commitment to emancipation. A Scottish friend who had lived in America warned him he would be despised if he allowed himself to be deceived by the Americans. "You may be sure," Garibaldi answered, "that had I accepted to draw my sword for the cause of the United States, it would have been for the abolition of Slavery, full, unconditional."[24]

In Garibaldi's mind emancipation was a hemispheric mission. That summer, in after-dinner conversation with his comrades at Caprera, he envisioned a general war of emancipation that would sweep from the American South to Brazil. "The battle will be brief," he predicted. "The enemy is weakened [*infrollito*] by his vices and disarmed by his conscience." After vanquishing the Southern slaveholders, "next, we will free the Antilles [Caribbean], so that miserable slaves will lift their heads and be free citizens, breaking those presidential seats, source of jealousies, quarrels, intestine wars, and public harm. And when, coming to the Plata River, we will have freed 42 million slaves." Garibaldi, it seemed, was contemplating a Pan-American campaign of universal emancipation extending well beyond enslaved Africans.[25]

Even as Sanford made his way back from Caprera, dodging the press at every step, Garibaldi took care not to air his differences with the Union over slavery and to see that the door to America was left ajar. He wrote to Quiggle, whose reliable indiscretion would ensure publicity, promising that if the war continued, he would "hasten to the defense of a people who are so dear to me."[26]

From Antwerp Quiggle was fully prepared to shift all blame for the failed mission to Caprera onto Sanford. Had secrecy been maintained, he had the gall to write Seward, "Garibaldi would now be on his way to the United States." Overreaching as always, Quiggle asked Seward for a private interview with President Lincoln "at the earliest moment practicable" after he returned to the United States.[27] Quiggle never got his audience at the White House, nor did he and Cordelia win the fame they had dreamed of in Antwerp. The Garibaldi affair eventually faded from the news and from America's memory of the war, revisited occasionally only as a bizarre curiosity.[28]

But it was more than that. Garibaldi's flirtation with the Union that first summer of war demonstrated the enormous power the press and public opinion were about to play in foreign relations and the vital importance their management would have in the diplomatic duel that was soon to unfold. Moreover, Garibaldi had raised a fundamental question about the purpose and meaning of the war that left the Union diplomatic corps confounded by its own uninspired message to the world that it sought only to preserve the Union as it was. The question was never *whether* Garibaldi was willing to fight for America; he wanted to know, what would he be fighting *for*?

Was this, Garibaldi asked, "like any civil war," just another internecine conflict over territory and sovereignty "in which the world at large could have little interest or sympathy"? The Union would have to find answers, and soon.

CHAPTER 2

WE ARE A NATION

The Confederate States of America have . . . formed an independent government, perfect in all its branches, and endowed with every attribute of sovereignty and power necessary to entitle them to assume a place among the nations of the world.

—ROBERT TOOMBS, CONFEDERATE SECRETARY
OF STATE, MARCH 16, 1861

THE SOUTH WOULD ALSO HAVE TO EXPLAIN TO THE WORLD WHAT it was fighting for. *Why* exactly had it determined to separate from a nation it had been a part of for eighty-five years? It would not do to explain that the Southern states simply did not like the outcome of the late election and preferred going their own way. Most modern wars, exposed to the scrutiny of political opposition and the press at home and abroad, require each side to come forth with some public explanation of the conflict's origin and purpose. Separatist movements bear a special burden of demonstrating just cause for their rebellion. As Thomas Jefferson put it in 1776: "A decent respect to the opinions of mankind requires that they should declare the causes which impel them to the separation."[1]

Respect for the opinions of mankind had a practical element as well, for in order to survive, aspiring nations needed to win international recognition as sovereign powers—or be relegated to the dustheap of lost causes. Until their country was recognized, Confederate emissaries could not expect to be officially received or be treated with the respect accorded other diplomats. Jefferson Davis huffed early in 1863 that Confederate envoys were left "waiting in servants' halls and on the back stairs," begging for an audience with European officials. He would have liked the crowns of Europe to send supplicants to the South, but the world of nations did not operate that way.[2]

Of course, recognition involved far more than all the courtesy, pomp, and plumage that surrounded formal diplomacy in the nineteenth century. Recognition meant that a nation was a legitimate sovereign power able to negotiate treaties, form commercial and military alliances, assume international loans, and enjoy all the rights of other nations under international law. Recognizing or aiding the South invited confrontation and possible war with the United States, as Secretary of State William Seward made emphatically clear. But once Britain or perhaps another Great Power led the way, and other countries followed, the Union itself would come under tremendous pressure to acknowledge the South's independence, especially if multiple European powers acted in concert to mediate peace, break the North's blockade of Southern ports, or perhaps intervene military. Recognition, in other words, quite likely meant independence for the South.[3]

Revolutions and separatist rebellions had already become well-worn paths to nationhood by the time the South seceded. Roughly half of today's nearly two hundred UN members originated as breakaway states. What is cheerfully referred to as the family of nations has been largely the product of hostile divorces, forced marriages, and patricidal violence. Questions as to the legitimacy of the newborn and doubts about life expectancy often loom like dark shadows over embryonic nations until the verdict of war or diplomacy decides their fate.[4]

The American Civil War is usually viewed as a military contest decided by major battles. Nationalist independence movements are not always decided by the fortunes of war alone, however. Rebels need not fully triumph on the field of battle so long as they can continue to field an army, wear down the enemy, and hope for international intervention of some kind. Davids often triumph over Goliaths in such struggles, precisely as Britain learned in the American Revolution and the United States would learn much later in Vietnam.[5]

The South's bid for independence took place within living memory of dozens of successful nationalist independence movements in the Atlantic world, including the wars for independence that gave birth to the Spanish American republics, all of which won international recognition despite the fulminations of imperial Spain. The Greek struggle for independence from the Ottoman Empire and the Italian Risorgimento were also widely admired by most European and American onlookers at the time. When Belgium broke off from the Netherlands in 1830, Great Britain and other European powers hastened to recognize it as an independent kingdom. Hungary, Ireland, and Poland had not achieved independence by the 1860s, but these nationalist aspirations also inspired enthusiasm abroad. By the time the Confederacy came upon the world stage, the idea that people possessed a natural right to govern themselves and pursue their own destiny had a firm basis in liberal philosophy and a clear precedent in international law. Confederate diplomats were eager to remind Europe of that.[6]

During the crucial first months of the conflict, the Confederacy was able to set the terms of debate by emphasizing its desire for national self-determination and free trade—not slavery—as the motive for secession. The principle of self-governance was closely joined to the legal argument that secession was a legitimate as well as peaceful means of separation. Far from being revolutionaries seeking to overthrow the existing government, secessionists insisted they were merely withdrawing from the existing "compact" of states and creating a government of their own among the other like-minded Southern states. We are a nation, and we exist already in fact and in law, the Confederate States of America proclaimed to the world. The self-declared new nation sent forth emissaries to the world asking nothing more than recognition of this fact. It went to war not to achieve nationhood, but to defend a fait accompli.

THE DEBATE OVER THE RIGHT TO SECEDE WAS A LEGAL QUARREL about the origin of the Union among states, the US Constitution, and the original intent of the founding fathers. That debate obscured a far more salient question as to the *reason* for secession. It was notable that the Confederacy never issued a Declaration of Independence that submitted "facts to a candid world." This was no mere oversight. During the

Secession Winter of 1860–1861, the radical secessionists, known as "Fire-Eaters," had been altogether forthright in arguing that secession was the only means of perpetuating slavery and white supremacy and that the alternative was racial holocaust and economic ruin under "Black Republican" rule. As they seceded, several states went on the public record with declarations of the causes of secession that spelled out the Republican Party's threat to slavery and to the peace and prosperity of the South and the world.[7]

The first state to secede, South Carolina, issued a Declaration of Immediate Causes on December 24, 1861, which was essentially a breach-of-contract suit that tediously outlined the grounds for termination. South Carolina in 1788, the declaration explained, had entered into a league with other states under certain well-understood terms, and the US government had repeatedly forsaken its obligations under this contract. Every one of South Carolina's grievances centered on slavery. The declaration complained of those in nonslaveholding states who "denounced as sinful the institution of slavery" and "encouraged and assisted thousands of our slaves to leave their homes." Worse yet, those slaves who remained were being incited by "emissaries, books and pictures" to engage in "servile insurrection." South Carolina's declaration also made allusions to Republicans "subverting" the Constitution by electing a president without Southern support and accused them of "elevating to citizenship" people, apparently immigrants, who were unfit to vote. Shifting to future tense, the declaration prophesied that, once in power, the Republican Party would wage war against slavery and deprive the South of the "power of self-government, or self-protection."[8]

South Carolinians of more diplomatic temperament thought it unwise to put slavery so boldly before the world. Robert Barnwell Rhett and Maxey Gregg, both proslavery secessionists, nonetheless understood that Southern independence would require European support. They urged their fellow delegates to tone down the hysterical rhetoric about abolitionism, play up the South's alienation over tariff policy, and place the South's desire for free trade with Europe front and center. But with more bravado than tact, the new Republic of South Carolina brazenly staked its claim to independence on the preservation of slavery.[9]

Mississippi followed in early January by cleverly joining the anxiety over the safety of slavery to alarming predictions of economic disaster for the world once the antislavery party took power. "Our position is thoroughly identified with the institution of slavery—the greatest material interest of the world," the declaration led off. The "imperious law of nature," it further explained, dictated that only blacks could bear the tropical sun. A "blow at slavery" will be "a blow at commerce and civilization." Mississippi had to choose between "submission to the mandates of abolition, or a dissolution of the Union."[10]

The other Deep South states fell in, one by one, during January and February: Florida, Alabama, Georgia, Louisiana, and Texas. According to plan, the legislature of each seceding state sent delegates to a convention in Montgomery, Alabama, on February 4, exactly one month before Lincoln took office. They gathered there to create what they unblinkingly called a "permanent federal government."[11]

Voices of caution urging the South to wait and see what Lincoln did were silenced by ominous warnings of a diabolical plot among the Black Republicans to ignite a race war on the model of the bloody revolt in Saint-Domingue (Haiti) during the French Revolution. The secessionist delegates in Montgomery were also determined to show that the South was not just bluffing in order to win concessions from the Lincoln administration. They came to create "a government of their own" and present the North and the world with a fully conceived new nation before Lincoln even took power.[12]

Within mere days the Montgomery convention assembled all the essential trappings of modern nationhood: a constitution, a president and vice president, a cabinet, money, a flag, even a motto—*Deo Vindice* (God Will Vindicate). For its constitution the delegates borrowed the US model, but with crucial alterations, including ones to safeguard slavery, restrict voting rights of foreigners, limit presidential terms, and admit new states. The new nation needed a name. One delegate proposed calling it the "Republic of the Southern United States," which would force everyone to distinguish it from the "Northern United States." In the end the delegates chose "Confederate States of America" to convey the core idea of a compact of sovereign states and one to which others might be added in due time.[13]

This was a provisional government organized under a provisional constitution. There was no time before March 4, secessionists insisted, to conduct plebiscites on the constitution and the presidency. Besides, the Confederacy was designed to do away with acrimonious party strife and rancorous election campaigns of the kind that had so plagued what they characterized as the "extreme democracy" of the North. To that end, under the Confederate government the president would serve only one six-year term. The Montgomery congress, having authorized itself as a sovereign body, nominated Jefferson Davis, former secretary of war and US senator from Mississippi, and Alexander Stephens, former US senator representing Georgia, as the provisional president and vice president. Elections were to follow in November 1861.[14]

ON FEBRUARY 18, 1861, JEFFERSON DAVIS GAVE HIS INAUGURAL address and, for the first time, presented to the world the official justification for the Confederacy and its claim to nationhood. On that frosty morning a procession formed in front of the Exchange Hotel in Montgomery to escort the nominee to the ceremony. A brass band led the parade, followed by militia groups in bright blue and red uniforms. Six iron-gray horses pulled an elegant carriage lined with saffron and white cloth, trimmed with silver, and carrying Davis, Stephens, and Howell Cobb, president of the provisional Confederate Congress. Behind them in carriages were other officials, followed by citizens in carriages and on foot, all forming a long procession that passed by cheering crowds. The band played "Dixie" as the convoy made its way to the Alabama statehouse where an anxious crowd of five thousand gathered to hear their new leader.[15]

On the portico of the statehouse, framed by high stone columns, Davis was introduced amid a storm of applause. Though he was only fifty-two, the strain of political life showed on his face. Hollow cheeks, thin lips, and weathered skin made him look "haggard, care-worn, and pain drawn," a British journalist noted. He suffered chronic nervous dyspepsia and a recurring facial neuralgia that intensified with stress, contorting the left side of his face and affecting a pained grimace. His left eye, covered with an opaque film, seemed nearly blind.[16]

Davis's wife, Varina, later remarked that, when Davis first received news that the Confederate Congress had chosen him to be the provisional president, he looked positively stricken. He was not a radical secessionist. He shared none of the illusions other secessionists propagated that the North would give up the South without a fight, and he warned the Fire-Eaters against precipitating a war they were not equipped to win.

4. Jefferson Davis's inauguration as provisional president of the Confederate States of America. (LIBRARY OF CONGRESS)

He arrived in Montgomery after five days of difficult travel from his plantation in Mississippi, giving speeches along the way, but he apparently gave very little time to preparing an inaugural address. It showed.[17]

After taking the oath of office, Davis pulled sheets of paper from his coat pocket and, with what the *Harper's Weekly* reporter described as his usual "soldierly bearing" and "rather stern manners," began a surprisingly

5. Jefferson Davis, imagined here as a dashing, young cavalier arriving at the Battle of Bull Run. (LIBRARY OF CONGRESS)

brief and perplexing speech. He opened by proclaiming the Confederacy as "unprecedented in the history of nations" and then invoked a familiar precedent: the Declaration of Independence. Echoing Thomas Jefferson on the right of the people to "alter or abolish" governments once they become "destructive of the ends for which they were established," he seemed to embrace the revolutionary model of 1776. Then he abruptly reversed course, denouncing as "abuse of language" the notion of some that Southern secession amounted to a "revolution." The Southern states, Davis rationalized, had simply "formed a new alliance," and "within each State its government has remained." The Confederacy's new constitution differed from its predecessor only "so far as it is explanatory of their well-known intent." When Abraham Lincoln described secession as a "sugar-coated" rebellion, it was exactly this kind of obfuscation that he had in mind.[18]

IT WAS LEFT TO THE CONFEDERATE VICE PRESIDENT, ALEXANDER Stephens, to provide a full, unguarded public exposition of the reasons for Southern independence without sugarcoating. It came in a widely published and much-discussed speech in Savannah, Georgia, about a month after Davis's unremarkable inaugural address.

A large, raucous crowd of men and women packed the Athenaeum hall the evening of March 21, 1861. Hundreds more were left outside, straining to hear. Stephens was afflicted by multiple maladies, ranging from neuralgia to pneumonia, which led one reporter to describe him as "painfully thin." He spoke in a sharp, shrill voice that did not carry well, but he was nonetheless a brilliant orator and much beloved by his fellow Georgians. The crowd outside began chanting, urging him to come address them since there were more outside the hall than inside.[19]

Stephens told them his frail health required him to remain inside at the rostrum. He began by setting forth the several "improvements" the Confederate government had made to the US Constitution. He rang off some of the more noncontroversial novelties in the new constitution, those involving the tariff, internal improvements, cabinet membership, and the one-term presidency. The boisterous crowd outside began remonstrating again, complaining they could not hear. They were about to miss a sensational moment of candor. If it did not register with those outside the hall that night, the rest of the world would hear it again and again during the next four years.

Stephens resumed speaking as the crowd quieted. He referred to one final "improvement" the Confederate Constitution had introduced, a brief but crucial clause that banned forever any "bill of attainder, ex post facto law, or law denying or impairing the right of property in negro slaves." "The new Constitution has put at rest, *forever,* all the agitating questions relating to our peculiar institutions—African slavery as it exists among us—the proper *status* of the negro in our form of civilization." This question, Stephens baldly admitted, "was the immediate cause of the late rupture and present revolution."[20]

Stephens then referenced Thomas Jefferson and other founding fathers who thought slavery to be something "wrong in *principle,* socially, morally and politically." Men of that day, Stephens explained, seemed to wish that slavery would somehow fade away in due time. "Those ideas were fundamentally wrong"; the whole idea of equality of the races was "an error," he told the crowd. The Confederacy had at last corrected Jefferson's mistake. "Our new Government is founded upon exactly the opposite ideas; its foundations are laid, its cornerstone rests, upon the great truth that the negro is not equal to the white man; that slavery, subordination to the superior race, is his natural and moral condition. This, our new government, is the first, in the history of the world, based upon this great physical, philosophical, and moral truth." The hall burst with applause.

This last passage gave the address its name—the Cornerstone Speech. It was astonishing. The vice president of the new nation had not only admitted that slavery was at the very heart of the South's rebellion, but also went out of his way to repudiate the underlying principle of democracy—human equality.

Stephens later claimed that he spoke extemporaneously, that the notes of the reporter were "very imperfect," and that he had been careless about correcting them before the speech was published. But it was untrue. He had given very similar remarks earlier and never repudiated a word. After the war he tried to explain what he really meant to say, but his rationalizations confirmed exactly what he was reported to have said. Stephens had committed a classic political gaffe: a politician telling the truth.[21]

Arguments against Jefferson, the "Godless ideas of equality," and the "fanatical egalitarianism" of the antislavery movement had been running through Southern proslavery rhetoric for years. Though Stephens did not go into the scientific basis for what he called "new truths" about Africans, he was undoubtedly alluding to Arthur Gobineau, the French author of *Essai sur l'inégalité des races humaines* (1853), a pioneering treatise on the inequality of human races that had been translated in 1856 by Henry Hotze, who would serve as chief Confederate propaganda agent in London. Hotze's coeditor was Josiah Nott, a Mobile physician whose science of race led him to propound the theory of polygenesis, by which Negroes were categorized as an altogether separate species from whites. Gobineau's work was applauded by proslavery Southerners for its scientific explanation of race as an immutable, biologically determined human trait. The "sentimental" antislavery fanatics of the North, Stephens told his Savannah audience, were blindly "attempting to make things equal which the Creator had made unequal." The South, instead, was embracing modern science.[22]

Stephens's Cornerstone Speech has been called "the Gettysburg Address of the Confederate South" because it neatly summarized the most salient principles of the Confederacy. It would become an important asset for Unionists abroad and was widely quoted in the international press. Use of the term *cornerstone* (*la pierre angulaire* in French) became a shorthand method of reminding foreigners of the real purpose of the South's rebellion. Stephens's speech was a gift to the Union, but its power was dampened at first by the Union's own diffident stance on slavery.[23]

MEANWHILE, MANY IN THE NEW CONFEDERATE GOVERNMENT WERE anxious to get their case before the world using less controversial arguments for self-government and free trade. The seceding states had hastily drafted a constitution, set up a government, and fielded an army, in large part to convince foreign nations that the Confederacy was a viable, permanent nation-state worthy of recognition. The next step was to send out emissaries to the nations of the world. On February 13, 1861, the Confederate Congress authorized two foreign missions: one to Europe and the other to Washington.[24]

The Washington "peace commission" was sent by Jefferson Davis with a letter addressed to the president of the United States introducing the commission's leader, Martin Crawford, and explaining that his mission was to establish friendly relations between the two countries. Davis took the occasion to date the letter the "27th day of February, A.D. 1861, and of the Independence of the Confederate States the eighty-fifth," a pointed reference to the Confederate theory that its independence was first established in 1776.[25]

Crawford and his fellow commissioners, Andre Roman and John Forsyth, went to Washington ostensibly to arrange an amicable political divorce, settle debts, divide property, and establish new commercial treaties going forward. This was also a Confederate public diplomacy ploy to demonstrate goodwill and win public sympathy at home and abroad.

Lincoln and Seward, once in office, wisely avoided the trap being set. They refused to meet with agents of rebellion or even to speak the name of what they insisted on calling the "so-called Confederacy." Seward effectively stalled Crawford and his commission, while Lincoln and his cabinet prepared for the confrontation over federal control of Fort Sumter, South Carolina. For the Confederacy, the Washington commission was a dress rehearsal for the delicate dance of diplomacy, an exercise in which Confederate envoys would often appear graceless, especially as they grew impatient with the lack of respect accorded them.[26]

WHEREAS THE WASHINGTON COMMISSION WENT NORTH TO SETTLE A divorce, the European commission went abroad to court marriage partners. The South, many thought, would need to propose rich dowries in the form of commercial treaties offering Southern cotton for European arms and supplies. The South would also need financial loans and military allies with naval prowess to break the blockade Lincoln inaugurated soon after the conflict began.

Cabinet member Judah P. Benjamin proposed that the government buy up as much cotton as possible and sell it to Europe in exchange for arms, supplies, and ships, thus fastening European creditors to the fate of the South. Others, such as Robert Toombs, Davis's first secretary of state, and Robert Barnwell Rhett, chair of the Foreign Affairs Committee in Montgomery, advocated generous long-term trade agreements, up to twenty years or more, with exclusive most-favored-nation status awarded to the first European nation willing to aid the South's struggle for independence.

The South would thus "make a league" with Europe's Great Powers and, in turn, promise not to poach their possessions in the American hemisphere. Toombs thought that Spain, the only European power still sanctioning slavery and with its rich sugar colonies in neighboring Cuba and Puerto Rico, was destined to become the South's natural ally. One cynic thought Toombs would favor "an alliance with Satan himself" if that is what it would take to win the South's independence. From the beginning there were serious differences within the Confederate government over foreign policy, and even some who thought diplomacy was a complete waste of time and resources. But most Confederate leaders accepted a common assumption: Europe's material self-interests, not constitutional arguments for secession and not moral defenses of slavery, were the vital key to winning recognition abroad.[27]

Jefferson Davis found it demeaning to plead for aid from Europe and remained convinced that the South would have to win its independence at arms without foreign aid. Instead of inducing European assistance by generous offers of cheap cotton, he adopted an opposite strategy by imposing an embargo on cotton exports, confiscating cotton, and even burning crops to force European nations to terms, or face cotton famine and social upheaval among their workers. Eventually, the tightening Union blockade rendered Davis's proposed embargo policy redundant, but the arrogant assumption that King Cotton would bring the world to heel was not soon forgotten abroad.[28]

Jefferson Davis typically betrayed a certain tone deafness when it came to diplomatic appointments and policy. To head the first Confederate commission to Europe he appointed William Yancey, a rabid proslavery extremist who had advocated reopening the African slave trade. The other two commissioners—Pierre Rost, a Louisiana judge, and Ambrose Dudley Mann, the only envoy with diplomatic experience—would prove of little help. They were, one historian would later conclude, the "poorest choices possible."[29]

Whomever Davis appointed to the European commission, their main problem, Robert Barnwell Rhett thought, was that they had nothing of substance with which to tempt foreign governments to risk aiding their bid for independence. "You have no business in Europe," he told a startled Yancey. "You have nothing to propose; and nothing therefore, to treat about." Rhett urged his friend Yancey not to accept the appointment on these terms and warned that his mission would meet with nothing but "failure and mortification."[30]

Yancey should have listened. A fiery Southern rights politician from Alabama with a marvelous reputation for oratory, a man who could hold a crowd for hours, Yancey was entirely out of his depth amid the intrigue of European diplomatic courts. He was ignorant of the world and, by his own admission, wholly unsuited by experience and personality to the gentle art of diplomacy. But Davis saw him as a political rival in the upcoming presidential contest and wanted him out of the country.

Why Yancey accepted, especially after Rhett's stern warning, is not clear. He was by reputation a quick-tempered, violent man. It was said he had killed a relative in an affair of honor. He "was not a winning or persuasive man," one Confederate envoy uncharitably described his colleague. He was "bold, antagonistic and somewhat dogmatical," never good traits for diplomats. Unrefined in deportment, he was "not at all impressive in personal appearance, and decidedly negligent in dress." This description, from a fellow Confederate envoy, leaves us only to wonder what the English made of Yancey.[31]

Pierre Adolfe Rost, another of the commissioners, was completely unknown outside Louisiana, where he had lived as a planter, politician, and judge. Born in France in 1797 and schooled in Paris, he had fled with his family to Louisiana after Napoleon's defeat at Waterloo. If nothing else, Rost's command of French ought to have recommended him to the post. But some found his accent a bit too Creole for the Parisian ear. "Has the South no sons capable of representing your country?" one French official asked. Among the diplomatic corps in Paris, Rost became something of a joke for strolling down the Champs-Élysées and greeting all who inquired about the Confederate fortunes in France with a jaunty *Tout va bien.*[32]

Alone among the three commissioners, Ambrose Dudley Mann had considerable diplomatic experience and extensive knowledge of Europe. Before the war he had won a string of appointments in Bremen, Hungary; Hanover, the German Confederation; and Switzerland. He had also served as assistant secretary of state in Washington. His command of French and other European languages and his understanding of diplomatic protocol made him indispensable to the Confederate mission, and he knew it. But his close friendship with Jefferson Davis and his wife, Varina, often led him to overestimate his influence with the president. In Europe Mann exhausted enormous amounts of ink and time penning lengthy dispatches to the home office, sometimes brimming with insights on European affairs, but just as often given to self-serving reports on trifling diplomatic triumphs and grandiose promises of glory ahead.[33]

Mann had foolishly decided to risk crossing the Atlantic from New York to London and, more foolishly still, to stop in Washington on the way to show off his copy of the new Confederate Constitution to friends. Seward nearly had him arrested before he rushed to New York and took the first ship for London, where he arrived in mid-April, two weeks before his colleagues.[34]

Yancey and Rost, meanwhile, were delayed in New Orleans by Yancey's chronic ill health. They sailed to Havana, then Saint Thomas, where they finally caught a ship to London, arriving April 29, just after news broke that the South was at war with the United States. Meanwhile, in London, Mann used his time and connections to open communications with the inner circle of Prime Minister Lord Palmerston's government. Arriving on a high tide of Confederate confidence, Yancey and his troupe were about to be initiated into the cunning world of European diplomacy.[35]

BRITISH PRIME MINISTER HENRY JOHN TEMPLE, THIRD VISCOUNT, otherwise known as Lord Palmerston, was the picture of England's aristocratic governing class. Born in 1784, he had been in one government office or another since 1807. "Pam," as he was affectionately known, instinctively feared the excesses of democracy and thoroughly detested the United States for inspiring British Radicals, Member of Parliament (MP) John Bright chief among them, to agitate for "universal suffrage." Palmerston still remembered the summer of 1792 when, as a child on holiday with his family in France, he witnessed the revolutionary fury of Parisian mobs.[36]

Palmerston viewed Britain's constitutional monarchy as the best and only proper model for good government, for it avoided at once the abuses of absolutist monarchy and the turmoil of democratic republicanism. "The History of the world in all Times and countries," he later wrote to his foreign secretary, John Russell, reflecting on the American crisis, "shows that Power in the Hands of the Masses throws the Scum of the Community to the Surface and that Truth and Justice are Soon banished from the Land." If Bright and company had their way in Britain, he groused, it would fare the same.[37]

John Russell, recently elevated to the peerage as an earl, also came from a prominent aristocratic family. Born in 1792, "Johnny," as some referred to him, shared Lord Palmerston's profound distrust of democracy. His icy aristocratic aloofness left diplomats on both sides of the American war suspecting that he wished them ill, and they were usually right. Like Palmerston, Russell had championed the Reform Act of 1832, which eliminated some "rotten boroughs" and ended the most egregious forms of aristocratic domination, but that was the first and last step toward democracy he was willing to see Britain take. Russell staunchly opposed Bright's movement to expand voting rights to workers. America's disaster seemed quite enough proof of the dangers of "Brightism" to the British way.[38]

There was nothing Russell and Palmerston feared more than being dragged into another war with the United States. Two wars with the belligerent American republic, in 1776 and 1812, had proved costly, fruitless, and humiliating. Now Britain faced a far stronger nation across a vast ocean, one with a powerful army and navy in the making. In the event of war, British Canada would be exposed to invasion by the United States across a long, unprotected border. Furthermore, as an imperial power with possessions in North America, the Caribbean, India, and the Far East, to say nothing of Ireland, the British government dared not side with rebel nationalists. "For God's sake," Russell implored his fellow MPs, "let us if possible keep out of it."[39]

Though Palmerston had no American-style democracy to contend with, the American question threatened to upset the thin majority on which his newly formed Liberal coalition government rested. He had to constantly mind the storms of public opinion aggravated by a free and boisterous press. And he had to keep an eye on the line of rival politicians eager to take his place as prime minister. For the same reasons that he feared democracy, Palmerston understood the danger of alienating public opinion. "What are opinions against armies?" one of Palmerston's political rivals had asked years earlier. "Opinions are stronger than armies," he famously answered. It was a lesson worth remembering as Britain grappled with the American question during the next four years.[40]

ON MAY 3, 1861, YANCEY, ROST, AND MANN MADE THEIR WAY through the crowded streets of London to meet with Earl Russell. He had invited them to his private home on Chesham Place in order to underscore the unofficial nature of their interview and, of course, to avoid antagonizing the United States. While Russell listened in stone-faced silence, Yancey, taking his cues from Toombs's instructions, rehearsed the history leading up to Southern secession, taking care to emphasize the desire of the South to free itself from the tribute it had been forced to pay in tariffs. Two months earlier the Republican-dominated Congress had passed the Morrill Tariff, which sharply raised duties on foreign imports, some said to raise revenue for the coming war. The new tariff followed rather than caused secession, of course, but it was a gift to Confederate diplomacy, and Yancey made it clear that an independent South would be devoted to free trade.

The "people," Yancey explained to the poker-faced foreign minister, "had thrown off one Federal Government and formed a new one . . . without shedding a drop of blood." He closed by expressing the hope that Great Britain, "for the benefit of industrial interests generally" and in "the highest interests of peace, civilization, and constitutional government," would recognize the independence of the Confederate States of America. Russell gave absolutely no hint of sympathy for either side, but he assured Yancey and the other commissioners that he would take the matter up with the cabinet. Without further ceremony, he showed them out.[41]

Ten days later, on May 13, Yancey and his fellow commissioners were thrilled to learn that Queen Victoria had issued a formal Proclamation of Neutrality. In the stroke of a pen, the queen's proclamation swept aside the Union's characterization of the conflict as a domestic insurrection and recognized instead two belligerent parties engaged in a regular war. Recognition of belligerent status was quite different from recognizing the Confederacy's national sovereignty, but everyone understood this to be a first step in that direction. France, the Netherlands, Spain, Belgium, and Portugal followed Britain's lead by the end of June (Brazil and even the Kingdom of Hawaii did so in August). Before any major engagements on the field of battle, it looked as though the Confederacy was marching toward a bloodless diplomatic triumph in the marbled courts of Europe.[42]

Soon after their interview with Russell, Yancey dispatched Rost to Paris, where he arranged an unofficial interview with the Duc de Morny, the illegitimate half brother and trusted confidant of Emperor Napoleon III. France and Britain had a long tradition of enmity and distrust, but during this period the two powers were operating on the tacit understanding that neither would act on the American question without at least informing the other. Morny gave encouraging assurances to Rost, who immediately reported to Yancey that the Confederacy "need apprehend no unfriendly action" from France and that recognition was "a mere question of time."[43]

Yancey and his fellow commissioners wrote the home office on May 21, 1861, to explain that while neither Britain nor France was quite ready to take the step of recognizing the South's independence, "England in reality is not averse to a disintegration of the United States," and both nations would act at the first sign of decisive military success. In June Yancey reported that the London press was "growing more favorable to our cause" and that public opinion was "more enlightened" than ever. The public remained divided on the right to secession, he wrote in July, but self-government was understood by all as "the great principle underlying the contest." By the end of the summer, Yancey's commission cheerfully reported to Richmond (the Confederate capital as of May 1861) that the "antislavery sentiment so universally prevalent here no longer interferes with a proper judgment of this contest." The South, by their account, seemed to be winning the war for public opinion in Britain, and, if it could defend the nation it had proclaimed, the "diplomatic solution" would soon be at hand.[44]

ROBERT TOOMBS, BORED WITH DIPLOMACY AND CROSS WITH DAVIS, resigned as secretary of state in July 1861 to take the field in command of an army. To replace him Davis appointed Robert Mercer Taliaferro Hunter, a strong-headed aristocratic Virginia politician whose career was notably devoid of experience in foreign affairs. Hunter assumed duties two days before the stunning Confederate victory at Bull Run on July 21, 1861. Here was the battlefield victory Yancey and the European commission were waiting for in London. But the new secretary of state did not get around to writing Yancey for a week, and then it was only to explain that he saw "no reason to make any change in the instructions" and merely wished to bring them up to speed on "such facts and events of recent date as are deemed of interest."[45]

Yancey had already received news of Bull Run weeks before Hunter's desultory message arrived and immediately recognized it as the "great victory" he and the other commissioners had been anticipating. Right away he requested another unofficial interview with Earl Russell. Russell, on vacation at his country estate, replied with a curt request that they "put in writing" anything they had to say.[46]

Yancey, Mann, and Rost worked diligently for a full week preparing a lengthy treatise on the case for recognition. Now, with victory at Bull Run to its glory, their appeal asserted, the South had met all the conditions for recognition. They had put a government in place and "raised, organized, and armed an army sufficient to . . . drive in ignominious flight from that field the myriads of invaders."

Inexplicably, their letter to Russell veered off topic to address "the antislavery sentiment so universally prevalent in England." Contradicting massive evidence to the contrary, they argued that "it was from no fear that the slaves would be liberated that secession took place." Referring to Lincoln's inaugural address, they pointed out that "the very party in power has proposed to guarantee slavery forever in the States if the South would but remain in the Union."

They should have left it there. Instead, the Southern commissioners seemed unable to resist scoring points by reminding Earl Russell of the shameful role Britain had played in introducing slavery to colonial America. The founding fathers were confronted with "two distinct races in the colonies, one free and capable of maintaining their freedom, the other slave, and in their opinion unfitted" to govern themselves. They "made their famous declaration of freedom for the white race alone" and created a government "resting upon that great and recognized distinction between the white and black man."

Still undercutting the commissioners' own claim that slavery was not at issue, the letter went on to extol the beneficial effects of slavery in the rich commerce between America and Europe. Slavery's destruction, they cautioned Russell, would be "disastrous to the world, as well as to the master and slave." They further warned that the Union might "resort to servile war" by pretending to emancipate the slaves, but far from "that high philanthropic consideration which undoubtedly beats in the hearts of many in England," Yankee abolitionism was motivated solely by a "baser feeling of selfish aggrandisement not unmixed with a cowardly spirit of revenge."

The letter closed by clumsily calling attention to the coming cotton harvest and warning that, should Britain decide the "Confederate States have not yet won a right to a place among the nations of the earth," it would be Europe that would suffer and not the South. The valiant Southerners would "buckle themselves to the great task before them with a vigor and determination," and Britain would be responsible for prolonging a conflict that would inflict suffering "upon millions of the human race."[47]

Russell must have groaned while reading this blustering epistle. He made Yancey's commission wait ten agonizing days before he replied on

August 24, and then only with a terse note that acknowledged the letter "on behalf of the so-styled Confederate States of North America," and he put the entire matter on ice by reminding them: "Her Majesty has considered this contest as constituting a civil war" and will maintain "a strict neutrality between the contending parties in that war."[48]

Yancey was deflated. In an unguarded letter to his brother, he gave a decidedly pessimistic review of his mission in England. "Anti-slavery sentiment is universal. Uncle Tom's Cabin has been read and believed." Though only forty-seven, he felt old and tired, and he missed his family. "I am fattening and growing gray," he told his brother. "My bowels are not right and my back pains me." For years he had suffered bouts of excruciating pain that at times immobilized him, and as usual he sought relief in strong drink. It was becoming clear to him that "the war will be a long one" and that British recognition would come only after a military victory brought the war to an end.[49]

Yancey wanted to go home. Not long after Russell's reply, he sent a message to Richmond, asking to be recalled. He found Mann's obsequious diplomatic groveling before the British ministers thoroughly disgusting. He also had sense enough to realize that his own training and temperament were ill-suited to diplomacy, and he much preferred the political arena at home. "I ought never to have come here," he admitted in a rare flash of self-doubt. "This kind of thing does not suit me. I do not understand these people or their ways well enough."[50]

BACK IN RICHMOND, JEFFERSON DAVIS HAD ALSO COME TO THE conclusion that the war would last far longer than the radical Fire-Eaters had so bravely forecast. By August 1861 he and Hunter had determined to expand diplomatic operations in Europe. They wanted to establish permanent posts in each capital rather than rely upon itinerant commissioners and had decided to send Mann to Belgium and Rost to Spain. To replace Yancey in London, they would send James M. Mason of Virginia, who as a US senator had extensive experience on the Foreign Relations Committee. For Paris Davis appointed John Slidell, a Louisiana senator with previous diplomatic experience in Mexico.

Since·May 1861, when Britain extended belligerent rights to the South, Seward's threats of war had effectively stalled further momentum toward full recognition, and Yancey and the Confederate European commission were thoroughly demoralized. All that was about to change. After midnight on October 12, 1861, Mason, Slidell, their two secretaries, and several family members sailed out of Charleston into a stormy night, trying to evade the US Navy ships that lay outside the harbor. They made it safely to Nassau, a British port in the Bahamas, and from there sailed to Havana, Cuba.

On November 7 Mason and Slidell boarded a British Royal Mail steamer, the *Trent,* for what would be the most fateful voyage of the Civil War. One day after they left Havana, a Union naval vessel commanded by Captain Charles Wilkes intercepted the *Trent* at sea. Boarding the British ship, Wilkes's officers announced they were there to arrest the two Confederate envoys and their secretaries. The *Trent*'s captain protested that this was an act of piracy and a violation of British neutrality. Mason and Slidell insisted they would have to be apprehended by force. An angry group of passengers, many of them Southerners, gathered on deck and howled in protest as the men were taken away. "This is the best thing in the world for the South," one of them yelled. "We will have a good chance at them now."[51]

The *Trent* affair was indeed a gift to the Confederates, so much so that some suspected it was all a setup to pull Britain into the war against the United States. Thurlow Weed, on assignment as special agent for the Union in London at the time, informed Seward that some viewed the capture of Slidell and Mason as "an understood thing" and that "the arrest was courted." Malakoff, the *New York Times* correspondent in Paris, reported that "the whole scheme was concocted at London." French insiders told Malakoff that "it was a trap laid for Mr. Seward, into which he incontinently stumbled."[52]

If there was a setup, Seward was not the only one taken in. The British press and many prominent political leaders roundly denounced the "wanton outrage and insult" to the British flag. They displayed remarkably little concern for Slidell and Mason, who were very comfortably billeted at Fort Warren in Boston Harbor, but the offense to British honor must be answered. When news arrived in London that ecstatic Northerners were crowing about the escapade and hailing Captain Wilkes as a great hero, it ignited even greater fury.[53]

The London *Times,* always happy to give vent to British indignation against America, published an eyewitness account from an officer on board the *Trent* that described "cowardly bullying" by the arresting officers. Whereas Weed's and Malakoff's informants detected Confederate or European intrigue behind events, the *Times*'s informants saw Seward's hand at work. Seward, they thought, was deliberately inciting the fanatical passions of the democratic mob and trying to reunite America against a foreign foe.[54]

Across Britain the drums of war began beating in the press, at public indignation meetings, and over dinner parties among the upper class. Young boys peddled miniature Confederate flags on the streets. Britain seemed to be getting ready for military retaliation. "The people are frantic with rage," Charles Mackay, an English friend, wrote to Seward from London on November 29. "Were the country polled I fear 999 men out of a thousand would declare for war."[55]

The Palmerston government had to do something to respond to the public clamor for war—and soon—lest the Tory opposition use the crisis to unseat the government. On November 30 Earl Russell began preparations to send ten thousand troops to Canada and bolster the British naval presence in the Caribbean.[56]

Yancey, still waiting in London to be relieved by Mason, immediately recognized the *Trent* affair as a windfall for the Confederacy and volunteered to stay at his post. On December 2, with British public indignation at full boil, he reported having "addressed to her Britannic Majesty's Government a solemn remonstrance against the outrage perpetrated by the United States." Yancey tried to goad Palmerston into demanding satisfaction, urging him to insist not only on an apology but also on reparations for the *Trent* outrage. To Richmond he sent clippings from British and French journals demonstrating the furor the *Trent* affair had caused. Yancey and most all the Confederate sympathizers in Europe were positively thrilled by the prospect of war between Britain and the United States.[57]

Eager as always to take credit, Ambrose Dudley Mann sent his own dispatch to Richmond, gloating over the triumph at hand. Great Britain was downright earnest "in her purpose to humiliate by disgraceful concessions" or punish the United States for its "flagrant violation of the integrity of her flag upon the high seas." Carried away by the moment, he gushed, "What a noble statesman Lord Palmerston! His heart is as young as it was 40 years ago."[58]

Pierre Rost wrote from Paris with equal élan, predicting that France would stay out of any war Britain commenced against the United States but would come in later as a mediator. France might delay in recognizing the South, he thought, "but a great change in public opinion has taken place here within the last six months." He immodestly added that Édouard Thouvenel, the French foreign minister, had confided that "no one could have done or accomplished more than I had."[59]

Tout va bien for the Confederacy in Europe. At the end of 1861 it appeared that a Union navy captain boarding a British mail ship on the high seas had done more for the Confederate cause than all its vainglorious envoys could have dreamed.

CHAPTER 3

WE WILL WRAP
THE WORLD IN FLAMES

If any European Power provokes a war we shall not shrink from it. A contest between Great Britain and the United States would wrap the world in fire, and at the end it would not be the United States which would have to lament the results of the conflict.

—WILLIAM HENRY SEWARD,
UNION SECRETARY OF STATE, JULY 4, 1861

BEFORE ABRAHAM LINCOLN HAD EVEN TAKEN OFFICE, THE Confederacy had already issued its claim to nationhood in February 1861 and set about explaining itself to the world. The new president and his secretary of state, William Seward, found themselves having to answer the Confederacy on its terms. To the Southern claim that secession was a legitimate path to nationhood, Lincoln and Seward would tell the world this was nothing more than treasonous rebellion. To charges that Republicans intended to abolish slavery and ignite racial conflagration, Lincoln answered that he had neither the constitutional power nor the intention to interfere with slavery in the states where it already existed. As for the South's appeal to the right to self-government, Lincoln repeatedly charged that the South was violating the most sacred principles of democracy: the sovereignty of the people and majority rule. Against the

South's right to secede, Seward would advance the fundamental principle of international law: the right to national self-preservation in the face of domestic insurrection.[1]

When the South threatened to deprive Europe of cotton unless Europe recognized its sovereignty, Seward answered with a far more ominous threat: any nation that dared to aid the rebellion would face the United States in war. "We will wrap the whole world in flames!" he told journalists and diplomats without hesitation. "No power is so remote that she will not feel the fire of our battle and be burned by our conflagration." He instructed his diplomats abroad to carry the same message: if the Great Powers dared to interfere on behalf of this rebellion, this civil war would "become a war of continents—a war of the world."[2]

In his March 4 inaugural address, however, Lincoln adopted a temperate, conciliatory tone. His speech would lay down the basic principles underlying domestic *and* foreign policy, and he used the occasion to place both on the firm foundation of national and international law. Above all, Lincoln knew he must avoid lending credence to hysterical claims that his party, once in power, planned to menace the South and violate the states' prerogatives regarding slavery.

The presidential inaugural represented the essence of democracy—the peaceful transition of power between champions of rival parties. It had been faithfully observed since 1800, when Thomas Jefferson defeated John Adams, a result that, at the time, met with shrieks of alarm among conservative Federalists. In elections ever since, the party in power had yielded peacefully to the loyal opposition. It was bracing testament to what Lincoln viewed as the most fundamental principle of popular government: leaders are chosen in free and fair elections by the will of the majority, and the losing party accepts the verdict of the ballot—until the next election.

That principle was the very opposite of the revolutionary idea behind secession, and without it democratic government simply could not work. The new president had a lesson to teach on March 4 about popular government and the rule of law.

LINCOLN ARRIVED IN WASHINGTON MORE THAN A WEEK BEFORE HIS inauguration and took rooms at Willard's Hotel, not far from the White

House. Willard's grand lobby was swarming with office seekers and reporters. Their cigars filled the air with smoke, and spit from chewing tobacco fouled the walls and carpets. Lincoln's young secretary John Hay described the president-elect sitting serenely in his rooms at Willard's receiving "moist delegations of bores" whose ardent demands failed to upset the "imperturbability of his temperament." That imperturbable temperament was about to be tested mightily.[3]

On March 4, 1861, the sound of drums and fife filled the streets of Washington. According to custom, the outgoing president, James Buchanan, called on the president-elect at Willard's to escort him in an open carriage to the Capitol. An estimated forty thousand people turned out for the procession. They lined Pennsylvania Avenue, some climbing trees and street poles to catch a glimpse of the new president.

Along with delegations of somber officials from the Supreme Court, the military, and the diplomatic corps was a gaily decorated carriage filled with thirty-four young girls personifying the states of the Union— including the seceding slave states. Military bands filled the air with music as the procession moved along Pennsylvania Avenue.

Yet this was no ordinary presidential inauguration. One reporter noted that the "usual applause was lacking" and that "an ugly murmur punctuated by some abusive remarks" could be heard. Poet Walt Whitman recalled that Lincoln's convoy was surrounded "by a dense mass of armed cavalrymen eight deep, with drawn sabres," with "sharp shooters stationed at every corner on the route." The parade made its way to the Capitol, whose unfinished dome stood high against the sun with unsightly scaffolding jutting above graceful neoclassical arches.[4]

James Buchanan looked "pale, sad, nervous," according to the *New York Times*. He rode next to Lincoln in silence except to complain about how much he longed to go home to Pennsylvania. As Lincoln took the oath of office, Buchanan "sighed audibly and frequently" and throughout the inaugural speech appeared "sleepy and tired" and "sat looking as straight as he could at the toe of his right boot."[5]

During four interminable months between Lincoln's election and inauguration, Buchanan, by sheer inaction and virtual abdication of power, had given the rebellion incalculable advantage. In his annual message to Congress in December, the outgoing president blamed the whole crisis on antislavery agitators and their "long-continued and intemperate

6. *The Outbreak of the Rebellion in the United States in 1861,* by Christopher Kimmel, depicts Liberty flanked by Justice, glaring at Jefferson Davis, while President Buchanan sleeps and Abraham Lincoln appeals to generous Northern supporters. (ALFRED WHITAL STERN COLLECTION, LIBRARY OF CONGRESS)

interference" in the slavery question. Overseas, several of Buchanan's appointees, still at their diplomatic posts, used their treacherous influence to encourage foreign governments to believe, as Buchanan maintained, that the federal government was powerless to stop secession and that the fragmentation of the republic was irreversible.[6]

Unlike Jefferson Davis, who had given an inaugural speech two weeks earlier that was hastily prepared and consisted mostly of party-line secessionist platitudes, Lincoln labored over his address for weeks, crafting every phrase, revising and practicing until the speech conveyed exactly what he wanted to say to an anxious nation—and world. Lincoln invited advice from his secretary of state, William Seward, who leaped at the opportunity and responded with six pages of line-by-line commentary. Seward had a well-earned reputation as a pugnacious adversary of the South, but at this tense moment his editorial suggestions all aimed at softening the language and soothing Southern nerves.[7]

Seward viewed the secessionists as an impulsive extremist fringe, and he wanted nothing in the speech that would lend credence to their claims that Republicans were about to abolish slavery or stir unrest among the slaves. He saw himself as a mentor to the president, who, except for one term in Congress a dozen years earlier, was a newcomer to Washington and a stranger to international affairs. Seward had been Lincoln's rival for the Republican nomination the previous summer, and the new president wanted him on the inside of the tent. Lincoln was also wise enough to recognize his own shortcomings and humble enough to seek advice. He instinctively trusted Seward and relied on his savvy grasp of politics and diplomacy. It was the beginning of a remarkable collaboration between two men who, working together, became masters of statecraft at home and abroad.[8]

When he took the podium on March 4, Lincoln appeared awkward, fumbling for a moment to find a place to set his top hat. Democratic senator Stephen Douglas, one of Lincoln's rivals in the recent election, made a gracious gesture of respect by offering to hold the president's hat. After putting on his reading glasses, Lincoln reached in his coat pocket and pulled out several sheets of paper, unfolded them on the lectern, and then unceremoniously placed his cane on the papers to hold them flat. Then, with remarkable poise, he "commenced in a clear, ringing voice," the *New York Times* reported, to tell Americans what their new president was going to do about the crisis engulfing the nation.[9]

What people heard that afternoon depended on what they were willing to hear. Douglas heard a conciliatory promise of "no coercion." Confederate telegrams to Montgomery fairly screamed that it was a virtual declaration of war. The significance of the speech lay in the ideological framework it provided for domestic and foreign policy. Most remarkable was that, with a few deft phrases, Lincoln managed to elevate the US debacle from a mere civil war to a crisis of momentous global significance.[10]

It was the underlying principle of international law, Lincoln declared, that all nations had a moral obligation to their citizens to preserve and perfect their nature as civil associations. Nations cannot set limits on their future. "I hold that in contemplation of *universal law* and of the Constitution, the Union of these States is perpetual," he affirmed. "Perpetuity is implied, if not expressed, in the fundamental law of all national governments." Secession, he insisted, made government practically unworkable and amounted to national suicide. No government provided "for its own termination." Why, he asked mischievously, might not the states of some "new confederacy" decide to "secede again," once the principle was granted? (Confederates in Montgomery, he may have known, had secretly debated provisions for secession and nullification in their own constitution and summarily rejected both as impractical.) The "central idea of secession is the essence of anarchy," Lincoln insisted. Majority rule was the "only true sovereign of a free people," and those who reject it must "fly to anarchy or to despotism."[11]

Next the president turned to slavery. Having argued that secession was implicitly unconstitutional, he had to reconcile this point with the sacrosanct American principle of the revolutionary right of people to overthrow governments that abused the natural rights of the people. He also had to lay to rest any reasonable just cause for revolution by insisting that the new Republican administration would not interfere with slavery in the states where it already existed. He cited the Republican platform that affirmed "the right of each State to order and control its own domestic institutions." Then Lincoln quoted from one of his own speeches: "I have no purpose, directly or indirectly, to interfere with the institution of slavery in the States where it exists. I believe I have no lawful right to do so, and I have no inclination to do so."

That the president had no constitutional authority to interfere with slavery in the Southern states was undisputed, but his denial of any *inclination* to end slavery in those states demoralized friends of freedom around the world. Lincoln then took it further by alluding to motions in Congress for a constitutional amendment banning federal abolition of slavery. On the very day of the inaugural, Congress had approved what would have been the Thirteenth Amendment. It was cosponsored by Seward in the Senate, and it would have guaranteed slavery within the United States *forever*. The price for perpetual Union would have been perpetual slavery. No wonder so many would question the moral purpose of the war—and of the Union, for that matter.[12]

SEWARD'S INITIAL FOREIGN POLICY MESSAGE TO THE WORLD ESSENTIALLY echoed Lincoln's inaugural address. The Union was fighting for national self-preservation against a treasonous rebellion, and a rebellion without cause, for abolition was not contemplated. However, his foreign policy also contained a firm warning. According to the rules of international law, any foreign gesture of support for a domestic insurrection would be considered an act of war. On March 9 Seward issued a circular to all US diplomats abroad, instructing them to exercise the greatest diligence in counteracting any designs for "foreign intervention to embarrass or overthrow the republic."

With this circular Seward also enclosed a copy of the president's inaugural address, which, he explained, "sets forth clearly the errors of the misguided partisans who are seeking to dismember the Union." He then laid out an oblique threat that discord and anarchy in such a well-established and widely respected government as America's could infect "other parts of the world, and arrest that progress of improvement and civilization which marks the era in which we live." Seward seemed to be issuing a cautionary advisory to foreign powers that America's troubles might become their own if they dared give encouragement to rebellion.[13]

Seward also busied himself in March and April advising Lincoln on appointments to dozens of diplomatic posts around the world. Once the disloyal appointees of previous administrations were replaced, the Union would enjoy a great advantage in the impending diplomatic duel because of its vast network of legations and consulates, a reliable system of intercontinental communication, and a corps of experienced civil servants as secretaries in all the main legations abroad. Seward and Lincoln understood that the men they appointed to these diplomatic posts would be the eyes and ears, as well as the voices, of America abroad. Seward firmly believed that listening would prove more valuable than "propagandizing," and he instructed all his diplomats to report on the press and public sentiment abroad as well as official government communications.

There was no time to waste. Eight years of pro-Southern Democratic presidents had left the diplomatic corps infested with Confederate sympathizers, several of whom were actively promoting the idea that secession was constitutional and irreversible. George Dallas, a Pennsylvania Democrat serving as US minister in London, did nothing to actively betray the Union, but his secretary Benjamin Moran recorded in his diary that "Dallas has some of the secession virus in him and he is clearly strong on the States Rights folly."[14]

Charles Faulkner, a Southern sympathizer from Virginia serving as the US minister to France, refused to relinquish his post until after his replacement arrived and was suspected of using his office to convince the French government that Southern secession was irrevocable. Seward quickly sent Henry Sanford, his most trusted man in Europe, ahead to Paris to control the damage. He authorized Sanford to speak directly with the French government and explain the Union side of things, but Faulkner used his position to delay Sanford's meeting with the French foreign minister. Thanks to Faulkner and his ilk, Sanford complained to Seward, it was now generally accepted in Paris that "the 'Secession' of the 'Confederate States' is complete." Upon his return to the United States, Faulkner was arrested on suspicion of procuring arms for the Confederacy while in Europe. The charges were not sustained, and Faulkner was released. He later served in the Confederate army as Stonewall Jackson's assistant.[15]

Eduard Maco Hudson, secretary to the US legation in Berlin, turned his talents to issuing a German-language pamphlet describing the Southern rebellion as the "second war of independence in America." An English edition was later published in London. The outgoing minister to Madrid, William Preston of Kentucky, put his remaining time to use nurturing friendly relations between Spain and the Confederacy and returned home to serve the Confederacy as brigadier general and later as envoy to Mexico. Henry Sanford was outraged to discover that the wife of Elisha Fair, his predecessor as US minister to Belgium, had stolen the legation seal and was using it on letters she sent out to encourage European support of the secessionist cause. She "is excelled by no secession agent abroad" in this ugly business, Sanford wrote to Seward. If the Union had "one half the amount of sharp activity the Secessionists have shown," instead of the betrayal or stony silence demonstrated by "those who profess to represent us," the South would never have made such headway convincing Europe that secession was fact.[16]

MEANWHILE, IN WASHINGTON, LINCOLN MOVED QUICKLY TO FILL key diplomatic posts with his own loyal men. Ministers to the Great Powers of Europe were handsomely paid, and the posts came with enviable status and perquisites. Lincoln was no different from other presidents in treating diplomatic appointments as political rewards for supporters. Remarkably little attention was paid to even such basic qualifications as prior experience abroad, knowledge of international law, familiarity with the host country's history, or even comprehension of its language. If

America's diplomats "talk abroad as they do at home," John Bigelow, future envoy to France, once wryly observed, "the fewer languages at their command the better."[17]

More than the candidates' qualifications, what often mattered was what state they were from, the political faction they represented, and how their appointment might help the party in the next election. Politics trumped diplomacy, but if diplomacy sometimes suffered, there would also be benefits to having men practiced in the arts of democratic politics and public persuasion ready for the contest of public diplomacy that was about to unfold overseas.[18]

One week after taking office, on March 11, Lincoln sent Seward a memo suggesting how he might fill what they anticipated correctly to be four key diplomatic posts. Britain and France were the most critical. These were the two leading naval powers in the world, and both were heavily dependent on cotton from the South for their textile industries. Spain was a feeble imperial power, but its colonies, Cuba and Puerto Rico, remained dependent on slave labor, and that made Spain a dangerous potential ally of the South. Mexico was crucial because of its seaports on the Gulf and its long border with Texas, which would provide a vital supply route, circumventing the Union blockade Lincoln was about to impose. "We need to have these points guarded as strongly and quickly as possible," Lincoln told Seward.[19]

For London, clearly the most critical post, Lincoln proposed William Dayton of New Jersey, an old Whig and the Republican candidate for vice president four years earlier. Dayton was an amiable if not always diligent man who had no diplomatic experience or any discernible knowledge of Europe to recommend him. For Paris, Lincoln wanted John C. Frémont, who ran for president on the Republican ticket with Dayton in 1856. He was the son of a French immigrant and was wildly popular with European liberals for his antislavery views. Cassius Clay, a colorful antislavery Republican from Kentucky known to pack pistols and a bowie knife, Lincoln thought fit to serve as ambassador at court in Madrid. For Mexico City, he wanted his old friend Ohio congressman Thomas Corwin, whose opposition to the US war with Mexico in 1846 made him hugely popular among Mexican liberals.

Seward concurred on Corwin, who would be heartily welcomed in Mexico by Benito Juárez, the newly elected president of a republic that had just emerged from its own civil war and still faced intransigent opposition from conservative monarchists and Catholics. For London, however, Seward persuaded Lincoln to appoint Charles Francis Adams of Massachusetts. He had a well-tempered mind, and politics and diplomacy ran in the Adams family blood; his grandfather, John Adams, and father, John Quincy Adams, had served as distinguished diplomats as well as presidents. Besides, Seward noted, a New England appointee would help Republicans in the next election. Seward had little use for Frémont because of his radical antislavery views, and instead he got behind Dayton for the Paris post, despite his utter lack of qualifications. Cassius Clay met the need for a border-state nominee, and they decided to send him to St. Petersburg, Russia.

Lincoln wanted to reward "our German friends" who had helped deliver the Midwestern immigrant vote to the Republicans. Carl Schurz, a radical who fled Germany for Wisconsin after the failed Revolution of 1848, had been a loyal campaigner, and he wanted the appointment to Italy. Seward distrusted Schurz, and the entire radical wing of the Republican Party for that matter. He argued that such an appointment would offend a conservative Catholic country, and he even tried to impose a general rule against the appointment of any foreign-born ministers to diplomatic posts. Lincoln relented and filled the Italian post with George Perkins Marsh, a Vermont Republican with a cultivated mind, a command of several languages, and years of successful diplomatic experience in Istanbul. But Lincoln insisted on sending Schurz to Madrid, a far more conservative Catholic nation than Italy.

Thus, politics and diplomacy commingled from the start, and not always with good results. Most of Lincoln's appointees, like those of the Confederacy, would begin as amateurs, learning the art of statecraft on the job. They were plunging into an uncharted world of public diplomacy, where their political instincts would often serve them well.[20]

In a democracy with a new party and president coming to power, everyone was learning on the job, not least Abraham Lincoln. William Howard Russell, the London *Times* correspondent, recorded a comical vignette of Lincoln and Seward at their diplomatic debut a few days after the inauguration in March 1861. Italy, following the annexations of Sicily along with several other small kingdoms and duchies, was applying anew for recognition as the Kingdom of Italy. Russell described Italy's dashing emissary to Washington, Giuseppe Bertinatti, who arrived at the White House dressed in full diplomatic regalia, with a "cocked hat, white gloves, diplomatic suit of blue and silver lace, sword, sash, and ribbon of the cross of Savoy." A tall, handsome, slim man, the Italian ambassador walked into the White House beside Seward, whose hair and clothes were, as usual, slightly rumpled.

Russell watched as Old World pomp encountered American rusticity. Seward and Bertinatti stood side by side at the center of the room as President Lincoln entered. Russell described a "tall, lank, lean man, considerably over six feet in height, with stooping shoulders, long pendulous arms, terminating in hands of extraordinary dimensions, which however were far exceeded in proportion by his feet." He was dressed in "an ill-fitting, wrinkled suit of black, which put one in mind of an undertaker's uniform at a funeral." His "strange quaint face" was topped by a "thatch of wild republican hair."

Lincoln walked across the room, greeting everyone with a smile, and then "was suddenly brought up by the staid deportment of Mr. Seward" and "the profound diplomatic bows of the Chevalier Bertinatti." Lincoln "suddenly jerked himself back, and stood in front of the two ministers, with his body slightly drooped forward and his hands behind his back, his knees touching, and his feet apart." Seward made his formal presentation, "whereupon the President made a prodigiously violent demonstration of his body in a bow," which Bertinatti answered with another bow and then read the message from his king, asking to be received in Mr. Lincoln's court. This ritual of recognition so readily accorded the newly constituted Kingdom of Italy was exactly what Confederate envoys longed for abroad.[21]

IT IS EASY TO UNDERSTAND HOW SEWARD SAW HIMSELF TUTORING Lincoln in the ways of Washington, the rituals of office, the strange pomp of diplomacy, for that was exactly what he was doing. In truth, Seward and Lincoln quickly formed an exceptional working relationship and learned from each other. Though not always in harmony, they came to embody complementary foreign and domestic policies, and the Union's eventual success at home and abroad owed much to the close understanding that developed between these two men.[22]

There is no denying that Seward was at first jealous and condescending toward the prairie lawyer who occupied the office for which Seward had been preparing all his life. "Disappointment!" he lashed out at one startled congressman that first spring. You speak of disappointment "to me, who was justly entitled to the Republican nomination for the presidency" and "had to stand aside and see it given to a little Illinois lawyer! You speak to me of disappointment!" But Seward soon came to admire Lincoln's gifts while flattering himself to think the president could not manage without him. "The president is the best of us," he wrote his wife, Frances, in early June 1861, "but he needs constant and assiduous cooperation."[23]

The president was willing to defer to Seward on the execution of foreign policy. "I don't know anything about diplomacy," he told one astonished foreign diplomat. "I will be very apt to make blunders." He also told Seward at the outset, "There is one part of my work that I shall have to leave largely to you. I shall have to depend upon you for taking care of these matters of foreign affairs, of which I know so little, and with which I reckon you are familiar."[24]

Lincoln reckoned correctly. Seward enjoyed years of experience on the Senate Foreign Relations Committee, and he had traveled extensively in Europe. He was conversant in French and well read on world affairs. An ardent nationalist, Seward foresaw America's future as a major world power. He was keenly aware that European monarchists harbored deep jealousy and resentment toward the United States, its democracy, and its success. At sixty years of age, with years of service before him, Seward was eager to assume an indispensable role as consigliere to the neophyte president, the knowing guide to the inner mysteries of Washington politics and to the peculiar world of diplomacy.

But Seward also earned a reputation for presuming too much authority over the new president, acting as though he were a prime minister and mistaking Lincoln's inexperience with an incapacity to manage the presidency. In a bizarre memorandum dated April 1, 1861, Seward took it upon himself to set forth "some thoughts for the President's consideration." The April 1 memo opened with an unfortunate tone of impatience, complaining that after a month, the administration was "yet without a policy either domestic or foreign." Seward quickly laid out his solution, numbering and underlining its main points. "My system is built upon this *idea* as a ruling one, namely that we must *Change the question before the Public from one upon Slavery, or about slavery* for a question upon *Union or Disunion.*"[25]

The secretary of state proposed that Fort Sumter be abandoned because in the public mind, it had become closely associated with the slavery question. The issue he wanted Americans to focus on was the menace of Spain in the Caribbean. Only two days earlier, news had arrived that Spain had launched an invasion of its former colony, Santo Domingo, and proclaimed its reannexation. Rumors were flying that the French were cooperating and poised to take over their former colony in neighboring Haiti. "I would demand explanation from *Spain* and France, categorically, at once," Seward advised the president. "I would seek explanations from Great Britain and Russia, and send agents into *Canada, Mexico* and *Central America,* to rouse a vigorous continental *spirit of independence* on this continent against European intervention." Then he came to the point: "If satisfactory explanations are not received from Spain and France," Lincoln should "convene Congress and declare war against them."[26]

Seward was possessed by an idea—a patriotic fantasy, in truth—that historians would later call his "foreign war panacea." Faced with a foreign enemy menacing America, Unionists in the North and South would reunite and rally around the flag. The "hills of South Carolina would pour forth their population to the rescue of New York," Seward told a home-state audience the previous December.[27]

During a dinner party at the home of British ambassador Lord Lyons not long before his April memo, Seward, cigar in hand and speaking loudly, told Lyons, Henri Mercier, the French ambassador, and Eduard Stoeckl, Russia's envoy, that "the best thing that could happen to America right now would be for Europe to get involved in some way in her affairs." It would create international upheaval, and "not a government in Europe would remain standing." Mercier thought he must have had too much to drink, but as he warned the home office in Paris: in vino veritas. Lyons also worried that Seward was itching for war. Among Northerners, he wrote to London, "a Foreign war finds favour, as a remedy for intestine divisions."[28]

It was never clear to foreign diplomats and reporters whether Seward was just blustering or if he actually thought he could resolve the domestic crisis by creating an international crisis. He was deliberately trying to frighten European powers from intervention in America's crisis by suggesting that he welcomed rather than feared war with them. If he was sometimes intemperate with language and drink, it seemed to serve his purpose of intimidation all the better. More than one foreign diplomat and head of state feared Seward precisely because they thought he was half-mad.[29]

There was no doubt that in his April 1 memorandum, Seward questioned Lincoln's command of the situation. He advised that, because the president was preoccupied with other matters, an experienced cabinet member might take charge of formulating clear domestic and foreign policies. "I seek neither to evade nor assume responsibility," he closed rather disingenuously.

Lincoln probably spoke with Seward about the memo, but for the record he also wrote out a careful reply that gave no hint of irritation yet explained firmly that his inaugural address had already delineated the administration's domestic policy. He saw no good reason to surrender Sumter. As for foreign policy, until now Seward's own policy had been conciliatory. Spain's Santo Domingo invasion was new, Lincoln admitted, but he saw no advantage in fomenting war over this incident. He added that while he valued advice from all cabinet members, whatever "must be done, I must do it."[30]

The story of Seward's "April Fool's Day memorandum," as his detractors would later call it, is usually told as an internal challenge to a novice president answered by Lincoln's bold assertion of command. But there was a good deal more to it. Seward and his confidant Thurlow Weed, a savvy New York political operator and newspaper publisher, had an elaborate plan to leak the memo to the *New York Times* and other newspapers and to launch a barrage of editorials and news stories that would incite public outrage against Spain and France. It was a revealing example of Seward's conflation of diplomacy and domestic politics, and it demonstrated his readiness to use the press as a tool of diplomacy. The episode also reveals Seward deliberately making use of loose talk, bluster, and brinksmanship to intimidate foreign adversaries as much as to arouse patriotic sentiment at home.[31]

Weed had come down to Washington several days earlier to help work out the plan with Seward. On March 31 Henry J. Raymond, editor of the *New York Times* and a stalwart Republican, joined them, arriving by train at midnight. James Swain, the Washington correspondent for the *New York Times,* brought Raymond to Seward's residence and then waited at his own house. Raymond instructed him to keep the telegraph lines open for a "marvelous revelation to the readers of the *Times.*" At four in the morning on April 1, Raymond finally showed up at Swain's house and asked for a drink. It was not until the second bottle, Swain remembered, that his boss revealed what was in the works.[32]

The plan was to publish Seward's memorandum to Lincoln, along with the president's reply, on the front page of the *New York Times* later that day. Seward and Weed both assured Raymond that the president "could not fail to be in accord with the suggestion of the Secretary." Meanwhile, Raymond was to return to New York, whip up a "vigorous editorial endorsement of the programme," and issue "an unmistakable *pronunciamento* that Seward alone" could carry it out. It sounded like Seward and his cronies were plotting a palace coup. Of course, Lincoln's cool response to Seward's April 1 memo forced a change of plans.[33]

On April 1 the *New York Times* contained no "marvelous revelation" of Seward's ascendancy, but it ran a robust editorial denouncing plans for predatory foreign intervention in the American hemisphere. Alluding to the alarming reports from Malakoff, the newspaper's Paris correspondent, that Britain, France, and Spain were preparing to send fleets of warships, supposedly "for observation" of America's coasts, the editorial painted a dark picture of the American republic besieged by its Old World nemeses.

> French fleets in American waters—Spanish cruisers hovering in our Gulf—English men-of-war along our coasts;—significant rumors from France of her assuming new relations with her old province of Louisiana— burning, secret sympathies of England with her enslaved black "men and brothers"—menacing attitude of the Spanish Government, . . . which now, in our time of trouble, taunts and defies us by stationing ten thousand troops within fifty miles of our shores, to keep eye upon us, and possibly, in the domestic melee she hopes for, to repossess herself of the splendid provinces which, as Florida, Texas, etc., we now call sovereign States of the Union.

The editorial closed with a rousing call for domestic unity in the face of foreign enemies, but if this was the fuse for Seward's scheme of a foreign war that would reunite North and South, it failed to light.[34]

SEWARD'S APRIL 1 SCHEME MAY NOT HAVE GONE ACCORDING TO PLAN, and his ambitions to become virtual prime minister were curbed, but the more important point is that Lincoln supported Seward's underlying foreign policy strategy. The main issue before the public was already "Union or Disunion," not slavery or abolition. In his April 1 memorandum, Seward proposed an aggressive, hard-power foreign policy whose cardinal feature was the blatant threat of foreign war, and to that Lincoln had no objection.

The next day, April 2, Seward began implementing his strategy by sending a menacing warning to the Spanish ambassador, Gabriel García Tassara, in which he promised a "prompt, persistent and, if possible, effective resistance" to Spain's aggression in the New World. At the same time, he wrote to the French ambassador in Washington, Henri Mercier, and to Lord Lyons, Britain's ambassador, to inform them of his protest against Spain and, by implication, to warn them against any cooperation or aggression on the part of their governments.[35]

Seward then put his mind to writing instructions to each of his newly appointed emissaries abroad. These were lengthy, complicated expositions tailored to the circumstances of each foreign country. They were meant to inform the ministers of the official policy of the US government and provide debate points for defending those policies. Underlying each of the sometimes rambling and philosophical letters of instruction were the core principles of Seward's foreign policy: First, the conflict was an American domestic insurrection taking place within one permanent and inviolable nation. Second, this was a rebellion without cause, pretext, or any defensible goal; the Union was focused upon "national self-preservation" and *not abolition*. Third, any nation recognizing or aiding the rebellion would risk war with the United States.

Seward's April 10 instructions to Charles Francis Adams went out more than a month before Adams would even get to London (he was home in Massachusetts attending his son's wedding). "You will not consent to draw into debate before the British government any opposing

7. William Seward and Abraham Lincoln, Currier and Ives.
(ALFRED WHITAL STERN COLLECTION, LIBRARY OF CONGRESS)

moral principles which may be supposed to lie at the foundation of the controversy between those States and the federal Union." (Ironically, this was essentially the same warning Toombs gave his Confederate European commissioners.) Adams was instructed to remind Britain of the dire consequences of recognizing the "so-called Confederate States." Should the rebellion succeed, there would be "perpetual war" within North America, because the "new confederacy" would, "like any other new state, seek to expand itself northward, westward, and southward." No part of North America or the Caribbean, he warned the British who had possessions in both places, could expect to remain at peace.[36]

It was April 22 before he sent instructions to William Dayton in Paris. Seward advised him also to "refrain from any observation whatever concerning the morality or the immorality, the economy or the waste, the social or the unsocial aspects of slavery." He was emphatic in making the French understand that slavery and abolition were not at issue. "Whether the revolution shall succeed or shall fail," he wanted Dayton to explain, "the condition of slavery in the several States will remain just the same."

Dayton was to tell the French that the goal of the South's revolution was "the overthrow of the government of the United States," whose establishment "was the most auspicious political event that has happened in the whole progress of history." Seward, apparently oblivious to the French Second Empire's antipathy toward republicanism, took this further by instructing Dayton to communicate that America's "fall must be deemed not merely a national calamity . . . but a misfortune to the human race." He then applauded France's valiant role in emancipating the American colonies from British tyranny and then, inexplicably, called upon Napoleon III's decidedly undemocratic regime to help defend their common principles of "universal suffrage" and "free popular government." It was a clumsy appeal to republican ideals the French government detested.[37]

By instructing extreme caution on the subject of emancipation, Seward clearly wanted to soothe anxieties among government leaders and business interests abroad that his government might plunge the nation into social conflagration, and throw world cotton markets into chaos, by some reckless edict to abolish slavery. But more was involved here. Seward's own deep reservations about radical abolitionist programs guided his foreign policy.

FEW KNEW THAT SEWARD CAME FROM A FAMILY OF SLAVE OWNERS AND grew up surrounded by the peculiar institution in New York, where slavery survived until 1827. His memoirs recalled with fondness the many hours he spent in the family kitchen listening to the family's slaves, enthralled by their astonishing tales of the supernatural. Yet he was equally impressed by the desire of slaves to be free. He never forgot Zeno, a slave owned by another family, who was among his childhood playmates. Zeno had run away after being "severely whipped" and was brought back with an iron collar fastened on his neck. He later stole away again, this time for good. Then one of the Seward family's slaves fled soon after Zeno left. "Something was wrong," Seward recorded in his memoirs, "and I determined, at an early age, to be an abolitionist." Seward's moral objections to slavery were genuine, but he steadfastly favored the New York model of gradual emancipation and consistently warned of the dangers of sudden abolition.[38]

As an aspiring politician, Seward became the protégé of Thurlow Weed, the savvy New York newspaper publisher and political operator who managed Seward's early rise from state senator to governor and then to the US Senate in 1848. That was the year Lincoln and Seward first met at a political rally in Boston. They wound up sharing a hotel room the next night in Worcester and talked deep into the night about politics and the slavery question. Seward told Lincoln that he had come to realize the time was right to speak out against the expansion of slavery. By Seward's account, his roommate was far more cautious. Seward continued talking that night in Worcester, until Lincoln finally conceded the point—whether out of conviction or exhaustion, it was never clear. That year Lincoln left Congress and retreated into the relative obscurity of Illinois politics for a decade. Seward, meanwhile, became the leader of the antislavery "conscience Whigs" and the voice of the rising Republican Party, on his way, so it seemed, to becoming its first president.[39]

In part to restore his health, but also to absent himself from the American press before the 1860 election and prepare for office, Seward embarked on an extended tour of Europe and the Middle East in May 1859. He was greeted abroad as the president-in-waiting. In December he returned to a troubled nation in time to prepare for the coming election. The best-laid plans of mice, men, and politicians sometimes go awry, and they did for Seward at the Republican nominating convention, held in Chicago in the summer of 1860.

Significantly, several key Republicans thought he was too radical on the slavery question; his recent speech on the "irrepressible conflict" between North and South and his earlier appeal to a "higher law" than the Constitution haunted his prospects for the nomination. Eager to win moderates and bring in disaffected Democrats, Republicans chose Lincoln over Seward, not because of any fundamental disagreements on the slavery issue (their sentiments and policies were not far apart) but precisely because Lincoln was less well known. For Seward, it was a severe blow. He was not going to let the slavery issue wreck his new career as secretary of state and adviser to the president.[40]

Seward and Lincoln were as one on the basic message that the Union was waging war only to preserve the Union and not to abolish slavery. In addition to delegitimizing the South's justification for rebellion, this policy accorded with both men's view that, whatever their moral revulsion toward human slavery, the institution was protected by the Constitution and vital to both the American and world economies. An "abolition war," they feared, would endanger support for the Union at home and abroad.

SEWARD'S MESSAGE ON SLAVERY AIMED AT REASSURING GOVERNMENT and business leaders, but his diplomatic corps abroad soon warned him that more liberal elements in the European public expected the Great Republic to seize the opportunity to destroy the cause of the rebellion and advance the cause of liberty. Europeans were genuinely puzzled by the Union's conservative, legalistic position and lack of moral purpose in waging war. Seward's ministers, whom he had instructed to report on public opinion, warned him that if the conflict was viewed only as an American quarrel over secession and territory, the world would just as soon see the Union dismembered.

"You must make up your mind to commense an anti slavery crusade in England," Henry Sanford, unofficial chief of public diplomacy operations in Europe, wrote Seward in May 1861. "Send over some good speakers, spend a little money and we can carry the country with us." Europeans, he told Seward, supposed the war was being waged for "the *Extinction of Slavery*," and they held no interest in local political contests or legal squabbles over the right to secession. The public, if not the governments and the press, Sanford assured him, would be with them once it was made clear that the Union was on the side of liberty.[41]

None of Seward's ministers was more prescient than Carl Schurz, writing from Madrid in September 1861. The Union, he advised Seward, must "place the war against the rebellious slave States upon a higher moral basis and thereby give us the control of public opinion in Europe." Conservative monarchies in Europe saw America's war as the "final and conclusive failure of democratic institutions," and they would find in this catastrophe "an inexhaustible source of argument in their favor."

The Union was forfeiting its most appealing moral assets, Schurz bluntly told Seward. Friends of liberty in Europe assumed that the war would "be nothing less than a grand uprising of the popular conscience in favor of a great humanitarian principle." Yet Union envoys were being sent abroad with instructions not to even mention slavery as "the cause or origin" of the war. Why, Schurz asked sarcastically, should Europeans support the North if its only goal was "the privilege of being re-associated with the imperious and troublesome Slave States"?

Confederate agents in Europe had learned to make their appeal in the liberal language the European public admired, Schurz noted. They, too, "carefully abstain from alluding to the rights of slavery," but they made alluring offers "of free-trade and cotton to the merchant and the manufacturer, and of the right of self-government to the liberal." The rebels were beating the Union at its own game by appealing to freedom. "It is my profound conviction," Schurz concluded his plea from Madrid, "that, as soon as the war becomes distinctly one for and against slavery, public opinion will be so strongly, so overwhelmingly in our favor, that in spite of commercial interests or secret spites no European Government will dare to place itself, by declaration or act, upon the side of a universally condemned institution. Our enemies know that well, and we may learn from them."[42]

These admonitions from Henry Sanford and Carl Schurz were the first of many coming back to Seward and Lincoln from abroad. These were not what the secretary of state wanted to hear. Though Union agents had been instructed to glean what they could about the foreign press and public opinion, their counsel was not always welcome when it contradicted Seward's stubborn conviction that Europe's governing classes feared an abolition war that would disrupt the cotton markets. Seward also instinctively distrusted radicals like Schurz, whom he accused of meddling in domestic and military policies that were not his concern.

Seward answered Schurz's impassioned tour de force from Madrid with a terse, icy message that essentially told him to mind his diplomatic business in Spain. In it the secretary of state feigned indifference to foreign opinion and blustered foolishly about the Union's capacity to take on all enemies. "I entertain no fears that we shall not be able to maintain ourselves against all who shall combine against us," he wrote. "This confidence is not built on enthusiasm, but on knowledge of the true state of the conflict, and on exercise of calm and dispassionate reflection." Schurz, Seward implied, ought to exercise his own dispassionate reflection.[43]

Seward was not as pigheaded as he sounded in his scolding letter to Schurz; nor was he indifferent to public opinion abroad. Even as he wrote it, that October he was busy launching a pioneering program in

8. Carl Schurz, appointed US minister to Spain, later served as major general in the Union army. (CARL SCHURZ, *REMINISCENCES*)

public diplomacy. The idea of employing unofficial agents to manage the press, lobby politicians, and persuade the foreign public was nothing new in the history of war and diplomacy. Efforts to shape diplomacy by influencing public sentiment had many precedents. Benjamin Franklin in Paris during the Revolution may have been the most famous of such ambassadors to public opinion, but he was neither the first nor the last.[44]

America's Civil War, however, witnessed the first organized, sustained government programs in which each side fielded special agents whose sole aim was to mold the public mind and, thereby, affect the foreign policy of other governments. It was a prolonged conflict, and each side had time to develop campaigns abroad. More important, the war took place at a time when mass-circulation newspapers and magazines flourished on both sides of the Atlantic. The vast expansion of print culture was accelerated by robust rivalry among political parties, each with its own journal, and aided by new communications technology—steam-driven printing presses, telegraphs, and steamships—that allowed rapid transmission of foreign news.

Large metropolitan newspapers hired foreign correspondents in major capitals, or they sent over traveling reporters and war correspondents. Malakoff and Monadnock (pseudonyms for *New York Times* reporters), William Howard Russell, Karl Marx, Ottilie Assing, and a host of other journalists were all part of a new phenomenon, the international press. These developments both created and served a vastly expanded readership and provided a powerful instrument by which foreign governments could at once take the pulse of public opinion and get their stories before readers. None understood the power of the modern press better than regimes such as Napoleon III's France, where articles were scrupulously censored and publishers fined for infractions.[45]

The rivalry between Union and Confederate agents abroad fueled the growth of public diplomacy campaigns. Agents on both sides warned their home offices that the enemy was beating them in the contest to manage the press and win public sympathy abroad. They implored their governments to send more money and men to counter the success of their rivals, and—without exactly knowing how to measure their own success—the commitment to swaying public opinion abroad grew apace.

Not all of their efforts were aboveground. Seward had given Henry Sanford a sizable purse for secret service operations throughout Europe. Much of his time and resources went toward building an extensive espionage program to gather intelligence on rebel procurement of arms and supplies, but he was also engaged in managing public information and launching the Union's public diplomacy campaign abroad. Soon after he arrived in Europe in April 1861, Sanford wrote to Seward, urging a covert public diplomacy program whose aim would be to "correct the public mind through the Press and refute the errors of fact or opinion so prevalent." From Paris he sounded an early warning that the "Southern (Creole) element here . . . has the power of influencing greatly the public press," which was "full of erroneous statements calculated to prejudice public opinion against the cause of the Union." Some of these press misstatements were the result of ignorance, Sanford allowed, but others were the product of "considerations" (bribes) issued by pro-Southern interests.[46]

Sanford wanted to offer his own "considerations" to willing foreign journalists. He hired A. Malespine, a Paris journalist for the liberal *Opinion*

Nationale. A devoted republican who had spent time in the United States and was fully in sympathy with the Union, Malespine was not above receiving a monthly stipend of five hundred francs for lending his pen to the cause. The "best way to discredit the South," Malespine advised Sanford, is "to prove that slavery is the cause of the war, and that the South fights only for the maintenance of that institution." In addition to his columns in the *Opinion Nationale,* Malespine published several pamphlets informing French readers about the war.[47]

Sanford was the first to sound the alarm that US diplomatic posts abroad were swarming with "men of doubtful loyalty," mostly Buchanan appointees. It was an early lesson in public diplomacy, for several of the disloyal diplomats had used their positions to persuade foreign officials and the press that the US Constitution actually permitted secession and that separation was inevitable in any case. That message of inevitability proved especially stubborn, and Sanford worked assiduously to counter it by working the press, hiring sympathetic authors, subsidizing influential journals, and seeing that erroneous views of the situation were promptly corrected by letters to the editor. But it would not be enough to simply "correct the public mind" on the errors implanted by rebel sympathizers. Union agents abroad still needed an appealing message to tell the world *why* they fought and why this was something more than just an American civil war.

BACK IN WASHINGTON, SEWARD ACCELERATED THE UNION'S COMMITMENT to courting favor among the European public after the embarrassing disaster at Bull Run in late July 1861. Seward was terrified that this humiliating Confederate victory would prompt European powers to recognize the Confederacy, and he desperately sought ways to arouse opposition among the European public. That was when he sent Sanford to Caprera on his ill-fated mission to enlist Garibaldi. In August Seward appointed John Bigelow, a well-traveled, savvy New York newspaper publisher and seasoned political operative, to assist Sanford and Dayton in France and Europe generally. Officially, Bigelow would serve as consul general to Paris, but off the record he was there to back up Dayton, Lincoln's choice for the post and one whose ignorance of the French language and politics worried Seward. Dayton knew his limitations, and to give him credit, it was his idea to bring over someone "accustomed to the use of the pen" and with good connections to leading men in the European press and

9. John Bigelow, US consul to Paris and unofficial chief of public diplomacy in France. (MATHEW BRADY PHOTOGRAPH, BRADY-HANDY COLLECTION, LIBRARY OF CONGRESS)

government circles. "If a little money were judiciously expended here," Dayton wrote to Seward in late May 1861, "it would go far to put the public sentiment right in certain quarters." Bigelow was one of Seward's most brilliant appointees, and he soon became a pioneering master of the arts of public diplomacy in Europe.[48]

When Seward learned in September 1861 that the Confederates were sending James Mason and John Slidell to Europe, he stepped up efforts in public diplomacy to counteract their influence. In October he organized the first of a procession of private citizens sent over as spokesmen for the Union cause. Seward's special agents were religious leaders, literary figures, financiers, businessmen, and politicians whose job it was to address the foreign public as well as meet with government officials, and in every way to "enlighten" the public mind about the "true nature" of the conflict in America.

Henry Adams marveled at the men Seward sent over. He "had a chance to see them all, bankers or bishops, who did their work quietly and well." To the outsider, he wrote, "the work seemed wasted and the 'influential classes' more indurated with prejudice than ever." But this was misleading: "The waste was only apparent; the work all told in the end."

Not least among Seward's public diplomacy innovations was his decision in late 1861 to launch the annual publication of the State Department's diplomatic correspondence with the president's annual message to Congress. Although carefully selected and edited, the publication of these dispatches created an extraordinary image of a government whose foreign policy aims were transparent to the world.

At the same time, Seward deployed numerous clandestine special agents whose job it was to shape the public mind overseas. Later, during the impeachment of Andrew Johnson in 1868, Seward acknowledged to the Senate Foreign Relations Committee that he had secretly paid for the services of twenty-two special agents (including Garibaldi, it turned out), for a grand sum of $41,193. Had the Union sent to England and France at the beginning of 1861 the men it sent later, Seward told the senators, the machinations by which the rebels gained belligerent rights might have been defeated. In retrospect, Seward testified, "the national life might have been lost" but for the services of these men.[49]

Seward's first public diplomatic mission of this sort included two religious leaders: Archbishop John Hughes, an immensely popular New York Catholic of Irish origin, and Bishop Charles McIlvaine, an Ohio Episcopalian who was well known in Europe and a former chaplain to the US Senate. Thurlow Weed, Seward's trusted confidant, came along at the insistence of his friend Archbishop Hughes, or so the story was told. Actually, Seward had a more important role in mind for Weed. Their mission, as Seward dexterously explained in his letter of introduction to Charles Francis Adams in London, was "to counteract the machinations of the agents of treason against the United States" and to do so "in a way and to a degree which we could not reasonably expect from you." At the last minute, this unlikely band of clergy and politicos was joined by General Winfield Scott, the venerable commander of the Union army and hero of the Mexican War, recently retired and on his way to meet his family in Paris. Scott had his own unofficial diplomatic mission in mind:

he confided to Seward that he planned to meet "in private circles" with European leaders to thwart "those arch-traitors Slidell and Mason."[50]

Seward's troupe of public diplomatists sailed out of New York on November 9, and after a rough fifteen days at sea they arrived at Le Havre, France, on November 24. It was three days later that news of the *Trent* affair reached them in Europe. The explosion of indignation from Britain suddenly cast a grave shadow over their entire mission.

US diplomats in Europe still had no official explanation from Washington, which left Adams and the whole legation in London paralyzed as the British press raged against their country. Adams confided to his diary that war was inevitable. He even pondered withdrawing from London, perhaps staying on the Continent until matters were clarified. The "policy of Lord Palmerston is to terrify America into such terms as he will dictate," Adams wrote. "He may be successful." The mood at the US legation "would have gorged a glutton of gloom," Adams's son Henry remembered. All of them felt "as though they were a military outpost waiting orders to quit an abandoned position."[51]

In Paris friends of the Union were equally demoralized by the prospect of war with Britain, while Confederate partisans were rejoicing over *l'affaire du* Trent. John Bigelow instinctively recognized it as a problem to be addressed through public diplomacy. On December 2, 1861, days after the *Trent* news arrived, he sought the wise counsel of Louis-Antoine Garnier-Pages, a stalwart member of the French republican opposition who stood by the Union and believed that "the future of republicanism in Europe depended upon the success of republicanism in America." Bigelow found his friend utterly despondent over the crisis, and he tried to ease his mind. As Bigelow explained, the *Trent* affair was probably nothing more than an ambitious naval officer acting on his own authority and not meant as an insult by the US government and certainly not a provocation of war. Garnier-Pages was visibly relieved; he urged Bigelow to sit down immediately and write up what he had just told him, and they would submit it to the newspapers the next day.

Bigelow told his French friend that in his official status, he could not sign such a letter, but he knew just the man who could. He hurried over to the Hotel de Europe and implored Thurlow Weed, who had just arrived, to persuade General Winfield Scott to sign a public letter that Bigelow would compose. "Old Fuss and Feathers," as General Scott was affectionately known, could be prickly, but on the voyage over Weed had bonded with the old man, and he assured Bigelow he would try working his charm. Weed found Scott holed up in his rooms at the Hotel Westminster, suffering a painful bout of rheumatic gout, a hand and leg badly swollen. Scott was in despair that America was about to be pulled into war with Britain and was already preparing to return to New York City to advise on preparing harbor defenses in the event of British attack. He told Weed he would sign the letter.

Meanwhile, Bigelow was back at his office, furiously drafting the letter. It was framed as an informal message from Scott to a fictitious friend, assuring him that there was no reason for concern that Britain and the United States might go to war. After scoring a few gently lodged blows against British transgressions on the high seas prior to the War of 1812, Bigelow's letter made a deft turn toward conciliation: "I am sure the President and people of the United States would be but too happy to let these men go free, unnatural and unpardonable as their offences have been, if by it they could emancipate the commerce of the world." Bigelow hurried the draft over to Scott's hotel room, and, to his enormous relief, the old warrior signed it with no changes.

The Bigelow-Scott letter was published the next day, December 3, appearing simultaneously in all the leading Paris and London journals. Miraculously, the letter met with an immediate calming effect, as though providing an excuse to avoid war with the Americans. As Weed later noted with obvious satisfaction, "It was accepted abroad and at home as an able and well-timed appeal to the judgment, reason, and good sense of both countries." Édouard Thouvenel, the French foreign minister, noted the dramatic shift in public mood: "There is a pacific current in the air," and both the British and the Americans "will think twice before fighting."[52]

Encouraged by these early signs of success but still in crisis mode, Bigelow and Henry Sanford huddled with Weed, Archbishop Hughes, and Dayton to work out how best to deploy Hughes as unofficial emissary from the Catholic Church. Napoleon III was sensitive to Catholic opinion in France, and his Spanish wife, Empress Eugénie, was an especially devout defender of the faith. It was decided Hughes should seek an interview with the emperor.

After getting the cold shoulder from a cordon of French officials, Hughes finally took it upon himself to write a private note directly to the emperor. It worked. On December 24, with the *Trent* crisis still unsettled, he met with Napoleon III and Empress Eugénie, who took "great interest, and no small part" in the discussion, Hughes noted. He urged Napoleon to offer his good offices to arbitrate peace between England and America. The emperor begged off, saying the dispute involved non-negotiable matters of honor. After more than an hour Hughes left, uncertain as to which side France might take in America's dispute with Britain and in its war with the South.[53]

"If I am not deceived," the archbishop wrote Seward from Paris, "the feelings of what we would call 'the people'" were not ill-disposed toward the United States, but "the tone of the papers here does not indicate any warm national friendship." Lincoln, he pointedly told Seward, "is winning golden opinions for his calm, unostentatious, mild, but firm and energetic administrative talents."

Hughes let it be known in Paris that he was planning an extended tour of Catholic Europe, which apparently worried Thouvenel, for the foreign minister pressed Dayton to reveal details of the archbishop's travels and intentions. He was worried that Hughes might arouse Catholic interest in the American question and, of course, in the Union's favor. Hughes went about his tour, spending several weeks in Rome visiting the pope and other Catholic officials, which at least gave the appearance of a welcomed visit from an unofficial spokesman for Catholic America. On his return journey to the United States the next summer, he came through London and then Dublin, where he was hailed as a returning Irish hero. The archbishop was helping to draw the Irish, and Catholic Europe generally, toward the cause of the Union.[54]

MEANWHILE, ON DECEMBER 5, THURLOW WEED, WITH SEVERAL COPIES of the Bigelow-Scott letter in his pocket, left Paris for London to try to calm Britain's war fever. Weed's reputation as Seward's close confidant gave him access to the inner circles of power in England, and it also invested what he had to say with unusual, albeit unofficial, authority. He was also a consummate manager of politicians and the press, full of confidence of a sort that left young Henry Adams in absolute awe. Once Weed took into his hands "the threads of management," Adams recalled, he did "quietly and smoothly all that was to be done." Weed began by writing

10. Thurlow Weed, political mentor to William Seward who sent him and two clergymen on an unofficial public goodwill mission to Europe. (LIBRARY OF CONGRESS)

a soothing letter to the London *Times* and then deftly arranged meetings with the inner circle of the Palmerston government. He was invited to a dinner party with a group of military and political leaders at the home of Sir James Emerson Tennent. Weed likened it to "a war party of gentlemen." One was a colonel about to leave for Canada with British troops who gave a lengthy toast dwelling "upon the duty of Englishmen to resent the insults to their flag."[55]

Returning to his hotel on Hanover Square, Weed found a friend waiting to tell him that a private audience with Earl Russell had been arranged for the next morning at the foreign secretary's country estate, Pembroke Lodge. Weed took an early train and arrived before lunch at the foreign secretary's country home. As usual, Earl Russell was frosty and led off the conversation with his view of things from what Weed described as a decidedly "ultra English standpoint." Weed answered by delicately referring to the many instances of Americans being apprehended at sea before they resorted to war in 1812. He then smoothly turned the conversation toward the earl's illustrious career in advancing the great Anglo-American Whig tradition, which they both had championed.[56]

Russell's indignation seemed to moderate. He made it patently clear that he wanted to avoid war. He feared that Seward's belligerence was such that he might actually welcome a foreign war. A story was circulating about Seward at a dinner party in Albany a year earlier, at which he allegedly told the Duke of Newcastle he looked forward to threatening Britain with war in order to rally political support for the Union at home. Seward denied any such comment, but the story corresponded with tales of his April 1 memo calling for war, and it offered further proof, if the British needed any, of the dangers of democratic mob rule. Russell understood that war with America would be a very dangerous business that would put at risk all of Britain's possessions in North America and perhaps the Caribbean. It might also topple the Palmerston government.[57]

Russell proposed to Weed that Mason and Slidell be set free. Weed allowed that their arrest on board the *Trent* may have been ill-considered, but he explained how exasperated Americans were with these men who had resigned their seats in the Senate to "inaugurate and lead a rebellion." "English noblemen had gone from the Tower to the block for offenses less grave than those which Messrs. Mason and Slidell had committed," Weed observed drolly. Russell had no retort. Weed then suggested an arrangement by which Britain would demand "in a friendly spirit" the release of the prisoners, the United States would comply, honor would be served, and the drums of war would be silenced.

This came at the end of a tense hour that, to Weed's mind, concluded with more sympathy than it began. The two men were called to lunch, and after the meal Weed saw Russell take his wife aside for a moment of private conversation. Then she invited Weed for a stroll in their garden. On their walk Weed asked about an unusual mound of about two or three feet. She told him to stand on top of it while she related a story: "You are now standing precisely where Henry VIII stood watching for a signal from the dome of St. Paul's church, announcing the execution of Anne Boleyn" (the king's second wife, who was beheaded in 1536 for high treason).

Resuming their walk, they passed a "mimic fortification" the children had built. Lady Russell paused, turned to Weed, and said: "Ladies, you know, are not supposed to have any knowledge of public affairs. But we have eyes and ears, and sometimes use them. In these troubles about the taking of some men from under the protection of our flag, it may be some encouragement to you to know that the Queen is distressed at what she hears, and is deeply anxious for an amicable settlement." It was one of those cryptic, entirely unofficial, but no less important communications in the game of diplomacy that Weed took as a comforting signal. He left Lady and Earl Russell's country home that day knowing that, for all the bluster in the press and over dinner tables in London, Britain was not going to war if the queen had anything to say about it.[58]

Queen Victoria, in truth, despised America and its democracy; it was her beloved husband, Prince Albert, who helped subdue the dogs of war that winter. Gravely ill with typhoid fever, he rose from his deathbed to soften the language of the demand Earl Russell was about to send to Washington. Albert died a short time later, on December 14, and the queen was stricken with inconsolable grief. There were still a few in the press beating the drums for war, but a somber spirit of mourning subdued Britain's war fever that winter.[59]

It was not until January 2 that news of Lincoln's Christmas Day decision to release Mason and Slidell finally reached London. The city was jubilant; the stock market soared. Everyone "but the confederates and the war party," Charles Francis Adams wrote in his diary, "seemed to be relieved."[60]

John Stuart Mill, a leading voice of liberal England, characterized the passing crisis poignantly: a cloud that had "hung gloomily over the civilized world" for a month had passed. Had America gone to war, it would have been "reckless persistency in wrong," he wrote, but for Britain, "it would have been a war in alliance with, and, to practical purposes, in defence and propagation of, slavery."[61]

THE *TRENT* CRISIS BROUGHT THE UNION TO THE BRINK OF WAR AND exposed the risks involved in Seward's hard-power strategy. At the same time, it revealed the dangers of letting one's enemies control the public narrative abroad. It also taught some timely lessons on the vital importance of the press and public opinion and on the urgency of having special agents, skilled in dealing with the press, on the ground and ready to put out fires. Bigelow's and Weed's adroit maneuvers at a time of peril proved critical in defusing the crisis. Archbishop Hughes's and Bishop McIlvaine's speaking tours also pointed the way toward a promising new path in semiofficial public diplomacy.

But the contest to win popular sympathy abroad would turn not on which side could spend more money, hire more pens, and otherwise control the public forum. What mattered more was what the Union had to tell the world about why it was fighting. After nearly a year of crisis, the questions Garibaldi posed the previous summer about the purpose of the war still loomed: Was the Union fighting only for its national survival, for territory and power? Or was there something more at issue, something that might matter to the world at large? If Americans would not address these questions forthrightly, there were foreigners who would.

PART II

THE AMERICAN QUESTION

11. *The Pending Conflict,* by Oliver Evans Woods, 1864, portrays Secession and Union fighting while Britain's John Bull, holding a bundle of clubs for Secession, and France's Napoleon III look on. (LIBRARY OF CONGRESS)

CHAPTER 4

THE REPUBLICAN EXPERIMENT

Every friend of despotism rejoices at your misfortune; it points
the moral and adorns the tale in every aristocratic salon; it is the
shame of them who have perhaps over zealously advocated the
absolute perfection of the great Republic.

—WILLIAM HOWARD RUSSELL,
TIMES (LONDON) CORRESPONDENT, FEBRUARY 4, 1861

WHILE CONFEDERATE AND UNION SPOKESMEN CRAFTED THEIR
messages to the world, foreign observers began formulating their
own interpretations of what became known as the American question.
European political leaders, intellectuals, workers, students, and people
of widely divergent ideological persuasions came to view America's Civil
War as part of a much larger struggle that had been taking place in the
Euro-American world since the late eighteenth century. This interpretation of the American conflict must be understood within the context of
alternating swells of revolutionary hope and reactionary oppression that
radiated through the Atlantic world in the Age of Revolution.

Spanning the American Revolution to the Revolution of 1848 and
beyond, the Age of Revolution witnessed the advocates of popular sovereignty, human equality, and universal emancipation locked in battle
against the defenders of dynastic rule, aristocratic privilege, and inherited
inequality. Though some took care to distinguish republicanism from

democracy, the latter entailing broad voting rights, the terms were not always used with careful distinction and were commonly conflated in the expression *popular government*. Whatever their precise political goals, many in Europe saw the failure of the Revolution of 1848 as the end of the revolutionary challenge to the old regime of dynastic oligarchies. Conservatives welcomed the American secession crisis, seeing it as the coup de grâce to the republican experiment in both hemispheres. For revolutionaries and liberals, America's war came to be seen as the crucial trial that would decide the fate of government by the people, the "last best hope of earth," in Lincoln's unforgettable words. At stake were not only systems of labor, but also whole systems of government and society. London *Times* correspondent William Howard Russell was hardly exaggerating when he wrote to his friend John Bigelow in February 1861 that the crisis about to unfold in America was "the most important social and political phenomenon of the later ages of the world, the result of which will be felt for good or evil to the end of time."[1]

One of most poignant testimonies to this idea of republicanism on trial arrived in May 1861 as an inauspicious letter of congratulation to President Lincoln from the Most Serene Republic of San Marino, a tiny rock-bound city-state nestled in the Apennine Mountains of Italy whose history of self-government stretched back to 1300. The Captain Regents, San Marino's governing body, represented the oldest surviving republic in the world. They were writing to honor the leader of the second oldest republic in the world, and at this moment certainly the least serene country in the world.

The letter from San Marino was dated March 29, but it was delayed for more than a month, probably because it was addressed to "Mr. Lincoln" in New York City, which the Captain Regents must have assumed to be the nation's capital. The letter was divided into two columns, one written in Italian and the other in imperfect but clear English.

"It is a some while since the Republic of San Marino wishes to make alliance with the United States of America in that manner as it is possible between a great Potency and a very small country." We "are sure you will be glad to shake hands with a people who in its smallness and poverty can exhibit to you an antiquity from fourteen centuries of its free government." The San Marino regents wanted to bestow an honor on a fellow republican across the sea. "Now we must inform you," the letter continued, "that the citizenship of the Republic of San Marino was conferred for ever to the President pro tempore of the United States of America and we are very happy to send you the diploma of it." (In honor of the 150th anniversary of this letter, President Obama's citizenship in San Marino was renewed in 2011.) "We are acquainted from newspapers," the regents gently added, "with political griefs, wich you are now suffering, therefore we pray to God to grant you a peaceful solution of your questions."[2]

On May 7 the president and Seward, who probably wrote the letter of reply for Lincoln to sign, took time in those hectic days to salute their fellow republicans across the sea. "Great and Good Friends . . . Although your dominion is small, your State is nevertheless one of the most honored, in all history. It has by its experience demonstrated the truth, so full of encouragement to the friends of Humanity, that Government founded on Republican principles is capable of being so administered as to be secure and enduring."

There was also a lesson Seward and Lincoln wanted their fellow republicans in Europe to consider: "You have kindly adverted to the trial through which this Republic is now passing. It is one of deep import. It involves the question whether a Representative republic, extended and aggrandized so much as to be safe against foreign enemies can save itself from the dangers of domestic faction. I have faith in a good result."[3]

THE REPUBLICAN IDEA HAD ANCIENT ORIGINS IN GREECE AND ROME and had been rekindled in Italian city-states, San Marino among them, toward the end of the Middle Ages. But it was not until the late eighteenth century that the modern experiment in popular self-government began. It grew out of ideas from the radical fringe of the Enlightenment in the latter half of the eighteenth century, the chief maxim being that all persons possessed basic natural rights, "unalienable rights," Thomas Jefferson called them. All humans were born with common needs, and they held in common basic rights to "Life, Liberty and the pursuit of Happiness," in Jefferson's felicitous phrase. It was to protect these rights that governments were formed. Such radical ideas were accepted nowhere before the American Revolution, but it was these principles that would inspire the Age of Revolution that swept through the Atlantic world between 1776 and 1848.[4]

Jefferson's "self-evident truths" served to delegitimize a king, who was accused of abusing the colonists' natural rights, and to bestow sovereignty on "the people," in whose name the new American republic was proclaimed. But the ideas were far more than rhetorical devices for the moment; natural, universal human rights constituted the core idea of popular sovereignty that formed the very foundation of the entire republican experiment. Such ideas also had radical implications for all forms of social inequality, not just hereditary monarchy and aristocracy. Jefferson himself understood the implications, as he acknowledged in a private letter: the "mass of mankind has not been born with saddles on their backs, nor a favored few booted and spurred, ready to ride them legitimately, by the grace of God."[5]

Everywhere in the Atlantic world political movements for national independence and popular self-rule inevitably became entangled with revolutionary social change that assailed the bastions of aristocratic privilege and hereditary power. The Confederate rebellion stands in retrospect as a conspicuous exception to the egalitarian spirit of the Age of Revolution.[6]

In Europe the experiment in human equality and self-government met with violent resistance from the ramparts of aristocracy and established religion. But in the Americas the republican idea was propelled by powerful waves of colonial national revolutions that swept monarchy and European imperial rule aside in the name of popular sovereignty. In the half century between 1776 and 1825, most of the colonial possessions of Britain, France, and Spain in the American hemisphere repudiated their imperial rulers and proclaimed independent republics.

Not all embraced republicanism. Brazil followed an unusual path to independence that transformed it into the seat of the Portuguese Empire when Napoleon I invaded Portugal in 1808, then an independent constitutional monarchy, the Empire of Brazil, in 1822. Mexico, too, experimented briefly with a homegrown version of monarchy, installing Agustín de Iturbide as emperor of Mexico at the end of its grueling war of independence. Iturbide's empire quickly collapsed, and in 1823 Mexico began its rocky experiment with republican self-government.

Republicanism and slavery were mutually antagonistic in theory but also in practice. With important exceptions, the new American republics abolished slavery not long after throwing off monarchical rule. The United States was both a leader and a laggard in this republican antagonism toward slavery. Several Northern states had passed laws to end slavery after the break with Britain in 1776, and in 1787 the federal government banned it altogether from the Northwest Territory above the Ohio River. The founding fathers, including many southerners, agreed that human slavery did not belong in their republic, that it was immoral, dangerous, and should be put on a path toward extinction. Alexander Stephens, the Confederate vice president, believed the founding fathers were wrong about all that, but he acknowledged this to be their belief.[7]

By 1860 the remaining strongholds of slavery outside the United States included Cuba and Puerto Rico, both of them Spanish colonies, and the Empire of Brazil. Significantly, all three were vestiges of European monarchies lacking strong liberal challenges to slavery from within. The American South presented the strange anomaly of a slave society organized around ideas of fixed, hereditary racial inequality flourishing within a robust democratic nation that was, in theory at least, based on the very opposite principles. "Neither hereditary monarchy nor hereditary aristocracy planted itself on our soil," George Bancroft, a Republican critic of the slaveholding South, remarked after the war. "The only hereditary condition that fastened itself upon us was servitude." Slavery was frequently denounced by American abolitionists as a vestige of aristocracy that the Revolution had failed to eradicate, and some would describe America's Civil War as the Second American Revolution.[8]

Though often beleaguered, especially in Latin America, the "vine of liberty," as George Bancroft put it, "took deep root and filled the land." The republican experiment flourished in the American hemisphere thanks in large part to distance from its aristocratic enemies in the Old World.[9]

In Europe, however, violent and repressive reaction followed the French Revolution of 1789. Beginning as a protest against absolutist monarchical power, the Revolution broadened into a radical assault on entrenched citadels of hereditary privilege and religious authority. At the heart of the French Revolution was the exaltation of the same idea embedded in America's revolution: popular sovereignty, derived from the *natural rights* of the people, must supersede monarchical sovereignty derived from the *divine rights* of kings.[10]

The American and French Revolutions differed in many ways, but they shared a common vocabulary of natural rights, equality, liberty, and self-government. The reverberations from both revolutions shook the pillars of church and crown throughout the Atlantic world. The old regime fought back hard, appealing to fears of disorder, decrying the anarchy of "godless republicanism," and mocking the arrogance of those who thought they could govern themselves without kings or God.[11]

The French Revolution provided critics with memorable lessons about the murderous violence and social disorder that ensued from attempts at radical reform. The French Republic descended into the Reign of Terror that sent thousands of aristocrats, clergy, and other enemies of the Revolution to their death at the guillotine. A bloodfest of reaction and revenge finally came to an end when Napoleon Bonaparte led a coup d'état in 1799. Later crowning himself Emperor Napoleon I and operating as military dictator of France, Napoleon set out to destroy the old regime of Europe.

As Napoleon's reign approached its end at the Battle of Waterloo in 1815, the monarchist leaders gathered in the Congress of Vienna, the bastion of Hapsburg absolutism. They redrew the map of Europe, returned dynastic rulers to their thrones, and restored the Catholic Church to its traditional position of authority. A cold blanket of repression and censorship settled over Europe. The only republics to survive were a handful of small German city-states, Swiss cantons, and, of course, *la serenissima* San Marino.

The revolution would not die, however. During "three glorious days" in 1830, the French people went to the barricades and deposed King Charles X, but this time they did not dare give republicanism another trial. They turned instead to Louis Philippe, of the liberal Orléans branch of the Bourbon dynasty, beseeching him to serve as "king of the French" under a constitutional monarchy. François Guizot, who later served as Louis Philippe's prime minister, summarized the views of many chastened French when he said, "Not to be a republican at twenty is proof of want of heart; to be one at thirty is proof of want of head."[12]

Many European monarchs operated within constitutional restraints and were checked by parliaments elected by citizens, whose voting rights were generally restricted to a narrow slice of the propertied male population. Though Britain had the strongest parliamentary tradition, only about one in five adult males could vote. Everywhere the exclusion of women was taken for granted. Constitutional monarchy, with parliaments of varying strength, became the European center, flanked on the right by absolutist monarchists in league with the Catholic Church and on the left by republicans, liberals, and radicals from among the workers and middle class.[13]

"Free England" became the asylum for republicans and revolutionaries from all parts of Europe, and it enjoyed freedom of speech and assembly unparalleled under most other European monarchies. On the Continent "red republicans," as the revolutionary element was known, were forced underground, where they met in secret societies, often Masonic lodges, or gathered at what were ostensibly public banquets where politically coded toasts and speeches were offered. They sang the French republican anthem "La Marseillaise" and waved flags modeled after the French tricolor but in various national colors. Some donned red Phrygian caps, an ancient emblem of liberty. They denounced the aristocracy, made surreptitious references to the justice of the guillotine, and waited for the day when the tinder of revolution might be ignited once again.[14]

That moment came unexpectedly in January 1848. Furious that their public banquets had been outlawed, Parisian revolutionaries took to the streets, threw up hundreds of barricades, and called for the ouster of King Louis Philippe and his prime minister, François Guizot. After police shot into a crowd, killing more than fifty demonstrators, the man once hailed as the "king of the French" abdicated and fled to Britain. Out of the ruins of the "July monarchy," the republican experiment was reborn in its French cradle.[15]

The Revolution of 1848 spread to most of the main capitals of continental Europe and into the rural countryside. Socialists played significant roles in many places, but this was essentially a movement of the educated middle class, whose motto was "Liberty, affluence and education for all." Students, professionals, and military officers threw up barricades, waved tricolor flags, and demanded constitutions based on popular sovereignty. In London thousands of veteran Chartists, a workers political reform movement of the 1840s, led a public march to protest for universal manhood suffrage before being turned back by a massive show of government force.[16]

Hailed as "the springtime of peoples," the Revolution of 1848 brought a brief resurgence of hope for republicanism in Europe. It did not last long. Weakened by internal divisions, the revolutionaries were defeated in one country after another. In France the Second Republic rested on a shaky coalition of radicals, socialists, constitutional monarchists, "pure republicans," and liberal Catholics. Leaders decided to rally behind Louis-Napoleon, the nephew of Napoleon Bonaparte, as candidate for president. His famous name won stunning popular majorities at the polls. Republicans saw an early sign of betrayal in 1849 when, in order to firm up Catholic support, Louis-Napoleon sent French troops to Rome to topple the Republic of Rome, drive out Garibaldi's army of Red Shirts, and restore Pope Pius IX to his temporal throne. Three years after being elected president, taking a page from his uncle's book, Louis-Napoleon staged a coup d'état and had himself crowned Napoleon III. Under the Second Empire he called for the revival of Bonapartisme, the French civilizing mission conceived by his uncle under the First Empire. France, the birthplace of liberty, equality, and fraternity, became a land of repression, censorship, and imperialism under Napoleon III.[17]

Republican hopes for Germany died painfully in Berlin in early 1849. Prussia's king, Friedrich Wilhelm IV, had conceded to popular demands for parliamentary representation, but his prime minister, Count Brandenburg, called in troops and declared a state of siege, and when revolutionary resistance spread he dismissed the assembly. By the spring of 1849, dissident revolutionaries were being rounded up and sent to prison at Spandau, on the edge of Berlin. Frederick Salomon, a young Prussian officer and architecture student, was among them but once officials realized they had mistaken him for his brother Karl, he was unexpectedly released in April 1849. Within days he and his brothers and sister fled to Bremen and then to America, making their way to Wisconsin, where the rest of the family would join them. The Salomon brothers would take up arms for republicanism again, but this time it would be in America.[18]

Thousands of other Forty-Eighters, as veterans of the Revolution became known, sought asylum in Switzerland, among the few republics to survive in Europe. Others fled to England, and tens of thousands made their way to America. All hopes for a liberal republican future for Germany had failed. Prussia would subsume the German states within a centralized authoritarian regime ruled by the "Iron Chancellor," Otto von Bismarck.

"The Revolution," the ongoing battle against dynastic sovereignty, was defeated across Europe. After 1848 the republican experiment seemed to be settled, at least as to which side had the stronger brigades. Many European liberals who believed in individual freedom, equal rights, free

12. Frederick Salomon. A German Forty-Eighter who commanded the all-German 9th Wisconsin Volunteers; he is the author's great-great-grandfather. (WILLIAM D. LOVE, *WISCONSIN IN THE WAR OF THE REBELLION*, COURTESY WISCONSIN HISTORICAL SOCIETY)

trade, and constitutional limits on government powers were questioning whether large, modern nations could ever be successfully united and ruled without a king and church. For conservatives, the fury and contagion of revolution that spring of 1848 left them with an uneasy dread that it might be reignited at any time.[19]

AFTER 1848 THE REPUBLICAN EXPERIMENT WAS UNDER SEVERE DURESS on the American side of the globe as well. Since independence the Spanish American republics had endured constant challenges from the combined forces of conservative landowners, military leaders, and the Catholic Church. By the 1860s most Latin American republics had succumbed to one or more cycles of peaceful constitutional democracy interrupted by *pronunciamento* (coup d'état), military dictatorship, civil war, and back again. The travails of Latin American republics gave critics all the proof they needed of the inherent instability of popular sovereignty, but they also presented undeniable evidence of a heroic, enduring commitment to republican ideals.[20]

There was a prevailing idea, shared by hopeful republicans as well as skeptical conservatives, that all the young American republics were little more than fragile experiments, subject to tumultuous discord and vulnerable to foreign intervention. Because the Latin American republics had declared independence during the upheavals of the Napoleonic wars in Europe, there was good reason to expect that European powers would attempt to restore their American empires once they had subdued republicanism in Europe.

As the new independent Latin American republics emerged, British foreign secretary George Canning looked upon the Euro-American world taking shape in 1825 with grave apprehension. The great danger of the time, he warned, was the "division of the World into European and American, Republican and Monarchical" nations with "worn-out Governments" on one side and on the other side "youthful and stirring" republics, foremost among them the United States. Canning, naturally, wanted to bolster the worn-out system, not give way to the brash young spirit of republicanism. During the 1820s the British tried to nurture Latin American monarchies under Simón Bolívar in South America and Agustín Iturbide in Mexico. Both failed as bulwarks against what the British saw as the insidious spread of republicanism and democracy emanating from the United States.[21]

It was in response to European monarchical schemes for recolonizing the Americas that the United States had issued the Monroe Doctrine in 1823. Monroe warned European nations that any further colonizing ventures in the American hemisphere would be regarded as an act of aggression against the United States. Later the Monroe Doctrine would become identified with American imperialism, but its origins were defensive and prorepublican, more a shield than a weapon.[22]

A glance at the map of the Western Hemisphere showed the United States surrounded by imperial monarchies: Britain in Canada and the Caribbean, Spain in Cuba and Puerto Rico, and Russia in Alaska and the Pacific Coast. While the Monroe Doctrine did not challenge the presence of existing European empires, it discouraged further encroachment and was intended to protect Latin America's frail republics from European enemies—that is, until the 1860s, when America's Civil War suddenly rendered the United States powerless to keep European predators at bay.[23]

Until the American Civil War, republicans everywhere looked to the United States as the best working example of how a free people, unfettered by aristocracy and established religion, might live in peace and prosperity. The most remarkable measure of republican success in the United States was its stability. Since the Constitution was established in 1789, power had been transferred peacefully from one elected president and Congress to the next over more than seventy years, through thirty-six congressional and eighteen presidential elections. The coups d'état, dictatorships, assassinations, and civil wars that plagued the dynasties of the Old World and the republics of Latin America did not appear in the US political world. Elections were often acrimonious, but Americans accepted their outcome without resorting to the sword—until the election of 1860.

Alexis de Tocqueville's widely influential book *Democracy in America* (1835) recognized America as the "great experiment," a valiant "attempt to construct society upon a new basis." "It was there," Tocqueville wrote, "that theories hitherto unknown, or deemed impracticable, were to exhibit a spectacle for which the world had not been prepared by history of the past." "Sooner or later," he thought, France and all of Europe "shall arrive, like the Americans, at an almost complete equality of condition." "In America I saw more than America," he told the world. "I sought there the image of democracy itself . . . in order to learn what we have to fear or to hope from its progress."[24]

Other European visitors came to America seeking to make a case against it as a model for the future. They decried its violence and vulgarity and mocked its pieties and hypocrisies. The aristocratic classes of Europe, one British defender of the United States noted, always sought to put republicanism in the worst possible light: "They recognize America as the stronghold of republicanism. If they can bring it into disrepute here, they know that they inflict upon it the deadliest blow in Europe."[25]

In 1861 European aristocrats were pointing to the conflagration of the so-called Great Republic as clear proof of democracy's doom. Sir John Pakington, an arch Tory MP, treated the large audience gathered at the Worcester Shire Hall for the annual Conservative Association dinner to a vivid portrait of an America destroying itself. Look across the Atlantic, he told them, and "see the sudden and, extraordinary collapse of that attempt to promote and increase the happiness and welfare of mankind by governing them on the principles of extreme Democracy." Let them ask any American, he taunted: "Had democracy succeeded? Had extreme democracy contributed to promote the happiness of mankind?" "Take warning from this country," he admonished the cheering crowd.[26]

British conservatives took delight in invoking the American disaster as a means of rebuking the Radicals, led by John Bright, who had been calling for the democratization of Britain and a vast expansion of voting rights to include the working class. British journalist William Howard Russell explained it all in his October 1861 letter to Massachusetts senator Charles Sumner in America: We are threatened with "Americanization which to our islands would be anarchy and ruin." America's troubles provide an ideal opportunity for politicians and writers to deal "deadly blows at Brightism."[27]

Sir Alexander James Beresford Beresford Hope, editor of the *Saturday Review,* took the lead in denouncing the United States for aggression against the valiant South. He gave a series of well-attended public lectures in which he applauded the South's secession and happily forecast further division of the "once United States." An impartial view of the map, he instructed his British listeners, shows that "the inevitable design of Providence" dictated that "the country should be divided into at least four great commonwealths," the Northeast, Midland, South, and Pacific. Such division, he proposed, would create a balance of power in North America much like that of Europe (conveniently ignoring centuries of bloodshed in the Old World). Each new fragment would have to maintain a standing army to guard its frontiers, instead of there being one nation menacing Canada and Mexico. "Every other country in the world does the like, and it is time that our bumptious cousins" did the same instead of displaying such "childish petulance" unbecoming to a mature nation.[28]

Hope saw the South fighting "with one heart and mind for independence from a hateful thralldom" against that "hotbed of anarchy" in the North. All those who want to see peace must recognize the independence of the Confederacy, though he groused that Palmerston's government was "too mealy-mouthed to say so." His lacerating critique of America's democracy met with loud cheers from English audiences, and published versions of the lectures went through multiple editions. America's spectacular disaster became an object lesson on the errors of democracy that conservatives were happy to teach.[29]

The Palmerston government was rejoicing "at the threatened dismemberment of the American Union," Malakoff grimly reported to *New York Times* readers in May 1861. "The feeling of hostility is no stronger against one section than the other; all they ask is to see each tearing the other to pieces." Rumors spread that Palmerston, now in his late seventies, wanted to see another war with America before he died, "such is his hatred of the insolent Yankees." Malakoff also accused Palmerston's foreign secretary, Earl Russell, of actively "prolonging and embittering" the fratricidal war in America and doing all he could to rekindle Britain's lingering hatred of its former colonies.[30]

Others in Britain's Parliament marked the lesson that America's debacle had for Britain. In a widely quoted comment, Tory MP Sir John Ramsden in May 1861 warned that Britain was "now witnessing the bursting of that great Republican bubble which had been so often held up to us as the model on which to recast our own English Constitution." The first duty of the British government, he advised, ought to be to strengthen "the great distinction between the safe and rational, and tempered liberties of England, and the wild and unreflecting excesses of mob-rule which had too often desecrated freedom and outraged humanity in America." When Ramsden's comments were repeated in an open session of Parliament, they brought cheers from some MPs.[31]

The Earl of Shrewsbury, a venerable Tory MP, speaking before a large crowd of party faithful at Worcester in October 1861, congratulated Britain on its aristocratic government and drew disparaging comparisons between it and the extreme democracy running amok in America. "In America they saw Democracy on its trial, and they saw how it failed." "Hear, hear!" the crowd cheered. The separation of North from South was inevitable, sooner or later, and the whole republican experiment would eventually face the cruel choice between "democracy and despotism." Those before him now, he prophesied, "who lived long enough would . . . see an aristocracy established in America."[32]

Such caustic remarks, coming from their English brethren in the freest country in Europe, puzzled American observers. "Monadnock," pseudonym for George Nicholls, the *New York Times* correspondent in London, tried to explain that "Londoners amuse themselves" with our struggles.

They seemed to take pleasure in accounts of the country's troubles, which showed "what a gigantic humbug the United States have been." Their enmity was "not directed against America merely," he tried to assure Americans. Ramsden's "bubble" remark was aimed at those advocating America's democracy as a model for Britain. Their "dread of John Bright and his Democratic principles" was so deep that "they cannot resist the temptation to pound him, to sneer at him, and to hold him up to the British nation as the man who wished to exchange their beloved Queen, and their ancient and glorious aristocracy, for a system of government like ours."[33]

Whatever their inspiration, such comments played a key role in framing the war as a contest between America's troubled democracy and the British monarchy it had forsaken in 1776. The rhetoric set a tone of mutual hostility between two peoples and two systems of government. The idea of the war as a clash between political ideologies and systems of government originated with European conservatives and was only later taken up by those on the Left.

In London US minister Charles Francis Adams recognized the origins of anti-American sentiment: "The secret of the ill will to us here is to be traced to the terror of democratic movement entertained by the aristocracy. They feel it hanging over their heads, and think they may evade it by appealing to the example of our failure." The question, he wrote later, "is of aristocracy and democracy. The former interest wishes us to fail because our success may ultimately be its ruin."[34]

FRENCH CONSERVATIVES TOOK THEIR OWN LESSONS FROM THE DISASTER in America. They saw in it exactly what they had opposed in France's violent history of revolutionary republicanism and positively gloated that *la Grande République* had finally arrived at the same sorry fate. "Your Republic is dead, and it is probably the last the world will see," one French cabinet officer, Achille Fould, brazenly announced to an astonished American in the fall of 1861. "You will have a reign of terror, and then two or three monarchies." The Marquis de Boissy told the French *Corps législatif* that he rejoiced at the news of civil war in America and prayed to God that both sides would be "irretrievably ruined."[35]

French critics saw America's democracy plagued by the same flaws that had doomed the first French Republic. In the North there was an aristocracy of wealth and another of "ultra puritan reverends" who led their flock beneath a mantle of hypocrisy and intolerance. *Le Monde,* an arch-monarchist journal, condemned the American experiment as a mistake from the beginning. Eighty years ago "the republican tree" had been planted; now "its spoiled fruits had fallen, and its roots were rotten." Behold slaveholding liberals crying *Vive la liberté!*[36]

Those among Napoleon III's French imperialist party were especially pleased to see the Great Republic pulled apart, and some were already hailing the result. French journalist Taxile Delord later wrote that some monarchists fantasized about "the White House transformed into a palace, and a deputation from Congress crossing the Atlantic to offer the crown of America to some available prince." The enemies of America, French historian Henri Soret, put it neatly, included those from whatever party who "look upon '89 as an evil date" and to whom ideas of liberty, equality, and self-government "have always meant horror." Like their British counterparts, the French conservatives' hatred for democracy, Soret concluded, made them "joyfully welcome" its destruction in America.[37]

Other European conservatives confirmed the view that popular sovereignty had come to its inevitable end in America. From Hamburg an American visitor reported that among intelligent circles, the crisis in America was understood to be the "natural consequence of unlimited freedom." The experiment in a federal republic had finally come to its inevitable end, and "the day for a monarchy in America has at last arrived."[38]

Spain's Catholic press was equally happy to pronounce the death of "the Revolution" in its American crib. In an especially vitriolic editorial, Madrid's *El Pensamiento Español* in September 1862 summarized the indictment: "In the model republic of what *were* the United States, we see more and more clearly of how little account is a society constituted without God, merely for the sake of men. . . . Look at their wild ways of annihilating each other, confiscating each other's goods, mutually destroying each other's cities, and cordially wishing each other extinct!" It mocked the "model republic" founded in rebellion and atheism, "populated by the dregs of all the nations in the world" and living "without law of God or man." Now America's republic stood doomed to "die in a flood of blood and mire" and serve as a rebuke to "the flaming theories of democracy."[39]

THE FOREIGN VIEW OF AN AMERICAN DEMOCRACY RUN AMOK resonated with the sharp distinctions Confederate sympathizers made between the South's aristocratic Anglo-Saxon landed gentry and the democratic "mobs" of the North polluted by the "scum" of Europe. James Spence, a Liverpool businessman and foremost defender of the Confederacy in Europe, explained that the US Constitution designed by George Washington and John Adams originally served as the basis for an aristocratic government by the nation's best men. Jefferson, unfortunately, was off in Paris imbibing Jacobin principles and "cultivating the acquaintance of Thomas Paine." The French "temple of infidelity was about to open its portals—in the purlieus of brooding socialism, in the coming shadow of the guillotine." The Constitution of the conservative founding fathers, by Spence's account, had been "subverted by this spirit of extreme democracy, imported from France." The effect of universal suffrage had also been aggravated by the flood of foreign immigrants "placed in the command of political power, without either training or association to fit them for it."[40]

"Universal suffrage tramples everything down to a dead level," railed another British Confederate partisan. "Infidelity is rampant" and "newspapers are violent, untruthful, scurrilous to a degree which we cannot imagine in this orderly old land."[41]

Many viewed Abraham Lincoln's election in 1860 as the culmination of America's descent into "extreme democracy" that witnessed unwashed immigrants and ignorant masses partaking of the "unqualified suffrage." Southerners justified secession as the last resort in the face of "Black Republican" rule, an aspersion that resonated with European conservatives in flight from the terrors of "red republicanism." Thus, black and red republicans were equally portrayed as incendiary revolutionaries whose aims were to level society and overturn natural hierarchies of race and class.[42]

Southern secessionists assumed that their hostility to extreme democracy would go over well with Europeans in the press and government circles, and some openly expressed preference for some form of monarchy. When London *Times* correspondent William Howard Russell toured the South in the spring and summer of 1861, he was treated again and again to ranting against universal suffrage, mob rule, and foreign influence in the North. What took him by surprise were the expressions of nostalgia for life under the British crown. His secessionist witnesses seemed especially eager to point to Abraham Lincoln as proof of a democracy gone so far astray that it would elect such a vulgar rustic frontiersman to the highest office of the land. The South, in contrast, was yet governed by its

13. William Howard Russell, special correspondent to America for the London *Times* and veteran war correspondent. He gave the world strong impressions of a permanently ruptured Union. (MATHEW BRADY PHOTOGRAPH, NATIONAL ARCHIVES)

"best men." All "the better classes in the South," Russell reported, display the "utmost dread of universal suffrage and would restrict the franchise largely to-morrow" should they win independence.[43]

South Carolina's leading men seemed especially eager to let Russell know of their feelings of kinship with the European aristocracy, whose landed wealth and habits of mastery alone bred the proper requisites for public leadership. Russell was fascinated by their repeated expressions "of regret for the rebellion of 1776 and the desire that if it came to the worst England would receive back her erring children or give them a prince under whom they could secure a monarchical form of government." (Louisianans, he later learned in his travels, preferred reunion with their former "mother country," France.) There was general agreement that this desire for reunion with Britain could not be practically gratified, at least not until independence was secured, Russell told his readers, "but the admiration for monarchical institutions on the English model, for privileged classes, and for a landed aristocracy and gentry, is undisguised and apparently genuine."[44]

When Russell's dispatches to the *Times* found their way back across the Atlantic and into print in the American press in the summer of 1861, Southerners hastily denied these pleas for monarchy or blamed them on a few eccentrics. Some even tried to quietly apply pressure through British diplomats to get Russell to issue a retraction—or at least not supply proof of his assertions. No doubt, they feared that such royalist sympathies would alienate their less aristocratic brethren in the border states and the West. Russell stood his ground. What he wrote, he told his editor, John Delane, in July 1861, "was in fact not half of what I had reason to state in reference to the pro-monarchy sentiments."[45]

The idea that the South was in rebellion against democracy itself had been running through numerous Northern newspaper accounts well before Russell began his tour of the South in April 1861. "The South to Be a Monarchy," a *New York Tribune* headline exclaimed on April 2, 1861. Based on testimony from a Tennessee Unionist, the story revealed secret plans to dupe the border states into joining the Confederacy under the terms of the old US Constitution, as modified in Montgomery in February. After a year under the provisional government, a constitutional convention would be called, the report revealed, and a new government would be formed "on a Monarchical basis." This is what the secessionist envoys were to explain to European governments, the Tennessee Unionist alleged. Republican government was to be abolished and "the last vestige of Democracy to be destroyed under the new order of things."[46]

In July 1861 New York's *Commercial Advertiser* charged that at the heart of the rebellion was a "strong aversion to popular government and a sinister purpose of repudiating the principle that the people, through the ballot-box, must be their own rulers." The right to secede was an invitation not only to anarchy but also to foreign incursion, for it meant that citizens claimed the right to "transfer allegiance to another government or system of government and thus bring to our very doors the corrupting and politically demoralizing influence of monarchy or despotism." The "lurking fondness for such a system, already betrayed frequently and in many quarters," points toward an alliance with European powers. Far more than separation was involved in the South's rebellion, as this report would have it; America's very existence as an independent republic was under siege.[47]

Similar reports were circulating in Europe. In early February 1861 from Paris, Malakoff issued an account of Southern monarchist leanings. It came from an entirely reliable source, he assured readers. Two "commissioners" from Mississippi and South Carolina had met with Napoleon III the previous August. They had implored the emperor to recognize the South should it secede and made it clear they were not only at odds with Republican Party ideas about ending slavery but also at war with republican principles of equality in general. They had complained that the radical "ultra Democratic" North was crushing the only class in America that "answers to the aristocratic classes of the Old World" and urged Europe to protect them. "Baiting their hook a little more heavily," Malakoff continued, "they intimated that the Southern people rather inclined towards a monarchy, and would like a prince to reign over them," Preferably a Bonaparte prince, so they flattered the French to believe. The South Carolina commissioner reminded His Majesty that his people "were largely descended from the Huguenots" and "felt a warm admiration of and affection for France as the 'mother country,'" and Louisiana's French legacy left it still a part of France in its culture and affections. In Paris another story broke in the summer of 1861 that Southern envoys had approached Jerome Napoleon Bonaparte, the American-born nephew of Napoleon I, to serve as "military dictator" of the South, for which he would be awarded a "crown with cotton lining."[48]

As rumors and denials of Confederate sympathy for monarchy continued to circulate, President Lincoln took the occasion of his first annual message to Congress in December 1861 to draw attention to this alarming report of Southern monarchism and to sharply define the Union's cause as the defense of democracy. "It continues to develop that the insurrection is largely, if not exclusively, a war upon the first principle of popular government—the rights of the people."

Lincoln mentioned unspecified "abridgments" of democracy, alluding to the lack of an election for president and vice president, never mind the absence of plebiscites on secession itself in most states. Lincoln noted also the "labored arguments" from the rebels "to prove that large control of the people in government, is the source of all political evil." Then he moved to the reports of Southern royalism: "Monarchy itself is sometimes hinted at as a possible refuge from the power of the people," and to this he felt compelled to raise "a warning voice against this approach of returning despotism."[49]

These hints of monarchist sympathies were also disturbing to democratic elements within the South. Not least, Confederate soldiers had reason to question if they were fighting to undo their hard-earned democracy. Rumors that the Richmond government was alleged to be plotting the "founding of a monarchy" with full support from the slaveholding elite circulated with disturbing effect among Confederate soldiers during 1862. An Alabama newspaper alarmed readers with reports that Confederate officials were proposing to "take their chances" under the government of Napoleon III.[50]

Various schemes to unite the South with a European empire would surface again at the end of the war, some of them floated by the *Richmond Sentinel,* the semiofficial organ of the Confederate government. The states of the Confederacy, one of its editorials recommended, "ought to repeal the old Declaration of Independence and voluntarily revert to their original proprietors—England, France, and Spain and by them be protected from the North." In January 1865 Governor George Allen of Louisiana sent representatives to meet with Napoleon III in what appeared to be negotiations for a separate peace by which Louisiana would seek the protection of its former mother country.[51]

Years later, evidence came to light of a mysterious unsigned letter sent in August 1860 to Sir Edward Archibald, British consul in New York. The letter invited Archibald to act as liaison in a plot to bring the Southern states back into the British Empire. Should the impending presidential election bring Lincoln and the Black Republicans to power, it explained, "we will either Secede from the Union and form a separate government or upon certain conditions at once *return to our allegiance to Great Britain our Mother Country.*" This plan, the anonymous royalist confided, had to be kept secret from the "gossiping newsmongers and babbling pothouse politicians," but was quietly gaining force among the leading men of the South. "*Select Dinner Parties* come off *every day* throughout the whole South and not one of them ends without a strong accession to our forces. I have even heard some of them address each other by titles already." The letter went on to offer Archibald a pivotal role in "accomplishing this grand object of returning to the dominion of our fathers' Kingdom" by bringing this plan to the attention of Lord Lyons, the British ambassador to Washington.[52]

The author withheld his name but told Archibald to reply to "Benjamin" at the US Congress. The obvious suspect was Judah P. Benjamin, US senator from Louisiana, future secretary of state for the Confederacy, and, not incidentally, a British subject by birth. When the letter was published in the 1880s, Benjamin (who fled to England after the war) denied authorship, but he could not resist taking credit for planting the idea. It was all a ploy, he suggested, to win support among British aristocrats who were convinced of the failure of republicanism.[53]

These and other clandestine overtures took place in the shadows of diplomacy and rarely with a traceable link to official authority. Some rumors may have been concocted by journalists or planted by agents working for various governments. The idea of the South's rebellion rising out of hostility to "extreme democracy," "fanatical egalitarianism," and "mob rule," however, was not all fanciful exaggeration and slander. The antagonism between the egalitarian ideals underlying democracy and the ideals of fixed hierarchy and inherited privilege that upheld monarchy paralleled the conflict between free and slave labor. The hints of monarchy emanating from the South, whether genuine or concocted, played into the emerging narrative of an epic battle between systems of government and society about to take place in America.

CHAPTER 5

THE EMPIRES RETURN

The terror of the American name is gone, and the Powers of the Old World are flocking to the feast from which the scream of our eagle has hitherto scared them. We are just beginning to suffer the penalties of being a weak and despised Power.

—*NEW YORK TIMES*, MARCH 30, 1861

THE EUROPEAN DEBATE OVER THE FATE OF THE REPUBLICAN experiment was not restricted to rhetoric in parliamentary speeches or town hall political meetings. As soon as the secession crisis surfaced, the Great Powers of Europe seized the opportunity to reverse the advance of popular government in the Western Hemisphere and more, to take back lost empires and restore the authority of church and crown.

From Paris on March 10, 1861, Malakoff reported for the *New York Times* that the French and British were "filling out a powerful fleet of war steamers for the United States" and would sail with sealed orders, supposedly as observers of "the struggle which is soon to take place between brothers and friends in the United States." The "ostensible errand" was to protect English and French subjects abroad, but Malakoff mused that the naval mission "may be intended as a sort of escort of honor for the funeral of the Great Republic."[1]

From its nearby base in Cuba, Spain was also busy mobilizing men, ships, and matériel to patrol the Caribbean. It had a more decisive target in mind. Within two weeks of Lincoln's inaugural, the Spanish launched an invasion and takeover of their former colony the Dominican Republic. Malakoff also reported intriguing rumors circulating in the Tuileries Palace that Louisiana, having "repudiated her allegiance to the Government of the United States," gave France "the right to reclaim her former Colony."[2]

Malakoff's grim report in the *New York Times* projected the very foreign menace that Seward alluded to in his April 1 memorandum to Lincoln. Above all, Malakoff's report from Paris gave proof that some insidious ideas were taking hold abroad, at least in the minds of government leaders: that the Union was dead, further fragmentation would follow, and the entire republican experiment was about to be dealt a fatal blow.

With the new Lincoln administration seized by the secession crisis, several Great Powers of Europe—Spain, France, and Britain, with support from Belgium and Austria—recognized their opportunities to reclaim lost American empires and shore up existing ones. Whatever power the United States previously had to enforce the Monroe Doctrine, it became a dead letter during the Civil War. While Britain nervously guarded its possessions in Canada and the Caribbean, Spain and France set out to conquer feeble Latin American republics.[3]

Spain seemed enthused by hopes for the return of imperial glory in the Americas, while France vowed to lead the global regeneration of the "Latin race" against the Anglo-Saxon Protestants. What came to be known as Napoleon III's "Grand Design for the Americas" had been gestating since the 1830s and was unveiled in the 1860s as a bold new program of nationalist aggrandizement impelled by the transnational concept of "Latin" racial and cultural ascendancy.[4]

France's Grand Design envisioned a Latin Catholic empire that would, in time, embrace all the failed Spanish American republics and include an alliance with the Empire of Brazil. It was the supreme expression of Napoleon III's Bonapartisme revival, which in the fullness of its ambition encompassed everything from Baron Haussmann's rebuilding of Paris to the colonization of Algeria, the construction of the Suez Canal in Egypt, colonial expansion in Indochina (Vietnam), and, the grandest of all, the founding of a new Latin American empire radiating from Mexico. Napoleon III's aim was nothing less than to create in France a major global power that spanned both hemispheres and the Atlantic and Pacific Oceans. Nowhere did his ambitions reach higher, and fail more spectacularly, than in Mexico.[5]

The Grand Design owed much to Michel Chevalier, one of Napoleon III's court intellectuals, an ardent French imperialist and devotee of historian Jules Michelet, who viewed Europe as divided into competing Latin Catholic and Teutonic Protestant races. During his travels in the United States and Mexico in the 1830s Chevalier recognized that similar divisions were being reproduced in the Americas, and always with unfortunate results for "Latin America," a term he helped invent. While Anglo-American Protestants had established a thriving republic in the United States, Latin America, infected by democratic ideas of equality and liberty that were wholly unsuited to its traditions and temperament, had degenerated into what Chevalier described as "an impotent race without a future." The regeneration of Mexico and all of Latin America would come either by means of an Anglo-American conquest or the beneficent tutelage of France as the ascendant leader of the Latin race. "Without France, without her intelligence, her elevated sentiments and her military power," Chevalier wrote, Latin nations "would long since have been completely eclipsed."[6]

Ideas about France as the redemptive leader of the Latin race and about Mexico as the geopolitical key to control of the Americas and the Pacific Ocean had evolved in answer to America's doctrine of Manifest Destiny, which prophesied the inevitable spread of democracy and Anglo-Saxon culture. The Latin race was an imagined community of peoples of Spanish, Portuguese, Italian, and French origin bounded by a common *Latinidad* (Latinity) that was grounded in their similar language, Catholicism, and opposition to the Teutonic races of northern Europe and North America.[7]

Suddenly, America's Civil War opened the way for France to fulfill its own manifest destiny in the Americas and to roll back the expansion of the United States. At its broadest conception, the Grand Design envisioned a Latin Catholic monarchical league dominating the Western Hemisphere from California to the tip of South America, with two powerful monarchies, Mexico and Brazil, forming the main axis and France and other allied European Catholic empires providing protection and guidance.[8]

More ominous for the United States was the idea that the success of Napoleon's Grand Design depended on an independent Confederacy to serve as a buffer state between the United States and Mexico. A sensational pamphlet entitled *La France, le Mexique et les États Confédérés* was published anonymously by Michel Chevalier in 1863 and translated into English for *New York Times* readers that September. In it Chevalier, obviously with Napoleon III's approval, blatantly announced that France's purpose was to help the Confederacy win independence, thwart US expansion, and shield Mexico from US interference.[9]

The "monarchical projects directed against America do not stop" at Mexico, the *New York Times* alerted readers as early as February 1862. There were plots "openly talked of in the Continental Courts" to establish monarchies in the Rio de la Plata region encompassing Paraguay, Uruguay, and parts of Argentina and Brazil, as well as in the Central American republics of Nicaragua, Costa Rica, and perhaps Guatemala and San Salvador. According to one report in Frankfurt's *Allgemeine Zeitung,* several Italian monarchs recently deposed by the Italian Risorgimento were candidates for Latin American crowns. Brazil's emperor, Dom Pedro II of the Braganza dynasty, was reported to be in full cooperation with these plans for the restoration of monarchy in his troubled Spanish American neighbors.[10]

Latin American conservatives much preferred the protection of France to dethroned Italians. In 1861 Ecuador's Gabriel García Moreno, styling himself the enemy of "godless liberals," invited France to protect his country from "the domestic disorder and anarchy . . . dishonoring and impoverishing the country" and against the "destructive torrent of the Anglo-American race." Paraguay's Francisco Solano López, assuming his late father's role as dictator in September 1862, inquired of French officials whether European royals would welcome him as monarch of a López dynasty. That was when he first learned of plans by France, Spain, and Italy to install a single European monarch over the discordant Rio de la Plata region. Ramón Castilla, the republican president of Peru, predicted that Latin America was about to witness a "war of the crowns against the Liberty Caps."[11]

THE CROWNS STRUCK THE FIRST BLOW AGAINST THE LIBERTY CAPS IN Santo Domingo in March 1861. Spanish officials in Madrid and Havana had been plotting with conservative forces in the Dominican Republic for months as the secession crisis ripened in the United States. The Dominicans had suffered an unhappy national life. They won independence from Spain in 1821, only to be taken over by their Haitian neighbors, who feared the reintroduction of slavery. Finally, in 1844 the Dominicans pushed the Haitians out and established an independent republic. But its seventeen years of independence had been plagued by foreign debt and wracked by internal strife that followed a familiar Latin American pattern: conservative white landowners, military leaders, and Catholic clergy pitted against liberal republicans in the middle class and peasantry, most of the latter former African slaves.[12]

Fresh off its conquests in Morocco, Spain was animated by a renewed sense of imperial grandeur. Ever since she ascended to the throne as an infant, Queen Isabella II had been challenged by the ultratraditional Carlists, who had no use for a female monarch and proclaimed Carlos VI as the legitimate heir to the throne. The Carlists waged war against her in the 1830s, again in the 1840s, and in 1860 mounted yet another failed revolt to oust the queen. Isabella II stood between two fires: reactionary Catholic legitimists, on one side, and liberal republicans, on the other.[13]

Spain's burst of imperialist enthusiasm, Carl Schurz reported from Madrid in September 1861, was "calculated to tickle national vanity." Courtiers flattered the queen by calling her the "second *Isabel la Católica*," whose destiny it was "to restore the ancient splendors and power of the Spanish Monarchy." Spain's resurgence in the Western Hemisphere, Schurz warned Seward, "seems to have been for some time a favorite dream of the dynasty."[14]

Spanish officials had long worried that the United States would seize the Dominican Republic and use it as a base of operations for taking over Cuba, the jewel in what was left of Spain's imperial crown. So did the Dominican Republic's conservatives, whose leader, the aging president Pedro Santana, had been secretly plotting with Francisco Serrano, the Spanish commander in Havana, to devise a plan to return their country to Spanish rule. According to plan, Santana fomented popular support for the takeover by whipping up fears of invasion, either by the United States or its dreaded Haitian neighbors. "Santo Domingo will be Haitian or Yankee," Santana exclaimed.[15]

When Spanish officials in Madrid stalled out of fear that the United States would retaliate, Santana became frantic. On March 18, 1861, he forced the issue by holding a sham plebiscite and proclaiming the "unanimous consent" of Dominicans for a return to the Spanish Empire. The Spanish flag rose above the capitol, and Santana ordered a 101-gun salute. On signal two Spanish warships lurking offshore landed and disembarked soldiers to secure the capital. The island that Columbus had claimed for *Isabel la Católica* in 1492 was thus reclaimed by Isabella II to the glory of Spain.[16]

Madrid was stunned by the news and braced for retaliation from the United States. Leopoldo O'Donnell, the Spanish prime minister, worried that Americans might "forget their internal discords" and make war on Spain's vulnerable American empire. But Gabriel García Tassara, the Spanish ambassador to Washington, assured his government that the Lincoln administration was far too distracted to take action against Spain. Spain's "grand hour," Tassara prophesied, "approaches again in America as in Europe." "The Union is in agony, our mission is not to delay its death for a moment."[17]

O'Donnell's fear of America uniting against foreign incursions was exactly what Seward had in mind in his notorious April 1 memorandum to Lincoln. Though he might be faulted for exaggerating what he supposed to be the remedial effects of foreign war to disunion, Seward clearly grasped the more important truth that Spain's aggression in Santo Domingo would open the door to more European incursions if it went unanswered. There were already signs of French cooperation with Spain, Seward warned. The next step would be the reinstatement of slavery over the entire island of Hispaniola, Santo Domingo, and Haiti.[18]

While Lincoln and the United States stood back, the republicans of Santo Domingo, many of them former slaves, took to the jungles to begin a fierce guerrilla war against what their April 1861 manifesto characterized as Santana's plot to "crush the Dominican people under the colonial yoke." One Dominican Republic leader, General José-Maria Cabral, sounded the alarm: "Tomorrow we will be slaves!" He enlisted Haitians to join them in a war to the death rather than submit to "slavery" under the Spanish occupation. The Dominicans also sent agents to Washington to urge the United States to stand up for its Monroe Doctrine, all to no avail. Seward refused to receive the desperate Dominican envoys for fear that any show of support might push Spain into the arms of the Confederates.[19]

The *New York Times* roundly denounced Spain's effrontery. "Our domestic dissensions are producing their natural fruits." Spain, feeling its "new-born power," would never have dared such a move had it not been for the secession crisis. This was only the first step in that haughty empire's desire "for resuming her position as a Power on the Western Continent."[20]

SEWARD HAD NO IDEA THAT IN MADRID, THE US MINISTER TO SPAIN, William Preston, a Buchanan appointee from Kentucky, was using his last months in office to aid the Confederacy. Preston did all he could to convince the Spanish foreign secretary, Saturnino Calderón Collantes, that Southern secession was legal, justifiable, and an accomplished fact. The secession of the slave states was just the beginning, Preston informed him. Before it was over, all but a few of the northeastern states, those infected by "ultra fanatical" abolitionism, would come under the Confederate constitution, and Washington would soon become the capital of the reconstituted proslavery nation.[21]

Seward learned all of this from Horatio J. Perry, the loyal secretary of the legation in Madrid, who had the courage to report his superior's treachery. Perry was married to Carolina Coronado, a popular Spanish writer and close friend of Queen Isabella II. Her literary salon brought Perry into close contact with Madrid's intellectual and political leaders, which made him aware of but powerless to counter Preston's insidious influence.[22]

"You cannot too quickly change the Legation at this Court," Perry advised Seward in early May 1861. Preston had been "working on the aristocratical prejudices of Courtiers and army and navy officers against the United States" and cultivating "considerable sympathy for . . . rebels in the name of slavery and aristocratical privileges." Preston also used his connections to plant a newspaper story, "rejoicing over the idea that the Confederate States have already entered upon the road" toward "a monarchical form of government." Upon leaving Madrid, Preston took the occasion to deliver a grandiose speech to Queen Isabella II, extolling Spain's recent triumphs in Africa and Santo Domingo.[23]

It was only later that Perry discovered Preston had also absconded with all of Seward's instructions, which left the legation at great disadvantage for weeks. Preston returned home to serve in the Confederate army and later would be appointed Confederate envoy to the Empire of Mexico at Maximilian's court. But it was in Madrid, while serving as US minister, that Preston performed his greatest service to the rebellion.[24]

Confederates were enchanted with the idea of alliance with Spain. It was the only European power still sanctioning slavery, and it was a vociferous opponent of America's Monroe Doctrine. Robert Toombs, the first Confederate secretary of state, saw Spain as a natural ally and instructed Martin Crawford, a member of the Confederate commission in Washington, to meet with Tassara, Spain's ambassador to the United States, and assure him "of the sincere wish of this Government to cultivate close and friendly relations with Spain." Tell him, Toombs instructed, "that we are fully sensible of the importance of a great European Power possessing slave holding colonies in our Neighborhood." Toombs also sent Charles Helm as envoy to Havana to establish friendly relations with local officials. After Helm finally arrived in October 1861, he reported cheerfully, "I find a large majority of the population of Havana zealously advocating our cause, and am informed that the same feeling extends throughout the island."[25]

From London William Yancey, head of the first Confederate commission to Europe, urged Richmond to send an envoy to Spain, but it took until late August for Toombs's successor, Robert Hunter, to authorize Pierre Rost, one of Yancey's fellow commissioners, to go to Madrid. Spain alone, of all the Great Powers, "is interested through her colonies in the same social system which pervades the Confederate States," Rost was instructed to point out to the Spanish government. The Confederacy, he added, would never "find any cause for jealousy or regret in the steady growth of the power and resources of Spain," a delicate allusion to the takeover of Santo Domingo.

As for the South's prior filibustering expeditions in Cuba, Hunter instructed Rost to explain that the only motivation for it was to maintain "something like a balance of power" with the North in Congress. An independent South would be relieved of all such concerns: "Of all the nations of the earth . . . there is none so deeply interested as Spain in the speedy recognition and permanent maintenance of the independence of the Confederate States of America." Then Hunter added a menacing threat: Spain had the choice of either assisting what will be "a great friendly power" or facing in the future a "formidable" rival in the Caribbean.[26]

The capture and detention of Mason and Slidell and the entire *Trent* crisis forced the Confederacy's initiative in Madrid to the back burner. Rost decided on his own authority to stay in Paris and did not get to Madrid until March 1862. In his interview with Calderon, the foreign minister, he found it difficult to persuade him that it was the North, not the South, that coveted Cuba. Rost did not help things when he began waxing eloquent about the Confederacy's hopes for a great tropical empire in league with Spain and Brazil. Together the three nations "would have a monopoly of the system of labor, which alone can make intertropical America" prosper. "Nothing in the past could give an idea of the career of prosperity and power which would thus be opened to us."[27]

THE SOUTH WOULD INDEED HAVE TO SHARE ITS DREAMS OF A TROPICAL empire if Europe's Great Powers had anything to say about it. Spain's takeover of Santo Domingo was the thin edge of the European imperialist wedge, the full dimensions and purpose of which soon became apparent. Having met with nothing more than feeble protests from a distracted United States, Spanish zeal for a *Reconquista* gained momentum. Mexico, once the heart of Spain's American empire, loomed as the next prize.[28]

During its forty years of independence since 1821, Mexico had undergone fifty changes in government, and the breach between conservative and liberal factions had never closed. Paralleling the rise of the Republican Party in the United States, Mexico's ascending Liberal Party had gained power in the 1850s. In what was known as la Reforma, the liberals introduced sweeping laws that vastly expanded the rights of citizens, limited the powerful grip of the Catholic Church on land and education, and culminated in the ratification in 1857 of a new constitution that liberals hoped would place Mexico on a firm republican foundation.[29]

Mexico's conservatives refused to accept la Reforma, the 1857 republican constitution, and the new liberal government elected under it. Pope Pius IX denounced the reforms, which included confiscation of church lands and secularization of education. The pope compared Mexico's liberals to Italian revolutionaries Giuseppe Garibaldi and Giuseppe Mazzini, all godless enemies of the church. Mexico's Catholic priests were instructed to deny absolution for any officeholder who had taken an oath to uphold the 1857 constitution. Conservative military officers defected and fomented a rebellion to oust the Liberals and vest power in the "church party." In January 1858 Mexico was plunged into a bloody civil war known as *la Guerra de Reforma*.[30]

Mexico's Reform War (1858–1861) foreshadowed the civil war about to break out in the United States. Though set in vastly different cultural contexts, both were instigated by conservatives rebelling against liberal republican electoral victories. After three years of war, Mexico's republican forces finally routed the enemy army outside Mexico City and resumed power in January 1861, just as Mexico's republican neighbor to the North was plagued by its own rebellion.

Benito Juárez, a lawyer from Oaxaca and a full-blooded Zapotec Indian, had played a leading role in *la Reforma*. He served as head of the supreme court of the first liberal government and then as interim president during the Reform War. Juárez would be called the "Abraham Lincoln of Mexico," for both men rose from abject poverty, believed deeply in the rule of law, and became leaders of embattled republics against rebellious conservative forces, one trying to secede, the other trying to supplant the republic with a monarchy.[31]

Mexico's conservative church party, as it was known, no more accepted the verdict of war than it had the verdict of the ballot box. No one was more zealous in his opposition than José María Gutiérrez de Estrada, who made it his life's ambition to overthrow the republic and install a European monarch in Mexico. Born to a wealthy Creole Yucatán family in 1800, during the 1830s Gutiérrez de Estrada served briefly as Mexico's minister to Vienna and became convinced that the only solution to Mexico's tumultuous republic was an absolutist Catholic monarch on the Hapsburg model. His monarchist views were scorned in Mexico, however, and sometime in the 1840s he went into exile in Europe to begin a career as a self-appointed diplomat. For twenty years he lobbied the Catholic monarchs of Europe, not least Pope Pius IX, to aid his scheme for Mexico's regeneration under a European prince.

While in Rome during the 1850s, Gutiérrez de Estrada met José Hidalgo, Mexico's minister to the Papal States and soon converted him to the cause of monarchy for Mexico. After being transferred to Madrid, Hidalgo developed a close personal relationship with the vivacious widow

14. Benito Juárez and Abraham Lincoln, portrayed together in a mural by Aarón Piña Mora, Government Palace, Chihuahua, Mexico. (PHOTOGRAPH IN AUTHOR'S COLLECTION)

of a Spanish grandee, Madam de Montijo, whose beautiful daughter, Eugénie, had married Napoleon III in 1853. Almost by chance, Hidalgo and Gutiérrez de Estrada had found a path to the inner circle of French power. Empress Eugénie would become an indispensable advocate for restoring Spain's wayward former colony to glory under a Catholic monarchy.[32]

Back in Mexico Juárez's republican regime was besieged by troubles. Though the Reform War had ended, in early 1861 outside Mexico City roving bands of brigands menaced the countryside, disrupted the economy, and obstructed transportation between the capital and the main port in Veracruz. Ravaged by war, deeply in debt to foreign creditors, Mexico would not be able to sustain payments on its international debts. In July 1861 Juárez announced the suspension of interest payments for two years. He was careful not to repudiate the debt itself, but this was all that was needed for the Great Powers of Europe to launch plans for intervention and bring to fruition the royalist plan Gutiérrez de Estrada and Hidalgo had been tirelessly promoting in Europe. With the United States descending into what appeared to be a prolonged internecine war, the door to Mexico was opened.[33]

AT THE END OF OCTOBER 1861 DIPLOMATS FROM SPAIN, FRANCE, AND Britain gathered in London to form the Tripartite Alliance. "Three States are combining to coerce a fourth [Mexico] into good behavior," the London *Times* explained it, *"not so much by way of war as by authoritative interference in behalf of order."* The alliance's professed purpose was the recovery of Mexican debts, many of them owed to cronies of Napoleon III, chief among them the Duc de Morny, his illegitimate half brother. There were also demands of reparations for alleged harms to European citizens in Mexico. But the undeclared design of the French and Spanish governments was to overthrow Juárez's republican government and install a European monarch in Mexico.[34] The British were owed debts from Mexico, too, but they were wary of mad schemes to install a foreign monarch there. Against the advice of his ambassador in Mexico, Earl Russell decided to take part in the alliance, supposedly to check the imperialist plots of Spain and France.

Napoleon III's plans for Mexico were no secret. In October 1861, days before the Tripartite Alliance meeting, Napoleon instructed his ambassador in London to explain to Palmerston and Russell that his aim was to establish a stable government in Mexico that would block American expansion. "The faction of Juárez will be overthrown, a national assembly will be convoked and a monarchy will be established." Furthermore, the French emperor revealed to the British, "I have put forward the name of the Archduke Maximilian," the younger brother to Emperor Franz Joseph of the Austrian Hapsburg dynasty. "A regenerated Mexico would form an insuperable barrier to the encroachments of the Americans of the North," he noted. He sent a similar letter to Leopold I, king of the Belgians and the uncle and adviser of Queen Victoria.[35]

The *Trent* affair conveniently consumed Lincoln's government during November and December 1861 while the Tripartite Alliance planned its invasion. Spain, with troops ready in Havana, eagerly led the way. Its armada of twenty-six warships steamed into the harbor at Veracruz on December 8, 1861. Six thousand infantry disembarked, while five thousand marines and sailors remained on board.[36]

General Don Manuel Gasset y Mercader, acting commander of Spanish expeditionary forces in Mexico, addressed his soldiers after they landed at Veracruz. "Soldiers: In every quarter the Spanish army meets with glorious remembrances of its valor and devotion. On these very sands exist the traces of Hernando Cortez, who with but a handful of Spaniards planted side by side with the standard of Castile, the ensign of the Cross and of Civilization, dazzling the world with his wonderful achievements. Today our mission is not less glorious; it is to exact from the Mexican Government satisfaction for insults heaped upon our flag." Some of the Mexican onlookers may have known that Cortés in 1519 had ordered his ships burned to prevent retreat before leading his army of conquistadores toward the Aztec capital to pillage its treasure and enslave its people. What lay ahead for Mexico, and its invaders, nearly three and one half centuries later, none could yet foresee.[37]

The British and French fleets did not arrive until January 6 and 8, respectively. Britain brought seven hundred marines. The French landed two thousand regular troops, not counting five hundred Zouave soldiers with their dashing uniforms of bright-red trousers and tasseled red fez caps.[38]

"Ambition grows by what it feeds on," the *New York Times* gravely intoned after the invasion began. Success in Mexico, it predicted, would encourage similar operations in other Spanish American republics. The allied powers were attempting "to establish this species of Monarchism on the ruins of the Democratic Governments founded in the Western World," which would set off "a grand struggle between the votaries of Republicanism and the votaries of Monarchy."[39]

THE TURMOIL IN MEXICO AND THE INVASION BY EUROPEAN POWERS created new challenges and opportunities for both the Union and the Confederacy to realign their foreign policies and redefine their messages to the world. For Confederates, hemmed in by the tightening Union blockade, Mexico would provide a vital lifeline to overseas shipments of essential supplies. Matamoros, a small port on the Rio Grande opposite Brownsville, Texas, became a bustling international center of trade. Most of the territory surrounding Matamoros was controlled by José Santiago Vidaurri Valdez, governor of the northern Mexican state of Nuevo León and the strongman who ruled the adjoining states of Coahuila and Tamaulipas. Known as the "Lord of the North," Vidaurri distrusted Juárez and the republicans and spoke openly of his desire to secede from Mexico and perhaps join the Confederacy.[40]

The Confederates immediately recognized in Vidaurri an important ally whose protection of Matamoros would be vital to their success and whose secessionist sympathies might open a path to expansion southward. In May 1861 Robert Toombs dispatched José Agustín Quintero as "agent and special messenger" to the Vidaurri government. A Cuban-born intellectual and journalist, Quintero had fled Cuba after falling afoul of Spanish censors and made his way to the United States, where he became active in Democratic Party circles and formed a friendship with Jefferson Davis. Toombs instructed his new envoy to inform the Lord of the North that Southerners "feel a deep sympathy with all people struggling to secure for themselves the blessings of self-government." Quintero was also authorized to arrange for purchase of arms and supplies through Vidaurri, a profitable reward for the Mexican chief's loyalty to the rebel South.[41]

Vidaurri promised Confederates a back door around the blockade, but northern Mexico might also provide a back door for the Union army to invade their vulnerable western borders. Recognizing the vital importance of Mexico in the coming conflict, Lincoln had shrewdly appointed Tom Corwin as US minister there. The Ohio politician and former US senator arrived in Mexico City in June 1861 already something of a hero for his opposition to the war with Mexico and especially his famous 1846 Senate speech warning that Mexico would receive America's invading armies "with bloody hands and hospitable graves."[42]

Juárez and Mexican liberals looked to the United States as their protector against European—and Confederate—aggression. Corwin, reassuming his role as defender of Mexico, warned the Juárez government that the rebel South aimed to spread its empire of slavery southward. If Europe invaded Mexico, he told Seward, it would embolden the Southern rebels and probably "aid them in procuring their recognition by European powers." Furthermore, European invasion would "so weaken Mexico that a very inconsiderable southern force could conquer in a very short time four or five Mexican States."[43]

Corwin proposed to fend off threats to Mexico from Europe or the Confederacy by having the United States pledge a generous loan to Mexico to pay interest on its foreign debt and build up the depleted Mexican army. The "Corwin loan" was to be secured by territories in northern Mexico, which would undoubtedly have led to vast acquisitions of Mexican land by the United States, including the rich mining districts in Sonora. Due to wartime strains on the economy, however, the US Congress was in no position to pour money into Mexico. Besides, Seward feared that siding with Juárez might push France to ally with the Confederacy. Corwin's gesture of support, nonetheless, benefited US-Mexican relations.[44]

As its envoy to Mexico City the Confederacy sent John T. Pickett, a rough-hewn Virginian who had served the Buchanan administration as US consul to Veracruz and had a shadowy career in Caribbean filibustering adventures before that. He began his Confederate service as secretary to the Confederate commission to Washington in March 1861. He was a favorite of John Forsyth, one of the commissioners and a former US minister to Mexico under Buchanan. "Mexican affairs have suddenly come to be very interesting to the Black Administration," Forsyth warned Jefferson Davis from Washington that March. Forsyth regarded Corwin as a traitor to his country, but he understood his appeal to Mexican liberals and advised Davis to respond swiftly by sending Pickett to Mexico.[45]

Forsyth asked Pickett to prepare a memorandum outlining for President Davis a Mexican strategy for the Confederacy. Pickett went to work crafting a policy that recommended by turns the Confederate overthrow of the Juárez regime and the wholesale takeover of the country. "So long as Mexico is governed, or attempted to be governed, by Mexicans alone," it will never have a stable government. Foreign intervention "in one shape or another" is the only remedy to the corruption, "gross ignorance and superstition of the people (if Mexico may be said to have a 'people')." The United States, Pickett advised, would do all it could to "exclude us forever from our natural inheritance in that quarter." The Union was likely to colonize Veracruz and close off access to the Confederacy in pursuit of its "long cherished design of surrounding African servitude by a *cordon* of flourishing free States." The right Confederate special agent, Pickett advised Davis, could "place Yankee meddlesomeness and Puritan bigotry in their true light," and if the "so-called Liberal party" in Mexico made terms with the United States that were "offensive to our dignity or interest," the South must take sides with conservative leaders and help restore them to power. The "boundless agricultural and mineral resources" of Mexico and its Isthmus of Tehuantepec, thought to be a vital path between the Pacific Ocean and the Gulf of Mexico, must remain open to Confederate expansion, Pickett further explained to Davis. "Southward is our destiny."[46]

President Davis apparently liked these ideas and recommended that Toombs send Pickett to Mexico in May 1861. Toombs instructed Pickett to inform the Juárez government that the Confederacy welcomed a friendly alliance with its neighbor. Pickett was also instructed to emphasize the compatibility between the two countries, being "principally engaged in agriculture and mining pursuits" and with similar institutions of slavery and peonage. The instructions also included some blunt advice on bribing Mexicans: "A million or so of money judiciously applied would purchase our recognition by the Government." Furthermore, "The Mexicans are not overscrupulous, and it is not our mission to mend their morals at this precise period."[47]

WHEN PICKETT ARRIVED IN MEXICO CITY IN JULY 1861, HE ENCOUNTERED few friends. Corwin's popularity in Mexico had, it seemed, closed off Confederate approaches to the Juárez government, and, in any case, Pickett soon managed to alienate all sides entirely on his own. His violent temper and ethnic bigotry, together with a weakness for strong drink, were a dangerous combination in a diplomat. Irritated by Corwin's favorable reception in Mexico, Pickett lashed out in what he thought was private correspondence, hurling racist slurs against the Mexican people, their political instability, and their military incompetence. One especially intemperate dispatch threatened that the South would invade and imprison Mexicans, who would "find themselves for the first time in their lives, usefully employed . . . hoeing corn and picking cotton."[48]

In another dispatch Pickett confided that he was purposefully deceiving Mexicans into thinking that an independent South would have no need to expand. He even let it be known that the Confederacy might consider a retrocession of territory stolen from Mexico in 1848 by the "late United States." This, Pickett assured the home office in Richmond, was all a ruse aimed at neutralizing Mexico and confounding the Union. If Mexico persisted in favoring the Union, however, it would present "a golden opportunity" for Confederates to fulfill the "inevitable destiny which impels them Southward."[49]

It never occurred to Pickett that the government he was insulting as inept might be intercepting his messages. Instead, when his dispatches went unanswered for weeks, he blamed it all on the incompetence of Mexican couriers, made copies of all his correspondence, and sent the copies by special courier through an agent in New Orleans. The agent, it turned out, was a Union spy. The entire packet was promptly forwarded to Seward in Washington.[50]

Pickett was, to say the least, in bad odor with the Juárez government, yet by late 1861 he hoped that the plans of the Tripartite Alliance to invade Mexico were about to tilt the game in his favor. "I little thought a few years ago ever to counsel a Spanish alliance," he wrote to Richmond in November 1861, "but revolutions bring us into strange company." The "Spaniards are now become our natural allies, and jointly with them we may own the Gulf of Mexico and effect the partition of this magnificent country."[51]

Acting as usual on his own authority, Pickett decided to abruptly sever relations with the Juárez government and realign the Confederacy with Mexico's church party and its European allies. In late November he swaggered into the office of an American named John Bennett and berated him for some alleged offense to the honor of a Confederate cabinet member's wife. Then he assaulted Bennett, striking him with his fists and kicking him as he lay writhing on the floor. Mexican authorities threw Pickett in jail. He protested diplomatic immunity; they released him and then arrested him twice again. He finally fled to Veracruz. Only Pickett would have the gall to claim this was all a deliberate diplomatic tactic, but indeed that is what he reported to his astonished superiors in Richmond.[52]

In early 1862 Pickett was in Veracruz, the bay full of warships and the troops of Spain, Britain, and France. Here they were, Pickett jubilantly reported to a friend in Richmond in February, "like buzzards on the house top, over the defunct carcass of the Mexican Nation." "The Monroe Doctrine, where is it?" At Veracruz he spoke with the French minister to Mexico, assuring him that the Confederacy welcomed any measures the European invaders might take that "would tend to give us a better neighbor and effectually exclude the Puritans from ever flanking us in this quarter."[53]

IF PICKETT AND THE CONFEDERATE HIGH COMMAND WERE COUNTING on Spain as their "natural ally" and new southern neighbor, their hopes were soon disappointed. Spain had sent General Juan Prim as commandeer of Spanish troops in the allied invasion of Mexico. Prim had served with distinction in the Morocco campaign in 1859 and was a popular political figure, especially among the liberal Progressista party in Spain. The conservatives, Carl Schurz thought, were trying to "get rid of a very dangerous man," and some even thought he might assume some leadership role in Mexico, perhaps as its new monarch. Prim was married to a wealthy Mexican woman whose uncle was Juárez's finance minister. But Prim was a thoroughgoing republican who thought the church, not the liberal government, should be blamed for most of the country's troubles and that it was absurd to impose a monarchy on the Mexican people whose traditions were strongly republican.[54]

Once Spain's allies landed at Veracruz in early January 1861, a five-man commission representing the three countries, with Prim as chair, issued a lofty proclamation that denied any intention of conquest and promised that the allied powers "shall preside impassibly over the glorious spectacle of your regeneration, guaranteed through order and liberty." It was when the commissioners tried to specify the terms of repaying the debt that the divisions among them appeared. The French insisted on demanding the full amount claimed, including many false and embellished claims made by French citizens. Prim and the British commissioners objected, and weeks of acrimonious wrangling ensued while the troops in Veracruz were wracked by illness, not least the *vomito* (yellow fever) that plagued the coast during the sickly season. The allied expedition had come four thousand miles, and its commissioners were now unable to agree on their objectives.

What ought to have been clear from the outset was that the French wanted to impose demands that would be impossible to satisfy and then provoke war with Mexico, march on the capital, bring Mexico's republic to its knees, and prepare the way for a European monarchy. France's allies were not prepared to go along with this, and when the French sent for more troops to Mexico and openly sided with the Mexican conservative leadership in early April 1862, Britain and Spain immediately withdrew from the alliance and pulled their troops out of Mexico.[55]

Now France faced Mexico alone. On the very day Britain and Spain withdrew from the alliance, April 9, 1862, the French notified Mexico that hostilities would begin. French forces, now augmented by reinforcements under the command of General Charles Latrille de Lorencez prepared to march on Puebla, the gateway to Mexico City. Acting as the political voice of the French Empire, the French minister to Mexico, Count Alphonso Dubois de Saligny, issued a proclamation that assured Mexico of France's benign intentions toward the "sound part" of the nation whom they sought to rescue from the tyranny and anarchy of the Juárez regime. Speaking as one who knew the country and its people, Saligny confidently promised General Lorencez that the Mexicans would welcome their "regenerators" with flowers and that the priests of Puebla would celebrate their arrival with a *Te Deum,* the Catholic hymn of praise to God.[56]

French forces marched on Puebla where, early on the morning of May 5, General Lorencez ordered his Zouaves to assault Mexican troops entrenched on the hill outside the city. They met ferocious resistance from the republican army under the command of General Ignacio Zaragoza. The French were widely regarded as the finest infantry in the world, and Lorencez was not about to back down from what he considered an inferior army of Mexicans. After a bloody day of battle, the French were repulsed, and the screams of wounded soldiers filled the night as Lorencez led his army in retreat.[57]

Cinco de Mayo became a celebrated national holiday for Mexicans. Tragically, soon after his stunning victory General Zaragoza, the hero of the day, died of typhoid fever. His funeral procession in Mexico City drew massive crowds of admirers who cheered and threw flowers on the coffin, as it passed before them, raised on a catafalque drawn by a handsome team of black horses. The French flag was thrown contemptuously at the foot of the coffin, while above it flew a banner proclaiming Zaragoza *el conquistador de los conquistadores.*

An army of Mexicans, most of them mestizos, had defeated what was purported to be the most formidable armed force in Europe. The Mexican victory at Puebla did not turn back the French, but it delayed their conquest for one crucial year. It was an unspeakable humiliation for Napoleon III, and his government censored details about the battle in the press. But the cries from Puebla that terrible night in May echoed all the way to Paris.[58]

Napoleon III was undeterred. He decided to teach the Mexicans a lesson in French military superiority. He reinforced the French army in Mexico to more than thirty thousand troops and sent one of his most trusted commanders, General Elie Frédéric Forey, to lead them. In a secret letter to General Forey, Napoleon III carefully instructed him on how

15. Cinco de Mayo, 1862, by Antonio González Orozco, Museo Nacional de Historia, Chapultepec Castle. (PHOTOGRAPH BY AUTHOR)

to carry out the subjugation of Mexico. Forey was to conquer the capital and then set up an Assembly of Notables from among the clergy and wealthy conservatives of the church party who supported the French mission. He was to empower this assembly to choose the form of Mexico's future government and suggest to them, should they choose monarchy, that Archduke Maximilian of Austria was available. "You must be master in Mexico without seeming to be," Napoleon III advised his general.[59]

All pretense surrounding the Mexican debt and other alleged injuries and losses suffered by French inhabitants of Mexico was forgotten. France's purpose, Napoleon explained bluntly to Forey, was to thwart the expansion and influence of the United States in Latin America. Mexico would become an "insuperable barrier" against US aggression and protect the possessions of "ungrateful Spain" in the Caribbean. Our "influence will radiate northward as well as southward" and create immense markets for French commerce and materials for its industry. "We shall have given back to the Latin race on the other side of the ocean its force and its prestige."[60]

A little more than one year after their inglorious defeat at Puebla, the French made their triumphal entry into Mexico City in early June 1863 as

Juárez and his republican forces retreated. Forey had no trouble filling the Assembly of Notables with reliable generals, Catholic clergy, and landowners. On July 10, 1863, with near unanimity and all according to script, the assembly declared Mexico a monarchy and elected to offer the crown to Maximilian. In case Maximilian refused, they agreed to let Napoleon III choose another prince to fill Mexico's throne. The notables also decided to send a delegation to present the offer to Maximilian in Austria.[61]

Mexico's conservatives embarked on their monarchical experiment in July 1863 just as their Confederate counterparts to the north met with stunning defeats at Vicksburg and Gettysburg. Juárez and his embattled republican followers hoped that the Union's eventual victory might yet rescue them, if only they could hold out long enough against the Mexican monarchists and their French protectors.

It seemed incongruous to choose an Austrian prince to lead the regeneration of the Latin race in Mexico, but in the cunning mind of Napoleon III this played perfectly into his design for French dominance in Europe. He had adopted Italy as something like a client state during its Risorgimento. Since 1849 French garrisons had defended Rome and the Papal States, and Napoleon III could not risk the furor of Catholics by abandoning the pope to the likes of Garibaldi. But he also needed to placate Italian nationalists who wanted to complete the Risorgimento and make Rome the capital of a united Italy. In 1859 Napoleon III deployed French forces to northern Italy to help oust the Austrians from Lombardy, which had been governed not incidentally by Archduke Maximilian. That left Venice still in the hands of the Austrians, and Napoleon III expected growing pressure from Italy to go to war with Austria again.

Archduke Maximilian had proved himself an able administrator of Lombardy. By Napoleon's calculation, having the younger brother of Hapsburg emperor Franz Joseph on one's side in Mexico might make it easier to acquire Venice without another war. "I have thought it in good taste," Napoleon III coyly put it in a letter of instruction to his ambassador in England, to propose "a prince belonging to a dynasty with which I was recently at war." There were other calculations in play as well. Maximilian's wife, Charlotte, was the daughter of Leopold I, king of the Belgians and confidant of Queen Victoria. Besides, the Hapsburg dynasty was Catholic and among the most prestigious in Europe. The Mexican monarchists, notably Gutiérrez de Estrada and José Hidalgo, had already vetted and approved Maximilian. As Napoleon III saw it, in one stroke Maximilian would bring in multilateral support from France, Austria, Belgium, Britain, and not least Mexico.[62]

Mexico's republicans worked frantically to arouse world opinion against the French intervention. Matías Romero, Juárez's ambassador to the United States, proved unusually adept in appealing to the American public. He was only twenty-three when he began diplomatic service in Washington. After the 1860 election determined Lincoln's victory, he rushed to Springfield to urge the president-elect never to allow Europe to build a monarchy next door. At the end of 1861, when the allied invasion began, the young diplomat grew impatient with the Lincoln administration's unwillingness to defend Mexico and stand behind the Monroe Doctrine, and he began working outside normal channels of diplomacy, making direct appeals to the American public. A true master of public diplomacy, with limited resources Romero performed the work of dozens, writing thousands of letters, and launching Spanish-language newspapers. In addition, he organized a vast network of Mexico clubs through which he raised money to send arms to Juárez and publish pamphlets alerting Americans of events in the imperiled republic to their south.[63]

Romero also staged well-publicized banquets with celebrity guests, then published the proceedings and sent them out to US congressmen and other influential figures. Some were staged at Delmonico's, the famous New York City restaurant. Romero hired a band that played lively Mexican tunes interspersed with "Yankee Doodle" and "Hail Columbia." Elaborate eight-course dinners were punctuated by dozens of spirited toasts and speeches denouncing the French and saluting the heroic struggle of Juárez and the republicans.[64]

There were two rebellions in North America, Romero relentlessly reminded Americans, and both were rooted in the same antipathy toward democratic ideals. The church party in Mexico and the slaveholders in America both called upon the monarchical empires of the Old World to sustain their cause. The French invasion and the Southern rebellion were both "parts of one grand conspiracy" in which the sponsors of absolutism and slavery "make common cause and strike a united blow against republican liberty on the American continent." The enemies of republicanism, Romero warned, must be defeated in Mexico and America before either republic would be safe.[65]

16. Matías Romero, the Republic of Mexico's ambassador to Washington. (NATIONAL ARCHIVES)

MAXIMILIAN WAS POOR MATERIAL FOR THE HARD BUSINESS OF RULING Mexico. He viewed himself as an enlightened aristocrat, an advocate of progress who disdained reactionary absolutists, whom he referred to as "Mandarins." As a boy of fifteen, he witnessed with undisguised horror the violence of the Revolution of 1848, which forced his father to abdicate and brought his older brother to the throne. The memory of those days left him convinced that monarchs must win the loyalty of their subjects out of respect, even love, not fear. As one of his conditions for accepting the throne in Mexico, Maximilian insisted upon some popular ratification of the Assembly of Notables' choice. The French complied early in 1864 by organizing a sham plebiscite in which leading citizens in every village were compelled to sign a petition endorsing the election of Emperor Maximilian. He came to Mexico naively believing he was the people's choice.[66]

Maximilian finally decided to accept the throne, and in April 1864 a Mexican delegation officially offered the crown to him at his magnificent

Miramar Castle, overlooking the sea near Trieste. According to some, it was Princess Charlotte who wanted nothing more than to be a queen and led her husband to accept the doomed "cactus throne" in Mexico. They were a couple starring in a romantic tragedy. She was not yet twenty-four, and he was only thirty-one years old that spring of 1864. He was tall, with deep-blue eyes that some described as dreamy. His thinning light-brown hair was parted in the middle, as was his flourishing beard. The day the Mexican delegation arrived, he dressed in his splendid blue Austrian admiral's uniform, while Charlotte wore a pink dress with a brilliant diamond tiara adorning her dark-brown hair. The head of the Mexican delegation, addressing them in French, offered the throne of Mexico to Maximilian, who accepted in his well-practiced Spanish. *¡Viva Maximiliano, Emperador de Mexico!* the delegation cheered; *¡Viva Carlota de Mexico!* Outside, the flag of Mexico was raised above Miramar and canons on the Austrian warship docked in the Trieste harbor fired a twenty-one-gun salute.[67]

The US minister to Austria, John Lothrop Motley, wrote to a friend that Archduke Maximilian "firmly believes that he is going forth to Mexico to establish an American empire and that it is his divine mission to destroy the dragon of democracy and re-establish the true Church the Right Divine. . . . Poor young man!"[68]

On their way to Mexico, Maximilian and Charlotte stopped at Rome for the blessing of Pope Pius IX. Then they sailed across the Atlantic in the Austrian ship *Novara,* arriving in Veracruz at the end of May 1864.

Meanwhile, Matías Romero had helped persuade Republicans in Congress to officially denounce "the deplorable events now passing in Mexico" and declare in April 1864 that the United States would never "acknowledge any monarchical government, erected on the ruins of any republican government in America, under the auspices of any European power." In France Napoleon III's government had done all it could to keep the French public from learning about US antagonism toward his Grand Design. From Paris Malakoff reported that news of the congressional condemnation fell "like a bomb in time of peace."[69]

Maximiliano and Carlota, as they would be known in Mexico, were welcomed in Veracruz by a lavish official reception, but the streets were empty and the few Mexicans they encountered maintained a stony

17. *The Arrival of Maximiliano and Carlota in Veracruz, 1864,* as imagined by Vienna artist V. H. Gerhart. (COURTESY ERIKA PANI)

silence as they passed. Before the royal couple came through Orizaba, Juárez supporters had distributed small sheets of paper exclaiming, "Long live the Republic, long live Independence, death to the Emperor." When they arrived in Mexico City, however, French troops saw to it that the streets were lined with cheering crowds. Mexico's monarchical experiment had begun.[70]

CHAPTER 6

FOREIGN TRANSLATIONS

> People at a distance have discerned this better than most of
> us who are in the midst of it. Our Friends abroad see it! John
> Bright and his glorious band of English Republicans see that
> we are fighting for Democracy or for liberal institutions. . . .
> Our enemies too see it in the same light. The Aristocrats and
> the Despots of the old world see that our quarrel is that of the
> People against an Aristocracy.
>
> —JOHN MURRAY FORBES,
> UNION SPECIAL AGENT, SEPTEMBER 8, 1863

B Y THE END OF THE FIRST YEAR OF WAR, THE LARGER IDEOLOGICAL
debate over the republican experiment that enveloped the American question and the incursions by European powers in the American
hemisphere made it clear to all that this was more than just another civil
war. Events, and the interpretation of those events, forced diplomats and
politicians on both sides to reconsider their message and the audience
for that message. Foreign governments would continue to calculate the
best course forward in light of their national interests as measured by
commercial profits and geopolitical strategy. But for their citizens, the
American question had become part of a much bigger debate about forms
of government and systems of labor, and about their future.

Though the Union and the Confederacy were not always clear or forthright about what they were fighting for, foreign politicians, journalists,

and intellectuals translated the meaning of events for themselves and reached their own conclusions about what was at stake in the distant war in America. The most lucid translations often came from the dissenting voice of the political opposition or the reformers who made the question about America's future one about their own.

"What *principle* is involved in the American civil war?" Europeans kept asking George Perkins Marsh, America's minister to Italy. Government officials were willing to honor a war waged to sustain "constitutional authority" and "established order against causeless rebellion," Marsh admitted, but the broad public found these matters rather uninspiring. Public support abroad, he warned Seward, depended on the belief that the war "is virtually a contest between the propagandists of domestic slavery and the advocates of emancipation and universal freedom." If the war proved to be protracted, he added, "I am convinced that our hold upon the sympathy and good will of the governments, *and still more of the people of Europe*, will depend upon the distinctness with which this issue is kept before them." If there were any concessions made to Southern demands on slavery, if the Union failed to demonstrate "at least, moral hostility to slavery," Marsh told Seward as bluntly as he dared, "the dissolution of the Union would be both desired and promoted by a vast majority of those who now hope for its perpetuation."[1]

As it moved into its second year, the American Civil War was about to become a pitched battle for public opinion abroad. This contest for public sympathy was fought on mostly uncharted ground, and both sides improvised as they went. Union agents abroad learned a vital lesson early on: they would need to enlist foreign intellectuals, journalists, reformers, and politicians who were eager to tell their people in their own language—and tell Americans—what they thought this war was *really* about, or *ought* to be about.

ONE OF THE FIRST FOREIGN INTELLECTUALS TO TAKE AN UNEQUIVOCAL stand in favor of the Union was Count Agénor de Gasparin, whose book *Un grand peuple qui se relève* appeared in Paris before the war even began. Malakoff alerted his *New York Times* readers as early as May 1861 that "there is in France one man at least who does not regard the American nation as going so rapidly into a decline." In Gasparin's view, instead of committing national suicide, the election of Lincoln heralded

18. Agénor de Gasparin, the first European voice in support of the Union. (PERMISSION OF LA SOCIÉTÉ DE L'HISTOIRE DU PROTESTANTISME FRANÇAIS)

an American resurgence. The Americans "have raised themselves up from the barbarism into which the slave power was drifting them, and placed themselves on nobler and more civilized ground." This was a reveille, a summons to battle, Gasparin announced. *La question d'Amérique* was a question Europeans *must* answer. Thanks to reviews in key French journals, Gasparin's book opened up a public debate on the American question in Europe and just at the time government officials and journalists seemed willing to accept the separation of the South as a fait accompli.[2]

Gasparin was a liberal Protestant politician, intellectual, and reformer from a prominent political family that originated in Corsica. Born in 1810, he had served in the Chamber of Deputies during the "July monarchy" of King Louis Philippe. He wrote prolifically as an advocate of religious freedom, prison reform, and the abolition of slavery. After 1848 Gasparin refused to support Louis-Napoleon and went into self-imposed exile in Switzerland. He became a supporter of the Orléanist faction, those advocating the restoration of Louis Philippe's grandson the Comte de Paris to the throne.

In September 1861, exactly at the time when Giuseppe Garibaldi was entertaining the invitation to serve the Union army, the Comte de Paris and his brother the Duc de Chartres, known as the Orléans princes, were visiting America with their father, the Prince de Joinville. The Orléans princes actually enlisted in the Union army and were attached to the command of General George McClellan. The Northern press was enthralled by these dashing young foreign princes fighting for the Union. Back in France, however, Louis-Napoleon, now Emperor Napoleon III, was irritated that these liberal pretenders to the throne were garnering such celebrity abroad, and he regarded all the fuss over them as an American insult. The Orléans princes in America and Gasparin from Switzerland were urging liberal France to embrace the Union cause, partly to bedevil their nemesis, Napoleon III, but also to renew the Franco-American bond of friendship.[3]

"Let us enlist," Gasparin summoned Europeans. This was Europe's conflict, too. "One of the gravest conflicts of the age is opening in America." "It is time for us to take sides." Now was the time, he wrote, "to sustain our friends when they are in need of us; when their battle, far from being won, is scarcely begun."[4]

His was the first European voice to proclaim without equivocation that, whatever Americans said about their war, at the heart of it was the greatest moral issue of the nineteenth century: slavery. How could it be denied? Southern rebels had inscribed slavery into their constitution, and their vice president, Alexander Stephens, had proclaimed slavery *la pierre angulaire* of their nation.

For most Europeans the legality of secession and the blockade, or even the stress on cotton manufacturing, held little popular interest. This was a moral struggle on the very highest plane of Christian ethics, Gasparin declared. He freely admitted he was viewing it all "from a distance" and that he had never been to America, but insisted that "there are things which are judged better from a distance than near at hand." The good news, in Gasparin's view, was that America was about to rise up (*se relève*) against the slave power. Friends of progress in Europe must stand by their friends. "Let others accuse me of optimism; I willingly agree to it," he wrote. "We need hope."[5]

Americans needed hope too, and they found it in Gasparin's distant voice telling them that their struggle to preserve the Union mattered greatly to the world. As one admirer put it, "He leaped manfully to the work of setting us right in the sight of Europe."[6]

Thanks to Mary Louise Booth, a young New York writer, Gasparin's message of hope became accessible to American readers during that summer of despair in 1861. As a child growing up in a small town on Long Island, she had devoured books in her father's ample library. Her maternal grandmother was French and had come over after the French Revolution. But Booth learned most of her French from diligent study of a grammar book and then mastered German by the same sheer determination. She taught at her father's school in Brooklyn for a while, and at eighteen, with what her biographer described as a gritty "disdain for obstacles," she moved to Manhattan, rented a small room, and immersed herself in the world of ideas and writing. She became a passionate abolitionist and feminist and took an active part in the woman's rights movement along with her friend Susan B. Anthony.[7]

Working by day as a seamstress and later as a secretary for a physician, at night Mary Booth wrote pieces for the *New York Times* and other publications. She translated French and German technical manuals to help pay the rent. Then in 1859 she published a history of New York City that was a popular success. Her publisher wanted to send her abroad to write similar books for all the European capitals. She was thirty years old and living on her own, and her writing career had suddenly opened an exciting new world of possibilities.[8]

Then the war came and changed everything. Booth watched her younger brother enlist and for a time she considered serving as a nurse. But when Gasparin's book appeared that spring, she found her calling; she would serve the Union with her mind and her pen.[9]

From Paris Malakoff had told *New York Times* readers about Gasparin's book and urged that it be translated "in order that the American public may see what an intelligent foreigner, who is our friend, says of us." It must have been Mary Booth who wrote the laudatory review of this "remarkable French book" for the *New York Times* in late May, not long after Malakoff's notice. Booth believed that the book deserved a full translation, which she proposed to do for Charles Scribner, a prominent New York publisher. Scribner was worried that the war would be over

19. Mary Louise Booth, an industrious translator who gave French pro-Unionists a voice in the English-speaking world. (LIBRARY OF CONGRESS)

soon, and he agreed to publish it under one condition: it would have to be ready for press in a week.[10]

Gasparin's book ran more than four hundred pages. Booth took it home to her small apartment, and with her desk lamp burning deep into the night she worked twenty hours each day. At the end of the week, with a few hours to spare, she brought Scribner a slightly abridged English translation ready for publication.

The Uprising of a Great People went to press in June 1861 and quickly gained a large audience. Booth's translation appeared just as demoralizing news from Europe was pointing toward early recognition of the Confederacy by Britain or France, and not long before London *Times* correspondent William Howard Russell's disturbing reports on Union disarray and Southern resolve were appearing in the American press in that miserable summer of First Bull Run. Gasparin's prophecy of national moral regeneration struck an opposite chord, and none too soon.

Charles Sumner, the Republican leader in the Senate, declared that Gasparin's book—and Mary Booth's translation, he might have added—was "worth a whole phalanx in the cause of human freedom." An anonymous reviewer for the *North American Review* was ecstatic about this unknown French voice that "comes to us from beyond the ocean." "We have as yet seen no American publication of any kind which can bear comparison." A man who had never set foot on American soil had grasped more fully than most Americans the real meaning of their conflict.[11]

An inexpensive abridged edition of *Uprising* was published in London in early July. Lest anyone miss Gasparin's point about slavery being at the heart of the matter, the British publishers added an appendix with extracts from Alexander Stephens's notorious Cornerstone Speech. A Dutch edition, *Een Groot Volk Dat Zich Verheft*, appeared later in the year. In the United States a book Charles Scribner had feared would be dated before long went through four editions in 1861 alone; it would go through seven editions in France. The second American edition, published during the *Trent* affair, appended Gasparin's special plea for peace, translated from his essay for the Paris *Journal de Débats*. In early 1862 Booth brought out a "new American edition" in which Gasparin made several small corrections and added a new preface. "I believed then in the uprising of a great people," Gasparin told his American readers. "Now I am sure of it."[12]

Meanwhile, Gasparin was working on a stirring sequel that appeared in Paris in March 1862. Galley proofs of *L'Amérique devant l'Europe* were sent to Mary Booth for immediate translation, and Scribner brought it to press in the summer of 1862 as *America Before Europe: Principles and Interests*.[13]

Gasparin had written to President Lincoln during the *Trent* affair, urging him to find a way to end the crisis peacefully, and the two men began a correspondence. Mary Booth sent President Lincoln a copy of Gasparin's second book, to which he responded with a brief note of thanks. But he may not have realized just how indebted the Union was to her for helping Gasparin and other French authors tell the English-speaking world what was at stake in America's war.[14]

"There is no such thing as distance today," Gasparin wrote in his second book. "The solidarity which today unites all peoples is so great, that nowhere can any question be agitated to which we may say that we are strangers." Gasparin's main point, as before, was that this was not just an American quarrel over petty local matters. "It is the house of our neighbor that is burning." "If liberal institutions come out victorious from a tempest where many hoped to see them perish . . . will this be nothing?"[15]

GASPARIN'S BOOKS ON THE AMERICAN QUESTION REOPENED A European debate that seemed to have closed around the assumption that separation of the South was irreversible, regardless of the moral issues involved. When John Bigelow, Lincoln's new consul to Paris, arrived in September 1861, he was dismayed to learn that the public sympathy of Europe "at court in the press in the clubs and in general society, was very largely with the insurgents." In the French *Corps législatif,* only Jules Favre and his stalwart clique of republicans, Les Cinq (the Five), as they were known, dared oppose the government and raise their voices for the Union. Bigelow's job was to do all he could to set the public mind in the right direction. Thanks to Gasparin, he found help among a number of France's liberal politicians and intellectuals.[16]

In early October the highly respected Parisian publication *Journal des Débats* ran a lengthy essay, "La guerre civile aux États-Unis." Ostensibly a review of Gasparin's first book and a book by Louis-Xavier Eyma, the review provided French readers with one of the first critical examinations of France's position on the American question. The author was Édouard-René Lefèbvre de Laboulaye, a professor at the Collège de France whom Bigelow recognized as France's leading authority on American history and constitutional law.[17]

Malakoff was also impressed by Laboulaye's essay, and he translated key passages for *New York Times* readers. "There has been nothing published in Europe showing so thorough an intelligence of all the aspects of the question," he wrote. These views, Malakoff thought, "cannot fail to exercise the most beneficial influence on European opinion."[18]

"We are not mere spectators of that civil war," Laboulaye told *Débats* readers. "It is not merely our commerce and our industry that are at stake; the grandest problems of politics are up for solution." What if the South wins independence? he supposed. "That act signalizes the advent into Christendom of a new society that makes Slavery the corner-stone of the structure" (another reference to Alexander Stephens's infamous speech).

20. Édouard Laboulaye, professor of history and law at the Collège de France, who spoke out for republicanism in America and France. (JOHN BIGELOW, *SOME RECOLLECTIONS OF THE LATE ÉDOUARD LABOULAYE*)

And if "the South wishes to reopen the Slave-trade" or "threatens to invade Cuba or Mexico," what will Europe do? Laboulaye pointedly reminded the French of the friendship forged with the United States during the American Revolution, when they joined in arms against the English and German Hessians. "Since that epoch, so glorious for both countries, France has remained the sister of America. This is a noble heritage, which we must not repudiate." France must be the "ally of liberty."[19]

Bigelow was greatly impressed by Laboulaye's "spirit of cordial sympathy with the North," but "what surprised me more," he later recalled, was Laboulaye's "singularly correct appreciation of the matters at issue." Bigelow understood the French well enough to know they would not welcome Americans trying to "educate" them on the proper view of America's crisis. What was needed instead were French authors like Laboulaye to make the Union's cause the cause of France. He immediately wrote to Laboulaye, complimenting him on the essay and asking to meet with him. Laboulaye replied that he would "be happy to serve in any way a cause which is the cause of liberty and justice."[20]

Visiting Laboulaye at his home at 34 rue Taitbout in Paris, Bigelow was shown into "rooms crowded with books and numerous tables groaning under all the apparatus and teeming with the confusion of active and prolific authorship." Bigelow was himself a scholar and felt completely at home with intellectuals such as Laboulaye. He gazed at the "curious and rare engravings" on the walls and dozens of books on American history and government. Soon a middle-aged, diminutive man entered the room, his thin hair smoothed against his head and framing an olive-colored face. He was dressed in what Laboulaye must have imagined to be the style of a common American, with a "high-necked Republican tunic of gray or black, with a thin line of white at the top." Bigelow later mused that it gave Professor Laboulaye a "slightly clerical appearance."[21]

During the 1850s Napoleon III's repressive censorship had forced Laboulaye to keep a low profile. Historian Jules Michelet, Laboulaye's colleague, had been fired for offending government censors. Laboulaye had become terrified of lecturing in public on American subjects. For a time he switched to teaching ancient Roman law. But when the crisis came in America in 1860, he returned to teaching his first love.[22]

Mary Booth described Laboulaye as *le plus américain de tous les Français* (the most American of all the French). Like Gasparin, he had never visited the United States. For Laboulaye, the Great Republic was an abstract ideal, a counterpoint to despotism and revolutionary tumult in France. In America he saw a successful, functioning model of self-government and an inspiration for France to resume its own republican experiment. He never tired of telling his students that since 1789, France had gone through fourteen constitutions and ten revolutionary changes of government, while America remained peaceful and prosperous under the same constitution—until now, his students must have thought.[23]

Laboulaye's lectures began drawing large crowds of students, foreigners, workers, and political reformers. Lines formed outside his lecture hall. "Until now I have lived and spoken in an honorable solitude, and for a small circle of devoted friends," Professor Laboulaye announced to his students one day. Now France needed "ideas that constitute the grandeur of man," and he admitted to great joy at being part of this "general reveille."[24]

In August 1862 Laboulaye wrote another two-part essay for *Débats,* a review of Gasparin's second book, *L'Amérique devant l'Europe.* Again, he used the occasion to offer an extended critique of French policy on America. Bigelow told Laboulaye that he thought these essays "will place Europe as well as the United States under permanent obligations to their author," and they "should enjoy a wider circulation." He asked Laboulaye's cooperation in preparing the essays as a pamphlet for general distribution at Bigelow's expense. Laboulaye agreed, saying, "I am completely at your disposal. I shall be charmed to serve a cause which is the cause of all the friends of liberty."[25]

Within days Laboulaye delivered an expanded essay running more than seventy printed pages. He ingeniously added appendixes documenting the French-American alliance in 1778 and Napoleon I's 1803 epistle to the French regarding their traditional enemy across the English Channel. In ceding Louisiana, Napoleon I explained, "I strengthen forever the power of the United States, and give to England a rival upon the sea, which sooner or later shall abase her pride." It was a clever swipe at Napoleon III, Napoleon le Petit, as Victor Hugo had dubbed the emperor, who blustered about his grand designs for Bonapartisme yet betrayed his uncle's legacy and France's historical friendship with America.

Laboulaye's pamphlet gave what Bigelow called "popular expression and currency" to three key points. First, the South's aim of "perpetuating and propagating slavery . . . was the true cause of the revolt." Second, secession was not a lawful constitutional process, and the rebellion had nothing to do with the South's rights having been violated. But Laboulaye's third point was most critical: French commercial and geopolitical interests depended on the success of the Union, not the South.[26]

Bigelow saw to it that the pamphlet, *Les États-Unis et la France,* was delivered to each member of the Institute of France (a prestigious academic group), the entire membership of the Paris bar, every foreign diplomat residing in Paris, prominent statesmen throughout Europe, and all the leading journals in Europe. "The effect of it was far greater than I had ventured to anticipate," Bigelow later recounted with satisfaction. "Friends of the Union multiplied and those who had been discouraged and silent before were now emboldened to come forward and confess their sympathy and their hopes." The *Journal de Débats,* which had been vacillating on the American question, also changed its editorial policy and gave over its columns on American matters to those who supported the North. An abridged English version of Laboulaye's essays was made available to American readers by the *Boston Daily Advertiser* in October 1862. It was a "masterpiece," Charles Sumner exclaimed. "Nothing better has been produced in Europe or America by the discussion of the war."[27]

Laboulaye, the quiet, diminutive professor, suddenly discovered a whole new audience for his work, and with it a renewed conviction to be heard. He continued to lend his valuable pen to the American cause, but it was America as a model for French reform that interested him most. The next year he came out with a witty fictional novel, *Paris en Amérique,* which he published under the pseudonym "Le Docteur René Lefebvre" and added in jest an absurdly long list of bogus international affiliations. The novel featured a Parisian who, in an extended dream, became magically transformed into an American in New England. The astonished Frenchman found himself in a country whose government actually protected freedom of religion and speech. It was Laboulaye's highly idealized image of America and, of course, a satire on France's oppressive Second Empire.

Mary Booth translated Laboulaye's novel for eager American readers as *Paris in America,* and it soon resonated with audiences on both sides of the Atlantic. The book went through thirty-four editions in French and eight in English. It sold twelve thousand copies by the end of 1863 alone. Accustomed to scholarly writing for a narrow audience, Professor Laboulaye was ecstatic with the success of his fanciful "extravaganza." "Artisans read my book in a loud voice at their working places," he gushed to a friend, and it has "done more for my name than twenty-five years of serious study."[28]

Laboulaye continued to translate the American question, always underscoring the common ideals France and America shared as champions of liberty, equality, and fraternity. In Laboulaye, John Bigelow discovered a powerful French voice for the Union. And in *la question amércaine,* Professor Laboulaye found the courage to trumpet a reveille for republicanism in France.[29]

THE CONFEDERACY WOULD ALSO ENLIST NATIVE AUTHORS, ENCOURAGING those who by conviction favored their cause. But in contrast to the Union, the Confederates generally preferred to control the message and get their own story before the foreign public. Their caution stemmed from a persistent distrust of antislavery sentiment abroad, and it was vindicated in part by their experience with James Spence, the Liverpool businessman who stepped forward entirely on his own and volunteered as Britain's most vigorous champion of the South.

Spence was in his mid-forties, with good experience in business and government affairs and a gift for polemical writing. Things had gone very badly for him during the panic of 1857, when several American firms that owed him money failed. His motives for favoring the South were both pecuniary and ideological. He had traveled extensively in America, knew it well, and had nurtured a heartfelt scorn toward its wayward democracy. His writings affected a knowing tone of familiarity, but also a certain condescending air of compassion for the errant ways of England's Anglo-American kindred. It was his professed desire to see Americans become "kinsman whom we can respect" that compelled him to write a scathing treatise on their failures.[30]

Spence would become active in numerous pro-South organizations and fund-raising activities, but he made his biggest mark with his pen. *The American Union* first appeared in early November 1861 and quickly went through four editions by March 1862. It was telling of the Confederate diplomatic corps that William Yancey and his fellow Confederate commissioners seemed not to take any notice of Spence's success. Nor is there any evidence that the State Department in Richmond knew anything about Spence and his book. It was only after James Mason, newly appointed Confederate commissioner to London, arrived that anyone thought to send a copy to Richmond. Even then, Mason admitted that he had "not yet had time to look into it," but "it is said on all hands to be the ablest vindication of the Southern cause."[31]

Much of Spence's book rehearsed the familiar arguments for the right of secession under the peculiar terms of the US Constitution. Predictably, he explained the growing conflict between the sections as those that naturally arise between agrarian and industrial societies. What made Spence's *American Union* so appealing to conservative European audiences, however, was its relentless critique of the evils of "unqualified suffrage" that had overwhelmed the American republic in a "deluge of democracy." Spence pandered to Britain's abiding hatred of the French by blaming America's travails on the early "infection" of French revolutionary ideas in the young republic, spread by Thomas Jefferson and his ilk. The insidious influence of continental radicalism had further perverted the Republic, due to the influx of immigrant rabble polluting Northern cities. Not only did they give the North political majorities over the South in the federal Congress, but the "overgrown foreign element" had also exercised an "injurious influence" on the entire nation. Spence portrayed the South, in contrast, as the valiant defender of the Anglo-Saxon race in America, taking its stand against the foreign hordes that had overrun the North.[32]

Spence addressed the slavery question with a boldness few Confederate envoys would have dared. In the South, he insisted, slaves received benign treatment, their "animal comforts" comparing favorably to the "suffering and hardship" of "many classes of European labour." "In Europe a man must work, or starve; there is the compulsion of necessity." Spence waded without hesitation into current anthropological theory on the inequalities among human races and argued his case for the "radical inferiority" of Negro "mental power." Armed with Arthur Gobineau's scientific racial theory, Spence ridiculed the whole notion of equality among human races as weak-minded nonsense propagated by sentimental philanthropists.[33]

In early 1862 Henry Hotze, who had been sent to Britain to generate favorable press for the Confederacy, arrived in London and immediately recognized the propaganda value of Spence's *American Union.* He was ecstatic. It "compares favorably in acuteness of penetration and closeness of reasoning with De Tocqueville's 'Democracy,'" he gushed to the home office in late February 1862. "The good effects of this book are everywhere perceptible," Hotze thought, and it proved that the soil was fertile for whatever "healthy seed" he might plant on his own. "I send a copy of Mr. Spence's book to the President," he wrote Richmond the next month, and "another for yourself . . . to multiply the chances of this valuable book reaching the Confederacy." "I am," he added with uncontained joy, "for the first time, almost sanguine in my hopes of speedy recognition."[34]

Once Mason got around to reading Spence, he too was powerfully impressed. "It has attracted more attention and been more generally read both here and on the Continent than any production of like character," he wrote to Richmond in May 1862. "Its general purpose was to enlighten the European mind as to the causes which brought about the dissolution of the Union . . . and to put an end at once to all expectation of reunion or reconstruction in any form." Mason also rhapsodized about

Spence's many labors on behalf of the South, not least as a "constant contributor to the London *Times* in articles of great ability, vindicating the South against the calumnies from the Northern Government and press and infusing into all classes in England sympathy with us."[35]

Meanwhile, Hotze went to elaborate efforts to have Spence's book translated into French and German for the benefit of continental audiences. Believing Southerners could also learn from Spence, Hotze arranged for a Confederate edition to be published in Richmond in early 1863.[36]

Astonishingly, neither Hotze, Mason, nor anyone else in the Confederate government seemed to have taken any notice of the heretical denunciation of slavery in Spence's book. No matter what could be said to justify slavery, Spence baldly acknowledged, "it remains an evil in an economical sense—a wrong to humanity in a moral one." Slavery, he went on, is "a gross anachronism, a thing of two thousand years ago—the brute force of dark ages obtruding into the midst of the nineteenth century."

Spence knew his audience. He was playing to British antislavery sympathies with a clever argument designed to confound abolitionists. It would become the party line among Southern supporters abroad: an independent South that was no longer menaced by incendiary Northern abolitionists would bring slavery to an orderly end far sooner and with more humane effect than the greedy, hypocritical North. Spence wanted to isolate the Southern cause of independence from the defense of slavery, and it was a smart strategy in a country that took such pride in its stance against slavery around the world. But Spence's heresy on slavery would vex Hotze and the Southern cause in Europe once Lincoln proclaimed emancipation as the Union's goal in the autumn of 1862.[37]

FOR BRITISH REFORMERS, THE AMERICAN QUESTION MESHED conveniently with their movements for democratizing suffrage and workers' rights. The *Trent* crisis inspired defenders of the Union to summon their countrymen to stand by the American "branch" of English civilization in its hour of peril. At the same time the Radicals, those who advocated universal suffrage, began to lacerate aristocratic politicians and journalists who rejoiced over America's troubles. The American question thus joined the British question on democratization.

The Union had dozens of vocal advocates across Great Britain and Ireland, but none more powerful than John Bright, the leading proponent in Parliament for suffrage reform. A successful cotton mill owner in Lancashire, Bright had inherited the business from his father and grew up in the comfort of a large country estate. Given his business interests and especially his dependence on cotton imports, Bright might have been expected to put his magnificent oratorical talents to work warning Britain of the coming "cotton famine" and urging recognition of the South. Instead, he became a champion of the Union cause. More than that, Bright told the British that at stake in the American contest was the universal emancipation of labor and the fate of democracy on both sides of the Atlantic.[38]

The Brights were Quakers, and from an early age John Bright had learned to follow an inner light. Throughout his long career in politics, he stood apart from any party organization and kept an arm's length from the upper classes. Quakers and other dissenters, in any case, were excluded from Oxford and Cambridge and from aristocratic social circles in general, which only made it easier for Bright to advocate democracy and rail against privilege.

As a young man Bright joined forces with free-trade liberal leader Richard Cobden in organizing the Anti–Corn Law League, a grassroots reform movement to end the protective tariff on wheat and make food more affordable for the British poor. Bright entered Parliament in the 1840s and soon rose as the leading voice for American-style "universal suffrage." But as a free-trade liberal, Bright despised the protectionist Morrill Tariff that America's Republican Congress had passed in March 1861. He also found little to inspire him in Lincoln's inaugural pronouncements guaranteeing slavery in the Southern states. He wondered if it might be better for the North to rid itself of slavery and the South to rid itself of the tariff. In this "American confusion," as he referred to it, Bright saw nothing but trouble for Britain.[39]

Bright came out for the Union in a speech on August 1, 1861, just before news of the Battle of Bull Run arrived in England. But he made the case for British support of the Union primarily on the conservative argument that any nation had the right to suppress rebellion. "Do you suppose," he mischievously asked, "that, if Lancashire and Yorkshire thought that they would break off from the United Kingdom," the British press "would advise the government in London to allow these two counties to set up a special government for themselves?" And what would they say to

Irish secession? He closed with a swipe at "those who wish to build up a great empire on the perpetual bondage of millions of their fellow-men."[40]

Bright was not certain that the United States would survive after the embarrassing defeat at Bull Run. Conservative adversaries were cheering for what they regarded as the "gallant little South," and Bright despaired to his friend Cobden that the North would have to recognize the South's independence. The Union seemed a lost cause.[41]

But in December 1861 with the *Trent* crisis looming over Britain, Bright's public stance on the American question changed radically. Bright's Quaker pacifism joined his democratic ideological convictions to produce a bold new construction of the American question. With the drumbeats for war sounding ever more loudly, Bright scheduled a public speech for December 4 in his hometown, Rochdale, in the heart of the Lancashire cotton mill district. It was the speech of his lifetime. The public hall was packed with 250 men who had gathered for a banquet; the galleries were filled mostly with women.[42]

Bright was extraordinary as an orator. A man of fifty, his round, cherubic face was framed by a high forehead, wavy graying hair, and bushy muttonchop sideburns. His voice had a "bell-like clearness," his biographer George Macaulay Trevelyan recalled. Even in the largest hall, "he never strained, and scarcely seemed to raise it." Bright spoke with zeal but always with a notable "absence of gesture." "There he stood foursquare and sometimes half raised his arm," Trevelyan described it, yet "he awed his listeners by the calm of his passion." Bright always struck a democratic chord, identifying with the people in opposition to the privileged classes who governed them, but he never stooped to demagoguery or personal vilification of the privileged. His appeal was to his fellow citizens, urging them to maintain the path of peace and freedom when political leaders seemed intent on leading them astray.[43]

At Rochdale that December, as war fever reached its peak in Britain, Bright gave a full-throated defense of the Union as the American branch of what he declared to be a "transatlantic English nation." This was not just America's civil war, he told the crowd; this was a conflict of global significance. Furthermore, Britain had played an ancient and shameful role in creating the conflagration by its role in introducing slavery into the American colonies. Within America's Christian democracy what began as a comparatively small evil had fomented an "irrepressible conflict." The "crisis to which we have arrived,—I say 'we,' for after all, we are nearly as much interested as if I was making this speech in the city of Boston or the city of New York,—the crisis, I say, which has now arrived, was inevitable."[44]

Bright closed with an impassioned call for solidarity with England's "brethren beyond the Atlantic." He was trying to defuse the *Trent* crisis, but in doing so he made ominous allusions to future conflicts with America. Whether the South won or not, the United States would again rival Britain. "When that time comes," he told the citizens of Rochdale, "I pray that it may not be said amongst them, that, in the darkest hour of their country's trials, England, the land of their fathers, looked on with icy coldness and saw unmoved the perils and calamities of their children."[45]

The Rochdale speech was the first and clearest bugle call that any prominent British political leader had sounded for the Union. It lasted a full hour and forty minutes, and if the reports of the cheers and applause are any indication, it left the crowd in a frenzy of enthusiasm for Anglo-American solidarity. The impact of the Rochdale speech rippled through Britain and across the Atlantic. New York publisher G. P. Putnam, always ready to give voice to European supporters of the Union, issued the full text as *A Liberal Voice from England.*[46]

John Lothrop Motley, the US minister in Vienna, wrote to Bright, praising "the breadth and accuracy of view, the thorough grasp of the subject and the lucid flow of argument by which your speech was characterized." That it was delivered during the bellicose madness of the *Trent* crisis, Motley added, made "it impossible for me to express my emotions in any other way than in one honest burst of gratitude to the speaker— Thank God!" Motley agreed heartily that British conservatives favored the South as a rebuke to democracy. "The real secret of the exultation which manifests itself in the *Times* and other organs over our troubles and disasters," he told Bright, "is their hatred not to America so much as to democracy in England."[47]

The day after his speech in Rochdale, Bright sat down to fuel the cause of transatlantic peace by writing his old friend Charles Sumner, who had spent considerable time in Britain before the war. Though the British decry the violence of the democratic mob in America, Bright mused, "our Government is often driven along by the force of the genteel and aristocratic mob." England is "arrogant and seeking a quarrel," he told Sumner bluntly, but your "great country" represents "the hope of freedom and humanity."[48]

Bright's letter made its mark. Lincoln invited Sumner to the cabinet meeting held on Christmas Day 1861 that would decide the fate of war between the United States and Britain. There Sumner read the letter from Bright and another from Cobden, both pleading for a peaceful solution. Bright opened up a path of direct communication with the president as well. Lincoln, for his part, so admired Bright that he had a large photograph of him in his office, a reminder that friends across the Atlantic stood by America.[49]

Bright continued to castigate the privileged governing classes for their hostility toward America and for their sympathy with the slaveholders of the South. But he also reached out to the working classes of England to enlist their support in what he viewed as an international struggle for democracy and emancipation of labor.

The war brought great hardship to mill workers, and as the Union blockade tightened its hold on the South, the prospect of a "cotton famine" became real. It is no wonder that cotton mill workers joined in voicing concern over the war or that some supported the South's bid for independence, just as Cobden and other free-trade liberals thought first of aligning with the South. The ultimate impact of the American crisis, however, was to unify workers across ideological and generational divides and form bridges between labor and middle-class reformers in opposition to slavery and in support of the Union. W. E. Adams, a veteran of the Chartist movement that advocated democratic reform during the 1830s, saw in the American war "the greatest question of the centuries. It was greater than the Great Rebellion, greater than the French Revolution, greater than the war of Independence . . . as great as any that has been fought out since history began." Support for the Union came to be regarded as a test of commitment among Radicals, who denounced opponents as Southern sympathizers. They even stormed some "Southerner" meetings and transformed them into spontaneous demonstrations for the Union.[50]

British popular support for the Union would eventually be galvanized by Lincoln's emancipation policy, once it was enacted in January 1863. By that time Bright and Radical labor leaders had already nurtured the idea of a shared interest in Union victory. Had Britain, instead, helped sustain a nation dedicated to slavery, one historian later speculated, "the example would have spread like the plague in a world ever susceptible to such infection." "John Bright saw it then, when the wise were blind; and he made half of England see."[51]

ANOTHER, AND FAR MORE UNEXPECTED, VOICE FOR THE UNION CAME from Karl Marx, an advocate of capitalism's demise. Living in exile in London, Marx spent most of his days at the British Library, researching his magnum opus, *Das Kapital* (1867). Marx shared little of Bright's concern for the salvation of bourgeois democracy or national unity. For him, the American war was the vanguard of the class struggle.

During the first volatile year of war and diplomacy, a large segment of the reading public in America and Europe learned about the war through this German-born communist revolutionary. Marx had been hired ten years earlier as a correspondent for the *New York Daily Tribune,* the largest newspaper in the United States and perhaps the world, with an estimated readership exceeding 1 million. Horace Greeley, the publisher, introduced his new European correspondent by saying Marx had "very decided opinions of his own," but he was "one of the most instructive sources of information on the great questions of current European politics." Greeley was a liberal reformer, an advocate of antislavery and the rights of workers and women. He and his managing editor, Charles Dana, were also deeply interested in the radical political movements that had stirred Europe during the Revolution of 1848. Dana had met Marx during the revolution, when he hired him to write for the *Tribune.*[52]

Accustomed to airing his views among small cliques of fellow revolutionary exiles over warm beer in a London pub, Marx welcomed the opportunity to reach such a vast American audience. He privately loathed Greeley as a bourgeois protectionist and white-haired armchair philosopher, but Marx was desperate for money, even five dollars per article, which was about his only income while he struggled to keep his family housed and fed.[53]

Marx had grown up in a prosperous middle-class Jewish family in Prussia. As a young law student in Bonn, he appeared to be more fond of beer than scholarship. His father made him transfer to the University of Berlin, where he met and eventually married a wealthy Gentile baroness, Jenny von Westphalen. It was also in Berlin that he got caught up with a political group known as the Young Hegelians and became thoroughly immersed in the world of radical political ideology. He lived by turns in Paris, Brussels, and Cologne.[54]

After the Revolution of 1848 failed, Marx and his wife fled to London and began a life of desperate poverty in the slums of Soho. Three of their six offspring died in childhood. With their surviving children, they moved from their squalid Soho hovel to a more spacious apartment in suburban Kentish Town. The rent absorbed most of his meager income from freelance writing, which left Marx begging money from friends, usually Frederick Engels, a fellow revolutionary, whose family owned a factory in the north of England. His letters to Engels were filled with financial and health woes. "A ghastly carbuncle has broken out again on my left hip, near the inexpressible part of the body," Marx shared with Engels in one such letter. Marx also successfully badgered Dana to raise his pay from five to ten dollars per article. But when the Civil War came, the *Tribune* decided to cut back on its coverage of overseas correspondents in order to focus more attention on the conflict at home. Dana directed Marx to write on European, particularly British, opinion regarding the American crisis.[55]

Frederick Engels was the coauthor, editor, and unpaid ghost writer of some of the weekly essays Marx published on the American Civil War with the *Tribune*. Marx was brilliant and well read, but his English was dreadful and his handwriting illegible. He depended on Engels to make sense of what he was trying to say and on Jenny to put it in legible form before sending the copy to New York.[56]

The *Tribune* articles, however, were only a fraction of what the two men wrote about the American war during the next four years. They became increasingly obsessed with the American war and constantly wrote letters to one another, sharing news from America. Maps of the United States covered the Marx family's dining room table, and newspapers were stacked high in every corner. Joseph Weydemeyer, a German immigrant who ran a journal in New York, sent Marx and Engels newspapers and kept them abreast of American affairs in lengthy letters. Engels considered himself to be an expert on military matters, while Marx took special interest in the economic factors underlying war and diplomacy. In addition to the *Tribune* articles, they coauthored a series of thirty-five essays published by *Die Presse,* an important German-language newspaper in

21. Karl Marx with his wife, Jenny. (COURTESY MARX-
IST INTERNET ARCHIVES)

Vienna. Together they worked out an unusually penetrating analysis of the American war and its meaning for the world.[57]

Their fascination with the war had much to do with the surprising contradictions it presented to their theories of class conflict and historical change. In their famous *Communist Manifesto,* published in 1848, Marx and Engels had asserted that the real conflict of the age was not between republicanism and aristocracy. Forms of government were but political superstructures underneath which were deeper structures configured according to the means of economic production. All of human history was the history of class struggles, which in turn were determined by the changing means of production, the *Manifesto* explained. Just as the capitalist class, arising out of modern forms of international commerce and industrialization, had supplanted the old landed aristocracy of feudalism, the next and final stage of history, they prophesied, would witness the triumph of the industrial working class. Marx and Engels had little sympathy for sentimental patriotism and nationalist allegiances, which they saw as manipulative devices employed by the ruling classes to distract workers from the class struggle.

What they saw in America, thought to be a land born free of Old World feudalism, was the last vestige of a feudal, landed, slaveholding class staging a counterrevolution against the industrial and mercantile bourgeoisie who championed free labor capitalism. "The present struggle between the South and North is . . . a struggle between two social systems, the system of slavery and the system of free labour," Marx wrote in October 1861. "It can only be ended by the victory of one system or the other." At stake was not only the death of slavery in America, but also the emancipation of labor everywhere.

Marx realized that slavery lay at the heart of the matter, regardless of what Lincoln declared to be the Union's policy on emancipation. The question was not "whether the slaves within the existing slave states should be emancipated outright or not, but whether the twenty million free men of the North should submit any longer to an oligarchy of three hundred thousand slaveholders." Nor was the question limited to the fate of the United States, for the slave oligarchy sought the "armed spreading of slavery in Mexico, Central and South America." In the American war Marx and Engels sided with the bourgeois North. They called for a revolutionary war against the South that would herald the general emancipation of labor and prepare the way for America to serve as the vanguard for the next stage of history.[58]

"The first grand war of contemporaneous history is the American war," Marx announced to *Tribune* readers in September 1861. The "highest form of popular self-government till now realized is giving battle to the meanest and most shameless form of man's enslaving recorded in the annals of history."[59]

Marx was determined to educate readers on the fundamental harmony of interests and values between the South and counterrevolutionary forces in Europe. He drew special attention to the intrigues of the British, Spanish, and French governments against the Juárez regime in the Republic of Mexico. The Tripartite Alliance's invasion of Mexico he judged to be "one of the most monstrous enterprises ever chronicled in the annals of international history," marked by "an insanity of purpose and imbecility of the means employed." He blamed the Mexican venture largely on Spain, whose "never over-strong head" had been turned by "cheap successes in Morocco and St. Domingo."[60]

During the stormy *Trent* crisis, Marx took special pleasure in exposing the venal hypocrisy of the British government and press. You may be sure, he warned *Tribune* readers, that Palmerston wanted "a legal pretext for a war with the United States." He excoriated the "yellow plushes" of the British press for their hysterical warmongering and posturing in defense of British honor. The whole affair, Marx insinuated, was stirred up by speculators who wanted to fleece unsuspecting investors in the stock exchange.[61]

Marx was especially scornful of France, "bankrupt, paralyzed at home, beset with difficulty abroad," and now pouncing upon the prospect of Anglo-American war as a "real godsend." France's "tender care for the 'honor of England,'" its fierce diatribes urging England to "revenge the outrage on the Union Jack," and its "vile denunciations of everything American" were as ridiculous as they were appalling.[62]

His very cynicism about the designs of British and French rulers during the *Trent* crisis led Marx to counsel peace to Americans, lest they "do the work of the secessionists in embroiling the United States in a war with England." Such a war, he cautioned, would be a "godsend" to Napoleon III, given "his present difficulties," and it would ignite popular support for him in France. Marx also took delight in lampooning William Yancey and the Confederate commission, which "exhausts its horse-powers of foul language in appeals to the working classes" to support a war with America.[63]

Marx praised the British working classes for their "sound attitude," all the more so for the striking contrast between them and the "hypocritical bullying, cowardly, and stupid conduct of the official and well-to-do John Bull." America must never forget, he insisted, that "at least the *working classes* of England" had "never forsaken them." They never held a public war meeting, even when "peace trembled in the balance" during the *Trent* crisis. This was due, he felt certain, to the "natural sympathy the popular classes all over the world ought to feel for the only popular government in the world."[64]

These tributes to transatlantic solidarity came from the last of Marx's articles published by the *New York Daily Tribune* in January 1862. Greeley wanted to give more space to military matters at home, and he was no doubt distressed by Marx's caustic tone and radical ideology. Though his direct conduit to American readers ended, Marx continued to interpret the American war for *Die Presse* throughout 1862.[65]

Later, in 1864, on behalf of the International Workingmen's Association, Marx hailed Lincoln's reelection victory at the polls. Slavery, a major obstacle to the emancipation of all labor, "has been swept off by the red sea of civil war." For this, he thanked Lincoln, "the single-minded son of the working class," who led "his country through the matchless struggle for the rescue of an enchained race and the reconstruction of a social world."[66]

OTTILIE ASSING (PRONOUNCED "AH-SING") TRANSLATED THE AMERICAN Civil War for European audiences at the side of one of the most important African American voices of the time. She grew up in Hamburg, where her Jewish father and Christian mother had defied convention by marrying. Her father converted to Christianity, changed his name, and had young Ottilie baptized after her birth in 1819. The family was nonetheless exposed to cruel anti-Semitism and scorned as *Halbjüdinnen* (half-Jews). Her German childhood imprinted in young Ottilie a defiant scorn toward prejudice of all kinds. After the untimely death of their parents, Ottilie and her sister moved in with relatives and later had a bitter falling-out with one another.

It was as much to escape family problems as political oppression in Germany after the failed Revolution of 1848 that in 1852 Ottilie, at thirty-three, single, skilled in several languages, and determined to make her way in the world, sailed alone to make a new life in New York. She was a passionate feminist and freethinking radical reformer who learned to live by her pen. She began writing about American culture and society for Berlin journals and then turned to the subject that consumed much of her life, the problem of race and prejudice.[67]

Assing became determined to translate for Europeans the authentic voice of the African American experience. After a false start with several essays on a black religious leader, she decided in the summer of 1856 to travel to Rochester, New York, to meet Frederick Douglass. What began with her translating his autobiography into German soon evolved into an intense intellectual and apparently romantic liaison between the married black abolitionist and the passionate German émigré intellectual that endured nearly three decades.

During the 1840s Douglass's autobiography and impressive oratorical skills had made him the leading African American voice of antislavery. Fearing that his fame might tempt his former master to try to abduct him, during the 1840s Douglass spent two years abroad in Ireland and Britain. He witnessed the suffering of the Irish during the potato famine and returned home with a more cosmopolitan view of social problems and with a broadened conception of emancipation as something that must be extended to all human beings, including women. He became involved in the woman's rights movement and spoke eloquently for woman suffrage at the Seneca Falls Convention in 1848. In Ottilie Assing, a half-Jewish, German radical feminist, Douglass discovered an extraordinary partner. They attended meetings and traveled together, read one another's work, and thought and wrote in tandem.[68]

In April 1861 Douglass and Assing were planning to move to Haiti to pursue what Douglass described vaguely as "a purpose, long meditated." He held little hope for the newly elected president, whom he believed was already bending his knees to slavery. American blacks might have to consider another means of exodus from slavery, and Haiti might be their New Canaan. For Ottilie Assing, the cosmopolitan milieu of Haiti offered a place where she and Douglass could live openly together.[69]

News of the attack on Fort Sumter came on the eve of their departure, and they immediately postponed their travel plans. Both of them threw their full energies into channeling the conflict over secession into a revolutionary war on slavery and a war fought by black men for their own emancipation. Assing wrote for European audiences, primarily through *Morgenblatt für gebildete Leser* (Morning journal for educated readers), a prestigious Berlin journal, while Douglass issued commentary through his own antislavery journal, *Douglass' Monthly*. They addressed parallel topics and issued similar arguments, at times borrowing heavily from one another's writings.[70]

Assing immediately interpreted the war as something much greater than a local conflict over secession or even the future of slavery in America. She told her German readers it was nothing less than the fulfillment of "the great revolution" that had failed in 1848 and was now about to sweep before it all forms of human inequality, oppression, and prejudice. "We have been at war for several months, but the great mass of the people have not yet understood that we are not fighting against a so-called rebellion." The war was "a revolution whose seeds were present at the founding of the republic and whose eventual outcome will determine the fate of the country and the nation." It is "quite simply and irreducibly the eternal war between slavery and freedom that has been repressed and postponed by halfway measures and compromises for more than seventy years and has now erupted with all the more force." Like Douglass, throughout the war Assing despaired at the efforts of Lincoln administration officials to "mislead themselves and the rest of the world" from what everyone understood to be the heart of the conflict.[71]

Ottilie Assing translated the meaning of Frederick Douglass and the American Civil War for German-speaking audiences, and at the same time helped interpret for Douglass the cosmopolitan context of the struggle that engulfed them. Meanwhile, against all odds, she sought to live out her ideal of love across the color line, which she viewed as the ultimate rebuke to the racial prejudice that lay at the heart of slavery. Emancipation, Assing hoped, might permit her to realize her desire to live as Douglass's "natural" wife. Douglass, however, remained bound to his actual wife until her death in 1882. He and Assing had parted ways in the meanwhile. Ottilie Assing was traveling in Europe and facing terminal breast cancer when she learned, sometime in early 1884, that Frederick Douglass had remarried. One morning in Paris, dressed elegantly as always, she walked to the Bois de Boulogne, sat on a bench, and swallowed a vial of potassium cyanide.[72]

EACH OF THESE EUROPEAN TRANSLATORS OF THE AMERICAN QUESTION came from different ideological positions: Gasparin was a constitutional monarchist, Laboulaye a French republican, Spence a conservative critic of democracy, Bright a Quaker reformer, Marx a revolutionary socialist, and Assing a radical freethinker. Each coupled the American crisis to current political debates within their own milieu. That none (save Spence and Assing) had ever visited America hardly mattered. For them, America was something more than a particular nation or people, and the Civil War was something more than a struggle over territory and sovereignty. They and many other foreign observers were translating the meaning of the war for the world at large—and for Americans.

CHAPTER 7

FOREIGN LEGIONS

Patrioti Italiani! Honvedek! Amis de la liberté! Deutsche Freiheits Kaempfer! The aid of every man is required for the service of his adopted country! Italians, Hungarians, Germans, and French, Patriots of all Nations. Arouse! Arouse! Arouse!

—GARIBALDI GUARD, NEW YORK 39TH INFANTRY, RECRUITMENT POSTER, APRIL 1861

WHILE FOREIGN POLITICIANS, JOURNALISTS, AND INTELLECTUALS took up their pens and raised their voices to translate the American question for foreign audiences, hundreds of thousands of immigrants and the sons of immigrants took up arms and risked—and often gave—their lives as Union soldiers.

US legations abroad were inundated with volunteers, many of them professional soldiers asking for commissions, others expecting enlistment bounties and free passage to America. During the first summer of war, Romaine Dillon looked out of his office window in the US legation in Turin, Italy, to see a long line of men, many wearing the red shirt emblematic of the Garibaldini. They had come to enlist in America's Risorgimento.

From Brussels Henry Sanford related the amazing story of George Nanglo. Born in New York and educated in France, he had served as a major in the Crimean War, fought with Garibaldi's Thousand in Sicily, and then wound up in the Turkish army. Now he was eager to return to his "native land" and raise his sword for the Union, and he needed Sanford's help to get back home.[1]

James Quiggle, the Antwerp consul, had sought to flatter Garibaldi by promising that thousands would rush to join him if he came to America. Whatever else Quiggle got wrong that summer, he anticipated one of the most remarkable features of the war. With or without Garibaldi, immigrant soldiers from all parts of Europe, Latin America, and elsewhere would volunteer for the American war. Several thousand fought for the Confederacy, but the lion's share of immigrant recruits formed the Union's foreign legions, and without them the Union might never have won.

Those who were recruited abroad during the war joined a much larger number of immigrants who had arrived since the late 1840s, refugees from the famines, repression, and failed revolutions that beset nineteenth-century Europe. By 1860 the United States had more than 4 million foreign-born inhabitants constituting about 13 percent of the population. They concentrated in the free states of the North, drawn by jobs in the urban economy, and they generally avoided the South, some out of moral antipathy toward slavery, others out of a practical preference not to compete with slave labor. In 1860 less than 6 percent (233,000) of the nation's foreign born lived in states that would join the Confederacy. Significantly, they were concentrated in cities such as New Orleans, Nashville, and Memphis, which fell under Union control before the South could draw on this foreign-born manpower.[2]

Immigrants and the sons of immigrants constituted well over 40 percent of the Union's armed forces. Germans and Irish made up nearly two-thirds of the Union's foreign-born soldiers, followed (in order) by those from Great Britain, Canada, France, Sweden, Norway, Hungary, Poland, Italy, Latin America, and elsewhere. Among the Union dead at Gettysburg was John Tommy, a Chinese immigrant who had been a favorite among his American comrades in arms.[3]

One night early in the war, General George McClellan was returning to camp when Union pickets challenged him. He could not make himself understood. "I tried English, French, Spanish, Italian, German, Indian, a little Russian and Turkish," all without success. McClellan most likely inflated the communication problem (and his language skills), but the polyglot nature of the army he led was no exaggeration. McClellan had toured Europe during the Crimean War and was quite familiar with the concept of foreign legions serving within national armies. But something new was taking place in the American war.[4]

The exact numbers and national origins of the foreigners who fought remain uncertain, but this much is clear: they were vital to Union perseverance and their participation underscored the perception of the war as an international struggle. Yet, despite their importance to the war's outcome, a legacy of bias and language barriers has conspired to leave immigrant soldiers in the shadows of America's Civil War narrative. During the war they were disparaged by fellow Unionists as well as by Southern detractors, who called them "mercenaries" and "soldiers of fortune," implying they had no honorable motive to enlist beyond earning a bounty or indulging a youthful spirit of adventure. Critics suggested that foreign recruits lacked patriotic valor and were unwilling to fight and die for a nation not their own.[5]

After the war immigrant groups answered rising nativist prejudice with a spate of publications celebrating the proud contributions of immigrant soldiers who fought America's wars. One of the recurring themes in such works portrays immigrants "becoming American" and earning their citizenship through sacrifice and military service. There was some truth to all this, but it is important to understand that many immigrant soldiers saw themselves fighting a war *in* America but not just *about* America.

For them, it was part of an ongoing struggle that they, or their parents, had fought and lost in the Old World. Many saw themselves fighting for broadly understood principles of liberty, equality, or democracy that transcended any particular nation. Benjamin Gould, the first to chronicle the immigrant soldiers' role in the war, credited the foreign-born enlistee with a "spirit of sympathy with a republic struggling for the maintenance of free institutions." More than soldiers of fortune, they were also soldiers of conviction who conflated the American war they *fought* with the international cause they fought *for*.[6]

IN THE SUMMER OF 1861, WHEN THE GARIBALDI GUARD, NEW YORK'S 39th Regiment, called for 250 volunteers, it did not matter what language they spoke. *Patrioti Italiani! Honvedek! Amis de la liberté! Deutsche Freiheits Kaempfer!* (Italian patriots! Hungarians! Friends of liberty! German

22. Recruitment poster for the Garibaldi Guard. (PERMISSION NEW-YORK HISTORICAL SOCIETY)

23. German recruitment poster. (PERMISSION NEW-YORK HISTORICAL SOCIETY)

freedom fighters!), "Arouse! Arouse! Arouse!" Another recruitment broadside called on New York's German immigrants: *Bürger, Euer Land ist in Gefahr! Zu den Waffen! Zu den Waffen!* (Citizens, your country is in danger! To arms! To arms!). Patriots of all nations were summoned to arms for "your country."[7]

Recruitment posters, broadsides, and speeches at rallies employed an array of languages, often mixing several, and made use of universally recognized iconography to call on immigrant soldiers to fight for their adopted country and for the one they had left behind. In a nation of immigrants, it was understood that patriotism was not always bound to a specific nation-state. It was a transferable sentiment, often a commitment to transcendent, universal principles rather than to one's place of birth. William Seward answered a controversy over the recruitment of foreign soldiers and officers unable to speak English with a pitch-perfect public declaration welcoming all adopted citizens: "The contest for the Union is regarded, as

24. Irish recruitment poster. (PERMISSION NEW-YORK HISTORICAL SOCIETY)

it ought to be, a battle of the freemen of the world for the institutions of self-government."[8]

Vorwärts Marsch!! (Forward march!), one poster for the 1st National Voluntairs of New York commanded its readers. A menacing-looking eagle, which could have as easily signified Germany as America, glared at them, flanked by symbols of commerce and industry. *Tretet ein! Lasst euch nicht zwingen!* (Come in! Don't let yourselves be forced!). A poster for Corcoran's Irish Legion featured a splendid Irish harp and a winged nude female figure, all surrounded by shamrocks and all in brilliant green ink.

Colonel Joseph Smolinski, the son of a celebrated military hero in Poland, invoked his father's legend to recruit volunteers for the First United States Lancers. The poster featured a cavalier astride a prancing white horse. Sporting long, flowing black hair and a thick mustache, the soldier was flamboyantly fitted out in a fur-trimmed tunic with lacy, puffed sleeves; headgear reminiscent of the Renaissance; buckled shoes; and what appeared to be white tights.

Many recruiting posters portrayed soldiers in dashing military uniforms of vaguely European origin. None were more colorful than the exotic Zouave uniforms, distinguished by their baggy red trousers, bright-colored sash around the waist, short open jacket with embroidered trim, spats or half-gaiters on the lower legs, and a tasseled red fez on top. French forces in northern Africa had borrowed this exotic mode from Berber tribesmen during the invasion of Algeria in the 1830s, and artists depicting French Zouave forces in battle in the Crimea and Italy during the 1850s helped popularize the fashion.

A poster appealing to volunteers for New York's Empire Zouaves featured a soldier wearing bright-red Zouave trousers and a puffed-sleeve shirt holding an American flag, his sword drawn and his foot on the chest of a fallen foe. In the background on one side were ravaged fields, a village aflame, and distraught women fleeing, while on the other side were a prosperous church, factory, and ships with a Union military unit in formation and a couple embracing beneath the American flag. No one needed to read English, or any other language, to understand what this poster was asking young men to fight for.

Among the international symbols found in the imagery of Civil War propaganda, one of the most ubiquitous was the Phrygian cap, a soft conical, usually red hat that had origins in ancient Rome, where emancipated slaves wore it as a symbol of their liberty. It also had links to the American and French Revolutions, which made the red cap of liberty a modern icon of revolutionary republicanism throughout the Atlantic world.[9]

The color red—whether in caps, shirts, bandannas, sashes, flags, or banners—became emblematic of the international revolutionary movement. The term *red republican* grew out of the French Républicain Rouge party that led the Parisian Revolution of 1848, and it was applied disparagingly by conservatives to radical revolutionaries whatever their country. After Napoleon III established his autocratic empire in 1852, he outlawed all displays of the red cap of liberty and even banned the singing of "La Marseillaise," the anthem of the French Revolution. It should be no surprise that this became a favorite marching song among European volunteers in the American Civil War.

25. Immigrant recruitment poster. (PERMIS-
SION NEW-YORK HISTORICAL SOCIETY)

Allons enfants de la Patrie,	Arise, children of the Fatherland,
Le jour de gloire est arrivé!	The day of glory has arrived!
Contre nous de la tyrannie,	Against us tyranny's,
L'étendard sanglant est levé.	Bloody banner is raised.[10]

The allegorical figure of Lady Liberty also became commonplace in Civil War recruitment broadsides. With ancient origins as the Roman goddess of liberty, she had become familiar in American iconography as "Columbia," a feminized symbol of the New World discovered by Christopher Columbus. But in Europe Liberty became recognized as an icon of red republicanism, nowhere more vividly than in artist Eugène Delacroix's 1830 painting *Liberty Leading the People*. Delacroix's canvas featured a bare-breasted Lady Liberty wearing a red Phrygian cap, the

French *tricouleur* in one hand and a musket in the other, leading armed citizens over the barricades.[11]

Just before the Civil War, many Americans thought there could be no more fitting symbol of a liberty-loving people than Lady Liberty atop the dome of the new Capitol, still under construction. The secretary of war, Jefferson Davis of Mississippi, however, rejected the idea as a rebuke to slavery as well as a foreign symbol of radical revolution. He was right, and it was with exactly these meanings in mind that Union recruitment posters featured Liberty and her red cap.[12]

PETER WELSH, BORN TO IRISH PARENTS IN CANADA, HAD MOVED WITH his wife to New York City, where he was struggling to make a living as a carpenter in the summer of 1862. While visiting relatives near Boston, he got into a family row and wound up on a long drinking spree that left him bereft of funds. It was to redeem his soiled honor, so he later recounted, that he decided to enlist in the 28th Massachusetts Volunteers.

A year later Private Welsh was writing to his father-in-law back in Ireland, and he had a lot of explaining to do. Written with imperfect grammar and spelling, his letter gave eloquent voice to powerful ideological motivation. It "should seem very very strange that i should volunteerly joine in the bloody strife of the battlefield. . . . Here thousands of the sons and daughters of Irland have come to seek a refuge from tyrany and persecution at home. . . . America is Irlands refuge Irlands last hope. . . . When we are fighting for America we are fighting in the interest of Ireland striking a double blow cutting with a two edged sword." We do not know how his father-in-law responded, but Welsh reenlisted in January 1864. He died from wounds sustained at Spotsylvania later that year.[13]

Even a small sample of the letters immigrant soldiers wrote home suggests the war meant more to them than bounties or adventure. August Horstmann was twenty-five and full of patriotic spirit when he wrote to his parents in Germany from the battlefields of Virginia in the first summer of war: "Even if I should die in the fight for freedom and the preservation of the Union of this, my adopted homeland, then you should not be too concerned, for many brave sons of the German fatherland have already died on the field of honor, and more besides me will fall!" "Much the same as it is in Germany, the free and industrious people of the North are fighting against the lazy and haughty Junker spirit of the South. But down with the aristocracy." Later that year he wrote home again to say, "The freedom of the oppressed and the equality of human rights must first be fought for here!" "To us the war is a war of sacred principles, a war that should deal the fatal blow to slavery and bow down the necks of the southern aristocracy." His zeal had not dampened by July 1864 when he wrote, "Believe me, this war will be fought to the end, the rebellion will be defeated, slavery abolished, equal rights established in *all America*, and then finally your Maximilian, Emperor of Mexico owing to Napoleon's grace, will be sent packing."[14]

Magnus Brucker had fled Baden, a small German state, for America after the Revolution of 1848. In September 1864 he wrote to his wife in Indiana from Atlanta to tell her that he did not care if neighbors called him a *"Blak Republicaner Abolitionist, Lincolnit* or *Yankee Vandal."* "I am satisfied with myself and am doing my duty as a citizen of this republic." He denounced the Copperheads, Confederate sympathizers in the North, as "cowardly traitors." Were it not for them, "the revolution would have been suppressed a long time ago, and time will tell and history will worship and honor the names of those who bled, fought and died for the *Republic*."[15]

Friedrich Martens "followed the drums when the first call to arms went out through the land" and gave his family back in Germany a cogent summary of why: "I don't have the space or the time to explain all about the cause, only this much: the states that are rebelling are slave states, and they want slavery to be expanded, but the northern states are against this, and so it is civil war!" Another German recruit gave an equally pithy explanation of the war he was fighting: "It isn't a war where two powers fight to win a piece of land," he explained to his family. "Instead it's about freedom or slavery, and you can well imagine, dear mother, I support the cause of freedom with all my might."[16]

One immigrant mother gave poignant testimony to why her seventeen-year-old son was fighting for the Union. "I am from Germany," Mrs. Chalkstone told the antislavery Women's Loyal National League convention in New York, "where my brothers all fought against the Government and tried to make us free, but were unsuccessful." "We foreigners know the preciousness of that great, noble gift a great deal better than you, because you never were in slavery, but we are born in it."[17]

THE LEGIONS OF IMMIGRANTS WILLING TO FIGHT AND DIE FOR THE Union were absolutely essential to the final outcome of the war. More would have to be recruited abroad if the Union army was to endure what became a grinding war of attrition—four hard years of massive battles, daily skirmishes, prolonged sieges, and appalling death tolls from combat and disease.

New estimates indicate that at least 750,000 men died on both sides, and another 470,000 were wounded, many of them maimed for life. The equivalent toll in today's US population would amount to a staggering 7.5 million deaths. Ultimately, victory in the American Civil War depended on which side could outlast the other. Contending sides had to replenish their armies, and it was here that immigrants gave the Union a decisive advantage.[18]

Lincoln once pondered the "awful arithmetic" that might allow the Union army, because of its overwhelming manpower advantage, to sustain enormous losses in one battle after another yet still win the war by grinding down the smaller Confederate army and exerting pressure on the South's civilian population. During four years of war, the Union army enlisted about 2.2 million men, versus approximately 850,000 who fought for the Confederate army. The Confederate estimate is less reliable, but it is clear the North enjoyed a manpower advantage in the field that exceeded 2.5 to 1 over four years.[19]

Both sides soon realized that it would be a protracted war and that they would require more than short-term volunteers. The Confederacy, with its smaller military-age male population, first resorted to a draft in April 1862, shortly after the massive bloodbath at Shiloh. It began by conscripting white men eighteen to thirty-five years of age and eventually expanded the range to include those between seventeen and fifty. Before it was over, the South would be forced to consider arming its slaves.[20]

The Union introduced a draft one year later, in April 1863. By then an array of bounties and other inducements at the state and local levels also encouraged enlistments. Another vital source of Union recruits resulted from the North's invasion of the South, which vastly expanded its pool of fighting men while diminishing that of the enemy. More than 76,000 whites from the Confederate states—mostly from nonslaveholding districts of the upper South, Texas, and captured cities—took up arms for the Union. Many of these were immigrants, especially in the cities that were captured.[21]

The Union's manpower advantage was substantial to begin with. The Confederate South had a much smaller population, and one-third of it was enslaved. The "military population" (defined as males eighteen to forty-four years of age) was only 1.06 million among whites in the eleven Confederate states in 1860, as opposed to 4.6 million in the rest of the United States—more than a 4 to 1 advantage. This meant that the South had to enlist virtually all of its eligible white males, while the North called less than half of its military population to arms. The pressure to field armies also exerted dangerous strains on the civilian population, revealed dramatically by the New York City draft riots in July 1863 and by the many desertions from the Confederate army. As the war dragged on, political opposition in the North found expression in the Peace Democrats' campaign for a return to the Union as it was.[22]

For the Union, one important means of lessening pressure on the civilian population was the expansion of its military population through the enlistment of 180,000 black men. About half were from the Confederate states, and most were former slaves willing to fight for the freedom of their people. None paid more dearly than the black soldiers who took up arms in the Union army, and a good number of their casualties would be attributed to the merciless slaughter of prisoners by Confederate soldiers who refused to give them quarter.

The ability of the North to attract enlistees from abroad during the war meant that, in striking contrast to the South, the potential expansion of its military population was almost limitless.[23] Even basic figures on how many immigrants fought in the Civil War and where they came from remain amazingly murky. Record keeping was not systematized across states and localities. At the outset no one thought it important to know where volunteers came from. It was not until quotas, bounties, and conscription came along that information on birthplace and citizenship became noteworthy.

Most of what is known about the ethnic origin and parentage of Union soldiers can be traced back to a massive tome of data compiled by Benjamin Apthorp Gould with the austere title *Investigations in the Military and Anthropological Statistics of American Soldiers*. Gould came from an eminent Boston Brahmin family, had been trained in Europe as an astronomer, and during the war served as the chief statistician for the United States Sanitary Commission, a nongovernmental organization that assumed a major role in tending to wounded Union soldiers. Toward the end of the war, he was charged with the task of compiling "anthropological statistics" on the age, height, weight, and other rather intimate physical measurements, along with information on national origin.[24]

Gould's task was complicated by the reluctance of Union officers to acknowledge how heavily they relied on foreign-born recruits. Union officials were embarrassed by repeated charges that their army was filled with foreign mercenaries and hirelings—the "dregs" of Europe, as critics described them. They were fighting a war that Yankee natives would not fight for themselves, so Southern partisans charged. Their embarrassment led to a good number of rationalizations and undoubtedly to underestimates of the immigrant contribution.

Conversely, Southern sympathizers did all they could to exaggerate the role of "foreign mercenaries" in the Union's army. The London *Times* correspondent reported in June 1862 that the Yankees "contributed several able generals and other officers to the war," but the rank and file were largely "Irish and the Germans who form at least two-fifths of the whole number of fighting men" and without whom the war could never be carried on.[25]

John Slidell, the Confederate envoy in Paris, told Napoleon III that "probably one-half of the [Union] privates were foreigners, principally Germans and Irish." Ignoring France's own reliance on its famous foreign legions, Slidell spoke of this as a point of shame. The South's troops, he told the emperor, "were almost exclusively born on our soil," which meant that Confederate losses on the battlefield carried "mourning into every Southern family." In the North, by contrast, "no interest was felt" for the "mercenaries who were fighting their battles," so long as they could get more of them.[26]

These distortions by Southern sympathizers complicated Gould's task. He was aware that old-stock, native-born Yankees tended to discount the contribution of foreigners, yet he also seemed captive to their bias. He included in his report dubious claims by Union army officials that foreign enlistees were slow to volunteer and came forth only when bounties were offered. Gould also lent credence to unproven charges that immigrants were notorious "bounty jumpers"—those who enlisted and collected a bounty, then failed to report for duty or deserted and signed up for another bounty in the next town or state. Such assumptions about bounty jumping played to stubborn suspicions about the patriotism of immigrants, and it led to groundless charges that the actual number of immigrant enlistees was inflated by three or four times.[27]

Long after the war, historians echoed these prejudices and discounted the contribution of immigrant soldiers to the Union victory. Nativist prejudice intensified in the late nineteenth century, while, at the same time, the North and the South sought to submerge their differences in a spirit of reconciliation. The prevailing historical narrative in postwar America came to emphasize a "brother's war" fought by Americans over uniquely American issues that were of consequence only to Americans. The immigrant soldier had no place in this epic American story about "our Civil War."[28]

The estimates of foreign involvement in the Union army and navy tell a different story. About 1 in 4 of the roughly 2.2 million men who served in the Union army were born outside the United States. Even Gould's conservative estimate put the number at 495,000; recent estimates raise the number to more than 543,000. The Union navy was even more cosmopolitan; 43 percent of its 84,000 members were born outside the United States. In addition, based on Gould's sample of Union soldiers and sailors, another 18 percent were American born but with at least one foreign-born parent. Taken together, immigrants and the sons of immigrants made up about 43 percent of all Union armed forces.[29]

Today the notion that so many foreign soldiers fought for the Union may strike some as simply another curiosity of the Civil War. But to understand who these immigrant soldiers were and why they fought—and in such numbers—is to understand why, for much of the world, this was so much more than an American civil war.

FAR FROM SHRINKING "FROM THE FIRST TOUCH OF LIBERTY'S WAR," as one poet wrote of an earlier conflict, American immigrants responded to the call to arms with extraordinary enthusiasm. Even before the rumors that Giuseppe Garibaldi was coming to America, the New York

39th Regiment adopted his name as a surefire way to draw volunteers. Hundreds of fighting men and dozens of wealthy New York sponsors were thrilled to send forth a regiment in the name of the Hero of Two Worlds. More than any unit, the Garibaldi Guard symbolized the cosmopolitanism of the Union's foreign legions. The regiment's marching song, modeled after one sung by troops of Napoleon I, captured the international esprit de corps:

> *Ye come from many a far off clime*
> *And speak in many a tongue*
> *But Freedom's song will reach the heart*
> *In whatever language sung.*[30]

The regiment was filled in less than a month with four companies of Germans, two of Hungarians, one of French, one of Spanish, one of Italians, and one of Swiss. Also among the ranks of the American Garibaldini were Latin Americans, including several Cubans, along with volunteers from the Netherlands, Russia, Alsace and Lorraine in France, Greece, Austria, Belgium, Scandinavia, and Slovakia. Rounding out the force was an Armenian, a Gypsy, and a free-black American. The mix of Catholics, Protestants, and Jews gave the regimental chaplain a hard day's work. Most of the volunteers were dockworkers and seamen, but there were also artisans from every conceivable trade, along with a few lawyers, doctors, and businessmen.

Several women served in the Garibaldi Guard as *vivandieres,* providing food and drink, and doubling as nurses when the time came. Acting in the European tradition of *figlia del reggimento* (daughter of the regiment), they dressed in blue frock gowns with gold lace, black-laced gaiters, red jackets, and hats with black and red feathers. Some were wives of men in the ranks, but among them were also young women who had run away from their New Jersey homes to serve with the Garibaldi Guard.

At a flag presentation ceremony held in New York City on May 23, 1861, the regiment pledged allegiance to the Union in no fewer than fourteen languages. Women presented an American flag to the company; then came the flags of Hungary and Italy, the latter emblazoned with Mazzini's famous slogan, *Dio e Popolo* (God and People), and said to be

26. *The Garibaldi Guard Marching in Review, Washington, July 4, 1861.* (*ILLUS-TRATED LONDON NEWS*, AUGUST 3, 1861; AUTHOR'S PRIVATE COLLECTION)

the same banner that Garibaldi had fought under during his heroic defense of the Roman Republic in 1849.

Regimental commander Colonel Frederick George D'Utassy spared none of the money his benefactors donated in fitting out his regiment with the most splendid uniforms the city had ever seen. The rank and file dressed in bright-red flannel shirts, dark-blue jackets and trousers, with republican-red piping. The most dashing feature of the uniform was the round, wide-brim black hat with a cluster of drooping dark-green cock feathers, which were fashioned after the hats of the famed Bersaglieri infantry who had fought gallantly with Garibaldi in Rome.[31]

The Garibaldi Guard left New York with a spectacular parade down Broadway to the docks. It was "a most moving spectacle," one witness recorded. "The mass of emotional humanity, waving and cheering and weeping, from housetop and curbstone, formed a great solemn aisle down which the Garibaldi Guard marched (a quick paced trot of the *Bersaglieri* backed by a fanfare of at least two score trumpets), with floating flags, flowing plumes, glittering gold, and flashing steel, singing *La Marseillaise* as they went. It was a proud thing to be of the Garibaldi Guard."[32]

GERMAN IMMIGRANT SOLDIERS MAY NOT HAVE BEEN AS FLAMBOYANT or cosmopolitan as the New York Garibaldini, but they contributed the largest numbers of any foreign-born ethnic group to the Union army. They answered the call to arms well above their quota of the military population and earned the often grudging respect of military men on both sides. Legend tells of Confederate general Robert E. Lee grumbling that if it were not for the "damned Dutch" (a common term for Germans), he could easily have whipped the Yankees. "The Germans, trained to war by the military system of their own little kingdoms and duchies, seem to sniff the carnage from afar," Confederate envoy Ambrose Dudley Mann wrote from Brussels. "They come over . . . ready material for the rough work of war, in which they receive more than double the pay of soldiers of Europe." Together with the Irish, Mann complained, they supply the Union with "at least two-fifths of the whole number of fighting men." These Germans "hang on the enemy" like bulldogs, one admiring Union officer observed.[33]

Gould estimated that there were 177,000 German-born soldiers in the Union army, but this is probably a significant undercount. Long after the war, Wilhelm Kaufmann, a German American journalist, mounted an elaborate case to prove that more than 215,000 Germans fought for the Union. The best current estimates are that 190,000 German-born, plus another 53,000 American-born sons of German immigrants, took up arms for the Union.[34]

Many of the Germans came to America with valuable military training and experience not found among other immigrant groups. Compulsory military service had been introduced in Prussia and other German states during the Napoleonic Wars. Dozens of German soldiers and officers arrived in the United States as seasoned veterans from the Revolution of 1848. Among them were the Salomon brothers of Manitowoc, Wisconsin, who furnished two generals and a private to the Union army, while a fourth brother served as governor of Wisconsin during the Civil War. For the Salomons and many Forty-Eighters, America's Civil War offered a second chance to fight—and this time to win.[35]

THE IRISH CLAIMED THE LARGEST SHARE OF FOREIGN IMMIGRANTS IN America, but they fell slightly behind the Germans in the numbers who served in the Union army. Political loyalties conditioned their enlistment to some degree. Mostly loyal Democrats, the Irish were naturally suspicious of a war sponsored by the Republican Party, which many associated with the nativist, anti-Catholic Know-Nothing movement of the 1850s. Republicans, many Irish suspected, wanted them to fight to free blacks who would then compete with them for jobs at the bottom of the American economy.

There was also a historic antipathy between the Catholic Church and republicanism that was rooted in ideological rather than ethnic antagonism. Anti-Catholics viewed the church, and Pope Pius IX in particular, as allies of reactionary monarchism opposed to secular ideals of individual liberty and religious pluralism. The main elements of anti-Catholicism were ingrained in American politics and culture well before the Irish arrived en masse after 1845. Some Protestants interpreted the Irish diaspora to America as part of a sinister Catholic plot to undermine the American republic. Scandalous and often fabricated exposés featuring sexually depraved priests and nuns sequestered behind convent walls inflamed Protestant fears. The "savage Irish" were disparaged for their ignorance, their proclivity for alcohol and violence, and their slavish obedience to the church and the Democratic Party. All but the most strident nativists might be willing to excuse the Irish as "ignorant and unfortunate" victims of their history and religion, but many continued to see the Catholic Church as the enemy of American republicanism.[36]

The Civil War at once eroded and confirmed ethnic and religious prejudices toward the Irish. Some hailed their willingness to serve the Union and praised their bravery and sacrifice in battle. For their part, many Irish took up the sword in America to prepare for the struggle against the British waiting to be waged back in Ireland. For the Fenian Brotherhood, a group of Irish nationalists formed among Union soldiers, America's war would be their training tour.[37]

One of the most prominent Irish nationalists, Thomas Francis Meagher (pronounced "Mahr") was a man with a sensational background. The attack on Fort Sumter left him "carried away by a torrent" of public opinion. He put aside his Democratic and pro-South sympathies and quickly emerged as a powerful Irish voice for the Union and an energetic recruiter for the famed Irish Brigade of New York. "The Republic, that gave us an asylum and . . . is the mainstay of human freedom the world over," Meagher told his fellow Irishmen, "is threatened with disruption." It was now the duty of Irishmen who aspired to freedom "in our native land" to defend it. "It is not only our duty to America but also to Ireland." Besides, he added, an Irish free republic could never come to be "without the moral and material aid of the liberty loving citizens of these United States."[38]

Meagher was born in 1823 to a wealthy and influential Catholic family in Waterford, Ireland. He honed his oratorical gifts at elite schools but held fast to his strong Irish brogue. He came of age enthralled by Daniel O'Connell, leader of a popular movement to liberate Ireland from British rule. Later he became caught up in the Young Ireland movement, one of the revolutionary republican movements inspired by Giuseppe Mazzini, with whom Meagher had become enamored during his travels on the Continent. In 1846 he vaulted to fame after a stunning speech in Dublin in which he renounced O'Connell's conciliatory policy by refusing to, as he put it, "abhor the sword."

"Meagher of the Sword," as he became known, then took a leading role in the Revolution of 1848. He rushed to Paris to witness the successful overthrow of Louis Philippe and returned to Ireland to take part in an unsuccessful uprising there. Meagher and several other republicans were arrested, convicted of sedition, and sentenced to be hanged, drawn, and quartered. Cautious British officials feared making a martyr of him and chose instead to deport him to the end of the earth, Van Diemen's Land, a British penal colony south of Australia, now known as Tasmania. Meagher somehow managed to escape the penal colony and by 1852 made his way to New York City, where he launched a prosperous career as a journalist and public speaker on Irish independence. In 1861, still only thirty-eight, he was the leading voice of Irish nationalism in America.[39]

Their Catholicism, their identity with the Democratic Party, and their instinctive distrust of a Republican abolitionist war all militated against the Irish embracing the Union cause. But there was also a centuries-old tradition of Irish volunteers fighting the wars of other nations. The legendary "Wild Geese" had fled British rule to fight in continental wars, usually for Catholic nations. The slogan emblazoned on the flag of the Union's Irish Brigade, "Remember Ireland and Fontenoy," celebrated the famed bayonet charge of the Irish volunteers who saved the day for France against English forces in 1745.[40]

Whether they fought for Ireland or America, or some transcendent notion of republicanism, before the Civil War was over, more than 144,000

Irish-born soldiers, according to Gould's conservative count, fought for the Union. Another nearly 90,000 American-born Union soldiers claimed at least one Irish-born parent. The Irish and sons of Irish constituted almost 12 percent of the Union army and by this measure were its most numerous ethnic group.[41]

THE VITAL STREAM OF IMMIGRATION TO AMERICA SUDDENLY SLOWED to a trickle during the first half of the war. During the 1850s an average of 500,000 immigrants arrived each year in the United States, all but a small fraction settling in the free states of the North. Immigration had slackened by the late 1850s, but when the war came it plummeted to below 92,000 and stayed there for two years. Immigrants had supplied much-needed labor as well as military recruits. They had always been disproportionately young and male; fully one-third of immigrants during the previous decade had been males of military age (compared to one-fifth of the general US population).[42]

It may have been fear of being dragooned into war or concern that jobs would not be waiting for them that led many Europeans to shun emigration to the United States in 1861 and 1862. But many others wanted to come over *because* of the war. Volunteers were banging on the doors of the US legation in Berlin. "I am in receipt of hundreds of letters and personal calls seeking positions in the American army, and asking for a means of conveyance to our shores," one harried diplomat there wrote to Seward. He finally resorted to posting a sign on the legation's front door: "This is the legation of the United States, and not a recruiting office." In Paris William Dayton begged for instructions on what to tell all the volunteers asking for a commission and passage. The legation in London had an intermittent stream of volunteers dropping in, among them not a few charlatans asking for commission far beyond their qualifications. From Hamburg the US consul reported daily crowds of men wishing to enlist in the Federal army and suggested paying their passage or deducting the cost from their bounties.[43]

The Union could not risk appearing to be recruiting a mercenary army to fight a war it had presented to the world as a defense of national integrity. Active recruitment abroad would also violate laws on neutrality and could redound to the benefit of the South. How could the United States protest foreign aid of the Confederacy when it was seeking recruits on foreign shores?[44]

The laws of neutrality, however, did not preclude normal commercial exchange or international migration. It was through this loophole that Seward and his diplomatic corps launched a remarkable campaign to replenish the Union army and score a clever public diplomacy coup in the bargain. In May 1862 Congress passed the Homestead Act, which promised 160 acres of virtually free western land to any settler willing to build a home and improve the land.[45]

The Homestead Act had been a campaign promise of Republicans for years, and it played a central role in their vision of a free-soil West for ambitious, poor farmers. But it was Seward's ingenious idea to transform a domestic policy designed to encourage settlement of the West into a powerful device for recruitment abroad. On August 8, 1862, Seward issued Circular 19 to all diplomatic posts. It instructed agents abroad to make known the generous terms of the Homestead Act and the abundant opportunities for immigrants in America generally. Far from discouraging immigration, Seward wanted it known that the war had created an "enhanced price for labor" due to the absorption of workers in the military. "Nowhere else can the industrious laboring man and artisan expect so liberal a recompense for his services." Seward authorized his agents abroad "to make these truths known in any quarter and in any way which may lead to the migration of such persons to this country." He added, with a nod to neutrality laws, that "the government has no legal authority to offer any pecuniary inducements to the advent of industrious foreigners."[46]

Seward unabashedly informed his diplomats that this offer of free land "deserves to be regarded as one of the most important steps ever taken by any government toward a practical recognition of the universal brotherhood of nations." Here was virtually free land being offered to anyone "irrespective of his nationality or his political or religious opinions."[47]

In Paris US consul John Bigelow understood immediately the public diplomacy value of Circular 19, and he knew enough not to ask for advance authorization as to how to make use of it. He quickly arranged for Seward's generous summons to America to be published in all the leading journals on the Continent. The French government at first tried to block Bigelow's publicity campaign, but it could not find any legal basis for banning a nation from recruiting labor abroad, and it relented. He reported jubilantly to Seward, "Nothing has been published here since the commencement of the war better calculated to reveal to the French people their true interests in our unhappy controversy." With an almost palpable wink, Bigelow added that there seemed also to be a great demand for information on bounties for enlistments, given the "numerous applications from persons desiring to emigrate and also to take service in the army."[48]

The effect of Circular 19 was magical and immediate. Malakoff reported to *New York Times* readers that "not only do European officers continue to flock to the American Legation in this city to obtain engagements in the army of the United States, but also workmen of the better class, who demand to be enlisted as common soldiers." He described them coming furtively "in squads" to the legation and sending in "only one of their number as spokesman, while the rest disperse" to avoid police, who were patrolling the street. Dayton confirmed the sudden rush to the legation and suggested to Seward that far more would come if the government could "induce" shipowners to lower passenger fares.[49]

Bigelow amplified the immigration campaign the next spring with his own publication, *Les États-Unis d'Amérique en 1863,* a five-hundred-page compendium brimming with statistics and information for prospective immigrants. He distributed it to governments, journals, and leading friends of America across Europe and Britain. By showing what the Union had accomplished, he wrote Seward, we "reveal the loss the world would sustain from Disunion."[50]

The stream of immigration across the Atlantic began to swell as the Union's surreptitious recruitment campaign had its effect. Arrivals in US ports nearly doubled in 1863 to more than 176,000 and continued rising to 248,000 by 1865. Tens of thousands also came across the border from Canada, according to Benjamin Gould, "animated by a kindred interest" in the Union cause.[51]

CONFEDERATES ANSWERED THE UNION'S OVERSEAS RECRUITMENT campaign by charging that Union agents were luring immigrants with deceptive practices ranging from false promises of civilian jobs to drugging and even kidnapping unsuspecting victims. Bounty brokers in

Europe were accused of inducing immigrants to enlist in the army, often under the influence of strong drink at dockside taverns. A notorious crowd of "runners" was alleged to be working on the receiving end in US ports, greeting bewildered newcomers with fast talk and charm, alcohol, even stupefying drugs. There were stories of drunken immigrants being escorted to recruiting stations and waking up the next morning, astonished to find themselves in uniform. Though some of these charges were apocryphal, profiteering from immigrant recruits proved to be a lucrative commerce rife with chicanery all around.[52]

A government investigation involving a group of immigrants brought to Boston in 1864 provided a revealing glimpse into the operations of this murky commerce. They had been recruited by Julian Allen, described as "a well-known citizen of New York." Allen was hired by a group of Boston investors, who insisted they were responding patriotically to a call from President Lincoln. In his 1864 annual message to Congress, Lincoln had hailed immigration as "one of the principal replenishing streams which are appointed by Providence to repair the ravages of internal war." Americans, the president urged, ought to do "all that is necessary to secure the flow of that stream in its present fullness." These civic-minded Bostonians may also have been facing the draft and seeking cheap substitutes to take their place.[53]

The investors supplied Allen with funds to pay sixty-four dollars in passage and a bounty of one hundred dollars for each of about two hundred immigrants, the "first experiment" in a program expected to bring about one thousand immigrants to Boston. Among the brokers Allen worked with in Europe was Louis A. Dochez of Brussels, who styled himself "agent for emigration to the United States." Dochez sent out circulars to the "burgomasters" of Belgium and posted advertisements calling for 800 "able-bodied unmarried men between the ages of twenty-one and forty." The advertisements made it blatantly clear that they would serve for three years in the US military in exchange for passage, one hundred dollars' bounty, twelve dollars per month in pay, and food and clothing during their service.

More than 900 men volunteered, and the first boatful with 213 recruits left Hamburg in April 1864. Before leaving each of the men signed, many with an X, a contract that was carefully worded to avoid any charge of illegal enlistment. "We hereby . . . bind ourselves and agree, on our arrival in the United States of America," the contract read, "to enter into any engagement, for a period not exceeding three years, with Julian Allen."[54]

It was after they sailed for America that trouble began. They took a circuitous passage to Hull, then Liverpool, crossing the Atlantic to Portland, Maine, and from there traveled by rail to Boston. Along the way "avaricious influences" in the form of bounty brokers, runners, and even Confederate agents harassed the frightened immigrants, offering inducements to renege on their contracts and enlist for more bounty with another unit or with the Confederacy. By the time they got to Boston, the number had dwindled to 60.

One of the recruits, a well-educated military officer named Jean Barbier Jr. was outraged to learn that he would be treated as an ordinary substitute and be enlisted as a private. Barbier and a few others filed formal complaints, and this forced a full investigation.

Confederate sympathizers in Europe seized upon the story with relish. An article in the *Courier des États-Unis* compared Dochez's enticement of unwitting immigrants to a "dealer in human flesh" who led his prey "to the shambles like a herd of slaves." Dochez answered what he characterized as a "Bonapartist pro-slavery" journal with an exculpatory account testifying that the men were fully aware they were going to America to enlist as soldiers. Union officials in Boston testified that all those who enlisted sang and cheered after taking the oath of allegiance. The only protests came from those who feared they might be rejected, and Barbier's only complaint was that he was being enlisted as a private and not an officer.

The investigation concluded that there had been no deception or illegal actions, and the sponsors of the Boston immigration program were encouraged to continue. Meanwhile, three more ships brought over more than 900 fresh foreign volunteers before the investigation was even concluded.[55]

SEWARD COULD HONESTLY STATE THAT THE GOVERNMENT PLAYED NO direct role in enlisting soldiers abroad, but he took pardonable pride in the extraordinary success of Circular 19. Without it, and without the foreign legions that had come before, the Union would have had to rely much more heavily upon its native-born population at grave cost to the political capital of Lincoln and the Republicans. Bigelow also looked back upon the success of Circular 19 with obvious satisfaction: "This circular deserves a place in this record if for no other reason than the light it throws upon the mysterious repletion of our army during the four years of war, while it was notoriously being so fearfully depleted by firearms, disease and desertion." Apart from its practical benefits in replenishing the army, the Union's overseas recruitment campaign was a triumph of public diplomacy. Nothing demonstrated quite so clearly the powerful appeal of the Union's cause than the lines outside US legations abroad and the ships full of immigrants, whether laborers or soldiers, who willingly became part of the "replenishing stream" that sustained Liberty's war.[56]

PART III

LIBERTY'S WAR

27. *The American Flag,* by Gilmour and Dean. These Scottish lithographers depicted Liberty in American dress brandishing a flag and sword and wearing a Phrygian cap. (LIBRARY OF CONGRESS)

CHAPTER 8

THE LATIN STRATEGY

The future destinies of the Latin race in the Old and New World may be wrought up into a magnificent conclusion, and the two master races, the Latin and the Anglo-Norman, typified by Mexico and the Confederate States in the Western Hemisphere, as by France and England in the Eastern, may be represented as clasping hands and marching breast to breast onward in the great career of civilization and true liberty.

—HENRY HOTZE, CONFEDERATE SPECIAL AGENT, AUGUST 23, 1863

As FOREIGN OBSERVERS TRANSLATED THE AMERICAN QUESTION according to their political agendas, and immigrant soldiers entered the fight with their own ideas of what America's war was about, both Union and Confederate strategists adjusted to unfolding circumstances, realigning foreign policy and reformulating their appeals to the public mind abroad. In 1862, as it approached the second summer of war, the Union began maneuvering to the left. It embraced the expectation abroad that the Civil War was indeed Liberty's war, a war to destroy slavery, but also presented it, in Lincoln's words, as "a people's contest" in defense of democratic principles. In the face of hostile or at best neutral European governments, the Union was fashioning a soft-power appeal that summoned the public overseas to defend the republican experiment against its aristocratic enemies.

Nothing helped crystallize the ominous narrative of slavery versus freedom, aristocracy versus democracy, so effectively as the Confederacy's shift to the right. During 1862 the South devised a new strategy to align its bid for independence with Napoleon III's Grand Design for a Latin Catholic empire in the Americas. This strategic shift involved new initiatives to get the South's message before the world through an active and well-funded program of public diplomacy.

By the spring of 1862, in the aftermath of the *Trent* crisis, Confederates were frustrated by Britain's refusal to recognize their independence, and they began to focus instead on cultivating support in France. Earlier emphasis on the kindred affinities between the English gentry and the South's landed elite gave way to appeals to the French as their natural ally. Confederate envoy to Paris John Slidell of Louisiana reminded leaders of the French government that the South was inhabited by the descendants of French Huguenots in South Carolina and Creole French in Louisiana. Henry Hotze emphasized that the French language, the Catholic Church, and the Latin temperament were all comfortably embedded in the South's "Anglo-Norman race."[1]

The South now portrayed itself as the main bulwark in the New World against the aggressive Anglo-Saxon "Puritan fanatics" and anti-Catholic Know-Nothings of the North. Confederate agents also made it known that their government repudiated the Monroe Doctrine, smiled upon French ambitions in Mexico, and welcomed a stable monarchy on their southern border. Without admitting that slavery was the main cause of secession, Confederate agents in 1862 also sought to "enlighten" the foreign public on the beneficent nature of Southern slavery, its suitability to the nature of the African race, and the baleful hypocrisy of sentimental Northern abolitionists.

ON FEBRUARY 22, 1862 (GEORGE WASHINGTON'S BIRTHDAY, NOT coincidentally), Jefferson Davis was inaugurated as president under the permanent Confederate government in Richmond, standing beneath a monument to the father of the country. This time he had been elected by the people, though few noticed that an election had even taken place. Confederate leaders loathed divisive party politics, and, by design, Davis ran unopposed. There had been, therefore, no noisy conventions, no nomination fights, no campaigns, no rallies or speeches, no groveling for popular support, and there were very few voters as a result. The scant commentary in the Southern press was devoted mainly to excusing the low turnout as due to so many men being off at war, but none saw the meager participation as problematic. In his inaugural address Davis denounced the "tyranny of an unbridled majority" as "the most odious and least responsible form of despotism."[2]

Moreover, rather than lament the South's frustrated appeal for recognition abroad, Davis fairly boasted about its "unaided exertions" to win its own independence. He nonetheless took the occasion of his inauguration to remind the "world at large" that rich stores of "cotton, sugar, rice, tobacco, provisions, timber, and naval stores will furnish attractive exchanges" for those willing to challenge the Union's blockade.[3]

William Yancey, returning from his unsuccessful mission in London about the same time, was far more candid. "There was not a country in Europe which sympathized with us," Yancey told a crowd in New Orleans. "They looked coldly on the South, because of its slavery institutions." He sounded a note of wounded pride and resentment that soon rang through debates in Richmond. "We cannot look for any sympathy or help from abroad," Yancey warned the South. "We must rely on ourselves alone." In Richmond Yancey proposed legislation to recall Confederate envoys from Europe, an idea that continued to smolder in the minds of disgruntled Confederates until the end of the war.[4]

Whether Yancey or Davis admitted it, however, Confederate hopes for survival depended more than ever on European intervention. After a year of desultory commitment, fluctuating leadership, and inept envoys, in the spring of 1862 Confederate diplomacy was about to change course. Since June 1861 the secretary of state, Robert M. T. Hunter, had been doing little more than warming the seat vacated by Robert Toombs, whose own tenure had been notable only for its lack of energy and success. Neither Hunter nor Toombs found Davis easy to work with, and each became vociferous critics of the president after leaving office. Southern secessionists disdained political parties as one of the diseases of extreme democracy, but in their place came factionalism, petty jealousies, and malicious backbiting among rivals whose political fortunes did not depend on party loyalty.[5]

In March 1862 Davis appointed his trusted adviser Judah P. Benjamin as the third secretary of state. Far more diligent than either of his predecessors, Benjamin made it his mission to have the Confederacy recognized among the nations of the world at whatever cost necessary. He had already made himself indispensable as a close counselor to Davis, and he had charmed his way into the good graces of Varina Davis, the president's wife.

Benjamin brought to the task a combination of intellectual agility and a rare cosmopolitan knowledge of the world. Benjamin had been schooled in the importance of impressing those in power. His ancestors were Sephardic Jews who had prospered in Spain as advisers to the Moorish rulers. When the Inquisition came they fled, first to Portugal, later to Amsterdam, and then to London, where his mother and father met. The parents migrated to St. Croix in the British West Indies, where Judah Patrick Benjamin was born in 1811. Later they moved to Wilmington, North Carolina, and eventually settled in Charleston, South Carolina.

Young Judah was a child prodigy. At fourteen, with help from a benefactor in Charleston, he went off to Yale University. Some embarrassing but never explained incident at Yale caused him to return home before graduating. At seventeen he moved to New Orleans and soon launched a lucrative career in law. Marrying into a wealthy Creole family, he acquired a large sugar plantation with 150 slaves. Benjamin also nurtured political ambitions and attached himself to John Slidell's political machine. In 1852 he was elected as one of Louisiana's US senators. Benjamin came late to the secession movement, but he rapidly ascended to power in the Confederate government.[6]

Benjamin became known as the "brains of the Confederacy," yet Davis was slow to make good use of his gifts. His first cabinet post was attorney general for a nation that had no federal judiciary. Davis then moved him to secretary of war, where he served as nothing more than a front behind which the president himself directed military strategy.[7]

As secretary of state Benjamin finally found his proper niche. He had command of several languages and was steeped in international law and world history. Far more than Davis, or anyone else in Richmond, Benjamin understood that protracted military struggle would involve politically unsustainable losses and that the quickest path to independence was diplomacy. He also understood that the South could not afford to wait for a cotton famine to bring Europe begging at King Cotton's throne. Recognition of the Confederacy as a sovereign state would demolish the Union fiction

28. Judah P. Benjamin, the third Confederate
secretary of state. (LIBRARY OF CONGRESS)

that the war was a mere insurrection. Once the Confederacy was recognized, according to international law, the Union blockade would have to be "effective," not just an edict on paper banning foreign commerce with the rebels. "Recognition will end the war," Benjamin wrote to his envoys, "from whatever quarter it may come, and . . . nothing else will."[8]

By April 1862, after less than a month on the job, Benjamin had committed more funds, personnel, and imagination to the diplomatic enterprise than any of his predecessors. And he instilled a new sense of urgency in the South's foreign policy. After a year of inconclusive military struggle, punctuated by recent horrendous losses at Shiloh, the Confederacy had no choice but to introduce a military draft. Concerned that such strain on the civilian population would eventually bring unbearable political pressure on the Confederate leadership, Benjamin realized that the South must win the war abroad or lose it at home.

Though European popular antislavery sentiment frowned upon the Confederate enterprise, the main problem in Benjamin's view was that the governments of Britain and France had a tacit agreement to act in concert on their American policies. Lord Palmerston and Earl Russell in Britain had good reason to fear that siding with the South would jeopardize Canada and agitate antislavery sentiment at home. Following the *Trent* affair, during which Britain drew dangerously close to war, Palmerston's government prudently adopted a wait-and-see posture on the American question, aware that Benjamin Disraeli and his Conservative opposition stood ready to take advantage of the slightest misstep.[9]

France, it appeared, was the South's best hope. Napoleon III and his government seemed indifferent to the slavery question and, in any case, less susceptible than the British government to pressure from public opinion on the matter. Furthermore, France's grand geopolitical strategy in Mexico required Confederate success. Despite the disastrous defeat at Puebla on May 5, 1862, Napoleon had decided to press forward with his Grand Design and conquer Mexico. He committed close to forty thousand troops to the Mexican expedition, including detachments from Belgium and Austria, and made it known he planned to depose Juárez in favor of a Catholic monarchy.[10]

After Britain withdrew from the tripartite expedition in Mexico, and just before the French disaster at Puebla on May 5, 1862, Benjamin had determined to drive a wedge between France and Britain. His strategy was to offer Napoleon III commercial inducements so lucrative that they could underwrite his venture in Mexico. It could even cover the cost of war against their "common enemy," the United States, which was likely to ensue should France take sides with the Confederacy.

Benjamin also played an instrumental role in launching a Confederate initiative aimed at "enlightening public opinion" in Europe. The first step came with the enlistment of Henry Hotze, a young Swiss-born journalist from Mobile, Alabama, as head of a new public information campaign in London. Hotze had been sent over by the War Department in the fall of 1861 to expedite arms procurement. Because Benjamin was then serving as secretary of war, Hotze reported to him when he returned in November. Hotze had an exciting new proposal to make. The South, he told Benjamin, must arm itself for a battle of ideas, not just bullets. William Yancey and the Confederate emissaries in London were getting nowhere with Earl Russell, and the South must move around him and get its story before the British people and government.[11]

Benjamin was impressed with Hotze, his cosmopolitan background, his brilliant mind, and his precocious knowledge of the press and public relations. Hotze persuaded Benjamin that the Union was winning the battle for public sympathy in London and that the Union's version of things was going unchallenged. What he proposed was a centralized, sustained program of public diplomacy that would use the press to get the South's version of events before Britain and all of Europe. Benjamin promptly turned the matter over to Robert Hunter, then secretary of state, who found the idea equally persuasive.

By January 1862 Hotze would be on his way back across the Atlantic with a commission as special "commercial agent" to London. "You will be diligent and earnest in your efforts to impress upon the public mind abroad the ability of the Confederate States to maintain their independence," Hunter's instructions stated, and "convey a just idea of their ample resources and vast military strength and to raise their character and Government in general estimation." Hotze had a grander vision of his mission than just rehearsing the case for the South's material and military strength. He aimed to place the South before the world on a strong moral foundation.[12]

Hotze's preternatural brilliance and poise made a strong impression on everyone he met. He was only twenty-seven, short in stature, pale of complexion, with weak, nearsighted eyes that were left strained beyond use at the end of each long day. Born in Zurich, in the German-speaking part of Switzerland, he had been educated in Jesuit schools before coming to the United States in 1850 while still in his teens. He settled in Mobile, where John Forsyth, a leading Democrat and newspaper editor who later became US minister to Mexico, took him on as a protégé at his newspaper and introduced him to the world of American politics. Thanks to Forsyth, Hotze also acquired valuable experience in the US diplomatic corps by serving as secretary and then chargé d'affaires with the US legation in Brussels.[13]

While in Mobile Hotze had become thoroughly immersed in the emerging field of "scientific" race theory. He collaborated with Josiah Nott, leader of the "American School of ethnology," who had advanced the theory of polygenesis, which argued that whites and blacks were created as separate species. Nott hired Hotze to prepare an American edition of Arthur Gobineau's *Essai sur l'inégalité des races humaines* (1853), which

Hotze translated as *The Moral and Intellectual Diversity of Races: With Particular Reference to Their Respective Influence in the Civil and Political History of Mankind* (1856).

Count Gobineau's theories about the natural superiority of the "Aryan master race" would later inspire Adolf Hitler. Gobineau warned that racial mixing led to the "degeneration" of whites, and that the very capacity of Europeans to conquer and subjugate inferior black and yellow races could lead to white degeneration as a result of imperial expansion. His views on racial hierarchy were also joined to strong prejudice against the leveling effects of democratic reforms at work in Europe and America.

In Gobineau Hotze discovered a wealth of ideas for his defense of the Confederacy in Europe. Gobineau's powerful critique of egalitarian democracy and liberal philanthropic sentimentality, together with his "scientific" argument for white supremacy, allowed Hotze to present the South not as a rearguard defender of barbaric slavery, but as a scientifically sound model of white supremacy for the new age of imperialism.[14]

Armed with a sharp mind, a facile pen, and the ability to communicate in English, German, and French, Hotze came fully equipped for his mission in London. By chance he wound up on the same ship that carried James Mason and John Slidell on their second, and less eventful, voyage to Europe. Their arrival at the end of January 1862 marked a new beginning for Confederate diplomacy abroad.

Once in London Hotze immediately set to work. Though operating on a shoestring budget of $750, he managed to make it go a long way. When money ran out he begged contributions from Southern sympathizers in London. While Hotze was not above dispensing gifts of whiskey and cigars to induce British journalists to get the South's story before the public, he decided to do the job himself. Like other Confederates, he was reaching the conclusion that European journalists were not reliable, especially on matters involving slavery and race.[15]

Hotze took the extraordinary step of establishing his own newspaper with the innocuous title the *Index, A Weekly Journal of Politics, Literature and News*. "I have now, after mature deliberation," he wrote to Benjamin in late April 1862, "concluded to establish a newspaper wholly devoted to our interests, and which will be exclusively under my control." The paper, he explained, will serve as "a machine for collecting, comparing, and bringing before the public with proper comments the vast amount of important information which is received in Europe through private channels." "I hope to cause you an agreeable surprise with the first number of the *Index*."[16]

Hotze's weekly newspaper was soon recognized as the semiofficial voice of the Confederacy abroad. As Hotze had predicted, James Mason was shut out from formal diplomatic communication with Earl Russell, and the *Index* became an essential conduit for making the South's case to the government as well as the public. Though its circulation never rose above 2,250, and many copies were distributed gratis to those in the press and government, the *Index* supplied news to other journals and managed to keep the South's side of things constantly before readers.[17]

Everyone understood that the *Index* was the mouthpiece of the Confederate government, but Hotze strained to make it a reasoned, temperate, and plausible forum for foreigners seeking to understand the American question. He thought it "essential to avoid the great error of American journalism, that of mistaking forcible words for forcible ideas," and to adopt a "tone of studied moderation." In revealing instructions to an Italian correspondent, he advised: "Always remember that you have to refute the suspicion of partisanship." Otherwise, "readers will always be disposed to make allowances for the tendency to represent facts as we wish them to be." Fortify yourself with facts, he admonished, "dates, names, and quotations," and avoid giving "undue importance" or "disproportionate prominence" to "isolated expressions of good will in favor of the South." But this cautious tone did not suit many Southern partisans, who faulted Hotze for "lukewarmness, timidity, or lack of spirit," and some simply refused to lend their fiery pens to the tepid *Index*.[18]

IN LATE FEBRUARY 1862, NOT LONG AFTER HOTZE ARRIVED IN LONDON, a smooth-talking man named Edwin De Leon arrived in Richmond to meet with his friend Jefferson Davis. A sycophant of the first order, De Leon (pronounced "Da-LEE-on") knew how to appeal to Davis's vanity and take advantage of his credulity when it came to foreign affairs. Before De Leon was finished, Davis had committed an astounding twenty-five thousand dollars from his own discretionary funds to launch a grandiose program to "educate" the public mind of Europe.

De Leon brought years of experience in journalism and diplomacy and a heavy dose of confidence to the task. Like Benjamin, he was the

29. Edwin De Leon, Confederate special agent, headed a well-funded public diplomacy campaign in Europe. (T. C. DE LEON, *BELLES, BEAUX AND BRAINS OF THE 60's*)

descendant of Sephardic Jews, whose ancestry traced back to León, Spain. His father had migrated to America and was a physician and successful politician who served as mayor of Columbia, South Carolina. Young Edwin studied law and literature at South Carolina College and later took up his pen in the cause of Young America, a nationalist movement modeled after Mazzini's Young Italy. By the 1850s De Leon's bellicose nationalism had found new channels in the emerging Southern rights movement. He moved to Washington and became the editor of a zealous secessionist newspaper.

Some thought it might have been in order to get him and his noisy secessionist views out of town that President Franklin Pierce in 1854 appointed De Leon consul general in Alexandria, Egypt. De Leon traveled widely in Europe during his service in Alexandria, visiting France, England, and Ireland, where he met and married an Irish Catholic woman.[19]

In Egypt, among the ruins of the earliest recorded civilization, early in 1861 De Leon learned of "the death-knell of the youngest of living nations." He resigned his post in Alexandria, made his way to Europe in May 1861, and threw his talents into assisting William Yancey and the Confederate commissioners in London and Paris. Operating as an unaccredited agent, De Leon wrote articles for the European press and, by his own self-serving account, vanquished all enemies of the South. From Europe he also took care to rekindle his friendship with Jefferson Davis, whom he knew from his Washington years. Assuming the self-appointed role as the president's personal envoy, De Leon sent lengthy confidential letters to Davis, advising him of "the exact position of things here" in Europe.[20]

In early 1862, after Confederate hopes for a diplomatic victory were dashed by the peaceful resolution of the *Trent* crisis, De Leon decided to return to Richmond, seek an audience with President Davis, and pitch a plan he had been hatching. Before leaving Europe he arranged for a handsome white Arabian horse to be shipped back with him to present as a gift to the president.[21]

De Leon's ingratiating approach to Davis stood in sharp contrast to his scurrilous criticism of others in the Confederate high command, which he judged to be infested with old men and old ideas. The Confederate "child was born lusty and vigorous," De Leon later recalled, but it was being "spoon-fed by ancient politicians" with their "narrow notions." De Leon had little confidence in Benjamin and less still in Slidell, whom he would grow to resent mightily. Though adept at political wire-pulling in Louisiana, these political hacks, De Leon sniffed, were simply "not the right men" to "advance the Confederate cause abroad."[22]

De Leon, of course, thought himself to be the right man for the job, and he seemed to know just how to steer Jefferson Davis's unworldly mind to the same conclusion. He presented his plan to Davis and Secretary of State Benjamin. Both men were interested in De Leon's proposal for a well-funded, centrally organized, hard-nosed campaign to "infiltrate the European press with our ideas and our version of the struggle," as he put it, and appeal "not to sentimental considerations" but to the "substantial interests" of European powers. De Leon also advised that France was disposed to "more friendly feeling towards us than England" and could be induced to aid the South.[23]

According to De Leon's retrospective account, he also warned the Confederate leadership that slavery presented the "great stumbling block" to foreign alliance and that antislavery feeling was possibly stronger in France than in Britain. De Leon would later claim that he suggested floating some vague promise of gradual emancipation to answer the cry abroad that this was a war to perpetuate slavery. He blamed the old fogeys of the Confederacy for not taking this sound advice, but there is nothing in De Leon's correspondence at the time, or in Davis's and Benjamin's papers, to lend credence to his claim. The truth was that, far from urging the South along the road to emancipation, De Leon saw his task as instructing foreigners on the benevolent nature of Southern slavery.[24]

The Confederacy, De Leon told Davis and Benjamin, must reach out to the European public with a vigorous program of education through the press. "Send ambassadors to public opinion in Europe" so that every foreign reader might "imbibe correct information . . . every morning, when he reads his newspaper at breakfast." Though France was no democracy, he informed Davis, the emperor "will march on with a firmer step, if the ground can thus be made solid beneath his feet."[25]

As he took control of the Confederacy's ill-starred diplomatic campaign in the spring of 1862, Benjamin fully agreed that an aggressive program of public diplomacy abroad was required. He also supported the idea of a strategic shift toward France. But Benjamin instinctively distrusted De Leon and preferred that his Louisiana friend John Slidell be fully in charge. He correctly anticipated that De Leon's very presence in France would irritate Slidell, who liked to work alone. De Leon convinced Davis, however, that it was essential to keep propaganda operations separate from Slidell's diplomatic efforts and that, with his experience in journalism, he was made for the job.

For the first time, Davis became directly involved in Confederate diplomacy in Europe by making a major financial commitment to further its success. Though he would report officially to Benjamin, De Leon saw himself as the president's man, and he would operate largely on his own instructions with little supervision from Benjamin, Slidell, or anyone else, and with sorry result in the end. Nor were De Leon's operations coordinated with those of Henry Hotze, who had launched the *Index* in May as the voice of the Confederacy abroad. De Leon arrived in Europe at the end of June with a large purse, an ego larger still, and an irrepressible jealousy toward the two men, Slidell and Hotze, who might have been the most help to his mission as Confederate ambassador to public opinion.[26]

Whatever his misgivings about De Leon, Benjamin was eager for the Confederacy to get its story before the European public, and he seemed to share De Leon's and Hotze's core idea that the message be controlled by Confederate agents and not left to foreign volunteers. "It is not wise to neglect public opinion," he wrote to his envoys on April 12, 1862, "nor prudent to leave to the voluntary interposition of friends often indiscreet, the duty of vindicating our country and the cause before the tribunal of civilized man." While Union agents such as John Bigelow were taking a strategic turn toward enlisting native advocates of their cause, the Confederacy turned inward to draw on its own talents and its long-insulated ideas about the morality of slavery.[27]

Benjamin's April 1862 instructions to Mason and Slidell explained that the dire situation of the Confederacy required "a more liberal appropriation" of funds for foreign service. "With enemies so active, so unscrupulous and with a system of deception so thoroughly organized as that now established by them abroad, it becomes absolutely essential that no means be spared for the dissemination of truth and for a fair exposition of our condition and policy before foreign nations." With Hotze's *Index* and De Leon's generous budget, the Confederacy was about to make use of a considerably larger megaphone. The question remained, what "truth" did the South want to broadcast to the world?[28]

JOHN SLIDELL AND JAMES MASON HAD ARRIVED IN EUROPE AT THE end of January 1862, nearly three months after their ill-fated voyage on the *Trent* began. The two men proved to be more helpful to the South as captives, inflaming the British sense of honor, than they were after their release. The British press and public displayed a cool indifference toward the Confederate envoys in London, and newspapers did little more than announce their arrival. Henry Hotze, who had come over with them, was disconcerted to learn that the London *Times* had recently scolded Mason and Slidell for being "persistent enemies and assailants of Great Britain and her interests throughout their public lives." Hotze blamed it all on

Seward's special agent Thurlow Weed, "who is said to have at his disposal a large secret service fund for that purpose."[29]

If Confederate fortunes depended on the reputation and charm of its diplomatic messengers, the choice of James Mason for London could not have been worse. Descended from Virginia aristocrats, he was the grandson of George Mason, who was hailed as the father of the Bill of Rights. James Mason instead was best known as the author of the Fugitive Slave Act of 1850. British readers of *Uncle Tom's Cabin* would recognize this odious law as the one that would have forced the fictional Ohio senator and his wife to return the runaway Eliza and her baby back across the icy Ohio River to slavery.

Although he enjoyed long service as chair of the Senate Foreign Relations Committee, Mason had no diplomatic experience, and it showed. He detested the "extreme democracy" that had overtaken America and made a point of telling his British acquaintances that he felt completely at home among their aristocracy.

The admiration was not mutual. Even ardent friends of the South in London described Mason as slovenly in dress and manners. One uncharitable observer described him as he sat in the gallery of the British House of Commons, appearing "coarse, gross, ponderous, vulgar looking," and "badly dressed." He chewed tobacco "furiously," and his spit "covered the carpet." Mason's tobacco habit also drew rebuke at a private party one evening when the host, though a fervent supporter, had to ask him to stop spitting in his home.[30]

Soon after his arrival, Mason managed to arrange a private interview with Foreign Secretary Earl Russell on February 10, 1862. As usual, Russell kept it unofficial by meeting at his private home on Chesham Place. Russell was as cold as ice, and he let Mason do most of the talking. As instructed, Mason explained that the blockade was ineffective and that Britain, therefore, had no obligation to honor it. This was coming from a man who had been abducted at sea and whose dispatches to and from Richmond would be routinely delayed for months or intercepted by the Union navy. If Russell was amused by the irony, his cold demeanor gave no hint of it. He promptly closed the meeting by saying they "must await events" and wishing Mason an "agreeable" stay in London. "On the whole," Mason summarized the meeting for Benjamin, "it was manifest enough that his personal sympathies were not with us."[31]

30. James Murray Mason, Confederate envoy to Britain.
(MATHEW BRADY PHOTOGRAPH, NATIONAL ARCHIVES)

MEANWHILE, JOHN SLIDELL'S WELCOME TO PARIS AT THE END OF January 1862 was far more auspicious. Paris was teeming with Southern expatriates, many of them Louisiana Creoles, *nos freres de Louisiana* (our Louisiana brothers), as they were known in the Tuileries Palace. A group of ebullient students, many from New Orleans, met Slidell at the Paris railway station and burst into song: *Bienvenu, notre grand Slidell, Au coeur loyale et l'âme fidèle,* euphoniously welcoming "our great Slidell, of loyal heart and faithful soul."[32]

Paris seemed captivated by Southerners, who often felt more comfortable among the French than among Londoners with their antislavery prejudices. Thomas Evans, an American expatriate who had won fame as the dentist to Europe's royalty, was gravely concerned about the influence of Southerners in Napoleon III's court. As Evans later recorded in his memoirs, "A very considerable part of the territory of the Confederacy once belonged to France," and many still regarded New Orleans as "a city of their own people." "Southern ladies, who formed a brilliant and influential society" in Paris, Dr. Evans lamented, "vied with each other in their endeavors to enlist in support of their cause everyone connected with the Imperial Court."[33]

One evening two weeks later, Slidell attended the Théatre Bouffes-Parisiens with Mathilde, his Creole wife, and his secretary, George Eustis. Southern partisans in the audience began applauding as they took their seats. Slidell rose and bowed graciously once and then again as the ovation continued. A little while later, when William Dayton, the US minister, entered the theater, some in the crowd began hissing loudly. Two gendarmes rushed to quell what they feared might become an unruly demonstration.[34]

This demonstration of Southern support may have been staged by parties unknown for the benefit of Emperor Napoleon III, who witnessed the entire affair from his box. At the intermission the emperor went backstage to pay his respects to the star performer known as Sophie Bricard, a *femme fatale* from New Orleans and a fiery partisan of the South. Mademoiselle Bricard seized the opportunity to introduce the emperor to Slidell as "the representative of my suffering country" (*Voilà, Sire, voilà le représentant de mon pays souffrant!*) "The South is fighting for freedom," she implored the startled emperor. "On my knees, I supplicate your Majesty. Give us the friendship of France!" Napoleon III stepped back, somewhat startled, and then turned and shook hands with Slidell without saying a word before making a hasty exit from this diplomatic faux pas.[35]

John Slidell could be arrogant and temperamental, sometimes for effect, but he was by far the savviest member of the Confederate diplomatic corps. Schooled in the cunning world of Louisiana politics, he was also a seasoned diplomat with experience as special agent to Mexico in the 1840s. Born in New York in 1793, Slidell attended Columbia University, went into business, and then moved to the bustling frontier city of New Orleans to make his fortune. He married Maria Mathilde Deslonde, heiress of a wealthy French Creole family, and soon emerged as a major figure in Louisiana politics. Slidell was fully equipped to navigate the labyrinth of European courts with a savoir faire no other Confederate agent came close to commanding.[36]

31. John Slidell, Confederate envoy to France. (MATHEW
BRADY PHOTOGRAPH, LIBRARY OF CONGRESS)

Not least of Slidell's assets in France were Mathilde and their two beautiful daughters, Marie Rosine and Marguerite Mathilde, whose marriages
to European aristocrats and bankers would soon become the toast of Parisian society. With his leonine mane of gray hair and his distinguished
bearing, Slidell cut an impressive figure in Paris. He spoke French with
fluency and seemed completely at ease among the aristocrats at court,
enjoying the camaraderie of gentlemen over card games at the casino or
at horse races at the elite Jockey Club. Despite his unofficial diplomatic
status, Slidell and his wife were invited to court receptions, where they
managed to endear themselves to Empress Eugénie, whose sway over her
vacillating husband made her a valuable asset.

Slidell cultivated other friends in high places. The Duc de Morny,
the emperor's half brother, enjoyed Slidell's company at the casino and
openly favored the South and promoted its recognition inside the court.
The Duc de Persigny, Napoleon III's zealous minister of the interior who

was responsible for press censorship, among other duties, also befriended Slidell and did all he could to help the Southern cause.[37]

Slidell operated with unusual advantage insofar as he learned everything that was going on inside the Quai d'Orsay, home of the French Foreign Ministry, thanks to an informant by the name of Pierre Cintrat. "I have a friend holding a high position in the foreign office and on the most confidential terms with Thouvenel," the French foreign secretary, Slidell discreetly reported to Richmond. As director of the foreign office archives, Cintrat saw everything, all the incoming and outgoing diplomatic correspondence, and he even knew how to decipher the encrypted messages. There is no hint that Cintrat received any inducement from Slidell, and he may even have been operating on instructions from the emperor. In any case, Slidell's mole at the Quai d'Orsay was guiding his every move.[38]

It did not take a spy inside the foreign office for Slidell to learn, as he reported dolefully to Richmond, that the French "regret that slavery exists amongst us" and hope for "its ultimate but gradual extinction." Slidell's usual response was to divert the conversation to "more agreeable topics." "I make it a rule to enter into no discussion on the subject," he wrote to Richmond, for many of "our best friends" "have theoretical views on the subject which in general it is not worth while to combat."[39]

Slidell would appeal to French national interest, not public sentiment. Immediately after arriving, he set up an unofficial meeting with Édouard Thouvenel, the French foreign secretary. He reported to James Mason afterward that "the Emperor's sympathies are with us" and "that he would immediately raise the blockade and very soon recognize us, if England would only make the first step, however small, in that direction."[40]

Not long after Slidell arrived, the Tripartite Alliance between France, Britain, and Spain fell apart in Mexico in early April. As France prepared to take on Mexico alone, it became clear that for the Grand Design to succeed, the South must also succeed. The Civil War would need to be continued while the French conquered Mexico, and beyond that Napoleon III wanted an independent Confederacy to serve as a buffer state between a powerful Anglo-Saxon republic to the North and a Latin monarchy in Mexico. In turn, if the Confederacy needed French support in its struggle, it would be forced to concede any ambitions of its own to take over Mexico or western sections of the United States.[41]

Precisely as the French took on their "civilizing" mission in Mexico in April 1862, in Richmond the new secretary of state, Judah P. Benjamin, was laying out the Confederacy's new French strategy. His instructions to Slidell began by gingerly pointing out that French and British interests were "distinct, if not conflicting." Slidell was to widen that distinction by offering what can only be described as a magnificent bribe to France.

The bribe involved a highly lucrative, long-term, and exclusive commercial treaty between France and the Confederacy. By this commercial "convention," Benjamin explained, France would be allowed to export its products "into this country free of duty for a certain defined period," but France would have to break the blockade to deliver its goods. French imports, including arms and powder, Benjamin estimated, would sell in the South at between two and five times what they cost to produce in Europe, which alone promised enormous profits to French merchants.

To sweeten the offer, and cover costs of a French naval escort to protect the merchant ships, Benjamin offered gratis one hundred thousand bales of cotton, worth approximately 63 million francs (more than $12.5 million) as a "subsidy for defraying the expenses of such expeditions." Together with the profits on European goods brought to the South, Benjamin estimated the total gain would "scarcely fall short of 100,000,000 francs" (about $20 million). "Such a sum," Benjamin spelled out, "would maintain afloat a considerable fleet for a length of time quite sufficient to open the Atlantic and Gulf ports to the commerce of France." The Confederacy was, in effect, offering to pay whatever it cost to hire the French navy to break the Union blockade.[42]

Alas, Benjamin's April 1862 instructions did not reach Slidell's hands until early July—underscoring how effective the blockade had in fact become. Fortuitously for the Confederates, news of their stunning victories against Union general George McClellan's abortive Peninsular Campaign to seize Richmond arrived at the same time. Slidell was ebullient, and he wasted no time in getting the offer before Napoleon III. Slidell's friend the Duc de Persigny helped arrange a private interview for him with the emperor on July 16 at the latter's private vacation home in Vichy, far from the prying eyes of the press. Aside from their brief backstage encounter in February, this would be the first meeting between the two men.

The emperor, Slidell recounted later for Benjamin, "received me with great kindness," "saying that he was very happy to see me and regretted that circumstances had prevented his sooner doing so." He "invited me to be seated," which was always taken as a good sign in the nuanced world of diplomacy. Napoleon III immediately confided in Slidell that, though he was officially neutral and valued the role of the United States as *contrepoids* (counterweight) to Britain, he personally favored the South because it was "struggling for the principle of self-government." More than once the emperor expressed irritation with Britain for failing to answer his repeated calls to recognize the South, mediate a peace, or otherwise intervene in the American war. What could be done, he wanted to know from Slidell, to bring the war to an end?[43]

This was the perfect entrée for Slidell to unveil Benjamin's proposal for a special relationship between their two countries and to lay out the terms of the cotton bribe. Knowing that Napoleon enjoyed speaking English, Slidell requested permission to proceed in "my own tongue." He then took command of the conversation while the emperor nodded in ascent and asked occasional questions. Slidell explained the terms of the exclusive commercial alliance and its handsome "subsidy" of one hundred thousand cotton bales. This "did not seem disagreeable" to Napoleon, Slidell reported.

"How am I to get the cotton?" the emperor inquired with apparent innocence. Slidell answered bluntly that France would have to send a naval fleet, break the blockade, and be prepared for war with the United States. He hastened to point out that this fitted nicely with France's plans to reinforce the Mexican expedition, which would, in any case, require "a fleet in the neighborhood of our coast strong enough to keep it clear of every Federal cruiser." The French navy, Slidell promised, would easily rout the fleet of "second-class" ships the Union had cobbled together. The emperor seemed quite flattered.

But Napoleon III was very concerned that his Mexican venture would provoke a clash with the United States, and he told Slidell as much. Going beyond Benjamin's instructions, Slidell took the opportunity to suggest something more than mere commercial alliance. Once Napoleon recognized the Confederacy, the South would be in a position to "make common cause with him against the common enemy" by supporting Napoleon's Grand Design for a monarchy in Mexico. The Confederacy had no Monroe Doctrine, Slidell made clear. It wanted nothing more than "a respectable, responsible, and stable government established" on its southern border and "will feel quite indifferent as to its form."[44]

When the emperor raised doubts about the wisdom of recognition at this hour, Slidell drew on the humanitarian plea Benjamin had rehearsed for him. Slidell implored Napoleon, as one who had "exercised so potent an influence over the destinies of the world," to act in the "interests of humanity" and help end the senseless strife that was ravaging both belligerents and threatening great harm to Europe's cotton industry. Britain, Slidell added shrewdly, "seemed to have abdicated the great part which she had been accustomed to play in the affairs of the world" and had adopted a "selfish" policy of national interest alone.

Warming to the task, Slidell played his Louisiana French card and with apparent magic effect on the emperor. "Your Majesty has now an opportunity of securing a faithful ally, bound to you not only by the ties of gratitude," but also of "common interest and congenial habits." "Yes," the emperor responded proudly, "you have many families of French descent in Louisiana who yet preserve their habits and languages." Slidell assured him (ironically still in English) that in his family, "French was habitually spoken," as it was in much of Louisiana.

The interview had gone on for an impressive seventy minutes, as Slidell carefully reported to Richmond. When he rose to leave, the emperor shook his hand. "I mention this fact, which would appear trivial to persons not familiar with European usages and manner," he informed Benjamin, "because it affords additional evidence of the kindly feeling manifested in his conversation."[45]

Slidell returned from Vichy thinking that, thanks to Benjamin's cotton offer and Napoleon's campaign in Mexico, he had suddenly opened the path to Confederate diplomatic victory. "While I do not wish to create or indulge false expectations," he told Benjamin, "I will venture to say that I am more hopeful than I have been at any moment since my arrival in Europe."[46]

WHILE SLIDELL WORKED HIS WAY INTO THE INNER CIRCLE OF FRENCH power, the Confederacy's continental public relations campaign was still awaiting direction from Edwin De Leon. The Southern ambassador to public opinion had been detained in Nassau, apparently by the blockade that was supposed to be so ineffective, and did not arrive in London until the end of June 1862. He stayed in London meddling in Mason's and Hotze's affairs; writing pieces for the London press; collaborating with James Spence, the South's advocate from Liverpool; and arranging a private interview with Lord Palmerston. De Leon quickly came to view Hotze's *Index* as utterly useless, since it was transparently an organ of the Confederate government, but he also seemed annoyed that Hotze had his own well-oiled, intelligent propaganda operation in place.[47]

In any case, De Leon was convinced that the Confederacy's fortunes lay in France, not England. He left for Paris in July 1862, quickly set up offices, spent money freely, and soon enlisted a large corps of French journalists and editors willing to hire out their pens to the South. Convinced that it was a waste of money to try to influence readers in Paris, where liberal opinion ran strong, De Leon concentrated on the provincial press, which he thought more important in bringing popular pressure to bear on Napoleon III's government. Within a short time he had well over two hundred French journalists on the Confederate payroll.[48]

While De Leon's "bought opinions," as he called them, were doing what they could to build public support for the Confederacy, he decided the French also needed to hear "the truth" from a native son of the South. He prepared a thirty-two-page pamphlet, *La vérité sur les États Confédérés d'Amérique,* for publication in Paris in August 1862. It came on the heels of Slidell's cotton bribe as well as welcome news from the front that Confederate forces were advancing into Maryland.[49]

De Leon's "truth" about the South offered French readers the perspective of a knowing witness to its valiant struggle for independence. He dismissed recent Union victories, including the capture of New Orleans, with the clever argument that these incursions would only inflame the South, "which battles for its homes and lands, for its liberty and the honor of its women." New Orleans was naturally of great interest to the French, and this last reference was one of several pointed reminders of Union general Benjamin Butler's infamous "woman's order," in which he warned that any woman caught insulting Union soldiers was "liable to be treated as a woman of the town plying her avocation," meaning she would be treated as a prostitute. Southern sympathizers abroad interpreted it as license to rape Southern women.[50]

Unlike Slidell, who preferred to divert arguments about slavery to more "agreeable subjects," De Leon set out to educate the French about the South's special brand of slavery. His pamphlet ridiculed "Madam Stowe's novel," which "represents the slave's goal to . . . massacre one's master." Instead, he emphasized the loyalty of the slaves who "have contributed greatly to the South's strength" by their resistance to such "false friends" from the North. "The negro knows very well by experience that the Yankee has no real sympathy for its race." Blacks were despised and segregated in the Northern cities, he told the French, and far from being liberated by the invading Union army, De Leon claimed, they were being forced to carry out hard labor as "contraband" of war. The pamphlet appeared not long before Lincoln's Emancipation Proclamation would transform many of these contraband laborers into Union soldiers.[51]

De Leon went on to draw a flattering portrait of Jefferson Davis, comparing him to the universally admired George Washington in his military valor and statesmanlike character. Readers of De Leon's booklet were also treated to an engraved portrait of Jefferson Davis that made him look noble, robustly healthy, and about twenty years younger. When meeting foreign dignitaries, De Leon made it a practice to hand them copies of the portrait, never failing to contrast the aristocratic bearing of the Southern leader with the homely, rustic visage of Abraham Lincoln.[52]

The most novel aspect of De Leon's booklet was his claim that the South was Latin, the same idea that Slidell had aired with some success at Vichy. Northerners, De Leon explained, descended largely from "the races of Anglo-Saxon origin," but "the South was principally populated by a Latin race." Those Anglo-Saxons who remain in the South, in any case, trace their origin to the royalist Cavaliers who defended England's King Charles against the overzealous Puritans.[53]

Thus, General Butler, the "descendant of the Puritans," now "applies himself in making war against women" in New Orleans, the bastion of French culture in the South. The Puritan North had built its army "in large part of foreign mercenaries" made up of "the refuse of the old world." Chief among these dregs of European society were "the famished revolutionaries and malcontents of Germany, all the Red republicans, and almost all the Irish emigrants to sustain its army." The South offered a bulwark against the tide of Northern Puritanism and the pollution of its immigrant hordes. "The seeds of discord" were of long standing, he added, and "France and England have never been as divided as the North and South have been in the past twenty years."[54]

De Leon was immensely satisfied with his effort to educate the French, and he wrote to Judah P. Benjamin in October 1862, eager to burnish his achievement. To counteract the pernicious efforts of the North in "the manufacture of public opinion," he explained, "I have been compelled to use extraordinary exertions, which I am happy to say, have wrought great results within the last two months." De Leon said he was surprised to find that the slavery question, which had "been dropped in England," was "made the great bugbear in France" and that friends of the South were "shuddering at the epithet *esclavagiste* [supporter of slavery], with which the partisans of the North were pelting them." He attributed this strange feeling for "the supposed sufferings of that race" to "the sentimental side of the French character." De Leon may not have noticed that among educated Parisians, especially the young, blacks enjoyed a level of acceptance unknown in America.[55]

If the French did not always take his lessons to heart, De Leon nonetheless felt confident that his pamphlet would serve as a "text book for our friends in the press." He summarized the most brilliant points of his argument for Benjamin: "The South is able to vindicate her independence without foreign assistance, and is rapidly doing so," and "has nothing to apologize for in her peculiar institution but has ever been the best friend of the black race."[56]

Even some of his fellow Confederates may have thought that the best thing that could be said for De Leon's tone-deaf pamphlet was that it went largely unnoticed by the French public. Paul Pecquet du Bellet, a Louisiana Creole who had lived in Paris for years, was sympathetic to the Southern cause but found De Leon utterly self-deluded. He was also annoyed that De Leon had not consulted him before going to print, for he had established good connections with French journalists while publishing his own pieces in support of the South. With one exception, French journals maintained a "disdainful silence" on De Leon's polemical pamphlet. As Pecquet du Bellet put it gingerly, De Leon was not quite au fait with the current state of conversation on the American question. Malakoff, the *New York Times* correspondent in Paris, remarked in a similar vein that De Leon, though pretending to offer a rare eyewitness account of the South, seemed unaware of how trite his arguments had become and what little effect they had on European opinion. Then there was the "peculiar style" of De Leon's French, which editors told Pecquet du Bellet was a bit too "Americanized" for French tastes, and was described by one editor as "broken" and indecipherable.[57]

The problem went much deeper than language and style, in any case. The French knew that slavery, not supposed cultural differences between a Latin South and Puritan North, lay at the heart of the American conflict. De Leon's effort to "enlighten" the public as to the "true" nature and benevolence of the South's brand of slavery was of little help to the Confederate cause.[58]

Though certainly no friend of the North, Pecquet du Bellet was immensely impressed with how its agents skillfully managed the French press on the slavery question. He credited Seward and Dayton (he apparently did not know of Bigelow's key role) for the skill with which the Union by late 1862 began to align its cause with the red republican cry for *Emancipation, Liberté, Fraternité, Egalité*. Eventually, he recalled sarcastically, newspaper editors "trembled at the mere idea of defending those 'Southern Cannibals' who breakfasted every morning upon a new born infant negro."[59]

Henry Hotze was also frustrated by the "sentimentality" and obstinacy of the French on the slavery question. Outside the emperor and his close circle of advisers, who he thought accepted the South's defense of white supremacy and slavery, "all the intelligence, the science, the social respectability, is leagued with the ignorance and the radicalism in a deep-rooted antipathy" against the South. In contrast to the French, Hotze found the English, "accustomed to a hierarchy of classes at home and to a haughty dominion abroad," and therefore able to grasp the "hierarchy of races." But the French, "the apostles of universal equality," are embarrassed by such ideas. The emperor dares not "offend so universal a feeling" and therefore could not act in the best interests of his country. That, Hotze summarized, was the problem the South faced in France. Financial interest, European rivalries, and the manifest destiny of Napoleon III's Grand Design all pointed toward a common cause with the South. The problem was the stubborn mind of the French people who would not accept the South's version of *la vérité*.[60]

CHAPTER 9

GARIBALDI'S ANSWER

Call the great American Republic. She is, after all, your daughter, risen from your bosom; and . . . is struggling today for the
abolition of slavery so generously proclaimed by you. Help her
to escape from the terrible strife waged against her by the trad-
ers in human flesh. Help her, and then place her by your side
at the great assembly of nations—that final work of the human
intellect.

—GIUSEPPE GARIBALDI,
"TO THE ENGLISH NATION," SEPTEMBER 28, 1862

THE SLAVERY QUESTION WAS AN OBSTACLE TO INTERNATIONAL
recognition of the South, but in the summer of 1862 it also bur-
dened popular enthusiasm for the Union overseas. A full year had passed
since Giuseppe Garibaldi posed the simple question that still seemed unanswered: why was America waging war against the slaveholders' rebellion without waging war against slavery?

The long summer of 1862 ended with the most serious threat of foreign
intervention during the entire four years of war. The most familiar narrative of this perilous season of war dwells on the Confederate invasion of
Maryland being turned back at Antietam, then Lincoln issuing the long-
awaited Emancipation Proclamation, which came in the nick of time to
upset plans among the European powers to end the war on terms of separation. But the truth is that initially the proclamation made intervention

more likely. *Because* of emancipation, which many leaders feared would ignite racial mayhem and throw the world cotton economy into chaos, some wanted to move quickly to mediate an end to war. It was not Antietam, nor was it Lincoln's emancipation decree that upset the Great Powers' plans to intervene. The tide of events was moving in favor of the South that summer and fall of 1862. As the summer wore on, the Union's Peninsular Campaign to capture Richmond lay in shambles. The Union army, led by General George McClellan, was in retreat, and the Confederate army was advancing northward to surround and capture Washington. Then, unexpectedly, a march on Rome led by Giuseppe Garibaldi and his army of Red Shirts created a public uproar across Europe, ignited huge riots in England, forced a shake-up in Napoleon III's government, and suddenly left Lord Palmerston's British cabinet to contemplate the unhappy prospect of facing the United States in war alone. Without ever leaving Italy, the Hero of Two Worlds and his band of Red Shirts inadvertently upended the plans of the Great Powers to intervene in support of the South.[1]

IN WASHINGTON ALL SUMMER THE LINCOLN ADMINISTRATION HAD been making a deliberate turn toward a war of abolition. During the secession crisis Lincoln had committed to safeguarding slavery in the Southern states in part to *delegitimize* in the eyes of the world what he and Seward characterized as a rebellion without cause. In the summer of 1862 Lincoln at last concluded that he must act against slavery to *legitimize* the Union cause, especially in the eyes of liberal foreigners who expected America to fight Liberty's war. Lincoln was slow to embrace emancipation in part because of constitutional constraints. He also feared that Northern soldiers and civilians simply would not be willing to sacrifice for a war to emancipate black slaves. Already pro-Southern Copperheads in the North were arousing opposition to emancipation and calling for peace and restoration of the "Union as it was." The voice of democracy was about to be heard in the November congressional elections. Lincoln had framed the war as a defense of democratic principles; ironically, it seemed that democracy might prevent him from using the one weapon he realized could win the war: emancipation.

William Seward had parallel concerns about overseas reactions to an emancipation edict. He was genuinely troubled that an emancipation edict would redound to the benefit of the South. Europeans viewed emancipation as a catastrophic threat to the cotton industry, he was certain, and instead of hailing emancipation as a higher moral cause, the world would see it as the last desperate act of a nation, unable to win on the battlefield, resorting to racial conflagration to save itself.[2]

One after another of Seward's diplomats abroad had tried to persuade him otherwise. The foreign public was perplexed as to why an antislavery party was fighting to maintain a union with slaveholders, yet Seward was instructing them to avoid any discussion of the moral principles involved in the war. This had "positively stripped our cause of its peculiar moral force," Carl Schurz, the frustrated US minister in Spain despaired. Seward's stance seemed to lend credence to the cynical view of Confederate sympathizers abroad that the war was merely a contest between Southerners who wanted to "be free and independent" and Northerners who "insisted on subjugating and ruling them."[3]

Schurz was the first to fully sound the alarm that European popular support depended on the Union placing the war "upon a higher moral basis" than simply defending its right to exist. No Union diplomat was more attuned to liberal Europe than Schurz. As a young student at the University of Bonn, he had been preparing for a quiet career as a history professor when the Revolution of 1848 suddenly changed everything. He joined the armed rebellion against the Prussians, and when it failed he sought asylum in Switzerland and later moved to Paris. After Napoleon III's autocratic regime expelled him for revolutionary activities, he moved again, this time to London, and in 1852, with his wife, Margarethe, he made his way to America and eventually came to Wisconsin. Schurz completely immersed himself in America's language, culture, and politics, and he channeled his revolutionary passion into tireless efforts on behalf of the Republican Party.[4]

To Schurz's impassioned plea from Madrid in September 1861 that liberal Europe would support a war against slavery and make it impossible for the aristocratic government leaders to favor the South, Seward had answered with a deflating rebuke that left Schurz in utter despair. "This struggle fills my whole soul," he wrote mournfully to Seward. "The cause which is at stake is the cause of my life. . . . I feel as if I wasted the rest of my strength and labor when not devoting it to the service of the country at a moment like this under these circumstances." He wanted out of diplomatic service, which he now realized was a misuse of his talent and experience so long as Seward controlled the message. He had already written to Lincoln asking to be recalled, taking the occasion to express "grave doubts" about the country's foreign affairs but not daring to say all he thought about Seward's uninspired leadership.[5]

Seward grudgingly granted Schurz a leave of absence, but he was not eager to have him back in Washington, filling the president's ears with his radical ideas. Schurz left Madrid in December as the *Trent* crisis was coming to its head. He stole across his native Germany by night and made his way to Hamburg, where Margarethe and his children were waiting. They made a rough, storm-tossed crossing and arrived in New York in late January 1862.

Schurz immediately headed straight for Washington, going first to the State Department to report to Seward. Busy with other duties, Seward asked him to wait and meet him later. Schurz promptly went next door to the White House. He was worried that Lincoln might be upset with him for leaving Madrid, a post Lincoln had battled Seward to secure for his German friend, and he was greatly relieved that Lincoln greeted him with the "old cordiality" and invited him to talk in his office.[6]

Assuming that Seward had not shown Lincoln his September plea for emancipation but feeling it improper to ask whether that was so, Schurz began to summarize its main points when suddenly the door opened and in popped the head of William Seward, who had found time to follow him there. "Excuse me, Seward," Lincoln said, holding up his hand, "excuse me for a moment. I have something to talk over with this gentleman." Seward realized that Schurz was going over his head and, no doubt, was troubled by what this radical was about to tell the president. But Lincoln wanted to hear what his German friend had to say. Schurz remembered vividly that Seward "withdrew without saying a word."[7]

Schurz resumed his exposition on the European situation while Lincoln "listened to me very intently, even eagerly," and without interruption. European governments wanted to see democracy fail in America, he told the president, but there was a vast public with liberal instincts waiting eagerly for the Union to place the war on a "higher moral basis" and proclaim emancipation as its goal. As he drew to a close, Lincoln sat "for a minute silently musing."

According to Schurz, it was as though he had been digesting his thoughts for some time: "You may be right. Probably you are," he said. "I have been thinking so myself. I cannot imagine that any European power would dare to recognize and aid the Southern Confederacy if it became clear that the Confederacy stands for slavery and the Union for freedom." These were almost exactly the words Schurz had written to Seward the previous September, and it seemed clear that Lincoln *had* read Schurz's plea from Madrid.[8]

Lincoln told Schurz he accepted the main point that "a distinct antislavery policy would remove the foreign danger." But he feared the American public was not "sufficiently prepared" and that a precipitous move toward an "abolition war" would undermine support. The Union had to defeat the rebellion militarily, Lincoln reasoned. Otherwise, any pronouncement against slavery would "be like the Pope's bull against the comet," a metaphor Lincoln used more than once to evoke the futile exercise of power.[9]

Schurz was among a growing coterie of passionate abolitionists who were exasperated with the administration's "dilatoriness" on the slavery question. But he came away from his meeting at the White House that day with a new understanding of the president's values and political instincts. Lincoln was not opposed to emancipation, nor did he scorn its advocates. Instead, he "rather welcomed everything that would prepare the public mind for the approaching development." Abolitionist critics Charles Sumner and Horace Greeley were, to him, more allies than adversaries. Lincoln typically answered them, sometimes in public letters, by engaging their arguments and posing questions rather than defending fixed ideas.[10]

The fundamental difference of opinion between Schurz and Seward reflected very different assessments about the way European powers decided foreign policy. Seward viewed European powers as motivated solely by national interests rather than moral sentiment. They calculated commercial or geopolitical advantage rather than the public good. Because monarchies were not as beholden to popular will, he reasoned, public opinion mattered less to European leaders than it did to America's democracy.

What Schurz was trying to explain to Seward and Lincoln was that European monarchies might wish the worst for the American republic and prefer to see it fragmented and weakened. But ideology and moral purpose mattered greatly to the broad European public, and though popular discontent might not be registered at the polls, European rulers still feared what might be unleashed at the barricades. Memories of 1848 still loomed over the crowned heads of the Old World, and the voice of opposition was never far away from the threat of revolution.[11]

Lincoln's domestic policy and Seward's foreign policy began from the same premise the president laid before the world in his first inaugural address: the Union was defending the basic right of a nation to self-preservation in the face of domestic rebellion. Yet long before emancipation was adopted, Lincoln in his public addresses and Seward in his diplomatic instructions were enveloping this narrow goal of national preservation within a loftier idea that the war was a trial of the broad principles of government by the people everywhere on earth. If a disgruntled minority was unwilling to abide by the will of the majority, the idea that people could govern themselves would be an utter failure. The outcome of the American contest would decide nothing less than the fate of democracy.[12]

Lincoln employed universalizing language to place the American Civil War within the broadest framework possible in space and time. This was "essentially a people's contest," he explained in his 1861 Fourth of July message to Congress. "On the side of the Union it is a struggle for maintaining in the world that form and substance of government whose leading object is to elevate the condition of men; to lift artificial weights from all shoulders; to clear the paths of laudable pursuit for all; to afford all an unfettered start and a fair chance in the race of life." "It presents to the whole family of man, the question, whether a constitutional republic, or a democracy—a government of the people, by the same people—can, or cannot, maintain its territorial integrity, against its own domestic foes."[13]

Seward also employed universalizing language in his diplomatic correspondence and referred often to the historic struggle and far-reaching consequences involved in the American conflict. Without endorsing emancipation, he frequently made broad appeals to the cause of human freedom, as in his instructions to Henry Sanford on negotiations with Giuseppe Garibaldi: "Tell him . . . that the fall of the American Union . . . would be a disastrous blow to the cause of Human Freedom equally here, in Europe, and throughout the world."[14]

Lincoln's goal of preserving the American Union was always much more than just an amoral placeholder for emancipation. From the outset, he and Seward had elevated the Union's right to exist to a higher plane as the defense of the universal republican experiment. While the idea of America's conflict as a trial of democracy resonated powerfully abroad, the appeal to ideals of liberty and equality rang hollow without emancipation.

IN THE SUMMER OF 1862 LINCOLN LED, AND SEWARD RESISTED, a decisive turn toward an emancipation policy that the president hoped would sharply define the Union's moral purpose and thwart foreign intervention. Lincoln did not need convincing that slavery was a great moral evil. Lincoln's moral abhorrence of human slavery never faltered from the time when, as a young man visiting New Orleans, he saw human beings sold at auction like livestock. His condemnation of slavery also drew on a strong republican political ideology. He hated slavery, as he explained in an earlier speech, "because of the monstrous injustice of slavery itself," but also "because it deprives our republican example of its just influence in the world." Slavery "enables the enemies of free institutions, with plausibility, to taunt us as hypocrites—causes the real friends of freedom to doubt our sincerity, and . . . forces so many really good men amongst ourselves into an open war with the very fundamental principles of civil liberty."[15]

Lincoln's moral and ideological condemnation of slavery remained firm and steady, but what he thought ought to be done about ending slavery took a crucial turn by the summer of 1862. Though the Constitution did not grant the president the power to end slavery, he came to realize that the war provoked by slaveholders handed him the best remedy to rid the republic of slavery *and* end the war. It was as commander in chief during a war to defend the republic against insurrection, not as chief executive, that Lincoln would proclaim emancipation.[16]

Grave political pressures arising from Northern advocates of peace, along with military reverses in the field, hastened Lincoln's reckoning with slavery. He later described the mood of that perilous summer of 1862: "Things had gone on from bad to worse, until I felt that we had reached the end of our rope. . . . [W]e had about played our last card, and must change our tactics, or lose the game!" Lincoln baldly admitted it was a desperate move motivated by military necessity, but he had been moving in this direction for some time.[17]

Lincoln and the Republican Party had been advancing piecemeal abolition measures for months. In March 1862 Congress passed legislation forbidding Union officers from returning fugitive slaves to their masters. In April the federal government exercised its local sovereignty to abolish slavery in the District of Columbia. In June it outlawed slavery in all federal territories. In July Lincoln signed the Second Confiscation Act, permitting the liberation of slaves of rebel owners. The president also publicly encouraged border states to pass legislation for the gradual emancipation of their slaves and even offered federal support for compensation to owners. The lack of cooperation from the states, however, helped set the stage for a presidential edict as the only viable path toward ending slavery. By midsummer 1862 Lincoln had all but given up on any possibility that the states would lead the way to legislating the end of slavery, even with federal inducements. At the same time, the president felt that a war-weary public, and especially the soldiers, would be more prepared to support abolition if that was what it took to end the war.[18]

On July 13, 1862, during a carriage ride in Georgetown, Lincoln explained what until now had been his secret emancipation plan for the first time to William Seward and Gideon Welles, the secretary of the navy. According to Welles, who recorded it all in his diary, Seward went along with the president at the time, saying his strategy was "justifiable" and "expedient." But Seward's private and diplomatic correspondence shows that he, in fact, remained firmly wedded to the view that emancipation, instead of defusing the "foreign danger," would inflame it.[19]

When Lincoln called a cabinet meeting for July 22 to present his plan for emancipation, Seward came fully armed and ready to play his hand. Lincoln's plan to free the slaves in rebel-controlled territory, by this point, had been linked to an even more controversial plan to enlist free blacks and slaves who made their way to the Union army. In a lengthy, passionate speech, Seward played on the alarming image that foreigners would have of slaves in arms. Foreign powers, some of whom had experienced their own colonial uprisings against whites, he cautioned, would see in this a frightening summons to "servile insurrection," arming slaves to slay their masters. Furthermore, he said, sudden emancipation and racial upheaval might disrupt cotton production for six decades. Instead of preventing foreign intervention, he warned the cabinet, Lincoln's emancipation edict would provoke the Great Powers of Europe to rescue the South.[20]

Seward was just beginning. He continued by pointing out to the president before the cabinet that emancipation, coming in the wake of the disastrous Peninsular Campaign in Virginia, would be viewed abroad as "the last measure of an exhausted government, a cry for help; the government stretching forth its hands to Ethiopia [the slaves], instead of Ethiopia stretching forth her hands to the government."[21]

Lincoln had made it clear to members of the cabinet at the beginning of the meeting that they were not there to debate the emancipation policy; his mind was made up. Seward shrewdly, if disingenuously, professed to approve of the policy in principle, but he insisted that now was not the time. The Union must wait for a decisive military victory. Pulling out the stops, Seward urged they wait until "the eagle of victory takes his flight," allowing the government to "hang your proclamation about his neck" in national triumph instead of desperation. Of course, Seward realized that a decisive military victory would render an emancipation decree less urgent.[22]

Lincoln remained determined to move forward on emancipation, and while Seward's dire predictions of Haitian-style racial conflagration did not change his mind, the president was concerned about the timing of his policy. As to Seward's prophecy of foreign outrage and intervention, it appears that by this time the president was more impressed with Carl Schurz's view that the foreign public would rally in support of emancipation. Lincoln understood fully that emancipation was a diplomatic as well as military necessity.[23]

THE LONG WAIT FOR UNION MILITARY VICTORY THAT SUMMER OF 1862 seemed endless. At the end of July Robert E. Lee's Confederate forces inflicted a second humiliating defeat on the Union at Bull Run. Emboldened by success, Lee decided to take the war into Maryland, humble the Union on its own soil, and surround the capital at Washington. This would demonstrate to the Great Powers of Europe that the South was capable not only of defending itself but also of capturing the very capital of the enemy. Lee ordered his troops to sing "Maryland, My Maryland," the defiant anti-Union anthem, as they advanced north on September 4, crossing the Potomac River no more than twenty-five miles northwest of Washington. On September 17 Lee's army joined battle with Union forces at Antietam Creek in western Maryland. It was the bloodiest single day of the entire war, indeed in all American history, and it ended in stalemate. The next day, however, Lee decided to withdraw his forces, and two days later they crossed back over the Potomac River into Virginia.[24]

Lincoln could make a plausible claim to victory at Antietam. With a draft of the Emancipation Proclamation in his hand, he opened the cabinet meeting on September 22 by saying he had "made a promise to myself and," he hesitated slightly, "to my Maker" that if the rebel army was driven out of Maryland, he would free the slaves. Then he read the lengthy and rather arid proclamation to a somber cabinet. Seward made no protest this time, and the next day he countersigned the final document.

Significantly, as soon as it was signed, Lincoln instructed his secretary of state to publish the proclamation as an official State Department circular and to send it immediately to all US legations and consulates around the world. Seward's cover letter for the circular employed cautious language. Given "a choice between the dissolution of this . . . beneficent government or a relinquishment of the protection of slavery, it is the Union, and not slavery, that must be maintained and preserved." But Seward's private correspondence indicates that he was still doubtful about the timing and international repercussions of the proclamation, and he was preparing to say, "I told you so."[25]

ALL THAT SUMMER SEWARD HAD WATCHED EVENTS UNFOLD WITH growing apprehension. Far from softening his hard-power policy in the face of Union reverses in Virginia, Seward had issued one of his most strongly worded threats to Britain a few days after Lincoln's July 22 cabinet meeting on emancipation. He instructed Adams to remind the British government that the Union army was growing with "new ranks of volunteers . . . daily increased by immigration." "Neither the country nor the government has been exhausted." In case anyone missed the point, he added: if "respect of our sovereignty by foreign powers" was violated, "this civil war will . . . become a war of continents—a war of the world."[26]

Seward feared the worst, that Britain and France were about to intervene and settle the war on terms of separation. He was right. In London when news of McClellan's reverses in Virginia first arrived in July, Lord Palmerston and Earl Russell quietly set in motion a plan for intervention.

They planned to act in concert with France and Russia, perhaps Austria as well, in hopes of presenting the North with a united coalition of Great Powers that would simply overwhelm Seward and all his blustering about a "war of the world."

According to this plan, a multilateral commission would extend its good offices to mediate a peace and on terms that would recognize the South's separation. This mediation offer would be presented as a human-itarian intervention to bring to an end the terrible carnage of the war and to alleviate the suffering of distressed cotton mill workers across Europe. International law specified that outside parties affected by prolonged wars could, with good cause, offer to mediate peace. When one side rejected peacemaking efforts, as everyone fully expected the Union would do, in-tervention in favor of the willing side became more justifiable. In any case, such an offer of humanitarian intervention, some thought, would help assuage public opinion if it came to war with America.[27]

All during the summer of 1862, Palmerston seemed to be signaling to the United States that Britain was preparing to abandon neutrality. In June he picked an unnecessary fight with Charles Francis Adams by writ-ing a personal letter denouncing Benjamin Butler's "woman's order" in New Orleans. Butler's order was controversial, but such matters were not the usual concern of foreign governments. "Palmerston wants a quarrel!" Adams realized.[28]

Also in June Lord Lyons, Britain's ambassador to the United States, left Washington for London, supposedly on personal leave to escape the oppressive heat, but some read his departure as a portentous sign. Con-federate agents in Europe certainly did. John Slidell wrote to James Ma-son in London, "There is every reason to believe that the event you so thoroughly desire and which we talked about when I had the pleasure of seeing you in Paris *is very close at hand*." "Lord Lyons returns to America on Oct 15th. Is it not possible that he may announce it?" His cryptic message, of course, was referring to the announcement of Confederate recognition by Britain and France, and it probably drew on secret infor-mation from his spy, Pierre Cintrat, inside the French foreign office.[29]

Another ominous sign of British bias came in July 1862, when, de-spite persistent protests from Union officials, the British government, either by subterfuge or by negligence, allowed a warship secretly built for the Confederate navy to launch from Liverpool in utter disregard of its own declaration of neutrality. The CSS *Alabama* would terrorize the Union merchant marine for the next two years; more ships were under way, according to reports.[30]

On July 18 MP William Lindsay, a stalwart of the "southern lobby," stood in Parliament to move that Britain extend its good offices to mediate peace and, in effect, recognize the South's independence. News of the Confederate victory in the Seven Days Battles had just reached London, and false reports that McClellan had surrendered the whole Union army circulated with stunning effect. Lindsay made his motion before a packed session of Parliament while members both jeered and cheered his resolution. James Mason sat nervously in the gallery, listening to the debate and chewing tobacco.

Palmerston slumped on the front bench and appeared to be snoozing while the MPs argued into the night. It was one thirty in the morning before old Pam finally rose from his seat as the members hushed. In a mildly scolding manner, he informed the MPs that discussion of this kind was fraught with great danger and that it was a matter best left to his cabinet to decide behind closed doors. Mason appeared sullen and dejected as the Parliament adjourned, but what he did not know was that Palmerston, though irritated by Lindsay's presumption, fully intended to intervene. Had it all gone as Palmerston and Russell planned, the South would soon have its long-sought independence.[31]

From the US legation in London, Adams wrote Seward that he had been informed that Britain and France were quietly conspiring "to get up a congress for the disposal of our affairs." He suspected Lord Palmerston to be the main instigator, but it was Earl Russell who actually took the more aggressive part in the turn toward intervention. Adams was already convinced that emancipation was "a positive necessity," and he told his diary that July that the ultimate purpose of the entire conflict must be "to topple the edifice of slavery." In late September Adams received a disturbing message from Seward, warning that recognition of the South was imminent. "The suspense is becoming more and more painful," Adams told his diary. "I do not think since the beginning of the war I have felt so profoundly anxious for the safety of the country."[32]

Like Lincoln in Washington, Lord Palmerston was waiting that September for military events to decide his course of action. On September 14 he made the first decisive move toward intervention after receiving news of Second Bull Run. He wrote almost gleefully to Russell, who was attending the queen while she was visiting her relatives in Gotha, Germany: "My Dear Russell," the Federals "got a very complete smashing," and it appeared "that still greater disasters await them," including the possible surrender of Washington or Baltimore. If all this should happen, Palmerston proposed, is it not time for England and France to "recommend an arrangement upon the basis of separation?"[33]

Russell answered three days later with equal alacrity, as though it all had been rehearsed for some time. "Whether the Federal army is destroyed or not, it is clear that it is driven back to Washington, and has made no progress in subduing the insurgent states." Russell readily agreed with Palmerston that "the time is come for offering mediation to the United States Government," and he added, "with a view to the recognition of the independence of the Confederates." Russell was not interested in simply ending the American war; he wanted to ensure the South's independence. If the North rejected mediation, he spelled it out to Palmerston, "we ought ourselves to recognize the Southern States as an independent State." Taking "so important a step," he advised the prime minister, required a cabinet meeting; October 23 or 30 would suit him.[34]

Palmerston was virtually rubbing his hands together as he replied to Russell on September 23. "Your plan . . . seems to be excellent," but the meeting should not be delayed. "France, we know, is quite ready and only waiting for our concurrence," and "events may be taking place which might render it desirable that the offer be made before the middle of October." What Palmerston had in mind, obviously, was exerting pressure on Lincoln and the Republicans before the congressional elections in early November. He also anticipated news of Union disasters in Maryland. If the Federals were defeated on their own soil, he told Russell, they would be "at once ready for mediation" before they lost more territory; "the iron should be struck while hot."[35]

Palmerston proposed that they invite Russia to join with Britain and France. This would make the offer of mediation more difficult for the North to spurn, but he also worried that Russia might be "too favourable to the North" if it actually came to mediation. Russell, in turn, let Palmerston know that the queen was favorable to the whole idea, but she urged them to bring Austria in on it as well to ensure broader European support for intervention. Whoever joined their plan, Britain was taking the lead to end America's war by separating the warring parties forever.[36]

News of the Emancipation Proclamation did not reach Europe until October 6 and 7, precisely as Palmerston's cabinet was preparing to meet to discuss plans for intervention. Seward's prediction that European governments would recoil in horror at what they would view as a call for servile insurrection and Carl Schurz's rival prophecy that the public would rally behind a Union war for liberty were about to be put to the test.[37]

If Earl Russell was any indication of Europe's reaction to the Emancipation Proclamation, Seward had been spot-on. Russell called the cabinet to its meeting with a circular dated October 13 that characterized the war as a regrettable stalemate between "military forces equally balanced, and battles equally sanguinary and undecisive." As for Lincoln's emancipation edict, Russell thought animosities between North and South would be "aggravated instead of being softened" by what he sarcastically referred to as the "large and benevolent scheme of freedom for four millions of the human race." It was nothing more than an incendiary device aimed at "exciting the passions of the slave to aid the destructive progress of armies."[38]

The question before them, Russell explained in his circular, was to decide if it was not Europe's duty "to ask both parties, in the most friendly and conciliatory terms, to agree to a suspension of arms for the purpose of weighing calmly the advantages of peace against the contingent gain of further bloodshed, and the protraction of so calamitous a war." In a private letter to William Gladstone, a key cabinet member brought into the plan, Russell spelled it out frankly: Britain, France, and possibly Russia would extend their good offices to both sides "and in the case of refusal by the North" would then propose that the South be treated "on the basis of separation and recognition."[39]

In France William Dayton had received the same instructions Seward sent to Adams: brace for mediation proposals and threaten war if there is even a hint of recognizing the South. Napoleon III, having met with John Slidell in Vichy on July 16 to plot possible alliance with the Confederacy, was eager for Britain to give the signal for some form of joint intervention by the Great Powers. Three days after the Vichy meeting, Napoleon had sent a telegram to his foreign minister, Édouard

Thouvenel, who was in London: "Ask the English government if they don't think the time has come to recognize the South."[40]

Napoleon III "is hovering over us, like the carrion crow over the body of the sinking traveler," John Bigelow, US consul in Paris, wrote to Seward that summer, "waiting until we are too weak to resist his predatory instincts." By this time France's Mexican adventure was deeply entangled with French policy on the American question, and France needed an independent Confederacy for the Grand Design to succeed.[41]

Meanwhile, at the Quai d'Orsay, Thouvenel had been poring over maps of North America, trying to delineate a boundary that might allow some peaceful coexistence of what he envisioned as two "federated confederacies." He had also come up with what he called a "possibly absurd ideas" for two republics that would govern their domestic affairs independently but act as one nation in foreign affairs and commercial policy. The United States of America would become a customs union, in other words. His office staff had been working on it since June, and Henri Mercier, the French ambassador to Washington, had proposed a similar plan to Confederate leaders in Richmond. Thouvenel thought that somehow the North and South had to learn to accept some form of peaceful coexistence.[42]

Thouvenel invited Dayton to meet with him on September 12 to assure him that, although there was no official change in French policy, he wanted to share his "personal views" as a friend of the United States. "I think that the undertaking of conquering the South is almost superhuman," he told Dayton bluntly. The South is so vast, "you can not hold it down if you conquered it." This may have seemed odd advice from an empire with occupying armies in Africa, Mexico, and Indochina, but Thouvenel's point was that "it is not the nature of a democratic republic like yours to hold so many hostile people in subjection."[43]

Dayton was only vaguely aware of Palmerston's plans for joint intervention when he met with Thouvenel again on October 2. This time he came armed with a discourse on the natural geopolitical unity of the United States and the Union's unswerving determination to maintain "one country" under one federal government. This was a life-or-death struggle for national existence, he explained earnestly to Thouvenel. The French minister allowed that Europeans such as he did not understand all that sustained America's concept of national unity, but as a practical matter, he told Dayton, "I must say I no longer believe you can conquer the South." Nor did any reasonable statesman in Europe believe the Union could succeed, he added.[44]

Then Thouvenel startled Dayton by nonchalantly asking, "Have you heard from Adams lately?" Dayton looked puzzled and said he had not. It appeared, Thouvenel informed the worried American, that "it will not be long before Great Britain will recognize the South." Dayton was visibly stunned, but far from speechless. He quickly responded, and according to Seward's script: if Britain recognized the South, Dayton warned, the United States would prepare for the "ultimate consequence." Union naval forces, he reminded Thouvenel, were "untouched" by the war and would be "better prepared than at any past period in our history." The Union would defend itself and its interests "to our last extremity," Dayton assured him.[45]

Thouvenel understood the threat was intended for France every bit as much as for Britain. He wrote to Mercier later that day, belittling Dayton's menacing remarks, obviously made at Seward's direction and with his boss's same overblown confidence. Dayton's "worried look betrayed his blustering language," Thouvenel wrote.

Then, as though thinking while he wrote, Thouvenel began to consider the consequences of French action and about the mighty naval force and ironclad ships the Union was building. Joint intervention would force the French to "do our share of the fighting along with England," he wrote, and "I admit to you that I would think a long while before doing it." Mexico, America, and Rome were "really too much all at once."

Dayton's warnings had more of an impact on Thouvenel than he knew, but he had found the whole conversation positively "alarming." That day he wrote to Seward to warn that France, with British cooperation, was about to make a move toward recognition of the South.[46]

WHAT NO ONE IN PARIS OR LONDON FORESAW THAT SUMMER OF 1862 was that Giuseppe Garibaldi and his band of Red Shirts in Italy were about to upset the mighty plans of Europe's Great Powers. Their actions in the remote south of Italy would create a crisis in the French government that would force Thouvenel from office and dash plans for joint intervention in the American war. Britain and France were about to receive a firm reminder of Palmerston's famous adage: "Opinions are stronger than armies."[47]

All during the summer Garibaldi had been rallying Italians to march on Rome and make it the capital of the new united Italy. French troops had been defending Pope Pius IX as pontiff of the Papal States since 1849. In Turin King Victor Emmanuel II publicly condemned Garibaldi's call to arms out of fear it would lead to war with France. Still, he and his government did little to silence Garibaldi that summer as he staged enormous public gatherings across Italy, issued bombastic speeches and militant statements to the press, organized citizen rifle clubs, and summoned Italians to fulfill their national destiny in Rome. There were rumors that the Italian government was secretly encouraging Garibaldi to arouse popular pressure to force Napoleon III to abandon Rome. Some said Garibaldi carried a sealed metal box with a signed letter from the king, authorizing his actions.[48]

Reenacting his spectacular invasion of Sicily two years earlier, Garibaldi sailed to Sicily late in June, and before an immense and enthusiastic crowd at Marsala he vowed, "Rome or Death!" *Roma o Morte!* the crowd chanted in response. *Roma o Morte!* It became the new slogan of the Italian Risorgimento.[49]

"Death if they like," Napoleon's devout Catholic wife, Empress Eugénie, replied, "but Rome never!" Napoleon III was less resolute than his wife. He was undergoing one of his common spells of indecision. The inglorious defeat of French forces at Puebla the previous May had inflamed opposition to his Mexican venture among the French public. Given his mounting problems at home, he might have been willing to let the pope fend for himself against the Garibaldini but for the fury it would set off among European Catholics—to say nothing of Eugénie. More than that, a humiliating retreat in the face of Garibaldi's red republican army would inflict incalculable damage to his prestige.[50]

In late August Garibaldi and his Red Shirts left Sicily, crossing the Straits of Messina to begin their march up the Italian peninsula toward Rome. The king, acting his part, dispatched units of the Italian regular army to stop them. The two armies met in southern Italy at Aspromonte (sour mountain) on August 29. When the Italian officers ordered them to surrender and lay down their arms, Garibaldi told his men only to hold their fire. In a dramatic moment that must have seemed endless, the great general, beloved by soldiers on both sides, stood in front of his men as they all cried out, *Viva l'Italia!*

Garibaldi expected the king's soldiers to come over, to join the march on Rome. Some said he was still shouting *Viva l'Italia* as two bullets, possibly ricocheting off nearby boulders, struck him, one in his ankle and another in his thigh. He was taken beneath a tree to lie down, and soldiers from both sides gathered around him, some openly weeping over the fallen hero. They took him down the mountain on a stretcher and then imprisoned him at Varignano, an Italian fortress near Spezia. The Italian prime minister, Urbano Rattazzi, was eager to maintain order and to appease France, and many feared that Garibaldi and his officers would be prosecuted for high treason and sentenced to death.[51]

The tremors from Aspromonte moved with alarming force across Europe that September, precisely as British and French leaders were planning to intervene in favor of the South. In Washington Lincoln was still waiting to proclaim a war of emancipation when news of Aspromonte arrived in mid-September. The wounded Italian hero, from his prison cell in Varignano, was about to play a crucial role in rescuing the Union.

Coverage of Garibaldi's debacle at Aspromonte was sensational. Rumors ran through the international press that Garibaldi had died, was about to be executed, or was being tormented in prison. Photographic and engraved images of the wounded hero were published widely. The press reported that thousands of admirers were sending letters, money, food, and gifts to Varignano and that hundreds of well-wishers were flocking there to visit the wounded hero or stand vigil outside the fortress walls.

Public interest began to fixate on the wounded ankle. Blood-soaked bandages became precious relics, and when the wound failed to heal some likened it to Christ's stigmata. An Italian cartoon portrayed Garibaldi nailed to the cross surrounded by his tormenters—duplicitous politicians and malevolent priests—while Pope Pius IX and Napoleon III danced merrily in the background. Eminent physicians from England, Russia, France, and Italy arrived at Garibaldi's bedside to inspect the wound. The distinguished French surgeon Auguste Nélaton became a hero in his own right after discovering that the bullet was still inside the ankle and providing his special probes for its extraction to save the foot from amputation.[52]

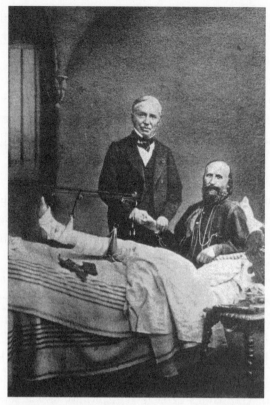

32. Giuseppe Garibaldi with Dr. Nélaton, the renowned French surgeon who saved Garibaldi's wounded foot. (COURTESY OF US NATIONAL LIBRARY OF MEDICINE, HISTORY OF MEDICINE DIVISION)

For George Marsh, the US minister in Turin, Garibaldi suddenly presented another ticklish diplomatic predicament. Rumors swirled through the Italian court that an American ship had conveyed men and munitions to the insurgents in Sicily, and the US consul to Ancona, one Mr. Mighari, was implicated. Marsh warned Seward of the "extreme jealousy" of the Italian government toward any "manifestations of sympathy" with what officials in Turin were characterizing as a red republican rebellion. No one knew what direction the growing uproar over the events at Aspromonte might take. Marsh moved with extreme discretion, communicating with Italian government officials through a trusted intermediary to negotiate amnesty for Garibaldi and his men and offer asylum in America. This, Marsh proposed, might provide the Italian government with a "convenient way of disposing of them," and they "would be willingly received" in the Union military.[53]

The invitation to Garibaldi of the previous year to lead a Union army was about to be renewed, and with equal sensation in the international press. Bowing to enormous public pressure, the Italian government finally granted amnesty to Garibaldi and his men in early October. Garibaldi immediately wrote to Marsh: "I am ill and shall remain so for some months; but I think continually of the disastrous war in America, my second country, to which I would gladly be of some use when recovered. I will go thither with my friends; and we will make an appeal to all the democrats of Europe to join us in fighting this holy battle."[54]

THE EUROPEAN UPROAR OVER GARIBALDI MIGHT HAVE REMAINED nothing more than a distraction from the American question, had it not been for an obscure American consul in Vienna named Heinrich Theodore Canisius. Borrowing from the memorable example of James Quiggle, the US consul in Antwerp who initiated the first invitation to Garibaldi one year earlier, Canisius took it upon himself to write to the heroic prisoner of Varignano.

Canisius was a German Forty-Eighter, a young doctor who had fled to America after the Revolution of 1848 failed. He published a German-language newspaper known as the *Freie Presse* in Alton, Illinois, and during the 1860 election struck a deal with Abraham Lincoln, who bankrolled the newspaper to help garner German votes. The newspaper later failed, and Lincoln felt he owed Dr. Canisius a favor. Though Canisius had no diplomatic experience, as Lincoln rationalized it to Seward, the Vienna consulship seemed to be a just reward: "The place is but $1,000, and not much sought, and I must relieve myself of the Dr." Now, a year later, from his humble post in Vienna, Canisius, with a wife and children, was hard up and complaining to Seward about his low salary and high rent. It may have been hope for pecuniary gain as much as ideological zeal that motivated Canisius to write to Garibaldi. Consul Canisius, in any case, was about to astonish the world and help upend the secret plans of the Great Powers of Europe to end America's Civil War and recognize the Confederate South.[55]

"General!" the Vienna consul wrote to the imprisoned Garibaldi on September 1, three days after the incident at Aspromonte. "As you have failed for the present to accomplish the great and patriotic work you lately undertook in the interest of your beloved father land, I take the liberty to address myself to you, to ascertain whether it would not be against your present plans to lend us a helping hand in our present struggle to preserve the liberty and unity of our great Republic. The battle we fight is one which not only interest ourselves, but also the whole civilized world."[56]

Garibaldi may not have known how to reply to this bold communication from an obscure, low-level consul in Vienna. He finally replied on September 14: "I am a prisoner and I am dangerously wounded." He told Canisius that he hoped to "be able to satisfy my desire to serve the Great American Republic, of which I am a citizen, and which today fights for universal liberty [*la libertà universale*]." Garibaldi had apparently made up his mind that his second country was fighting for emancipation, whatever Lincoln decided to do.[57]

Once Canisius received Garibaldi's reply, on September 18 he wrote to Seward, saying he had "hastened" to inform his superior about his self-appointed diplomatic mission. With only a terse cover letter that simply stated what he had done, Canisius sent copies of all his correspondence with Garibaldi. Seward received the letters in early October, about the same time that he was reading them in the *New York Times,* and he must have been furious. Canisius had gone public with his rogue diplomatic mission and given copies of the correspondence to the *Wanderer,* a Vienna newspaper. By late September the story had spread like wildfire through the international press.[58]

Seward was in a bind. He could not risk offending Italy and France by allowing a US consul to publicly praise a jailed rebel leader. He had little choice but to disown Canisius's overtures as unauthorized and to circulate news to all his ministers in Europe that Canisius had been sacked. His icy letter of dismissal, dated October 10, pointed out to Canisius that not only had he egregiously exceeded his authority, but he had also violated the very principle on which the Union was waging war: he was praising a rebel for his "great and patriotic work" against his own government.[59]

Canisius was out of line, but his bold personal diplomacy project was paying rich dividends by linking Garibaldi, whose popularity was soaring among liberal Europeans, to the Union cause. Public demonstrations in support of Garibaldi and against Napoleon III, the pope, and the Italian government broke out across Italy and then spread through Europe. "The whole peninsula is shaking as if a volcano were about to blaze forth," Caroline Marsh, wife of the US minister in Turin, confided to her diary, "and the death of Garibaldi from his wounds, or any severity towards him on the part of the government would be very likely to scatter the throne of Victor Emmanuel to the four winds of heaven."[60]

In France dissent smoldered, stringently censored by Napoleon's regime, but in England violent riots broke out in London's Hyde Park, Birkenhead, and elsewhere. On Sunday, September 28, a group of about fifty working-class Radicals going by the name Workingmen's Garibaldian Committee gathered at a large earthen mound in Hyde Park to speak in support of Garibaldi and the cause of republicanism. About one thousand people gathered around them, and as the oratory got under way, a gang of a hundred or more Irish Catholics—men, women, and children—rushed the mound, wielding bludgeons and shouting, "Long Live the Pope!" A brawl ensued for thirty minutes before the crowd dispersed, but the battle would be resumed the next Sunday.[61]

From prison Garibaldi and his coterie of advisers dexterously managed the press. In a public letter entitled "To the English Nation," dated September 28 and published in British newspapers on October 3, he hailed England as the refuge from autocracy and tyranny and called upon the English to lead the world toward a new era of peace and liberty. He urged the English to rebuke Napoleon III and his imperialist designs. "Call the French nation to cooperate with you." "Tell her that conquests are today an aberration, the emanation of insane minds."

Then he embraced the Union cause unequivocally: "Call the great American Republic. She is, after all, your daughter, risen from your bosom," and "is struggling today for the abolition of slavery so generously proclaimed by you." Garibaldi's letter appeared in British newspapers on October 3, three days *before* news of Lincoln's emancipation decree reached London. Garibaldi was proclaiming emancipation before Lincoln. "Aid her to come out from the terrible struggle in which she is involved by the traffickers in human flesh," he implored the English nation. "Help her, and then make her sit by your side in the great assembly of nations, the final work of the human reason."[62]

Garibaldi's letter "To the English Nation" arrived as Garibaldi meetings, some quite raucous, were taking place throughout Britain. In London Radical workers planned a second large Garibaldi demonstration in Hyde

Park on Sunday, October 5. Crowds estimated at eighty to one hundred thousand gathered in the park, and many thronged around the speaker's mound, which the Garibaldians dubbed the "Hyde Park Aspromonte." Again the Garibaldians on the mound were assailed by "Irish roughs" armed with bludgeons, and a full-pitched battle ensued, leaving dozens of busted heads and several stilleto wounds from Italians who "made free use of the knife." "It was not a mere squabble," according to the alarming report in the London *Times*. "It was a battle, lacking only the smoke and the lines and squares." The *New York Times* had a field day mocking the Hyde Park melee. "Had it occurred in Central Park instead of Hyde Park," it would have "been cited as a melancholy proof of the decadence of public morals incident to Republican institutions, and as a new motive to intervene 'in the interest of humanity and civilization.'"[63]

Charles Francis Adams hastened to inform Seward after the first Garibaldi demonstration, "A serious riot took place in Hyde Park on Sunday last, where a meeting in favor of Garibaldi was attempted." "All this contributes to divide the attention heretofore so much concentrated on America," and a good thing too, he might have added. "Less and less appears to be thought of mediation or intervention," he wrote, and "all efforts to stir up popular discontent" against the Union and in favor of ending the war "meet with little response." For the first time Adams was profoundly struck by the depth of popular support for the Union. "I am inclined to believe that perhaps a majority of the poorer classes rather sympathize with us in our struggle," he told Seward, "and it is only the aristocracy and, the commercial body that are adverse."[64]

The bonds between Garibaldi and the Union, the pope and the Confederacy, were reinforced as news flashes from Italy intersected with those emanating from Washington in early October. Garibaldi's full-throated endorsement of the Union cause roused popular support just as news of the Emancipation Proclamation broke in Europe. The shots fired at Aspromonte shook the foundations of power in Italy, France, and Britain. In Italy genuine fears of popular unrest forced King Victor Emmanuel to free Garibaldi and his men and summarily dismiss Prime Minister Rattazzi, who was blamed for the Aspromonte fiasco.

In Paris Garibaldi had become the hero of the hour. "Garibaldi has been vanquished," Malakoff told *New York Times* readers, but his name has grown grander and more monumental than ever!" "Daily bulletins of his health are published and sent over the world by telegraph, as if he were, as he really is, the only universal monarch." Garibaldi "represents a principle," and people were afraid that the principle, as well as the man, was wounded. Dr. Nélaton, the surgeon credited with saving Garibaldi's foot, met a boisterous lecture hall full of students clamoring for a full account of their professor's encounter with their hero. "Half the Police of the town could not prevent a demonstration," had Nélaton given them the least encouragement, Malakoff mused.[65]

Henry Sanford, writing from Paris in early October, was heartened by the surge of support coming from France's liberal public, "whose will is respected because its revolutions are feared." There were rumors that Garibaldi might raise the republican banner in Italy and that this would set off similar movements in Paris. France's history showed "what one day's excitement may do in the atmosphere of this inflammable and inconstant city," Malakoff noted. Coincidentally, rumors of a plot by Italian revolutionaries to assassinate Napoleon III led to widespread arrests in Paris that October. The Garibaldi imbroglio also caused a crisis in Napoleon III's cabinet. In order to appease Catholics and Empress Eugénie, he replaced Thouvenel with Édouard Drouyn de Lhuys, a veteran of the Quai d'Orsay and a conservative Catholic who believed fervently in the absolute power of the pope as pontiff of Rome. For now, France would continue to stand by the pope.[66]

CONFEDERATE HOPES, MEANWHILE, PLUMMETED AFTER ASPROMONTE. From Paris Edwin De Leon wrote to Benjamin, despairing that "the tide which was setting in so strongly toward our recognition . . . was turned by the frantic folly of Garibaldi in Italy." Slidell also lamented that Napoleon III "could do nothing until Garibaldi is disposed of" and that with the change of foreign ministers in France, it was clear "for the time our question has been lost sight of." Though Drouyn du Lhuys was far more conservative than Thouvenel on the Roman question, he proved even more determined than his predecessor to keep France neutral on the American question. He was dubious about the Mexican venture and not about to expose France to the risk of another war across the Atlantic.[67]

In October 1862 Judah P. Benjamin was dismayed to learn that the French were making overtures to Governor Francis Lubbock of Texas by way of encouraging his state to break away from the Confederacy.

It appeared that the French wanted a buffer to protect them from their Confederate buffer. The French backed away from Texas, but it reminded Benjamin and Slidell that the French could as easily become rivals as allies and that there were many levels to this game of secession and international intrigue.[68]

In London Palmerston and Russell were also backing away from intervention. Charles Francis Adams met with Russell in early September after news of Aspromonte arrived, and, in a rare moment of levity, Russell made a joke that Adams must feel relieved to learn that Garibaldi and his band had thwarted "any idea of joint action of the European powers in our affairs." Adams returned the favor by saying, "I was in hopes that they all had quite too much to occupy their minds" without looking for trouble on the other side of the Atlantic.[69]

Palmerston's plans for multilateral intervention had foundered. The Garibaldi crisis distracted the French government, and Russia, nursing its lingering enmity toward France and Britain following the Crimean War, kept aloof. Czar Alexander II regarded the Americans as Russia's friends, and some said that Lincoln's election inspired him to change his country's despotic image and emancipate Russia's serfs. He had no intention of moving backward by recognizing a nation whose cornerstone was slavery.[70]

The commotion in Paris, the eerie silence from St. Petersburg, the news of Confederate retreat from Maryland, and the Garibaldi riots in England left Palmerston with the terrifying thought that Britain might face an American army and navy more powerful than ever—alone and with doubtful popular support. By late September Adams wrote Seward with great relief that, for the moment at least, the Garibaldi affair seemed to have eclipsed interest in American intervention.[71]

But Adams spoke too soon. The British lion was about to roar through the ungoverned throat of Chancellor of the Exchequer William Gladstone, eager aspirant to power as Palmerston's successor. During a speaking tour that brought him to Newcastle in northern England, Gladstone decided to test public reactions to the idea of intervention in the American war. Early in the speech Gladstone bemoaned the misery America's war had visited on England's workers and then predicted that "the success of the Southern States" was inevitable. "Hear, hear!" the crowd cheered.

It was October 7, and news of Lincoln's Emancipation Proclamation had already broken in the British press. Gladstone knew this, but he chose to cast doubt upon the sincerity of Lincoln's proclamation, and proposed that an independent South would free its slaves more swiftly and with more benign effect than a decree issued by the North. Just as Seward might have predicted, Gladstone went on to say that Lincoln's emancipation edict would bring unimaginable racial strife to the South.

The time might come, Gladstone said, when it would become the "duty of Europe" to offer its "friendly aid in composing the quarrel." "We know quite well that the people of the Northern States have not yet drunk of the cup—they are still trying to hold it far from their lips—the cup which all the rest of the world see they nevertheless must drink of." Then Gladstone offered the lines that quickly reverberated around the world: "We may have our own opinions about slavery; we may be for or against the South; but there is no doubt that Jefferson Davis and other leaders of the South have made an army; they are making, it appears, a navy; and they have made what is more than either—they have made a nation."[72]

The press, unaware that Palmerston was losing interest in intervention, took Gladstone's speech as a signal that Britain was about to move toward recognition of the South. London financial markets experienced violent turbulence at the prospect of war. *New York Times* correspondent Monadnock also thought it was Palmerston's scheme: "The whole game is prepared, and the first move was the speech of Mr. Gladstone at Newcastle. It is the beginning of the end." Charles Adams, who a few days earlier had thought Garibaldi had derailed the intervention threat, told his diary on October 9, "We are now passing through the very crisis of our fate."[73]

Some thought Gladstone was trying to force the decision on Palmerston and the cabinet by demonstrating public support for intervention. He may also have been trying to bring glory to his own career as sponsor of a humanitarian solution to America's "terrible war." If so, the plan backfired very badly. Palmerston resented his younger rival's overreaching and quickly distanced himself from the speech. If he still harbored any thoughts about the wisdom of intervention, the press reaction gave no encouragement. Even pro-South organs such as the London *Times* and *Saturday Review,* condemned Gladstone for putting British neutrality at risk. Friends of the Union lambasted him for hailing a nation "made" to preserve slavery and took pains to point out that it was not Jefferson Davis "making" the Confederate navy so much as the British, who had recently allowed the *Alabama* to be built and launched in violation of its own professed neutrality.[74]

Gladstone's Newcastle speech was another supreme example of a politician's gaffe: stating honestly what he was not supposed to say in public. Gladstone's defenders insisted that he had been misunderstood and that he had no intention of speaking for the government. Little of this was true. Gladstone's own diary entries made it clear that his Newcastle remarks, far from being a "hasty impromptu utterance," had been "long and well considered" and expressed exactly what Palmerston, Russell, and Gladstone himself had been scheming out of public view. If the speech was a trial balloon to test public opinion, the air went out of it very rapidly. The British people did not want to wage war in support of slavery.[75]

Inside Palmerston's cabinet there was also rising opposition to taking sides with the South. On October 14 George Cornewall Lewis, the secretary of war, made a public speech against intervention and three days later circulated a lengthy, forcefully argued position paper against intervention in the American war. Palmerston was distressed by the negative reaction to Gladstone's Newcastle peroration, and he realized that, despite all the denunciations of the emancipation decree in the press, Lincoln had now declared war against slavery, and any policy favoring an independent South would be seen as an effort to rescue slavery from its doom.[76]

Looming over all of these concerns was John Bright and the Radicals' call for the democratization of Britain. The Garibaldi riots in Hyde Park and Birkenhead, similar demonstrations in Italy and elsewhere, and the rumors of revolutionary unrest on the Continent must have been much on Palmerston's mind when he wrote to Russell at the end of October, complaining of the "Scum of the Community" rising to the surface. But Palmerston was also chastened by recent events and gave clear signs of appeasement. Lady Palmerston made a public show of sending a special bed to Garibaldi and she made entreaties to Charles Francis Adams and his wife to attend parties at the Palmerston home again. Meanwhile, Prime Minister Palmerston was quietly retreating from anything that looked like intervention on behalf of the slave South.[77]

Inside the British and French governments, quiet discussions of the American question continued into the fall and winter of 1862–1863. France's new foreign minister, Édouard Drouyn de Lhuys, assumed the lead in efforts to bring an end to the American war, first with another attempt at joint intervention and then with a unilateral offer of mediation. Lincoln's Emancipation Proclamation had done nothing to discourage the Great Powers from privately wishing to bring the war to an end or from hoping for the ultimate success of the South. But with public opinion apparently turning against intervention, none had the spine to try using a rejected offer of mediation as an excuse to recognize the South.[78]

In January 1863 an uprising in Poland against Russian rule suddenly brought new strains to relations among the Great Powers, which further discouraged meddling in American affairs. Most European government leaders still expected the Union to exhaust itself, financially if not militarily, and they began placing their hopes for an end to war on the rise of the antiwar movement in the northern United States. In 1864 Democrats, deeply divided over the war and emancipation, nominated General George McClellan to challenge Abraham Lincoln for the presidency, taking as their motto "The Union as it was." The Peace Democrats within the party wanted to nullify the Emancipation Proclamation, end the war, and restore the Union with slaveholders. Though McClellan did not agree with them on all points, the election of November 1864 became a plebiscite on war or peace, Union or secession, freedom or slavery.

MEANWHILE, THEODORE CANISIUS WAS STRANDED IN VIENNA WITH a wife and young children and, at thirty-six years old, without a job or funds to get home. Far from remorseful over his diplomatic venture, Canisius felt fully vindicated by all the "commotion" he had caused and was indignant at being fired. He wrote an unapologetic defense of his actions to Seward, making the point that hundreds of military officers from all nations had enlisted in the Union army, and Garibaldi, not least among them, had been officially invited by Seward the year before.

More than seeking Garibaldi's military aid, Canisius explained, he was enlisting his moral support. "I thought the time had come to let the world know what the great Hero of the Castle of Varignano thinks of us and our cause." Referring to the "great Garibaldi demonstrations in England"

and Garibaldi's letter "To the English Nation," Canisius argued that his endorsement had greatly "strengthened our cause throughout Europe." "I was anxious to affect this at the time when almost everybody seemed to turn against us."

Canisius had a point, and Seward had to realize the great service his impulsive consul in Vienna had performed. The Italian government, eager to calm the waters, encouraged Seward to forgive Canisius's breach of diplomatic protocol. No doubt Lincoln, who followed the Garibaldi affair with great interest, agreed, and Seward reinstated Dr. Canisius in December 1862.[79]

Just as Canisius predicted, in Turin that autumn Marsh was besieged by volunteers, many of them veterans of Aspromonte, wishing to fight for the Union. One public letter from a Garibaldian colonel volunteered "four to six thousand men, commanded by two hundred good officers, and all of them veterans." A *New York Times* editorial welcomed "Garibaldi's Braves" to join Liberty's war in America. "Dynastic and aristocratic Europe has chosen to bestow its sympathies upon the South" and make it a "war in favor of a privileged class; a war upon the working classes; a war against popular majorities; a war to establish in the New World the very principles which underlie every throne of Europe." What they despised, the *Times* said, was "the spectacle of successful democratic institutions, which this country, until two years ago, happily presented," and they supported the Southern oligarchy "to prove, if possible, the democratic experiment a failure."[80]

In late October 1862 Marsh wrote to Garibaldi, still expressing hope that America would "have the aid both of your strong arm and of your immense moral power in the maintenance of our most righteous cause." But the wounded hero would return to his home on Caprera to convalesce, and would never again walk without aid of crutches or cane.[81]

It would be another year before America heard from Garibaldi again. In August 1863 he sent a public letter on behalf of the Italian liberals congratulating Lincoln as the world's "pilot of liberty." Comparing him to no less than Jesus Christ and John Brown, the letter hailed Lincoln as the great emancipator. "An entire race of men, bowed by selfish egotism under the yoke of Slavery, is, at the price of the noblest blood of America, restored by you to the dignity of man, to civilization and to love." While

America "astonishes the world by her gigantic daring," old Europe "finds neither mind nor heart to equal her's."[82]

America would no longer have need of Garibaldi's "strong arm," as George Marsh put it, but in that perilous autumn of 1862, his "immense moral power" had played a crucial role in the war now being fought for Union *and* Liberty.

CHAPTER 10

UNION AND LIBERTY

Privilege thinks it has a great interest in this contest, and every
morning, with blatant voice, it comes into your streets and
curses the American Republic. Privilege has beheld . . . thirty
millions of men, happy and prosperous, without emperor,
without king, without the surroundings of a court, without
nobles, except such as are made by eminence in intellect and
virtue, without State bishops and State priests.

—JOHN BRIGHT, BRITISH REFORMER, MARCH 26, 1863

ONE HUNDRED DAYS PASSED BETWEEN THE FIRST ANNOUNCEMENT
of Lincoln's Emancipation Proclamation and its implementation
on January 1, 1863. During this interim, debate on the American question took place inside government cabinets and parliaments and in the
press, cafés, taverns, and union halls across Europe. Initial overseas reactions to Lincoln's proclamation were often cynical and, predictably,
reflected class and political biases. "There they are," Thomas Carlyle, a
favorite among conservatives, remarked at a posh London dinner party,
"cutting each other's throats because one half of them prefer hiring their
servants for life, and the other by the hour." Carlyle's sarcastic comment
conceded more than he realized, for the once murky distinctions between
the North and South on the slavery question were about to become emphatically clear in the public mind by the end of 1862.[1]

The first reactions in the foreign press confirmed Seward's very worst expectations. The conservative journals were filled with shrieks of alarm over impending servile insurrection and race war, and even liberal newspapers engaged in scurrilous ridicule of Lincoln's moral pretensions. In early October 1862 Monadnock reported to *New York Times* readers from London that the proclamation "has satisfied nobody." Critics vilified Lincoln, saying that, unable to beat the South in war, he now "invokes the aid of the savage negroes, and wishes to excite an insurrection, like that of St. Domingo," another vivid reference to Haiti's violent revolution in the 1790s. Just as Seward anticipated, the press even invoked comparisons between Lincoln and Nana Sahib, the murderous leader of India's Sepoy Rebellion against the British in 1857. "It is a great mistake," Monadnock concluded, "to suppose England wishes immediate or violent emancipation."[2]

To no one's surprise, the London *Times* mocked the president's moral posturing, focusing on the preservation of slavery in nonrebel territory: "Where he has no power Mr. Lincoln will set the negroes free; where he retains power he will consider them as slaves." The *Times* warned of the "massacres and utter destruction" certain to attend the coming "servile insurrection" of blacks. Lincoln, it prophesied with lurid imagery, "will appeal to the black blood of the African; he will whisper of the pleasures of spoil and of the gratification of yet fiercer instincts; and when blood begins to flow and shrieks come piercing through the darkness . . . he will rub his hands and think that revenge is sweet."[3]

A month after news of the proclamation arrived, Henry Hotze, the Confederate publicist in London, remained smugly satisfied that the proclamation had utterly failed to do anything but expose the Union's venal hypocrisy. The Federal decree, he assured Secretary of State Judah P. Benjamin, "has been received by the English press in a manner which leaves nothing to desire." Most have understood it as a disingenuous bid for European sympathy that has not "the slightest merit of sincerity." James Mason, the Confederate envoy in London, concurred, reporting in early November that Lincoln's ploy had badly disappointed "the antislavery party here and met with general contempt and derision."[4]

It was true that among the British antislavery movement especially, some were openly disappointed and puzzled by Lincoln's limited and legalistic emancipation edict. "The principle is not that a human being cannot justly own another," the liberal London *Spectator* noted, "but that he cannot own him unless he is loyal to the United States." To prevent disunion, the liberal champion Richard Cobden charged, the North would "half ruin itself in the process of wholly ruining the South" and achieve victory by enlisting slaves in "one of the most bloody and horrible episodes in history." These were the views of the Union's *friends*.[5]

Karl Marx was among the few to appreciate the ingenious lack of "idealistic impetus" in Lincoln's proclamation. "He gives his most important actions always the most commonplace form." Others claim to be "fighting for an idea," when it is really about "square feet of land." Lincoln, in contrast, "sings the bravura aria of his part hesitatively, reluctantly and unwillingly, as though apologising for being compelled by circumstances to 'to act the lion.'" Even his most impressive proclamations appear intended to look like "routine summonses sent by a lawyer to the lawyer of the opposing party, legal chicaneries." What Marx saw in Lincoln's September emancipation decree was "the most important document in American history since the establishment of the Union." It was an achievement that would place this "plebian . . . average person of good will" next to Washington in the history of mankind.[6]

In Paris news of the emancipation decree met with less criticism and with welcome relief, at least among republicans and liberals. Malakoff reported that just before the news arrived, in early October 1862, Confederate agents and supporters had gathered with John Slidell to hail the long-awaited diplomatic triumph of the South. Rumors had been flashing through the European press that Confederate forces had seized Washington, Lincoln was gravely ill, Lee had advanced north across the Potomac again, and New York City was proclaiming secession. These false reports, which Malakoff suspected of being ginned up by Confederate agents in England, took hold with remarkable speed in this "small and inflammable community, ready to grasp at and magnify every shadow of a hope for their side." Even after news of the Emancipation Proclamation arrived, some Confederate stalwarts were willing to believe that it would guarantee victory of the opposition peace party in the November 1862 congressional elections.[7]

The French press, according to the reliably astute assessment of Malakoff, divided along predictable ideological grounds. Conservative imperialist journals denounced the "bloody butchery" that sudden emancipation portended, taking their cue from the London *Times*. But the liberal press in France saw it as a major breakthrough. *Opinion Nationale,* a leading republican journal, predicted that Lincoln "has now put himself upon the platform which will secure him the sympathies of all the Liberals of Europe, and render intervention an impossibility." *Siècle,* the largest republican journal, applauded the president for "entering at last into the heart of the question" by announcing the end of slavery. The "liberal Press and public unanimously approve of the Proclamation," and the idea of French intervention in the war found no popular support in Paris, Malakoff reported. Liberal journalists across France now enjoyed "an immense advantage" and were "making good use" of it, he added. Henry Sanford, who was visiting Paris when news of the emancipation policy broke in October, also felt certain that Lincoln had secured the sympathies of European liberals. It "gives now a basis for our friends here to work upon and to appeal to the sympathies of civilized Europe." It was exactly what friends of the Union had been waiting for: a cause they could fully embrace and promote without apology.[8]

IF MUCH OF THE INITIAL PRESS REACTION WAS AS CYNICAL AND alarmist as Seward predicted, he had himself largely to blame. For the past year, by way of excusing Union inaction against slavery, he had been instructing his emissaries to warn of the racial strife and economic havoc that emancipation would bring.[9]

But once the emancipation policy was in place, Seward skillfully played it to full advantage. Whatever doubts foreigners had about Union motives, Seward told his envoys to remind Europeans that Lincoln's proclamation made intervention tantamount to rescuing American slavery from its doom. Seward advised William Dayton to taunt the French foreign minister by asking, "Are the enlightened and humane nations Great Britain and France to throw their protection over the insurgents now?" "Will they interfere to strike down the arm that so reluctantly but so effectually is raised at last to break the fetters of the slave, and seek to rivet anew the chains which he has sundered?" "Is this to be the climax of the world's progress in the nineteenth century?" He gave similar instructions to Charles Francis Adams in London, noting that "the interests of humanity have now become identified with the cause of our country," and it was the rebel Southerners who brought emancipation upon themselves.[10]

By January 1863 the cynical criticism of Lincoln's proclamation seemed to be softening, in part because the extravagant predictions of bloody slave uprisings and racial mayhem began to collapse from sheer lack of evidence. If Seward had been correct in anticipating Europe's worst reactions, Carl Schurz's prophecy that liberal Europe would embrace the Union's cause was about to be validated as the new year opened.

It helped that Jefferson Davis issued one of his most draconian decrees in late December 1862 when he raised the black flag of war to the death. Davis singled out General Benjamin Butler, infamous in the South for encouraging runaway slaves and his harsh treatment of civilians in New Orleans, as "an outlaw and common enemy of mankind." Beast Butler and all commissioned officers serving him were to be executed by hanging immediately upon capture. What shocked the world far more was Davis's decree that "all Negro slaves captured in arms," and all white officers leading "armed slaves in insurrection," would be handed over to the states for execution. Davis's edict suddenly cast the South, not the North, as the instigator of race war.[11]

In mid-January 1863 the news reached Europe of Lincoln's signing the Emancipation Proclamation into law. From Paris Malakoff told *New York Times* readers that the president's order "has given an immense advantage to the liberal writers." Despite some moderation in government censorship, in France public political meetings and demonstrations were still suppressed, and the press strictly monitored, but in the spring of 1863 the liberal opposition found bold new ways to register its support of the Union and Liberty, the popular new slogan of the North. In March nearly seven hundred French Protestant ministers issued a widely published petition addressed to British clergy in which they boldly denounced the Confederacy. "No more revolting spectacle has ever been set before the civilized world than a confederacy, consisting mainly of Protestants, forming . . . a confederacy which lays down as the corner-stone of its constitution the system of slavery." The French ministers called upon their fellow Protestants in Britain to raise their voices in prayer that soon the "coloured man" in America will be "free and equal with the whites."[12]

In Britain where freedom of speech and assembly was protected, hundreds of public meetings were called by emancipation societies, women's antislavery groups, Radicals, workers, Quakers, and other religious dissenters. Some expressed impatience with the press for not fully covering the popular antipathy in Britain toward the South and slavery, and they began using public meetings as newsworthy devices for getting their message out. What the press did not report, the groups themselves publicized by disseminating pamphlets filled with speeches and resolutions. "Opinion here has changed greatly," pro-Union spokesman John Bright wrote an American friend. "In almost every town great meetings are being held to pass resolutions in favor of the north, and the advocates of the South are pretty much put down."[13]

Lincoln involved himself in public diplomacy by issuing a reply to a meeting that took place in Manchester, England. He thanked the "Workingmen of Manchester" for their heroic support, despite the "sufferings" the war had brought to them, and he neatly framed the common cause they supported. "It has been often and studiously represented that the attempt to overthrow this government, which was built upon the foundation of human rights, and to substitute for it one which should rest exclusively on the basis of human slavery, was likely to obtain the favor of Europe," he wrote. Then Lincoln commended their "sublime Christian heroism" as, "indeed, an energetic and reinspiring assurance of the inherent power of truth and of the ultimate and universal triumph of justice, humanity, and freedom." Adams saw to it that Lincoln's reply was ceremoniously hand-delivered to the mayor of Manchester. The letter appeared in British newspapers the next day and quickly made its way into the international press.[14]

Lincoln also sent to Bright a draft resolution, ready for endorsement by public meetings, that neatly summarized the Union cause. "Whereas, . . . for the first time in the world, an attempt has been made to construct a new Nation, upon the basis of, and with the primary, and fundamental object to maintain, enlarge, and perpetuate human slavery, therefore, Resolved: that no such embryo State should ever be recognized by, or admitted into, the family of Christian and civilized nations; and that all Christian and civilized men everywhere should, by all lawful means, resist to the utmost, such recognition or admission."[15]

In London the circumspect Charles Francis Adams found himself pushed into the limelight of public diplomacy that he had always instinctively shunned until now. On January 16, 1863, a deputation from the newly formed London Emancipation Society visited him at the legation to issue resolutions of support for the Union and emancipation. Adams found himself called upon to make some remarks. He was very encouraged, he told them, to see "growing here and in Europe generally, a better conception than has heretofore prevailed of the principles involved in the struggle." "I had not anticipated the probability of being called to say any thing," he recorded in his diary late that night, "but as it opened a chance for perhaps putting in a seasonable word, I made use of it at once. May the words so hastily summoned be productive of fair fruit!" The society had its resolutions embossed on velum, and Adams forwarded them to the president; meanwhile, they were published in newspapers everywhere. Fair fruit indeed.[16]

The London Emancipation Society organized a branch in Manchester to mobilize workers across the north of England. Together they sponsored publication of no fewer than four hundred thousand copies of books and pamphlets and sent scores of speakers, many of them university professors and prominent politicians, to meeting halls across the country to summon British men and women to stand by their American brethren. More important, they denounced those in the British press for their "systematic perversion of facts."

Emancipation Society speakers also assailed the government for its brazen violation of British neutrality by permitting the construction of warships for the slaveholding republic of the South. In January 1863 intercepted diplomatic correspondence from Richmond brought to light negotiations between British shipbuilders and Confederate agent George Sanders for the construction of six ironclad warships. Behind its pose of neutrality, it seemed evident, Palmerston's government was secretly in collaboration with the Confederacy. Above all, the speakers and resolutions angrily vilified the Southern rebellion and cast it as the enemy of the freedom-loving British. "The so-called 'southern chivalry' is waging war against a free, popular government, with the intention, unblushingly proclaimed, of forming a new confederation, whose chief corner-stone shall be the execrable system of human bondage."[17]

In early 1863 the air was filled with news of hundreds of emancipation meetings in all parts of Britain. "Just now I am getting the resolutions of very many public meetings in response to the President's proclamation," Adams told his diary in mid-January. "It is quite clear that the current is now setting pretty strongly with us among the body of the people." Now was the time "to strike the popular heart here," he told himself, and "to checkmate the movement of the aristocracy." The legation in London was flooded with notices and invitations that winter and spring, and its bookshelves fairly groaned with copies of the published speeches and resolutions from all parts of Britain and many from the Continent, along with private letters from individuals expressing solidarity with the Union and Liberty. Adams was inundated with requests to speak at or attend meetings, but he hastened to assure Seward, "I have taken no part whatever in promoting these movements, having become well convinced that the smallest suspicion of my agency would do more harm than good."[18]

What amazed Adams were the spontaneous displays of support coming from the common people and from the pulpits of dissenting religious leaders. The Reverend Charles Spurgeon, an immensely popular Baptist minister, was in the throes of a sermon before thousands of parishioners at his Metropolitan Tabernacle in South London when he suddenly raised a spontaneous prayer for America. "Now, oh! God, we turn our thoughts across the sea to the dreadful conflict of which we knew not what to say, but now the voice of freedom shows where is right. . . . *God bless and strengthen the north!* . . . Now that we know their cause, we can but exclaim God speed them." The most remarkable thing, Adams delighted in telling Seward, was that the audience responded to this with a robust "Amen."[19]

Seward replied in early March 1863 by assuring Adams that President Lincoln was moved by the expressions of support from the working people of Britain. And without any hint of repentance for his earlier doubts, he added that the "moral opinion of mankind, now happily awakened to the real nature and character of the contest," would stand by the United States.[20]

Whatever reticence liberal England had demonstrated before, a contagious enthusiasm for the Union and Liberty swept across the British Isles in the spring of 1863. John Bright had earlier been tepid in his support of Lincoln's proclamation, fearing that sudden emancipation would bring catastrophe and that the "remedy for slavery would be almost worse than the disease." But all that changed by early February 1863 when he stood before his fellow townspeople in Rochdale to give a rousing speech linking the Union to the universal cause of human freedom. The American contest was for more than the emancipation of the South's slaves, or even those of Cuba and Brazil, he told the cheering crowd. The "question of freedom to men of all races is deeply involved in this great strife in the United States." Then he quoted from the *Richmond Examiner,* which had announced, "The experiment of universal liberty has failed. The evils of free society are insufferable," and "therefore free society must fall and give way to a slave society." "Shame!" the crowd thundered. These slave owners, buyers, and slave breeders, Bright reminded them, had sent envoys to their country, where "they are met with at elegant tables in London, and are in fast friendship with some of your public men . . . and are here to ask Englishmen—Englishmen with a history for freedom—to join hands with their atrocious conspiracy."[21]

Bright, of course, was cleverly coupling the Union cause to his own crusade for democracy in Britain. He saved his most lacerating attack on the British aristocracy for the huge meeting of Trade Unions of London that gathered at St. James Hall on March 26. Karl Marx helped organize the meeting, and he might have taken pleasure in hearing Bright's assault on the privileged class that each morning "curses the American republic" because they saw in it "thirty millions of men, happy and prosperous, without emperor, without king, without the surroundings of a court, without nobles, except such as are made by eminence in intellect and virtue." "Do not," Bright admonished the workers before him, "give the hand of fellowship to the worst foes of freedom that the world has ever seen."[22]

Southern sympathizers in Britain did all they could to belittle what the conservative *Saturday Review* called the "carnival of cant" in celebration of emancipation. "All persons of social and political respectability have held aloof" from the emancipation meetings, Henry Hotze assured Benjamin. The London *Times* likewise dismissed the meetings as unimpressive crowds of middle- and working-class "nobodies." "They do not indeed belong to the high and noble class," Charles Francis Adams wrote to Seward, fairly steaming with indignation, "but they are just those nobodies who formerly forced their most exalted countrymen to denounce the prosecution of the Slave Trade . . . and who at a later period overcame all their resistance to the complete emancipation of the negro slaves in the British dependencies." If these "nobodies," Adams went on, "become once fully aroused to a sense of the importance of this struggle as a purely moral question," all sympathy in Great Britain for the rebellion would end.[23]

The hundreds of well-publicized demonstrations that rippled across Britain in early 1863 signaled a turn in public sympathy that neither the Palmerston government nor the Tory opposition could safely ignore. Nor could other conservative monarchies on the Continent fail to take notice of the depth and direction of public sentiment in opposition to the Confederacy. By early July 1863 Union military successes at Gettysburg and Vicksburg encouraged Union supporters to think the North might prevail militarily as well as morally. A conversation once dominated by upper-class rejoicings over the failure of the Great Republic, solemn pronouncements of its inevitable dismemberment, and predictions of democracy's failure was now encountering exuberant voices of hope among those in the middle and working classes who saw the Union's struggle as their own.[24]

MEANWHILE, CONFEDERATE SYMPATHIZERS WERE SLOW TO ADMIT the popular success of the Emancipation Proclamation abroad, in large part because they were sorely out of touch with the "nobodies," as the London *Times* characterized them, who were turning out for meetings and signing resolutions and petitions. In mid-January 1863 Henry Hotze was still pronouncing the Emancipation Proclamation a stupendous failure and gloating over the futility of Lincoln's appeal to European antislavery sentiment. "More than I could have accomplished has been done by Mr. Lincoln's emancipation proclamation," which appears only to have "awakened the fears of both Government and people."[25]

To Hotze's dismay, however, James Spence, the Confederacy's English champion, seemed willing to embrace emancipation as the proper cause of the South. In his book *The American Union,* Spence had intended to confound antislavery sentiment by turning it in favor of the South, instead of trying to correct its errors or deny its strength, as Hotze, De Leon, and others seemed intent on doing. The North's endemic greed and hypocrisy, Spence predicted, would weld the slaves' fetters anew and might even lead to the reopening of the African slave trade. When assailed by fanatical abolitionists from the North, he admitted, the South had resolutely defended slavery. But once the South was independent and standing foursquare before the court of world opinion, Spence promised, "emancipation would come gently as an act of conscience."[26]

In the fall of 1862 Spence began airing these same views at public meetings and in the press in an effort to deflate British enthusiasm for Lincoln's emancipation policy. This was hardly the kind of help the Confederacy welcomed at this moment. Henry Hotze, who had earlier gushed about Spence's genius, began complaining to Judah P. Benjamin in October 1862 that their former champion "has of late rendered the idea of ultimate emancipation unduly conspicuous." This was no time to apologize for slavery, Hotze admonished. The public mind did not "expect any promises of this kind from us," and it undermined the entire defense of slavery to accept the premise that it was evil and would end soon. Spence seemed to be bragging that "his moral influence with the Southern people" would persuade them to accept a plan for emancipation. Though he may have been sincere in his "friendship . . . and devotion to our cause," Hotze warned Benjamin, "I almost dread the direction his friendship and devotion seem about to take."[27]

Spence's problems with the Confederacy went beyond what Hotze referred to as his "philanthropic convictions" about slavery. In fall 1862, as a reward for his assiduous promotion of the Southern cause, and at the recommendation of Hotze and Mason, Spence had been appointed financial agent for the Confederacy in Europe. This sinecure ought to have put Spence in line for handsome remuneration. The Confederacy had devised a plan to finance a substantial loan that would be backed by the sale of Confederate cotton bonds, certificates redeemable in cotton at steeply discounted prices, once the war was over or the blockade was broken. The Confederate cotton bonds promised lucrative rewards to European investors, and thus linked their fortunes to those of the Confederacy.[28]

Spence came to his new assignment full of high expectations, but these were soon deflated by news that John Slidell had already arranged for the sale of 3 million British pounds sterling worth of cotton bonds with Paris financier Baron Frédéric Emile d'Erlanger, scion of one of the most powerful banking houses on the Continent. Slidell had persuaded Richmond that Erlanger's prestige in Europe would prove an invaluable political asset to the Confederate cause. Spence thought the terms of the deal favored no one except Erlanger, who profited by generous commissions and discounts. It did nothing to relieve Spence's suspicions when he learned through the press, in January 1863, that Slidell's daughter had become romantically involved with Emile d'Erlanger and that agents of the financier were in Rome imploring the pope to annul the marriage to his first wife so he could wed Mademoiselle Slidell.[29]

Furthermore, in January 1863 several intercepted Confederate dispatches were published in the Northern press, revealing, among other things, that Spence was on the Confederate payroll. His previous pose as the disinterested champion of the Southern cause was ruined. At the same time, his deviant views on slavery and emancipation became the subject of ridicule in the pro-Union press abroad. Confederate officials could neither disown him nor defend him without damaging their cause.[30]

Meanwhile, Spence's heresy on emancipation was not playing well back in Richmond. At Hotze's suggestion, a Confederate edition of *American Union* was published in early 1863 with an unsigned preface that did its best to explain the author's unorthodox views on slavery. The *Richmond Enquirer* applauded Spence's understanding of the South's constitutional rights but regretted the "bigotry" evident in the "slime of that British philanthropy" which was "the source of all our woes." "Here we are paying a man for abusing us as a nation of criminals steeped in moral evil!" the same newspaper bellowed in May 1863. Are we unsure that our "institutions and principles" are "sound and rightful" "until Europe has passed on them?"

Spence continued undeterred in his efforts to reconcile the Southern cause with British antislavery sentiment, and in late 1863 he published a pamphlet in which he proudly proclaimed himself an earnest opponent of slavery. Hotze was thoroughly embarrassed by Spence's "unnecessarily large concessions to the antislavery prejudice," and he found it "exceedingly gratifying" when Benjamin finally fired Spence as Confederate financial agent in early 1864. As Benjamin baldly explained it to Spence, no government could justify itself in selecting agents "who entertain sentiments decidedly adverse to an institution which both the government and the people maintain as essential to their well-being."[31]

THE HOPES OF SOUTHERN SYMPATHIZERS FOR RECOGNITION HAD not died in Britain, however. In early June 1863 Hotze reported that he was busying himself putting up placards all over London with an image of the Confederacy's recently adopted second national flag "conjoined to the British national ensign." He clutched at every signal of popular support among the English, including a subscription drive to memorialize the fallen general "Stonewall" Jackson, which a group of eminent English supporters was promoting. The "death of no foreigner has ever so moved the popular heart," Hotze assured officials in Richmond. The organization of various "Southern Clubs" in the manufacturing districts also led him to predict that "a people's movement and a people's champion in favor of recognition" were taking form. The clubs, in truth, seemed to consist of little more than factory owners and merchants distributing handbills and placards among intimidated workers.[32]

At the end of June 1863, with news of Robert E. Lee's army marching northward into Pennsylvania, MP John Arthur Roebuck, a gadfly backbencher, thought the moment for recognition of the South had at last arrived. Roebuck, together with MP William Lindsay, a stalwart of the Southern lobby, hatched a plan to bring the question before Parliament. Earlier that month Roebuck and Lindsay had paid a personal visit to Napoleon III in Paris, who apparently gave them assurances that he would recognize the South if England stood with him. As French forces entered Mexico City to realize the emperor's Grand Design, Napoleon III was flirting again with taking a bold initiative to recognize the South. Slidell met with him on June 18 and could tell that inside Napoleon III's vacillating mind, the risk of US intervention in Mexico was being weighed against the advantage of Confederate alliance.[33]

On June 30 Roebuck stood before Parliament to deliver a lengthy speech that defended Southern slavery, blamed its introduction on the British, decried the prejudice and hypocrisy of the North, and boldly proclaimed Napoleon III's commitment to recognize the Confederacy. The whole speech met with rude shouts of derision and humiliating outbursts of laughter. John Bright rose from his seat to rebut, and before he sat down he had eviscerated Roebuck and embarrassed the entire Southern lobby. Henry Adams watched with glee from the gallery. As he later described it, John Bright, "with astonishing force, caught and shook and tossed Roebuck, as a big mastiff shakes a wiry, ill-conditioned, toothless, bad-tempered Yorkshire terrier." Even Henry Hotze admitted it was an absolute "farce" and reported to Richmond with unrelieved despair. "The whole armory of sarcasm, denunciation, and worst of all, of ridicule, has been exhausted upon their devoted heads," he lamented to Benjamin.[34]

Meanwhile, the Confederate's own envoy was receiving little more respect than Roebuck in London. Foreign Secretary Earl Russell had kept James Mason at bay for months, answering his pleas for interviews with a diplomatic coolness that Mason and Benjamin came to view as an affront to Southern honor. The howling ridicule of Roebuck's speech in Parliament, which echoed through the liberal press, pushed Benjamin over the edge.

In early August 1863 the exasperated secretary of state shut down the Confederacy's mission to Britain. He informed Mason that the "Government of her Majesty has determined to decline" our offer of "friendly relation." "Under these circumstances, your continued residence in London is neither conducive to the interests nor consistent with the dignity of this Government."

Then, after waiting for some weeks with no apology forthcoming from London, Benjamin dropped the other shoe: he expelled all British consuls residing at Southern cities. They had all been accredited solely by the US government, since Britain refused to recognize Confederate sovereignty, and they had continued at their Southern posts, acting as unofficial liaisons between Britain and the rebel government. But if Britain did not recognize the Confederacy, Benjamin reasoned, its agents had no business being there. King Cotton, having withdrawn from Her Majesty's court, now tossed her emissaries out of his realm.[35]

For nearly a year Confederate politicians in Richmond had been urging the recall of all Confederate envoys in Europe. Jefferson Davis complained that Southern commissioners "now waiting in servants' halls and on the back stairs" were being dishonored. In a widely published speech, William G. Swann of Tennessee also decried the humiliation of Southern envoys abroad. "If these foreign powers will not recognize our nationality, shall we recognize theirs?" "Our independence is to be of our own making and is to be in our keeping," Swann argued. "We have no friends in this world."

In April 1863 Swann had sponsored a joint resolution to recall Mason from Britain but narrowly failed to get the required two-thirds majority. That spring the Confederate Congress had refused to approve Davis's appointment of L. Q. C. Lamar as envoy to Russia. A "deep-seated feeling of irritation at what is considered to be unjust and unfair conduct of neutral powers toward this Confederacy prevails among our people,"

Benjamin explained to Lamar. From Paris Edwin De Leon urged the general recall of Confederate envoys, advising that the money to sustain their missions abroad would be better spent on weapons.

But Benjamin was not going that far. By September 1863 he was willing to show Britain he was fed up, but he had no intention of withdrawing from Paris. French consuls in the Confederacy were welcome to stay, and Benjamin instructed Slidell to make this preferential treatment crystal clear in Paris. France was now the Confederacy's last best hope.[36]

AFTER NEWS OF GETTYSBURG AND VICKSBURG ARRIVED IN JULY 1863, even Slidell was losing confidence in the Confederacy's Latin strategy. "The time has now arrived," he wrote Mason on July 17, 1863, "when it is of comparatively little importance what Queen or Emperor may say or think about us." The South might have to win its independence without help from Europe. "A plague, I say, on both your houses."[37]

Whatever the failings of his mission, Slidell was still enjoying the high life of Parisian society and his affiliation with the Erlanger financial fortune. He was well received at court and was as determined as ever in his efforts to curry favor with Napoleon III. While vacationing at the emperor's seaside resort in Biarritz in September 1863, Slidell seemed to take cruel pleasure in gloating about his triumphs at court to Mason, who was now sulking in Paris. "My family and I have been twice to the receptions of the Empress," he wanted Mason to know. "She sympathises most warmly with our cause and so expresses herself without any reserve. I mention these facts because the Empress is supposed, I believe with truth, to exercise considerable influence in public affairs. . . . I forgot to mention that the Emperor at the second reception of the Empress was present—he came to me and shook hands and conversed very cordially for several minutes."[38]

Slidell was still shaking hands with royalty, but he was of little help to other Confederate envoys abroad. Indeed, the jealousy and discord that permeated the Confederate diplomatic corps had proven a crippling disadvantage. Slidell thought De Leon had done nothing to advance the cause despite his huge slush fund and vaunted press experience. It had not helped that Slidell discovered that during his Atlantic crossing, De Leon had opened sealed letters to Slidell inside the diplomatic pouch Benjamin had entrusted to him. Slidell kept his contact with De Leon to the very minimum and did not share intelligence from his mole, Pierre Cintrat, inside the Quai d'Orsay.

De Leon, in turn, denounced Slidell as an arrogant, self-indulgent, old fool who was living high in Paris and making lucrative alliances with the likes of Baron Erlanger while his country was bleeding to death at home. In an unctuous, self-serving letter to Jefferson Davis in November 1863, De Leon dealt several oblique blows against Slidell, Benjamin, and all those who had failed to appreciate his talents. "Military ability of the highest order our revolution has produced; but of diplomatic talent it has been most singularly barren." "The old men of the old regime," he went on to tell Davis, "like the Bourbon, seem 'to have learned nothing, and forgotten nothing.'" "I may seem to speak bitterly," he waded deeper, "but I see on this side so much pitiful self-seeking and worthless greed in the swarm of speculators and blockade breakers and swaggering shufflers from danger, who call themselves Confederates."[39]

De Leon's resentment was compounded by his own frustrations with the French, and he saved his harshest words for them. The French, he groused to Jefferson Davis, "are a far more mercenary race than the English, and we must buy golden opinions from them if at all." All France wanted was money, he sniffed indignantly. This from an agent who had showered huge sums of money on French journalists and publishers and bragged about the success of his bought opinions.[40]

It was most unfortunate for De Leon's diplomatic career that several of his candid letters were intercepted by the Union navy. In November 1863 they appeared in the *New York Times* and the *Daily Tribune*. The Northern press, naturally, had a field day ridiculing De Leon and celebrating the failings of the rebel mission abroad. Benjamin seized the opportunity to rid himself of this meddlesome, self-aggrandizing rival for the president's confidence. He wrote to De Leon in early December 1863, expressing his "painful surprise" upon reading the letters, and summarily fired him.[41]

De Leon, for his part, was marvelously indignant in his reply. "I cheerfully accept the withdrawal of a commission I have never exhibited, of a title I have never used, and of a salary which I have never accepted." He was now free, he went on, to advance on his own the Southern cause, "to which the better part of my life has been devoted," adding pointedly that his devotion to the cause had commenced "some years before you took an active interest in the Southern Question."[42]

Slidell was thrilled to learn of De Leon's demise. He considered having Benjamin's dismissal letter published in Paris journals, supposedly to assuage French public opinion, but it was obviously to further disgrace De Leon. De Leon would stay on in Europe, operating on his own authority as an unaccredited agent and after the war published a self-serving account of his exploits to save the South from the foibles of the "old men of the old regime" that led it to defeat abroad.[43]

BY THE END OF 1863, WHATEVER PERILS LAY AHEAD IN THE DIPLOMATIC intrigues of the Great Powers, in the fortunes of arms, or in the political challenge Lincoln faced in the election of 1864, the North had successfully aligned the causes of Union and Liberty. It had also effectively polarized the American question in the public mind abroad into one of slavery against freedom and linked that, in turn, to the trial of democracy. Lincoln's agonizing decision to embrace emancipation would also force the South to reckon with its own dilemma over slavery.

CHAPTER 11

THE UNSPEAKABLE DILEMMA

If slaves will make good soldiers our whole theory of slavery is
wrong. . . . Better by far to yield to the demands of England
and France and abolish slavery, and thereby purchase their aid,
than to resort to this policy, which leads as certainly to ruin
and subjugation as it is adopted.

—HOWELL COBB, CONFEDERATE GENERAL, JANUARY 8, 1865

THE POPULAR APPEAL OF THE UNION'S EMANCIPATION POLICY
had become undeniable to all but the most obstinate Confederate
sympathizers abroad by the summer of 1863. It would not be until the
eleventh hour, more than two years after Lincoln's initial emancipation
decree, that Confederate leaders considered answering with their own
promise of emancipation. The main obstacle to their diplomatic success,
Confederates grudgingly admitted, was the stubborn prejudice abroad
that human slavery was morally reprehensible and their own admission
that slavery lay at the very cornerstone of the national edifice they were
trying to build. In the second half of 1863, Confederate leaders conceded
defeat in Britain and found growing opposition in France. They turned
to Rome to enlist Pope Pius IX and his Catholic flock in the cause of
peace and Southern independence, only to encounter the same reservations about slavery. Emancipation, the Confederacy's last desperate card,
was played in large part behind closed doors in Richmond, Paris, and

London beginning in late 1864 and with utmost secrecy. It was the unspeakable dilemma: in order to win independence, they would have to renounce the main reason they had sought independence in the first place.

In July 1863 news from Gettysburg and Vicksburg dealt powerful blows to an abiding confidence, both in the South and abroad, that if the Confederacy could not win on the battlefield, it could at least outlast the North. These crushing defeats were "so unexpected," Henry Hotze wrote from London, that a "general dismay" quickly spread across Britain not only among active sympathizers "but even among those who take merely a selfish interest in the great struggle."

The prices of Confederate bonds, which had been brought to market in March 1863 to finance the Erlanger loan, provide a telling barometer of confidence in Confederate fortunes. Though public sentiment seemed to be turning in favor of the Union and Liberty, hard-nosed investors in Europe were betting heavily on the success of the Confederacy. The Confederate bond sales were oversubscribed within days of their initial offering and continued into July selling near their opening price at about 90 percent of face value. News of Vicksburg and Gettysburg sent prices plummeting to 60 percent by mid-September and, after a brief recovery, down to 38 percent of face value by the end of 1863.[1]

That September the frustrated Confederate commissioner in London, James Mason, having finally received his instructions from Secretary of State Judah P. Benjamin, informed Earl Russell that he was withdrawing his mission from London. Henry Hotze carried on alone in London, publishing his *Index* and casting the most favorable light possible on the news from America. After Edwin De Leon, the self-styled ambassador to public opinion on the Continent, was sacked at the end of 1863, Benjamin instructed Hotze to expand operations to France, Italy, and Germany. Hotze accepted his new duties with his irrepressible confidence. Let "our armies and our currency hold out a little while longer," he wrote to Benjamin at the end of 1863, "and we shall enter the assemblage of nations without being asked to wash the robe of our nationality 'of a foul stain.'"[2]

The Confederacy's envoy to France, John Slidell, remained comfortably ensconced in the beau monde of Parisian society, and was, to all appearances, unperturbed by signs of the crumbling fortunes of the South in Europe. He gloated over the loan financed by his future son-in-law, Baron Frédéric Emile d'Erlanger, and pronounced the early success of the cotton

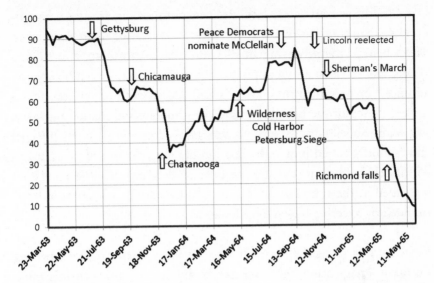

33. Confederate cotton bond prices. (DATA FROM MARC D. WEIDENMIER, "THE MAR-KET FOR CONFEDERATE COTTON BONDS," *EXPLORATIONS IN ECONOMIC HISTORY* 37 [JANUARY 2000])

bonds on European markets as tantamount to "financial recognition of our independence." Slidell allowed himself to be deluded that in the course of time, the North would eventually exhaust itself and the South would win its independence whatever sacrifice it endured in the meantime. When the French press began to shift its tone in favor of the Union, he convinced himself it was due to nothing more than bribes from Union agents.[3]

The change in the French mood was real, however. In the parliamentary elections of June 1863, the liberal opposition won stunning victories against the imperial party, and the embattled opposition known as Les Cinq (the Five) was now enlarged to eighty-four seats in the Corps législatif, all more or less opposed to Napoleon III's policies on Mexico, Rome, and perhaps America. The emperor had taken measured steps toward liberalization since 1860, but it seemed to arouse only bolder opposition. France, with its muzzled press and legislature, Malakoff told *New York Times* readers, is "ashamed to see all the nations around her enjoying more liberty than she does."[4]

Slidell seemed strangely unmindful of the tide of public sentiment and liberal political opposition setting against the South. On New Year's

Day 1864 he and his wife, Mathilde, were out strolling near the Champs-Élysées when a group of brash schoolboys, several of them Americans, fell in behind them, waving small Union flags, catcalling, and singing "Hang Jeff Davis to a sour apple tree." It had obviously been planned in advance, for they held up a crude sign: "Down with Slidell, the Slave-driver." Some of the boys brandished peashooters and blasted him with spit wads. Slidell wheeled around and grabbed one of them by the coat and "soundly cuffed him." The boy nimbly wriggled out of his coat and left Slidell holding it, cursing the boys as they ran off. The man once serenaded at the train station and toasted by Parisian society stood surrounded by a jeering crowd of onlookers.[5]

EVEN AS THE UNION'S EMANCIPATION POLICY GAINED FAVOR IN THE European imagination, the Confederacy did not seriously consider moderating its message or outflanking the enemy with its own promise of gradual emancipation, as James Spence and other foreign sympathizers were suggesting. Instead, Confederate foreign policy gravitated in the opposite direction, seeking to align the South with the conservative opposition to abolitionism, radical egalitarianism, and revolutionary republicanism. In 1863 Confederate diplomats began their shift to the right by going to the epicenter of reaction in Europe: the Vatican.

Pope Pius IX, or Pio Nono, as he was known to Italians, was monarch of the Papal States surrounding Rome and shepherd to millions of Catholic faithful in Europe, Latin America, and North America. Rome and the Papal States, however, stood besieged by the Italian Risorgimento against which Napoleon III's garrisoned French troops defended the pontiff's realm. Italians nationalists, not least Garibaldi and his followers, wanted nothing more than to drive out the French and make Rome the capital of a fully united Italy. Only the uncertain support of Napoleon III, bolstered by his devout wife, Eugénie, kept Garibaldi and Italy at bay. While the Union was courting Garibaldi and his Red Shirt republicans, the Confederacy sought to align its cause with their nemesis, Pio Nono, and his vast Catholic flock.

The pope had been duly alarmed by the enormous popular enthusiasm aroused by Garibaldi for his fateful march on Rome in 1862 and by the subsequent displays of adoration for the wounded hero. Catholic leaders in Europe and America had involved the church in the American conflict, whether they intended to or not. Following Archbishop John Hughes's tour of Europe in 1861–1862, Patrick Lynch, the Irish-born Catholic bishop of Charleston, South Carolina, and an ardent defender of the Confederacy and slavery, publicly berated Hughes for arousing support of the Union cause instead of counseling peace. In July 1862 Lynch made public a lengthy report he had sent to the pope detailing the many sufferings in his diocese due to the war. He successfully beseeched Pio Nono to call for peace in America.[6]

It was not uncommon for a pope or other religious leaders to appeal for peace among nations at war, but Pope Pius IX chose to counsel peace at a time when peace meant victory for secession. Moreover, the pope's call for peace conveniently coincided with the British and French plot to intervene in the autumn of 1862.[7]

In October 1862 Pio Nono began issuing public letters to Catholic leaders in America, calling for an end to the "destructive civil war." He sent letters to Archbishop John Hughes in New York and Archbishop John Mary Odin in New Orleans, deploring "the slaughter, ruin, destruction, devastation, and the other innumerable and ever-to-be deplored calamities" by which the "Christian people of the United States of America" are suffering by their "destructive civil war." The pope urged the archbishops to "apply all your study and exertion" with people and their rulers "to conciliate the minds of the combatants." He sent similar letters to Catholic bishops in Cincinnati and Chicago, and in these he alluded to alleged Union atrocities against Catholics and deprecated "the heavy afflictions brought upon us by the wicked designs and machinations of those men who wage an unholy war against the Catholic Church." In late November 1862, as British and French plans for intervention were faltering, the pope met with Richard Blatchford, the new US minister to Rome, and offered the Vatican's good offices for mediation.[8]

Slidell recognized a promising new opportunity. Early in 1863 he wrote to Benjamin to propose augmenting the South's Latin strategy, which aimed at building an alliance with France, by sending a mission to the Vatican. Slidell was intrigued by the report of his friend Charles S. Morehead, former governor of Kentucky, who was visiting American friends in Rome when he met with Cardinal Antonelli, the pope's shrewd consigliere on international affairs. Morehead came away with a strong impression that Antonelli favored the South and might be willing to bring the influence of the Catholic Church to bear on the peace movement in America.[9]

Benjamin found all of this to be "very interesting," and he wrote back to Slidell, instructing him to make the most of recent reports of sacrilegious acts by Union soldiers plundering and defiling Catholic churches in Louisiana. This is due, he suggested, to "the detestable Puritan spirit which . . . originated this savage war," an intolerance that is "just as hostile to the Catholic religion as the ultra abolitionists are to slaveholders." Benjamin saw a promising new vein of propaganda that could be effectively retailed to Catholics at the docks of Ireland and the recruiting stations and battlefields of America. But it would have more impact if the pope would lend his voice to the cause.[10]

In August 1863, with news of Union triumphs at Gettysburg and Vicksburg at hand, Pope Pius IX renewed his plea for peace. It came to light that Archbishop Hughes had done nothing to publicize the pope's October 1862 letter, and the Vatican decided this time it would go directly to the Catholic press by asking the *Tablet*, a newspaper sponsored by the Brooklyn diocese, to belatedly publish the pope's "lost" plea for peace. The pontiff's call for an end to America's war appeared in newspapers across the United States in August 1863.[11]

In Richmond Benjamin finally recognized in the pope's epistle for peace a timely pretext for the opening of relations with Rome. In September 1863 he instructed Ambrose Dudley Mann, the Confederate envoy stationed in Brussels, to go in person to Rome and deliver a letter from President Jefferson Davis, thanking the pope for his kind efforts in support of peace. Mann was eager and ready for this mission to Rome. For more than a year he had been pestering Benjamin to send him to Italy, where his son and personal secretary, W. Grayson Mann, had been sounding out what he felt certain were promising new diplomatic channels.[12]

Pius IX's reign would be remembered as a rebellion against everything modern. He was elected in 1846, ironically by liberal-minded cardinals who hoped he might help the church adapt to the new democratic spirit of the age. Those hopes were dashed after Mazzini's revolutionaries captured Rome, declared it a republic, and drove the pontiff into exile. That was when Louis-Napoleon sent French troops to Rome to restore the pope to his Vatican throne.

34. Pope Pius IX, with his court (Cardinal Antonelli, *third from right*). (COURTESY MARCO PIZZO, MUSEO CENTRALE DEL RISORGIMENTO, ROME)

From that point forward, Pio Nono became the archenemy of the Italian liberal state and everything to do with "the Revolution." His most shocking assault on liberal secular beliefs was the "Syllabus of Errors" of 1864, which listed no fewer than eighty heresies of the modern world that all Catholics must renounce, among them freedom of speech, press, and religion; separation of church and state; and the very idea that "the Roman Pontiff should reconcile himself to progress, liberalism, and modern civilization." Later, Pius IX's First Vatican Council would declare the pope to be infallible. Besieged by Garibaldi and the Risorgimento, protected only by Napoleon III's French forces, the pontiff of Rome summoned the faithful to repudiate the modern world.[13]

Mann and his son arrived at the Vatican in early November 1863, carrying with them the sealed letter of thanks from President Davis. Mann's intricately detailed report to Benjamin revealed an unctuous gratitude for even the smallest gesture of respect. Accustomed to meeting secretly in private homes as though he were an unwelcome supplicant, Mann was impressed by the diplomatic courtesy that Cardinal Antonelli and the pontiff accorded him. He drew Benjamin's attention to the "strikingly majestic" conduct of the Papal States "in its bearing toward me when contrasted with the sneaking subterfuges . . . of the governments of western Europe." Mann was pleased to report how he and his son, Grayson, who acted as translator, were admitted to the pope's audience "ten minutes prior to the appointed time," invited to "stand near to his side," and treated to an audience of "forty minutes duration, an unusually long one." The whole interview was marked by such consideration as "might be envied by the envoy of the oldest member of the family of nations."[14]

Grayson Mann read Davis's letter aloud to the pope, translating it into Italian and giving every sentence "a slow, solemn, and emphatic pronunciation," while his proud father monitored the pope's every change of expression and gesticulation. Davis's letter to the pope lamented the suffering of the South and, implicitly, asked His Holiness for help. "Every sentence of the letter appeared to sensibly affect him," Mann solemnly assured Benjamin. The pope's "deep sunken orbs, visibly moistened, were upturned toward that throne upon which ever sits the Prince of Peace," a sign to Mann that the Holy Father was "pleading for our deliverance from that causeless and merciless war which is prosecuted against us."

Once Grayson Mann finished reading the letter, the pope asked his father pointedly if "President Davis" was Catholic. "No," Mann had to sheepishly confess. Nor was he, the pope also gently forced him to admit. The pope moved on to a far more awkward matter by alluding to the North's proclamation of emancipation and suggesting that "it might perhaps be judicious in us to consent to gradual emancipation." Mann gave no comfort to His Holiness on this matter either and instead defended the South's right to slavery and lambasted "Lincoln and Company" for their heinous plan "to convert the well-cared-for civilized negro into a semibarbarian." Mann went on to extol the loyalty of "our slaves," who wanted nothing more than "to return to their old homes, the love of which was the strongest of their affections." The Confederate emissary saw nothing but "approving expression" and "evident satisfaction" in the pope's reaction.

Pivoting to the subject of the pope's suffering flock in Ireland and Germany who were being recruited into the Union army, Mann lamented that "these poor unfortunates" were being tempted by bounty money to enlist against the South. Were it not for these foreign recruits, the North would have failed long ago. "His Holiness," Mann reported, "expressed his utter astonishment, repeatedly throwing up his hands." The pontiff promised that he would write a letter that Mann's government would be welcome to publish. He then held up his hand "as a signal for the end of the audience." "Thus terminated one among the most remarkable conferences that ever a foreign representative had with a potentate of the earth," Mann breathlessly reported to Benjamin. "And such a potentate! A potentate who wields the consciences of 175,000,000 of the civilized race, and who is adored by that immense number as the vice regent of Almighty God in this sublunary sphere."[15]

Pio Nono kept Mann waiting in Rome for the next month before delivering a brief letter, in Latin, deploring the *fatale civile bellum* (fatal civil war) and the cruel *intestinum bellum* (internal war) and hoping that God would "pour out the spirit of Christian love and peace upon all the people of America." What thrilled Mann, however, was that on the outside of the envelope, the pope had addressed the letter to *Illustri et Honorabili Viro,* Jefferson Davis, *Praesidi foederatarum Americae regionum.* Mann took some liberties in translating this as "Illustrious and Honorable, Jefferson Davis, President of the Confederate States of America." He eagerly informed Benjamin that in the pope's few precious words, he had attained exactly what the Confederacy had been awaiting for two and a half years. "Thus we are acknowledged, by as high an authority as this world contains, to be an independent power of the earth."

Mann was absolutely ecstatic. "I congratulate you," he told Benjamin. "I congratulate the President, I congratulate his Cabinet; in short, I congratulate all my true-hearted countrymen and countrywomen, upon this benign event. The hand of the Lord has been in it, and eternal glory and praise be to His holy and righteous name." This was the turning point, Mann felt certain. "The example of the sovereign pontiff, if I am not much mistaken, will exercise a salutary influence upon both the Catholic and Protestant governments of western Europe. Humanity will be aroused everywhere to the importance of its early emulation."[16]

One can almost hear Benjamin groaning in his February 1864 reply to Mann. The pope's address to "President Davis," he explained, was nothing more than "a formula of politeness to his correspondent, not a political recognition of a fact." He also had to point out that, far from being a sign of recognition of Southern sovereignty, by referring to the conflict as an "intestine or civil war," the pope was implying quite the opposite. Though he was not Catholic in faith, Jefferson Davis had been educated at a Catholic school, and he knew enough Latin to see that Mann had misconstrued the translation as well as the intent of the pope's entitlement of "President Davis" and the nation he purported to lead.[17]

Mann was probably incensed by Benjamin's interpretation, but he remained utterly convinced of his triumph at the Vatican. Writing to Davis, his old friend, in February 1864, he confided that the "pope is well pleased with that which he has done in emphatically recognizing you as the Executive of a nation. The good old man is willing to do more, and is disregardful of consequences." Garibaldi, he assured Davis, is "no longer in favor, except with the vulgar," while "*Pio Nono,* himself, really has no enemies anywhere."[18]

After months of holding onto the original Latin letter, Mann sent it by a trusted special courier to Jefferson Davis in May 1864. "This letter will grace the archives of the Executive Office in all coming time," his cover letter informed the president. "It will live forever in story as the production of the first potentate who formally recognized your official position and accorded to one of the diplomatic representatives of the Confederate States an audience in an established court palace, like that of St. James or the Tuileries."[19]

Ambrose Dudley Mann may have been deluded as to the pope's intentions, but he recognized in the letter a gold mine for Confederate public diplomacy. Early publication of the letter in Europe, he told Benjamin, was of "paramount importance to the influencing of valuable public opinion, in both hemispheres, in our favor." Mann had a point; used appropriately, the pope's letter could leave a plausible impression that he supported the Confederacy in its "holy war" against the "infidel Puritans" and the revolutionary republicans of the North. It would also help highlight the anti-Catholic bigotry that infused both of those enemies of the South.[20]

The pope's letter was soon featured in the Confederate campaign against Union enlistments in Ireland and northern Europe. Edwin De Leon, whose wife was Irish, had alerted the Confederate government to the Irish problem as early as July 1862 when Archbishop Hughes was touring Europe. In Dublin "Bishop Hughes is busily beating up recruits in Ireland and haranguing for the North." "He boasts he can bring 20,000 men to the rescue of the North."

Thanks to Seward's Circular 19 publicizing the Homestead Act, a brisk traffic in recruits had picked up in late 1862, especially from Ireland and the German states. The Confederates were slow to respond to Seward's recruitment initiative, due in part to what Benjamin referred to as the "imperfect communication" between Richmond and agents abroad. It was not until July 1863, nearly a year after Circular 19, that Benjamin sent J. L. Capston, an Irish-born Confederate, to Dublin with instructions to use "every means you can devise" to persuade the Irish against enlisting. Thereafter, the Irish recruitment problem was a major focus of Confederates abroad. Mason and Hotze came over from London and De Leon from Paris to help expose the Union's "deception" of the Irish.[21]

In September 1863 Benjamin stepped up efforts in Ireland by sending over Father John B. Bannon, a Catholic chaplain in the Confederate army who was legendary for his oratorical prowess. Bannon carried instructions to use "all legitimate means to enlighten the population as to the true nature and character of the contest now waged on this continent." "Explain to them," Benjamin told Bannon, "that they will be called on to meet Irishmen in battle, and thus to embue their hands in the blood of their own friends and perhaps kinsmen in a quarrel which does not concern them." Tell them of "the hatred of the New England Puritans" for Irishmen and Catholics and the shameful burning and desecration of Catholic churches by New England soldiers.[22]

Father Bannon arrived in Dublin in late October 1863 and immediately put in place a Confederate counteroffensive to Circular 19. He enlisted Catholic priests in country churches to speak out against the Union recruitment effort from their pulpits. And he hired Irish agents to hover about the docks, visit port-side taverns, call on boardinghouses, distribute thousands of handbills, and put up posters warning immigrants against the Union recruiters.[23]

"Caution to Emigrants, Persecution of Catholics in America," one broadside warned, citing atrocities by Massachusetts troops against a Catholic church in Louisiana. "The Priest imprisoned, and afterwards exposed on an Island to Aligators and Snakes! His house robbed of everything!" Others proclaimed the South as the friends of the Irish. "The Southern people are, by race, religion and principles, the natural ally of

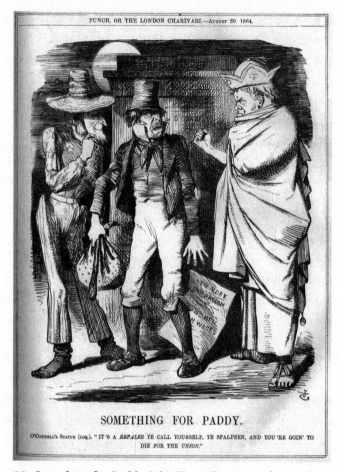

PUNCH, OR THE LONDON CHARIVARI.—August 20. 1864.

SOMETHING FOR PADDY.

O'Connell's Statue (loq). "IT'S A *REPALEE* YE CALL YOURSELF, YE SPALPEEN, AND YOU'RE GOIN' TO DIE FOR THE *UNION*."

35. *Something for Paddy.* John Tenniel's cartoon for London's *Punch*, August 20, 1864, depicted an Irish immigrant being recruited by a Union agent resembling Lincoln, while Pope Pius IX glowers at both of them. (COURTESY ALLAN T. KOHL, MINNEAPOLIS COLLEGE OF ART AND DESIGN)

the foreigner and Catholic," one flyer in Dublin exclaimed. "They sprang from Spanish, French and Irish ancestors."[24]

Copies of the pope's letter to Archbishop Hughes and his epistle to "President" Jefferson Davis were posted as though they were papal bans against enlisting in the Union army. Ambrose Dudley Mann happily credited the papal letters with igniting "formidable demonstrations" in Ireland. He promised his once-skeptical secretary of state that it "will accomplish little less than marvels" by depriving the North of Irish cannon fodder. "To the immortal honor of the Catholic Church, it is now earnestly engaged in throwing every obstacle that it can justly create in the way of the prosecution of the war by the Yankee guerrillas."[25]

Benjamin had to concede the effectiveness of the pope's apparent support, and he soon determined to redouble the effort to win more formal recognition from the Vatican. In March 1864 Benjamin appointed Patrick Lynch, the outspoken Catholic bishop of Charleston, South Carolina, as special envoy to the Papal States. Father Bannon, his mission in Ireland completed, came to Rome to aid Lynch, whose mission was to pursue recognition from Rome and European governments generally and to spread "enlightening opinions and molding impressions" among the public. Lynch was encouraged when the pope granted a private audience to him in July 1864. "It is clear that you are two nations," the pope assured Lynch. "But still," he gently advised the Confederacy for the second time, "something might be done looking to an improvement in position or state [of the slaves], and to a gradual preparation for their freedom at a future opportune time."[26]

Like Mann, Bishop Lynch saw the pope's advice on emancipation as a sign that he did not fully understand the Christian character of the South's peculiar institution. He immediately set his mind to working up a lengthy essay depicting "the actual condition and treatment of slaves at the South." Lynch's "A Few Words on Domestic Slavery" grew into an eighty-three-page booklet that advanced a proslavery argument tailored to his European Catholic audience. Sidestepping several of the church's admonitions condemning slavery, Lynch offered a sunny picture of a "patriarchal" domestic institution that, in practice at least, was in full harmony with the Catholic mission to rescue Africans from their violent heathen origins.

Lynch's pamphlet first appeared in Italian in late 1864, published anonymously as *Lettera di un missionario sulla schiavitù domestica degli Stati Confederati di America* (Letter of a missionary on the domestic slavery of the Confederate States of America). Lynch made contact with the deposed but still active Edwin De Leon, who volunteered to translate it into French. De Leon urged Lynch to put his illustrious name to the publication, but the author demurred. Through an acquaintance at the Vatican, Lynch also arranged for a German translation, which was published in early 1865. Though Lynch had copy prepared for an English edition, as the war ended it remained unpublished, but Henry Hotze filled the void by summarizing Lynch's main points for English-speaking readers of the *Index*.[27]

The owner of nearly one hundred slaves, most of them bequeathed to the diocese by deceased parishioners, Bishop Lynch noted that many of the leading Catholic clergy and laymen in the South were fellow slave owners. The slave South, by Bishop Lynch's account, served as a bulwark against the bigotry and fanaticism of the abolitionists, whom he was quick to identify as rabid anti-Catholic Know-Nothings. Turning to the familiar arsenal of American proslavery arguments, Lynch charged that these abolitionist hypocrites cared nothing for the genuine welfare of the Negro and were trying to use them to ignite a Haitian-style revolution across the South. Appendixes to all editions of his pamphlet included reports on horrible treatment of blacks by the Union army.[28]

Bishop Lynch's reply to the pope's concerns about slavery was revealing of the fixed mind of the Confederate South. For Lynch and the entire Confederate leadership, slavery was beyond debate. It was the cornerstone of the Southern nation, the foundation of King Cotton's prosperous realm, and the guarantor of white racial supremacy. Lynch's tract was the last gasp of the South's effort to repudiate liberal principles of human equality and align itself with the Latin Catholic regimes of the Old and New Worlds against what Pio Nono called "the Revolution."[29]

THE CORNERSTONE OF SLAVERY NOW HUNG LIKE A MILLSTONE around the neck of the Confederacy. Those who tried to challenge the dogma of slavery from within the Confederacy were quickly silenced, as Confederate general Patrick Cleburne learned in a cold tent in Georgia in January 1864. Cleburne was born in County Cork, Ireland, to a Protestant family, migrated to the United States in 1849, and settled in Helena, Arkansas. He brought military experience from service in the British army, and when the war came he rose quickly through the ranks to major general. In the winter of 1863–1864, with Sherman's invading army pressing Confederates into retreat in northern Georgia, Cleburne became convinced that Southerners now faced a cruel choice between arming their slaves or becoming enslaved to the North. It was telling that, once again, it took a foreigner to voice what the Confederate leadership dared not speak out loud.[30]

Cleburne's passionate plea, dated January 2, 1864, and cosigned by several other officers, addressed two key problems facing the Confederacy: the perilous shortage of fighting men and the failure to win support abroad. Southerners, his memorandum began, "have spilled much of our best blood," while the enemy draws on a vast supply of "his own motley population," "our slaves," and "Europeans whose hearts are fired into a crusade against us by fictitious pictures of the atrocities of slavery."

Their friends in England and France had strong incentives to "recognize and assist us, but they cannot assist us without helping slavery," Cleburne's memorandum continued. Slavery must be sacrificed for independence, he insisted; the Southerner must decide to "give up the negro slave rather than be a slave himself." Cleburne called for the outright abolition of slavery followed by the recruitment of blacks willing to fight for Confederate independence. "One thing is certain," he argued, "as soon as the great sacrifice to independence is made and known in foreign countries," there would be a complete change "in our favor of the sympathies of the world."[31]

The "Cleburne Memorial" was kept secret for a month before his commanding officer forwarded a copy to Richmond. The cover letter denounced the "incendiary document," and Jefferson Davis promptly ordered his secretary of war to suppress any further discussion of the matter. Cleburne would die at the Battle of Franklin in late November 1864, precisely as the unthinkable notion of freeing and arming slaves came to life again—this time at the center of power in Richmond.[32]

ON NOVEMBER 8, 1864, ABRAHAM LINCOLN WON A STUNNING reelection victory over George McClellan, his former general whose party called for the restoration of the "Union as it was." Confederates had pinned most of their hopes on the Northern peace movement. So had European investors: prices for Confederate bonds more than doubled from a low of 38 percent of face value at the end of 1863 to nearly 85 percent in the autumn of 1864. (See cotton bond chart, page 259.) Democrats had appealed to white racial fears and to resentment against the emancipation of blacks who, they predicted, would come North to compete for jobs and drive down wages. But Lincoln and the Republicans had prevailed in the election, and this finally forced the high command in Richmond to consider the very alternatives Cleburne had proposed.

By November 1864 Jefferson Davis and Judah P. Benjamin decided to cut the Gordian knot. They secretly agreed that the only way out was to force the South to sacrifice slavery for independence. Soon after Lincoln's reelection, Davis dared to broach the subject of arming and freeing slaves in his message to the Confederate Congress. He framed it as a solution to the need for manpower in the army and left the irritating diplomatic problem aside. Richmond newspapers friendly to the government helped prepare the public mind by defending the idea. Benjamin was more interested in winning international recognition, but he quietly enlisted support for the idea of arming and freeing black soldiers. "Public opinion is fast ripening on the subject," he wrote to one supporter, and the government would soon be able to inaugurate the new policy.[33]

In London Henry Hotze still found the whole subject of Confederate emancipation distasteful, but he dutifully published stories on the emancipation debate in the *Index*. Mason, who had returned from Paris to London, reported in December that the Southern Independence Association at Manchester "fully approves the proposed plan of arming the slaves." In January 1865 he assured the home office that supporters in England agreed that "our people would have no fear of bringing our slaves into the field to fight an enemy common alike to them and to their masters" and had no doubt that "our slaves would make better soldiers in our ranks than in those of the North." But there were, he cautioned Benjamin, grave reservations in Europe that promising freedom to enslaved soldiers would be "the first step toward emancipation" of all slaves, not least because it would cause "great mischief and inconvenience" to have so many "free blacks amongst us."[34]

By early 1865 rumors of Confederate emancipation plans were coursing through Europe. Under pressure from Benjamin, Robert E. Lee endorsed the idea of emancipating those slaves willing to serve, but only, he advised, "with the consent of their owners."[35]

For many Confederates, freeing slaves proved less contentious than proposals to arm them. The very idea of putting slaves on an "equal footing" with white soldiers fighting for their country was appalling to them, but the notion of giving slaves or free blacks guns was positively terrifying. Georgia's Howell Cobb, serving as a major general, put the matter succinctly in his letter to the Confederate secretary of war: "You cannot make soldiers of slaves, nor slaves of soldiers." "The day you make soldiers of them is the beginning of the end of the revolution. If slaves will make good soldiers our whole theory of slavery is wrong."[36]

Robert M. T. Hunter, the former secretary of state, sneered at the idea of succumbing to what he viewed as the false philanthropic zeal for abolition abroad. Before a large, boisterous meeting in Richmond, he admitted that "the world, if not in arms against us, is against us in sympathy." He summoned the white South to vindicate itself by winning victory before the "frowning face of all Europe." "What did we go to war for, if not to protect our property?" he asked poignantly. "The shades of our departed heroes hover over us and beckon us on. . . . [T]he enemy is far spent. . . . Let us stand firm" and not "commit suicide."[37]

"If the Confederacy falls," Jefferson Davis told one stubborn senator who was certain slaves would not fight, "there should be written on its tombstone, 'Died of a theory.'" Davis was desperate to save the South, but he was also facing a virtual mutiny against emancipation on any basis in the Confederate Congress. "If this Government is to destroy slavery," Henry S. Foote, a Tennessee congressman, asked, "why fight for it?" "Gloom and despondency rule the hour," Howell Cobb wrote in January 1865, "and bitter opposition to the Administration, mingled with disaffection and disloyalty, is manifesting itself." It would be far better, he argued, "to yield to the demands of England and France and abolish slavery, and thereby purchase their aid," than to resort to arming blacks.[38]

Benjamin, meanwhile, persuaded Davis that the most urgent problem they faced was not manpower but their desperate need for international support. If they conquered the diplomatic problem, he reasoned, the manpower problem would become less imperative. What Benjamin proposed was a secret diplomatic experiment in which emancipation would be promised to Britain and France in exchange for recognition. If that worked, Benjamin argued, Davis could then issue a presidential emancipation edict, justifying it as a "military necessity" dictated by national self-preservation. It had a familiar ring to it, and, indeed, Benjamin was borrowing a page from Lincoln's book. But he took it even further by making a dubious legal argument: the very de facto status of the Confederate nation, Benjamin reasoned, permitted the president to act outside of the constitution.

Davis was worried not only about violating the cornerstone of the Confederate Constitution, but also about the political risk of flouting the will of the elected Congress. The *Richmond Sentinel,* widely acknowledged to be Davis's unofficial mouthpiece, tested the waters by calling for bold action "over and above the constitution." Remarkably, it even went so far as to recommend subordination of the South to European governments under some form of protectorate, if it came to that. "Our people would infinitely prefer an alliance with the European nations . . . to the dominion of the Yankees." "*Any* terms with *any* other, would be preferable to subjugation to them." As the Confederacy entered 1865 it was about to play its last card to win independence at any cost.[39]

OUT IN LOUISIANA, SENSING THE DESPERATE SITUATION OF THE Confederacy at the end of 1864, Confederate leaders seemed prepared to pursue a separate peace and, some later charged, to invite French recolonization. General Camille de Polignac, a French prince from a renowned noble family, had come over to serve in the Confederate army and soon rose to the rank of major general and was hailed as the "Lafayette of the South." During that dark winter of 1864–1865, he was in Shreveport, Louisiana, and growing despondent over the South's declining fortunes and the steady stream of deserters taking French leave of the army. The South's last hope lay in his homeland, he told his commanding officer, General Kirby Smith, and he asked for personal leave of six months to return to France and rally support there. Smith conferred with Louisiana governor Henry W. Allen, who immediately decided to transform Polignac's leave into an officially sanctioned diplomatic mission to save Louisiana, if not the Confederacy.[40]

Governor Allen and the generals decided that time and faltering lines of communication did not permit consultation with Richmond. Allen, acting on his own questionable authority, appointed his aide-de-camp, Colonel Ernest Miltenberger, as Louisiana's envoy to France. He was instructed to accompany Polignac, whose close friendship with the Duc de Morny would allow him to serve as liaison. Allen gave Miltenberger a sealed letter to present to Napoleon III. The letter obliquely reminded the French of "the strong and sacred ties that bound France and Louisiana" and noted also "the imminent danger" a Union victory would pose to the French in Mexico. Before departing, Allen took Polignac aside and gave him instructions he dared not commit to writing. The enemy was fielding an army of "foreign mercenaries" and "kidnapped" blacks, Allen instructed Polignac to communicate, and as governor he planned to "arm the negroes" of Louisiana. "Of course," he added almost as an afterthought, "we must give them their freedom." Polignac and his troupe of ersatz diplomats left for Europe in early January and made their way circuitously to Matamoros, Havana, Cadiz, Madrid, and finally Paris in late March, just as the final curtain was about to close on the Confederacy.[41]

Unknown to Governor Allen and Prince Polignac, Benjamin and Davis in Richmond were at the same time, December 1864, secretly enlisting another Louisianan, Duncan F. Kenner, to carry out a secret mission to Europe where he would offer the promise of emancipation in exchange for recognition. Ever since Lincoln's Emancipation Proclamation was enacted, Kenner had tried to persuade Confederate leaders to consider a plan to arm and emancipate the slaves to save the South. Davis and Benjamin had quashed Kenner's proposal and refused to discuss it publicly, but it now seemed to them that Kenner, one of the largest slaveholders in the South, was the perfect messenger for this desperate diplomatic mission.

Benjamin also astutely realized that Slidell and Mason would be neither willing nor credible couriers of an emancipation proposal, which would require them to repudiate everything they had been defending for the past three years. With all the intercepted correspondence between Richmond and Europe, it would prove embarrassing beyond measure and politically dangerous at home for an emancipation proposal to fall into enemy hands. It was imperative that Kenner go to Europe and that his mission should remain secret—not only from Europeans and Northerners, but also from the Confederate Congress and the people of the South.[42]

Benjamin sent instructions to Mason and Slidell, referring obliquely to Kenner's mission, details of which were to be explicitly spelled out to Slidell and Mason in the encrypted instructions Kenner carried with him. The message to Slidell and Mason conveyed a strong current of resentment toward Europe, which he apparently wanted them to make known to the governments of France and Britain. "No people have ever poured out their blood more freely in defense of their liberties and independence nor have endured sacrifices with greater cheerfulness than have the men and women of these Confederate States," Benjamin asserted. The South might have won had it only been up against the United States, he hypothesized, but Europe's western powers have been lavishing "aid, comfort, and assistance" upon their enemy. The South had been "fighting the battle of France and England" against an aggressive enemy that now prepared to attack the French in Mexico and the British in Canada. The ulterior purpose of Lincoln's cry, "one war at a time," would now reveal itself in aggression against its neighbors as soon as the United States was "disengaged from the struggle with us."

Alluding to Sherman's March through Georgia, Benjamin complained of the barbaric assaults being carried out by "armies of mercenaries" that were now resorting to "the starvation and extermination of our women and children" and the wanton destruction of farms and cities. Slidell and Mason were instructed to ask, did the Great Powers propose never to recognize the Confederacy under any circumstances? If so, the South deserved to know. "If on the other hand," Benjamin finally circled back to the main point of the Kenner mission, "there be objections not made known to us, which have for four years prevented the recognition of our independence . . . , justice equally demands that an opportunity be afforded us for meeting and overcoming those objections, if in our power to do so." This was as close as Benjamin dared bring himself to spelling out the unspeakable proposition that Kenner was to explain to Slidell and Mason.[43]

As the Confederacy entered its eleventh hour, everything seemed to conspire to prevent the encrypted message that Kenner carried with him from ever reaching its intended audience. It was more than two full months since he left Richmond before Kenner finally crossed the Atlantic, and his troubled journey was symptomatic of the failing fortunes of the Confederate nation. Fort Fisher, which protected Wilmington, North Carolina, the last Atlantic port open to the Confederacy, fell to Union forces on January 15, 1865. Rather than run the blockade and go by way of the Caribbean, Kenner decided to embark from New York. It was highly risky. He was well known and easily recognized, not least by his very prominent bald head. He traveled incognito under an assumed name and wearing an absurd-looking brown wig. He hid out in the Metropolitan Hotel in New York, waiting to hear the results of an ill-fated peace conference that took place between Union and Confederate officials at Hampton Roads, Virginia, on February 3. One week later he boarded a ship for England. During the voyage he dodged federal officials on board by pretending to be a Frenchman. He arrived at Southampton on February 21 and hurried to London, expecting to find Mason, only to discover he was in Paris with Slidell. Kenner sent a telegram to Slidell, asking that Slidell, Mason, and Mann meet with him in Paris.[44]

By the time Kenner arrived in Paris on February 24, rumors of some major Confederate diplomatic move had surfaced in the European press. They may have been deliberately planted. Hotze had already run a story in the *Index,* anticipating "quite a turn to affairs in America" as a result of secret negotiations. In Paris Union envoy John Bigelow was hearing rumors in late January that England and France would "unite in recognizing the Southern Confederacy on condition that they will emancipate and arm their slaves." "I mention this rumor," he wrote to Seward, "not out of any respect for it, but to show . . . of what contortions the wounded carcass of secession is capable in its expiring agonies."[45]

Kenner met Mason and Slidell at the latter's office, a room in the sumptuous Le Grand Hotel, a palatial facility built as part of Baron Haussmann's redesign of Paris. Kenner explained to Slidell and Mason the purpose of his mission, which left both men stunned. Sensing their opposition, Kenner asked Slidell's secretary to decode the encrypted instructions signed by President Davis. Letter by letter, sentence by sentence, the instructions were slowly deciphered until Slidell and Mason were forced to confront the unpleasant reality that their government was about to sacrifice the very reason for its being.

The distraught diplomats were irritated by the messenger as much as by the message. True to character, Slidell demanded to know why Davis would send over Kenner when the South had seasoned diplomats in place. The answer to that became obvious when Mason refused outright to execute the plan. Kenner was prepared for that possibility. On Benjamin's advice he had been given power to dismiss any diplomat who refused to cooperate, and he let Mason know that. Mann, arriving late, quickly read the mood and fell in line with Kenner and the home office.[46]

Slidell and Mason, however, were not about to allow themselves to be treated as lackeys by the likes of Kenner, whatever powers the president had vested in him. They had long since made up their minds that any offer of emancipation would be fruitless. What ensued over the next few days amounted to Mason and Slidell effectively sabotaging the Kenner mission. Kenner deserved some of the blame, for he inexplicably deferred to the two veteran diplomats and did not take part in negotiations in Paris or London.

Kenner, Slidell, Mason, and Mann huddled in Paris for nearly a week before deciding to approach Britain first. No soon had Kenner and Mason arrived in London on March 3 than Mason began second-guessing the plan and managed to persuade Kenner to reverse course and have Slidell, who remained in Paris, go first. On March 4 Slidell met briefly with Napoleon III, who, almost routinely by now, declared that he would not act without England's cooperation. Slidell took the opportunity to tell him frankly the terms of Kenner's proposal, and he asked directly whether an offer of emancipation would make any difference to France. According to Slidell's account, which conveniently sustained his own argument against emancipation, Napoleon III told him the slavery question had never entered into France's policy on the American question. Maybe it would make a difference to the British, the emperor casually added.[47]

Inexplicably, Slidell delayed two days before reporting to Kenner and Mason, who waited anxiously in London. More than a week passed before Mason set up an unofficial interview with Palmerston. More than two and a half months had passed since Benjamin and Davis had authorized the Kenner mission. Here was the Confederacy's last chance for recognition among the powers of the earth.

Yet Mason seemed in no great hurry and admitted to waiting "a few days" before arranging a private interview with Lord Palmerston. Late in the morning on March 14, Mason went alone without Kenner to meet with Palmerston at his private residence, Cambridge House, at 94 Picadilly. There in Palmerston's home, Mason, with full authorization to spell out an exchange of emancipation for recognition, managed to turn what should have been a plea for British aid into a threat of war. In fairness, he was following Benjamin's instructions to warn Britain and France of Northern aggression once the South was conquered. But in Mason's hands, it sounded like a Southern threat. If forced to choose between the "continued desolation of our country, or a return to peace through an alliance committing us to the foreign wars of the North," he warned the prime minister, the South might choose to side with the North against Europe.

Turning at last to the urgent matter at hand, the emancipation proposal, Mason turned strangely reticent. He could do no more than repeat, more than once, the opaque language of Benjamin's written instructions: if there might be "some latent, undisclosed obstacle on the part of Great

Britain to recognition, it should be frankly stated and we might, if in our power to do so, consent to remove it." Mason simply could not bring himself to speak the actual words—*slavery, emancipation, recognition*—that would have made the Confederate proposal clear, even as he pressed Palmerston to speak frankly.

As Mason later painfully admitted to Benjamin, he had not "unfolded fully" the exact terms of the proposal: "I made no distinct proposal," he admitted in his encrypted dispatch to Benjamin. Indeed, it was as though he refused to decode the desperate plea for help Kenner had been sent to Europe to deliver. Mason later explained candidly that he was simply dumbstruck by "extreme apprehension" that word of this conversation might reach the ears of their enemies and that "the mischief resulting would be incalculable." He was tongue-tied by fear of humiliation and dishonor—of the South and of himself—once it became known that the Confederacy was repudiating the cornerstone on which it had proclaimed itself a nation.[48]

Mason dallied in London another two weeks, wracked with self-doubt that he had squandered his chance with Palmerston by not being forthright. He sought counsel with the Earl of Donoughmore, "a fast and consistent friend to our cause," to ask whether a more forthright offer of emancipation might make a difference. Donoughmore replied that perhaps earlier, in the late summer of 1862 when Lee's "army was at the very gates of Washington," it might have made a decisive difference; "but for slavery," the South "should then have been acknowledged."

"But for slavery" the South might not have tried to secede or plunged into the chasm of civil war so willingly. Mason sighed, replying with a Latin proverb: *Sic transit Gloria Mundi* (Thus passes the glory of the world). Thus also passed the Confederacy's bid for independence. Mason's March 31 explanation of his meetings in London arrived in Richmond well after Benjamin and Davis had abandoned the capital as it went up in flames.[49]

Meanwhile, Prince Camille de Polignac, the noble emissary from Governor Allen in Louisiana, finally arrived in Paris sometime around March 22. He was counting on his friendship with the Duc de Morny, Napoleon III's half brother, but he had died earlier that month. Polignac arranged an interview with the emperor, who received him cordially, at least until the conversation turned to official matters.

Polignac waxed eloquent about the Southern people's determination to fight on and told the emperor that their "ties of blood had ever since kept alive a natural sympathy with France among the descendants of the first settlers." Napoleon sat in studied silence. Polignac then told him that he came with an emissary bearing a letter from the governor of Louisiana. "What does he tell me in that letter?" the emperor asked. Polignac asked to return the next day with Colonel Miltenberger, who handed the sealed envelope to Napoleon. The emperor coolly laid it on the table unopened and, without even inviting the Louisiana envoys to sit down, told them that, although he had wanted to intervene on behalf of the South, Britain's reluctance prevented him from doing so. Now it was too late.[50]

Years later, Robert Toombs lamented that the South had not promised an end to slavery earlier in the war, for both France and Britain would have rushed to its support. John Bigelow was not about to let that rest. If the South had been willing to end slavery, he replied to Toombs in a popular magazine, "there would have been no war, and the Confederate maggot would never have been hatched."[51]

CHAPTER 12

SHALL NOT PERISH

Now we are engaged in a great civil war, testing whether that nation or any nation so conceived and so dedicated can long endure. . . . [W]e here highly resolve that these dead shall not have died in vain—that this nation, under God, shall have a new birth of freedom—and that government of the people, by the people, for the people, shall not perish from the earth.

—ABRAHAM LINCOLN,
GETTYSBURG ADDRESS, NOVEMBER 19, 1863

WHILE THE CONFEDERATE HIGH COMMAND WAS PLAYING ITS last cards in Rome, Paris, and London, the Union was honing its appeal to world opinion. Lincoln's own words were among the Union's most valuable assets in its public diplomacy campaign abroad. He had an unusual gift for articulating the meaning of the war in universalizing terms that resonated with the international vocabulary of republicanism as much as it did with the American troops and citizens at home. In his speeches and public letters, Lincoln repeatedly referred to the war's implications for "the whole world," "the earth," "the whole family of man." He spoke, too, of the struggle being "not altogether for today—it is for a vast future also."[1]

The idea of the war being part of a much larger historic struggle was not Lincoln's alone; it ran through much of William Seward's diplomatic communications as well. Their views on the war as an epic clash of fundamental principles also emanated from well-rehearsed Republican Party rhetoric that portrayed the aristocratic Slave Power assailing the will of the common people. It was a romantic drama and one that resonated with foreigners who reframed the national narrative into an international one of popular sovereignty locked in a life-or-death struggle against the advocates of hereditary sovereignty and servitude.

While some Unionists criticized the readiness of European conservatives to see America's crisis as proof that the republican experiment had failed, Lincoln often seized opportunities to frame the war as a trial of democracy and one with vast consequences for the world's future. Nowhere did he do this more masterfully than in the "brief remarks" he delivered at the dedication of the National Cemetery at Gettysburg, Pennsylvania, in November 1863.

Lincoln opened by linking the Gettysburg battle, and the war itself, to Thomas Jefferson's 1776 declaration of a nation based on human equality. "Fourscore and seven years ago our fathers brought forth on this continent a new nation, conceived in liberty and dedicated to the proposition that all men are created equal." Every schoolchild in America knows the words, and by now most are familiar with the moral journey they signified for the president who once insisted that the war was fought for no higher purpose than to preserve the Union. At Gettysburg that day he proclaimed the nation's "new birth of freedom."[2]

The "new birth" is commonly interpreted as a reference to the Emancipation Proclamation, but it carried a broader political meaning as well. "Now we are engaged in a great civil war," Lincoln told the Gettysburg crowd, "testing whether that nation, or *any nation so conceived,* and so dedicated, can long endure." The simple phrase "any nation so conceived" imbued America's war with universal meaning. That point was made emphatic when he closed by saying that the war's purpose was to ensure that "government of the people, by the people, for the people, shall not perish *from the earth.*"

The words and thoughts were quintessential Lincoln, but they connected with the language of international republicanism. His most unforgettable phrase at Gettysburg—"government of the people, by the people, for the people"—bore a familiar ring to European ears. The cadence "of, by, for" the "people, republic, nation" had been employed by other American orators, including Theodore Parker and Daniel Webster, but the phrasing had been popularized much earlier by the Italian nationalist Giuseppe Mazzini, who in 1833 called on Young Italy to make revolution "in the name of the people, for the people, and by the people." Mazzini used similar language in 1851 when he explained Italy's historic mission by asking "what does it mean if not a living Equality, in other words, Republic of the People, by the people, and for the people?"[3]

Some in the audience at Gettysburg on that cold November day in 1863 could not hear Lincoln's surprisingly brief remarks. The photographic evidence shows Lincoln engulfed by a sea of soldiers and civilians surrounding the speaker's platform. His voice may not have reached all of them that day, but in due time his printed words reached a world far beyond the restless crowd in front of him.

Lincoln had modestly asserted that "the world will little note nor long remember what we say here, but it can never forget what they did here." "He was mistaken," Charles Sumner later noted. "That speech uttered at the field of Gettysburg and now sanctified by the martyrdom of its author is a monumental act." "The world noted at once what he said and will never cease to remember it. The battle itself was less important than the speech. Ideas are always more than battles."[4]

Goldwin Smith, an Oxford University history professor, commented from England, "Not a sovereign in Europe, however trained from the cradle for state pomps, and however prompted by statesmen and courtiers, could have uttered himself more regally than did Lincoln at Gettysburg."[5]

Lincoln's understanding of the war as a "trial" of democracy and "a new birth of freedom" pervaded the understanding of the war both at home and abroad by the time he stood for reelection in November 1864. The Republican Party deliberately made the election into a national plebiscite on the war and the future of slavery in America. The party platform squarely denounced slavery as the cause of the war and condemned it for being inherently "hostile to the principles of Republican Government." Emancipation was not to be just a wartime measure; the Republicans called for slavery's "utter and complete extirpation from the soil of the Republic." Another prominent plank in the Republican platform denounced attempts by European powers to "obtain new footholds for

Monarchical Government, sustained by foreign military force, in near proximity to the United States."[6]

From Paris on the eve of the election Professor Édouard Laboulaye put his pen to an eloquent public appeal to American voters to uphold the Great Republic in its hour of trial. He deftly differentiated those sustaining a democracy of labor and freedom and those defending an aristocracy of idleness and slavery, and he left no room for compromise. Laboulaye also warned of the world's stake in the election. "The Presidential election may insure the triumph or ruin of the North," Laboulaye put it bluntly. "America may regain peace and become the model of free countries, or she may fall into that incurable anarchy which has made the Spanish Republics the prey of wretched despots, the laughing-stock and plaything of Europe."

"The world is a solidarity, and the cause of America is the cause of Liberty." All the world would be watching, Laboulaye wanted Americans to know. "So long as there shall be across the Atlantic a society of thirty millions of men, living happily and peacefully under a government of their choice, with laws made by themselves, liberty will cast her rays over Europe like an illuminating pharos." Then he warned of dire consequence if they failed to keep liberty's torch aflame. "But should liberty become eclipsed in the new world, it would become night in Europe, and we shall see the work of Washington, of the Franklins, of the Hamiltons, spit upon and trampled under foot by the whole school which believes only in violence and in success." America's cause was the cause of all nations, Laboulaye told America and the world.[7]

Soldiers in the field came to Lincoln's aid in the election of 1864 by voting for him (three to one) and encouraging family members at home to support him. Lincoln's victory owed much both to the soldiers' affection for him and to their apparent ideological zeal for Union and Liberty. One Union marching song captured the spirit of both:

We are coming, Father Abraham, 300,000 more,
From Mississippi's winding stream and from New England's shore. . . .
You have called us, and we're coming by Richmond's bloody tide,
To lay us down for freedom's sake, our brothers' bones beside;
Or from foul treason's savage group, to wrench the murderous blade;
And in the face of foreign foes its fragments to parade.[8]

THOUGH AMERICAN WOMEN DID NOT HAVE VOTES, THEY BROUGHT their voices to bear on the election of 1864 by endorsing the cause of Union and Liberty. The Women's National Loyal League, organized by Elizabeth Cady Stanton and Susan B. Anthony, fomented a powerful campaign that defined emancipation as the culmination of American republicanism. Angelina Grimké Weld, the daughter of South Carolina slaveholders and a renowned abolitionist, told the assembled women at the inaugural convention in May 1863 that the nation had been founded on "the great doctrine of brotherhood and equality" and that Lincoln's 1860 election had sounded the clarion call to complete the work of the founding fathers by ending slavery. The Women's National Loyal League launched a massive mail campaign that left pamphlets and petitions "scattered like snowflakes from Maine to Texas." In addition, their mammoth petition drive in support of the Thirteenth Amendment, which would abolish "slavery or involuntary servitude" in the United States forever, gained more than four hundred thousand signatures. "Here they are," the petitioners announced in February 1864, "a mighty army, one hundred thousand strong, without arms or banners; the advance-guard of a yet larger army." The petition affirmed that slavery was the "guilty origin of the rebellion," and remains "a *national enemy,* to be pursued and destroyed as such," and that "to save the national life, there is no power, in the ample arsenal of self-defense, which Congress may not grasp."[9]

LINCOLN HAD GOOD REASON TO INTERPRET HIS REELECTION IN November 1864 as a popular mandate to destroy slavery and "save the national life." The Emancipation Proclamation was a wartime measure that was necessary but insufficient, for it left slavery intact in areas outside rebel control. The proclamation also remained clouded by legal uncertainty, and Lincoln feared the courts might strike it down or Congress might overturn it, perhaps as a means of luring the Southern states back into the Union. The Thirteenth Amendment had been passed by the Senate in April 1864, but the House of Representatives remained deeply divided over the question. In January 1865 Lincoln, Seward, and a team of lobbyists and politicians, including radical Republican leader Thaddeus Stevens, began cajoling, inducing, and, when necessary, bribing congressmen to get the necessary two-thirds majority in the House.[10]

It was in the midst of this furious lobbying campaign that Francis Preston Blair Sr., a venerable Maryland Republican moderate, asked Lincoln for permission to approach his old friend Jefferson Davis and try to bring the South to the peace table. Two of Blair's sons, Frank and Montgomery, were prominent Republicans, and the latter was a member of Lincoln's cabinet. That must have helped because Lincoln, though he had reason to be skeptical about the Confederacy's good faith, was willing to grant the senior Blair safe passage to Richmond.

On January 12, 1865, Blair made the grim journey through the lines to Richmond, passing starving soldiers deserting from Robert E. Lee's army as he went. He met his old friend Davis at his office and, without delay, read to him the "suggestions" he had prepared for peace and reconstruction. Blair's plan was a half-mad tour de force that sounded remarkably like Seward's infamous foreign war panacea, repackaged to serve postwar reconciliation. In short, the South would rejoin the Union, and Jefferson Davis, whose military career began in the Mexican War, would lead an invasion of Mexico with legions of Confederate veterans at the vanguard. They would topple Maximilian from his throne, restore Juárez to power, and reunite Americans in a patriotic war for democracy in North America. Blair hinted that Davis might even conquer northern Mexico for the United States and become military dictator there.

It was a bizarre plan, but Blair's main point was that the Confederate cause of preserving slavery was doomed. Even the Confederacy, Blair told Davis, had now acknowledged that "all the world condemns" slavery. He alluded to the mission of Duncan Kenner, who, he somehow knew, was on his way to Europe to sacrifice slavery and "appeal for succor to European potentates." They were offering to sacrifice slavery in order to "enslave themselves" to "foreign protection under the rule of monarchy!" The South was aligning itself with the enemies of American democracy, Blair concluded. Thus, the "War against the Union becomes a War for Monarchy." He went on to excoriate Napoleon III's despotic designs to make the Latin race supreme in North America. If Davis followed Blair's proposal, the rebel leader could become the hero of the hour, "the fortunate man" who can counter Napoleon's "formidable scheme of conquest" and "at the same time deliver his country from the bloody agony now covering it in mourning."[11]

Davis was apparently not dazzled by dreams of glory in Mexico, nor would he concede Confederate independence. He told Blair only that he was willing to negotiate peace between "our two countries." Francis Blair, undaunted, returned to Washington full of optimism that he had opened the path to peace, and he persuaded a skeptical Lincoln that, though Davis was unyielding, there were many in the Confederate leadership he spoke to in Richmond who realized their situation was hopeless and would come to terms. A meeting between unnamed representatives of the warring parties was agreed to for February 3 at Hampton Roads, Virginia.[12]

Meanwhile, the House of Representatives passed the Thirteenth Amendment. Lincoln signed the bill on February 1, but it would not be law until three-quarters of the states ratified the amendment. Would Southern states be able to come back into the Union and block ratification? Might they even dictate the final terms of slavery's death and possibly secure compensation from an exhausted Union? Radicals were furious at the thought of Lincoln making concessions to the South at this, their hour of triumph over the Slave Power. Blair and his crowd were willing to pardon rebels, restore confiscated property, award compensation for slaves, and return the Southern states to the nation as if they had not led a rebellion against it for four years.[13]

On February 3 three Confederate commissioners—Vice President Alexander Stephens, Senator Robert M. T. Hunter, and Assistant Secretary of War Robert Campbell—were escorted through Union lines. As they crossed over the no-man's-land, soldiers from both sides climbed out of their trenches, cheered, and began chanting, "Peace! Peace!"[14]

There were additional signals that the Confederate commissioners might accept reunion in defiance of their president, and Lincoln therefore decided at the last minute to join Seward at Hampton Roads. The five men met on a steamboat, the *River Queen,* where Lincoln greeted the Confederate commissioners warmly and joked with his old friend Alexander Stephens as they sat down to talk.

Lincoln opened the discussion by saying that the restoration of the Union was the main prerequisite for peace, and that was the basis for their meeting. Stephens, as head of the commission, was eager to talk about Blair's plan for a united invasion of Mexico. Lincoln explained that Blair's proposal was unauthorized, as everyone knew, but Stephens kept returning to the subject and began waxing patriotic about the "sacred" principles of the Monroe Doctrine. He proposed a cease-fire, followed by an allied Union and Confederate invasion of Mexico. Sometime after rescuing Mexico, the Southern states could come to some kind of "settlement" with the Union.

Lincoln had to make it clear, once again: they were there to discuss terms of reunion, not an armistice between two nations. Stephens then asked what was to become of the slaves, the great majority of whom remained unaffected by the Emancipation Proclamation. That is when Seward pulled out a copy of the recently passed Thirteenth Amendment.

Lincoln said there was some question as to role of the "insurgent states" in ratifying the amendment. If it required three-quarters of all states, the South might defeat the amendment. Lincoln also tempted the Confederate representatives by speaking of the possibility of compensation for slaves if the South agreed to end its rebellion. When Seward protested, Lincoln magnanimously admitted that the North shared in the blame for slavery and must now share in paying for its abolition.[15]

There was never any real chance for peace at Hampton Roads. Davis had not authorized any terms of peace that involved reunion or emancipation, while Lincoln insisted on an end to armed rebellion, full emancipation, and full restoration of the Union. The Confederate commissioners had no intention of defying Davis. The meeting ended after four hours, and the war continued to its bitter end.[16]

SHERMAN'S ARMY RESUMED ITS CRUEL MARCH INTO SOUTH CAROLINA that February. Some thought it was in revenge for the false gesture toward peace at Hampton Roads that his army left the state's capital, Columbia, in smoldering ruins on February 17. One Confederate general likened Sherman's invading army to that of Julius Caesar for its ravaging speed. Meanwhile, Grant's army had entrenched around Petersburg. After months of siege, Robert E. Lee's army was running short of men, as death, disease, and desertion took their grim toll.

Lincoln's second inaugural address took place one month after Hampton Roads. It is often lauded for its conciliatory offer of "malice toward none, charity for all," but that came at the end of a much sterner speech. Lincoln reminded people that the rebellion's purpose was "to strengthen, perpetuate, and extend" slavery, and he speculated that the Almighty had brought "this terrible war" as the only way to remove slavery. "If God wills that it continue, until all the wealth piled by the bond-man's two hundred and fifty years of unrequited toil shall be sunk, and until every drop of blood drawn with the lash, shall be paid by another drawn with the sword," so be it.[17]

Confederate diplomats in Europe, meanwhile, were preparing to rescue the South by winning foreign intervention, not by accepting peace and reunion. As Lincoln spoke, Slidell was in Paris, James Mason and Duncan Kenner were in London, and Prince Polignac was en route to France from Louisiana, all bearing offers to sacrifice slavery for independence, or so they were instructed.

In Richmond Jefferson Davis resolved to never surrender, to hold out for aid from Europe, and to keep his cabinet intact so that Kenner, Mason, and Slidell would still represent a government that Europe could recognize. But when Lee warned the president that Petersburg was about to fall and Richmond had to be evacuated, Davis wasted little time. On April 2 he and his cabinet officers boarded a train packed with official papers and gold and silver from the Confederate Treasury. Late that night a government in exile, riding in what was called the "Cabinet Car," pulled out of Richmond. On Davis's orders Confederate soldiers set off enormous explosions of munitions after the train left. The fires illuminated the city as desperate mobs of people poured into the streets, plundering, drinking whiskey, and looting whatever the flames did not devour.[18]

Two days later Lincoln traveled by boat to Richmond, the smoke still rising from its ruins. He walked unescorted through the rubble-strewn streets flanked by scorched chimneys, holding the hand of his young son, Tad. Word of his arrival spread quickly through the city, and large crowds formed. Blacks greeted him with awe, some kneeling, kissing his hand and clothing. In an astonishing gesture of equality, Lincoln removed his hat and bowed before one grateful black man. Union soldiers were frightened that someone might assail the president and at one point stepped in with bayonets to keep the crowds back. Lincoln finally made his way to Jefferson Davis's home, the Confederate White House, and sat at his desk, pondering the end of a long, hard war.[19]

On Sunday, April 9, Robert E. Lee surrendered his army to Grant at Appomattox Court House, marking the effective end of the fighting. That day Lincoln was visiting the troops at City Point, outside the capital.

In honor of a visiting French official, the Marquis de Chambrun, Lincoln asked a military band to play "La Marseillaise," the French republican anthem banned under Napoleon III's regime. He told Chambrun he had always liked the tune and noted the irony of a Frenchman having to come to America to hear it. Chambrun, a thorough republican in sympathies, appreciated the gesture, and Lincoln had them play it again. Then the president graciously asked the band to play "Dixie," which the French visitor had never heard. "That tune is now Federal property," the president joked, but "it is good to show the rebels that," quite unlike France, "with us they will be free to hear it again."[20]

Even after the news from Appomattox finally reached him in Greensboro, North Carolina, on April 13, Jefferson Davis rejected his generals' advice and refused to surrender. He now led a fugitive government, whose armies were melting away. Davis held on to dreams of a last stand west of the Mississippi River. "The cause is not yet dead," he told weary Confederate soldiers in Charlotte. "Determination and fortitude" would yet bring victory.[21]

In Washington a stage actor named John Wilkes Booth was not ready to see the South surrender, either. For weeks he had been conspiring with others, including agents of the Confederate government, to kidnap President Lincoln, hold him hostage in Richmond, and negotiate the return of prisoners. When that plot failed, and some of the conspirators abandoned him, he turned to an assassination plot whose aim was to decapitate the Union government by killing Lincoln, Vice President Andrew Johnson, Secretary of State Seward, and even General Grant. Booth wanted to avenge the South and redeem it from humiliation and defeat, but he also hoped to reignite the South's will to fight.[22]

Grant and his wife did not join the Lincolns at Ford's Theatre the night of the assassination, and Johnson was spared by a failure of nerve on the part of Booth's coconspirator. Seward survived only because another assassin's gun failed, but he was attacked with a knife that left a horrible gash on his face. Booth was the only one to fully carry out his part of the assassination conspiracy that Friday evening, April 14.[23]

Jefferson Davis was in Charlotte, North Carolina, when he learned of the assassination four days later on April 19. He had just delivered a brief speech to a sullen, war-weary crowd. "The cause is not yet dead," he told them. "We may still hope for success." Someone handed him a telegram with the news. Davis did not openly rejoice, as some accused, but he coldly observed that there were a great many others he would sooner have seen assassinated.[24]

The assassination gave diehard Confederates new hope, just as Booth had intended. Confederate general Wade Hampton of South Carolina, one of the largest slaveholders in the South, pleaded with Davis to lead a last stand in the West. "We are not conquered," he implored. "If you should propose to cross the Mississippi I can bring many good men to escort you over." "If Texas will hold out, or will seek the protectorate of Maximilian, we can still make head against the enemy." "My plan is to collect all the men who will still stick to their colors, and to get to Texas."[25]

Davis wrote to his wife, Varina, on April 23 to tell her he was heading for Mexico, where they might "have the world from which to choose." Francis Blair's earlier promise of glory in Mexico must have stayed with him, and it was known that Maximilian was welcoming Confederate refugees. Before he was killed, John Wilkes Booth also planned to seek asylum in Mexico.[26]

Those members of Davis's government in exile who remained with the fugitive government were reduced to begging shoddy quarters from citizens or camping out in tents. Judah P. Benjamin decided to say farewell to Davis and made his way to Florida, hired a boat to Havana, and from there sailed to England to begin a new life. Davis was finally captured on May 10 in southern Georgia, camped in tents with his wife and a small military guard. Federal troops arrested him as he tried to escape while disguised in a woman's coat and shawl, a detail that invited merciless ridicule in the press. He was charged with high treason and imprisoned at Fort Monroe, near Washington, DC, to await his fate.[27]

Meanwhile, the Union was overcome with grief. News of Lincoln's assassination struck with painful force, all the more for coming at the jubilant moment of hard-earned victory at war's end. In many quarters his death was instantly transformed into a narrative of Christian martyrdom—the visit to Richmond the previous week, the assassin's attack on Good Friday, the slow death that came early Saturday morning all sustained a Christian parable of a man chosen by God to die for the nation's sins so that others could be free. That Easter Sunday hundreds of sermons interpreted the tragedy as God's plan for America, the price paid for the sin of slavery and the blessings of returning peace and liberty.[28]

After the assassination Lincoln's body lay in state underneath the Capitol dome, the coffin open as tens of thousands of grief-stricken citizens filed by. An enormous funeral procession took place in Washington on Wednesday, April 19, a hallowed day in national history marking the beginning of the American Revolution ninety years earlier. A funeral train returned the body to his home in Springfield, following a circuitous route that took nearly two weeks over seventeen hundred miles of track, moving at a glacial pace at times as people stood through the night with torches lit in silent tribute to the fallen leader as the train slowly passed. Citizens dressed in black and wearing black veils or armbands stood in lines for hours to mourn their slain president.[29]

Walt Whitman captured the mood as only a poet could:

> *Coffin that passes through lanes and streets,*
> *Through day and night, with the great cloud darkening*
> *the land,*
> *With the pomp of the inloop'd flags, with the cities draped*
> *in black,*
> *With the show of the States themselves, as of crape-veil'd*
> *women, standing,*
> *With processions long and winding, and the flambeaus*
> *of the night,*
> *With the countless torches lit—with the silent sea of faces,*
> *and the unbared heads,*
> *With the waiting depot, the arriving coffin, and the*
> *sombre faces,*
> *With dirges through the night, with the thousand voices*
> *rising strong and solemn*[30]

News of the assassination did not arrive in Europe until April 26. Immediately, long lines of mourners formed outside US legations, and in the coming days and weeks hundreds of condolence letters poured into diplomatic posts in all parts of the world. Some were the obligatory obsequies from one government or head of state to another. Not a few

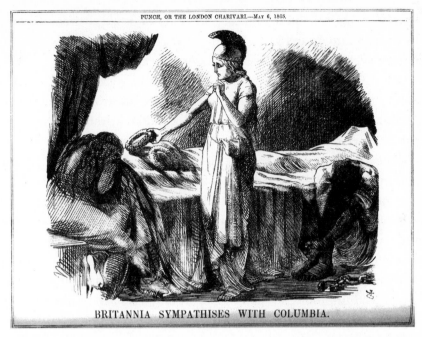

PUNCH, OR THE LONDON CHARIVARI.—MAY 6, 1865.

BRITANNIA SYMPATHISES WITH COLUMBIA.

36. *Britannia Sympathises with Columbia,* by John Tenniel, for *Punch,* May 6, 1865. (COURTESY ALLAN T. KOHL, MINNEAPOLIS COLLEGE OF ART AND DESIGN)

government leaders affirmed—not always honestly—their unwavering support of the Union and their faith in its leader.

What impressed American diplomats abroad, however, were the popular demonstrations of grief and support for America that swept through large cities and distant villages. The letters of condolence and public resolutions, coming from all levels of society and from remote corners of the globe, gave remarkable evidence that people everywhere had been closely following events in America all this time. Their letters revealed an intimate knowledge of Lincoln's life story, his words and ideas. Even seasoned diplomats who had led the Union's public diplomacy campaign abroad were surprised by the profusion and boldness of demonstrations of sympathy for Lincoln and America.

There were more than one thousand foreign letters of condolence sent to US legations or directly to Washington. The overwhelming majority were from ordinary citizens, ad hoc town assemblies, Masonic lodges, workers' trade unions, student organizations, women's groups, and a wide array of antislavery and reform societies. They came largely from the major cities of Europe and Latin America, but also from small rural villages, and not a few arrived from the Caribbean, Africa, and Asia.[31]

John Bigelow was overwhelmed by the public reaction in Paris, not least by the demonstration on April 28 when hundreds of students came through the streets in defiance of the police and broke through their cordon to enter Bigelow's house and express their sorrow and conviction. "I never saw all classes so entirely moved by any occurrence in a foreign country," he wrote to his old friend Thurlow Weed. "Strange to say," he went on, "what has astonished people most is the perfect ease and quiet with which Mr. Lincoln was replaced and the utter uselessness of the crime as a political remedy." Instead of showing popular government as inherently weak and fragile, America's trial by war, including the assassination, presented the very opposite lesson. "The mysterious power of republican institutions was never so highly estimated here as now, never," Bigelow added. "They are compelled to admit that we have found a political secret which none of the Old States of Europe possesses."[32]

The letters of condolence emerged from a welter of emotions— jubilant celebrations of triumph for republicanism and emancipation, grief and anger over an assassination that foreigners recognized as the familiar instrument of despots and revolutionaries everywhere. They often expressed admiration for America, the Great Republic, not as an exceptional phenomenon, but rather as the vanguard of a universal struggle for equality and popular government. One eulogy in France's *Avenir National* avowed that "Lincoln represented the cause of democracy in the largest and the most universal acceptation of the word. That cause is our cause, as much as it is that of the United States."[33]

The citizens of Acireale, a small fishing village on the east coast of Sicily, wonderfully expressed a similar idea: "Abraham Lincoln was not yours only—he was also ours, because he was a brother whose great mind and fearless conscience guided a people to union, and courageously uprooted slavery." "In President Lincoln," a group of French medical students proclaimed, "we weep for a fellow citizen; for no country is shut up now." "We are the fellow citizens of John Brown, of Abraham Lincoln, and of Mr. Seward." "Your history is the same as ours," the citizens of Abruzzo, Italy, avowed. "From Lincoln and Seward to Garibaldi and Mazzini, the tradition of the great struggle between good and evil, liberty and slavery, civilization and barbarism, national autonomy and the rule of foreign despots, has ever been the same."[34]

Political demonstrations were still prohibited in France, but Lincoln's death provided an exquisite opportunity to cloak political protest as mourning. Lincoln had once considered joining a Masonic lodge in Springfield and then decided against it out of fear it might harm his political fortunes. But that did not bother the Masonic brotherhood of France. Freemasonry had long been a refuge for liberalism and anticlericalism, and the opportunity to mourn a fallen brother across the ocean provided a welcome occasion to give the emperor a thumb in the eye. The French Masons draped their lodges in black crepe, wore black armbands, organized full Masonic funeral processions, fired salvos, and published declarations of sympathy laced with unsubtle digs at the Second Empire.[35]

"Abraham Lincoln died like a mason, to elevate humanity outraged by slavery," one lodge proclaimed. Mourning would carry on for months, even years. The Clement Friendship Lodge vowed to fire a "mortuary salvo" at each session during the next three months to honor him "not only as a brother, but as a friend of the whole human race." None surpassed the Admirers of the Universe lodge, which vowed to fire a salute on the anniversary of Lincoln's assassination over the next ten years.[36]

In late May Bigelow learned from the US consul in Nantes that a popular subscription had been taken up to present a medal to Mrs. Lincoln. It became known as the "two sous' subscription" because all contributions were limited to ten centimes (two sous under the old monetary system) as a way of broadening public participation. It said as much about the nervous state of Napoleon III's regime as it did about the enthusiasm of the French that police moved in, banned further fund-raising, and confiscated the money and subscription lists. Bigelow acidly remarked to the consul in Nantes that he was sorry that the police "did not think it safe for the people of his commune to express two sous' worth of sympathy for the widow of our murdered president."[37]

The two sous' subscription soon became a cause célèbre, and a group of illustrious republicans calling themselves the Committee of the French Democracy, among them exiled novelist Victor Hugo, took up "the people's subscription." Over the next several months they secured no fewer than forty thousand pledges and would have gotten many more were it not for continued government harassment. The medal had to be struck in Geneva,

37. The French medal for Mrs. Lincoln, presented by the Committee of the French Democracy. (AUTHOR'S PHOTOGRAPH, COURTESY OF MICHELLE KROWL, ABRAHAM LINCOLN PAPERS, LIBRARY OF CONGRESS)

Switzerland, and it was not until the end of 1866 that the "most eminent republicans of France" presented the medal to Bigelow.[38]

"If France possessed the liberties enjoyed by republican America, it is not by thousands, but by millions that would be counted, with us, the admirers of Lincoln, and the partisans of those opinions to which he devoted his life, and which are consecrated by his death," the committee's letter accompanying the medal explained. On behalf of the Committee of the French Democracy, Eugène Pelletan presented the medal to Bigelow in a small purple velvet box and said, "Tell Mrs. Lincoln that in this little box is the heart of France."[39]

The medal, now in the Library of Congress, was struck in solid gold, over three inches in diameter and more than a quarter of an inch thick.

On one side was a profile of Lincoln with an inscription in French around the edge: "Dedicated by the French democracy to Lincoln, twice elected President of the United States." On the other side was the image of an African American man and boy and a mourning angel flanking a tombstone that was inscribed, "Lincoln, an honest man, abolished slavery, reestablished the union, saved the Republic without veiling the statue of liberty." Below was the French revolutionary slogan, *Liberté, Égalité, Fraternité*. If the medal represented the heart of France, it also signified the resurgent ideological zeal of French republicanism.[40]

IN APRIL 1865 JOHN BIGELOW BECAME US MINISTER TO FRANCE. The previous December his predecessor, William Dayton, was found dead, apparently from a stroke, at the Hotel de Louvre in the apartment of a certain Lizzie St. John Eckel, whom Bigelow described as a "rather pretty and decidedly enterprising widow" who had fled an unhappy past in Canada and New York for Paris. There she soon became engaged to a man some eighty years old, "a count of some sort," Bigelow thought. The American doctor summoned to the scene was a family friend, and he quietly arranged a carriage to secretly transport the corpse back to the US legation. Then, in collusion with Dayton's son and perhaps his wife, the doctor concocted a story about too much pumpkin pie contributing to a tragic death during a late night at the office. Dayton was never known for his diligence in office, and Madam Eckel's reputation as an adventuress and the mystery surrounding Dayton's death naturally fed the Parisian appetite for scandal.

Paris gossipers were not the only curious ones; after Bigelow sent the report on his investigation, Seward pressed him to disclose more about the character of Madam Eckel and the physician's opinion as to whether anything occurred "by which the apoplexy may have been occasioned." Bigelow had gone along with the Dayton family story to shield them from embarrassment, but he wrote a highly confidential letter to Seward that he asked him to read and burn. Based on the state of Dayton's clothing, as Bigelow delicately put it, the doctor had indeed surmised that "something had been going on to which neither party could afford to have witnesses." Madam Eckel had also confided to Bigelow that Mr. Dayton was "fond of her and in the habit of using endearing language to her when they were together." The doctor had also told him that she betrayed her misconduct by falling on her knees before the doctor and hysterically begging him to "protect her reputation." No doubt she was concerned with what her aging fiancé might make of all this. Bigelow reported further that other parts of the Dayton family's story were false and that the rumors in Paris clubs and at the police station were that "his death was the consequence *de faire amour* [of making love] too soon after dinner."[41]

Bigelow had become accustomed to covering for Dayton's lapses as a diplomat during the previous four years; now he found himself filling the void entirely. In early April he was appointed to succeed Dayton as US minister to France.

As July 4, 1865, approached, Bigelow decided to make Independence Day a magnificent celebration. He magnanimously offered to stand treat for a giant fête champêtre, an outdoor garden party in the Bois de Boulogne, a grand Parisian park. Every American in Europe that he knew, or even heard of, was invited. So, too, were the entire foreign diplomatic corps in Paris; prominent members of the French government, along with their wives, children, and domestic servants; and any others they might wish to bring. The invitation list exceeded five hundred, and upwards of seven hundred showed up. They crowded into an immense tent festooned with American flags and bunting; inside were banquet tables, a band, and an enormous carpet rolled out for dancing.

In his welcoming remarks Bigelow reveled in the glory of the day. The American Union was safe again, he told the crowd, and "democratic-republican Government is no longer an experiment." The Fourth of July, he added, had "now acquired an importance in the eyes of mankind which it never possessed before."

The celebration rounded off with music, entertainment, and dancing into the night. Guests gathered outside the tent to sing "The Star-Spangled Banner" and watch a stupendous display of fireworks. The grand finale featured an enormous American eagle, with Daniel Webster's famous words ablaze: "The Union now and forever, one and inseparable." As Bigelow's fireworks lit up the sky over Paris, lusty republican cheers went up from the Bois de Boulogne that might have been heard as far as the Tuileries Palace.[42]

REPUBLICAN RISORGIMENTO

The newspapers and the men that opposed the cause of the great Republic, are those like the ass of the fable that dared kick the lion believing him fallen; but today as they see it rise in all its majesty, they change their language. The American question is about life for the liberty of the world.

—GIUSEPPE GARIBALDI, MARCH 27, 1865

THE SPIRIT OF BIGELOW'S FOURTH OF JULY CELEBRATION THAT fabulous night in Paris glowed across much of the Atlantic world in the coming years. The trial of democracy, it seemed, had returned a very different verdict from the one conservatives had relished four years earlier. "Under a strain such as no aristocracy, no monarchy, no empire could have supported," one English Radical noted, "Republican institutions have stood firm. It is we, now, who call upon the privileged classes to mark the result." The Union's triumph, which had been so long doubted by its detractors, sent an exhilarating thrill of vindication through reformers on both sides of the Atlantic. For the moment at least, there was something of a republican Risorgimento, a season of resurgent hope for popular government and universal emancipation.[1]

From London Giuseppe Mazzini, the champion of Italy's Risorgimento, summoned America to carry on as the leader of what he proposed as the "Universal Republican Alliance." It would form a "moral Atlantic

Cable," uniting republicans on both sides of the Atlantic. "You must," he told Americans, "be a guiding and instigating force, for the good of your own country and that of Humanity." Mazzini had in mind more than moral force; he called on America to lead the republican international brigades in an invasion of Mexico to overthrow this "outpost of Caesarism."[2]

Americans were weary of war and did not answer Mazzini's call to arms, but his dream of an international republican resurgence was about to be realized in other ways and on many fronts. In the American hemisphere the hostile constellation of slavery, monarchy, and empire that had ringed the United States in 1860 was defeated or in retreat by the end of the decade. The Confederate rebellion had been vanquished, and Reconstruction would proceed on the basis of free labor and the enfranchisement of former slaves. By 1867 it appeared that the Republican Party was determined to defend the hard-earned freedom of black citizens with an ongoing military occupation of the defeated South.

In the Caribbean Spanish dreams of imperial revival died hard in the jungles of Santo Domingo during the spring and summer of 1865. The Santo Domingo republicans, many of them former slaves, had bled the Spanish invaders during four grueling years of guerrilla warfare. Spain's prime minister denounced the proposal to withdraw as a "humiliating declaration of impotence." But in April 1865, facing a severely strained treasury, growing signs of unrest in Cuba, and the threat of US naval power in the Caribbean, Queen Isabella II finally called an end to Spain's experiment in recolonization. Thousands of Dominican collaborators scrambled to board Spanish ships as they departed for Cuba that summer.[3]

Spain was also forced to withdraw from reckless imperialist ventures in Peru and Chile that had begun with the military seizure of Peru's guano-rich Chincha Islands in 1864. This eventually led to the blockade and bombardment of Valparaiso, Chile, and Callao, Peru, supposedly in answer to insults to the Spanish flag. By the end of 1866 Spain welcomed the good offices of the United States to help mediate its retreat from the South American morass it had entered.[4]

In Madrid General Juan Prim, former commander of Spain's Mexican expedition and leader of the Progressista party, denounced the imperialist government for making Spain "the laughing stock among foreign nations" and in June 1866 led a military revolt. Prim was forced into exile when the rebellion failed and rumors circulated that he was meeting with John Bigelow to arrange for US support of a republican revolution in Spain in exchange for the sale of Cuba. In September 1868 Prim and others led Spain's Glorious Revolution, which overthrew Queen Isabella II and forced her into exile in France. "The Bourbons are abolished," the *New York Times* cheered; finally, Spain stood before the world as "a State without a King and a Government existing by popular will."[5]

Simultaneously, a republican independence movement erupted against Spanish rule in Cuba. During America's Civil War, slaves in Cuba's sugar fields could be heard chanting, *Avanza, Lincoln, Avanza, tu eres nuestra esperanza* (Onward, Lincoln, Onward, you are our hope). Since the 1810s Cuban slaveholders had been loyal to the Spanish crown out of fear that a revolution for independence would unleash a Haitian-style uprising among their slaves. All that changed one morning in October 1868 when Carlos Manuel de Céspedes, a wealthy Cuban sugar planter and liberal intellectual, told his astonished slaves they were free and then invited them to take up arms for Cuba's freedom. This was the beginning of Cuba's Ten Years' War, which failed to emancipate Cuba but succeeded in putting slavery on the road to extinction, first with a "free womb" law in 1870 that granted freedom to children of slave mothers; complete abolition followed in 1886.[6]

In January 1864 Brazil's emperor, Dom Pedro II, wrote to one of his senators that "the successes of the American Union force us to think about the future of slavery in Brazil." So long as the United States sustained slavery, "we were shielded," as one Brazilian senator put it. By 1871 there was no need for a war to end slavery, another politician poignantly explained. "The world laughing at us was enough; becoming the scorn of all nations . . . was enough." In 1871 Brazil passed the Rio Branco law, which freed all children born to slave women, but it was not until 1888 that Dom Pedro's daughter Princess Isabel signed the Golden Law that abolished slavery completely. The next year the last American monarchy was overthrown, and Brazil embarked on its own republican experiment.[7]

Union victory had already doomed the monarchical experiment in Mexico. In April 1865 Emperor Maximilian took the occasion of Lincoln's assassination to send a conciliatory letter of sympathy and friendship to the new president, Andrew Johnson. It went unanswered. So did his second letter, and his third. In June 1865 Maximilian sent an envoy to Washington, but Johnson refused to receive any representative of the illegitimate usurpers of power in Mexico.[8]

With the threat of a Franco-Confederate alliance gone, William Seward, who stayed on as Johnson's secretary of state, thought time was his best ally in Mexico. He gave no satisfaction to those calling on the United States to invade Mexico and help overthrow Maximilian.[9]

Matías Romero, the Republic of Mexico's young ambassador to Washington, impatient with Seward's inaction, went around him by enlisting support from Union commander Ulysses S. Grant, who had long sympathized with Mexico's plight. In June 1865 Grant sent a lengthy memorandum to President Johnson, warning him that "a monarchical government on this continent" sustained "by foreign bayonets" constituted an act of hostility against the United States. The spirit of the Monroe Doctrine as defender of American republicanism lived again. Grant was alarmed by news that diehard Confederates were bringing slaves and arms to "New Virginia," a colony in the Mexican state of Sonora. Maximilian had issued a decree allowing what amounted to slave labor in the Sonora mines. The beleaguered emperor wanted the Confederate exiles to form a bulwark against US invasion. Grant suspected worse, and he warned Johnson that Confederate "rebels in arms . . . protected by French bayonets" were preparing to take control of northern Mexico. If Maximilian's regime was allowed to endure, he prophesied, America would "see nothing before us but a long, expensive, and bloody war," with enemies of America "joined by tens of thousands of disciplined soldiers" from the South embittered by four years of failed war.[10]

Grant ordered General Philip Sheridan to take command of some fifty thousand Union soldiers on the Texas-Mexican border to thwart the plans of Confederate diehards rumored to be mounting a last stand from northern Mexico. Grant told Sheridan, "The French invasion of Mexico was so closely related to the rebellion as to be essentially part of it." Both men were committed republicans, and they shared a quiet understanding that US forces were also there to intimidate the French, possibly precipitate war with them, and aid Benito Juárez's beleaguered republican army. Carefully avoiding blatant acts of aggression, Sheridan's troops left large stores of arms and munitions on the banks of the Rio Grande, which mysteriously disappeared before daybreak. "Grant may yet be the La Fayette of Mexico, the Garibaldi of this continent," a speaker at one of Romero's New York banquets proclaimed. "Let the torches of civil war in the United States and Mexico be extinguished in the blood of the minions of Napoleon."[11]

Across Mexico Sarah Yorke Stevenson, a young American living in Mexico City, recalled that a new spirit of resistance "vibrated throughout the land" in the summer of 1865. Panic spread among conservatives, who feared the United States was about to come to Juárez's rescue. Emperor Napoleon III was reviewing his troops in Algeria when news of the Union's final victory reached him. With close to forty thousand troops committed to Mexico, another twenty thousand guarding the pope in Rome, and some eighty thousand in Algeria, the French Second Empire was stretched thin. Meanwhile, a powerful united Germany, forged in "blood and iron" by Prussia's Otto von Bismarck, loomed menacingly across the Rhine River.[12]

Maximilian had no intention of abandoning Mexico. On the contrary, he took extraordinary steps to establish an enduring dynasty. After eight years of marriage Maximilian and Charlotte had no children, and unflattering rumors of venereal disease or other "difficulties" circulated freely. Maximilian seized upon a bizarre solution that would "Mexicanize" his Hapsburg line; he would adopt the infant grandson of Mexico's first emperor, Agustín de Iturbide, whose career had ended in 1824 before a Mexican firing squad.[13]

One of Iturbide's sons had married an American woman, Alice Green, from Washington, DC. Their son, Augustín, named in honor of his grandfather, was born in Mexico City one year before Maximilian and Charlotte arrived. It must have occurred to Maximilian that a prince with dual citizenship might be a diplomatic asset if he wanted peace with the United States. In September 1865 Maximilian offered to adopt young Augustín and confer upon him the title of prince. The parents were to receive a handsome pension, but by agreement they would leave Mexico and return only with Maximilian's permission.

On her way to Veracruz a few days later, Alice Iturbide was tormented by a mother's change of heart. She returned to the capital and sent a heart-rending message to Maximilian, imploring him to allow her to reclaim her child. The emperor sent a carriage to pick her up, but instead of being delivered to the royal palace at Chapultepec, the distraught mother was taken to Veracruz, deported, and banned from ever returning to Mexico.[14]

Prince Iturbide did Maximilian little good. Mexican conservatives were outraged that he had chosen the infant grandson of a deposed tyrant over one of their own aristocratic families. Many were already furious over Maximilian's refusal to repeal the liberal laws that confiscated church lands and secularized public education. Maximilian still wanted to be an enlightened monarch; he even tried to bring Juárez into his government as prime minister. Mexico's conservatives wanted a strongman who would crush the godless republicans, not make peace with them.

With US forces on the Mexican border and Juárez's army scoring victories in the north, Maximilian sought to solidify conservative support by issuing the Black Decree in October 1865. The "time for indulgence has passed," the decree announced; the "national will" had ratified the monarchy, and "henceforth the struggle must be between the honorable men of the nation and bands of brigands and evil-doers" who would be summarily executed when apprehended.[15]

Meanwhile, Seward had instructed his minister in Paris, John Bigelow, to meet with the French foreign minister, Drouyn de Lhuys, in April 1865. Bigelow gave assurances that the United States preferred not "to meddle with the experiment which Europe was now making in Mexico." He pointedly used the word *experiment* at least eight times and added that his government thought it was in "the interest of all the world that this should be an *experimentum cruces*," meaning decisive and final proof.[16]

In January 1866 Napoleon III stood before the Corps législatif to announce that its "civilizing" mission in Mexico had been completed. French troops would begin withdrawing in stages later in the year. He wrote to Maximilian to explain that Mexico was now sufficiently strong to stand on its own without French aid. No one believed that, least of all Maximilian.[17]

Maximilian was tempted to return to Miramar Castle near Trieste and live out his days in peace, but his more resolute wife, Empress Charlotte, would have none of it. In July 1866 she embarked on a vain mission to seek aid from the Catholic thrones of Europe. Mexican republicans satirized Maximilian's plight in a popular song that featured the emperor standing at the shore sadly watching as his empress departed: *Adiós, Mamá Carlota, Adiós mi tierno amor, Se fueran los frances, Se va el emperador* (Good-bye, Mama Carlota, Good-bye my tender love, The French have left, The emperor will go, too).[18]

Napoleon III and Empress Eugénie received Charlotte in Paris, but only to encourage her to persuade her husband to return to Europe. She then went to the Vatican and begged Pope Pius IX to stand by the mission to restore Catholic authority to Mexico. The pope gave her no comfort, either. She began rambling incoherently about a scheme of Napoleon III to poison her and then started pleading for asylum at the Vatican. She had been slowly going mad for some time, everyone seemed to conclude in retrospect, but she was not deluded about those who had betrayed her and Maximilian.[19]

The last of the French forces marched out of Mexico City in early February 1867. Mexicans lined the streets, watching in eerie silence. General François Achille Bazaine, the French commander, invited Maximilian to return with him to Europe, but by this time the emperor of Mexico had decided to accept his fate and stay on in Mexico. With a small band of soldiers he left the capital and prepared to make a last stand near Querétaro, where in May 1867 the republican army took him prisoner, tried him on charges of treason, and sentenced him to death. Garibaldi and Victor Hugo were among the many prominent liberals who pleaded for clemency as a gesture of republican humanity. But Juárez risked rebellion within his own ranks if he dared pardon the author of the Black Decree.[20]

Early on the morning of June 19, 1867, Maximilian was brought before a firing squad outside Querétaro. Thousands of Mexican soldiers looked on as he made a short speech in Spanish that might serve as an epitaph for the entire Grand Design: "Mexicans! Men of my class and race are created by God to be the happiness of nations or their martyrs." "Long live Mexico!" All six bullets struck their mark.[21]

News of Maximilian's execution sent a "painful thrill" throughout the Euro-American world. It arrived in Paris on the day Napoleon III awarded prizes at the Paris International Exposition, which was intended to showcase the city Baron Haussmann had revamped to the glory of the Second Empire. Napoleon said not a word about Mexico that day, and reports of Maximilian's execution were withheld from the press for some time. Monarchs across Europe denounced Juárez and the Mexican liberals for their "savagery" and even spoke of sending troops to avenge Maximilian's death. But the shots from Querétaro sent a mournful echo through the courts of Europe, and calls for retaliation soon fell silent. Charlotte never fully regained her sanity, and she lived out her days at

38. *The Execution of Emperor Maximilian of Mexico, June 19, 1867,* by Édouard Manet. (STAEDTISCHE KUNSTHALLE MUSEUM, PHOTO CREDIT ERICH LESSING, ART RESOURCE, NY)

Miramar and later in Belgium, where she died in 1927. Shortly before his capture, Maximilian, sensing the end, had arranged for Prince Augustín to be returned to his mother, who came to America with the last prince of Mexico.[22]

JEFFERSON DAVIS HAD LANGUISHED IN PRISON FOR TWO YEARS AS Union officials weighed the potential consequences of punishment and martyrdom and debated his fate. He was released in May 1867 at the same time as the curtains were closing on Maximilian in Querétaro. During Davis's time in prison Pope Pius IX sent a token of his esteem, an inscribed photograph of His Holiness that Davis displayed on the wall of his cell. This gesture of respect from one victim of international liberalism to another stood in striking contrast to the pope's notable silence upon the death of Abraham Lincoln.[23]

Theories of Catholic involvement in the Lincoln assassination circulated in the United States and abroad, fueled by unfounded rumors that John Wilkes Booth was a fervent convert and knowledge that Mary Surratt, whose boardinghouse in Washington served as a meeting place for the conspiracy, was devout and was attended at the gallows by Catholic priests. Her son John Surratt, also implicated in the conspiracy, absconded to Montreal, where he was given asylum by a Catholic priest. He later fled to Rome and enlisted in the pope's Pontifical Zouave army. Rufus King, the US minister to Rome, learned of Surratt's presence and demanded his arrest. Surratt was detained, but mysteriously escaped from prison and was only later apprehended and brought back to stand trial in the United States. Unlike his fellow conspirators, Surratt was tried in civil court and set free by a jury of his peers in heavily Catholic Maryland.[24]

Catholic conspiracy theories were sensationalized in a book by Charles Chiniquy, a defrocked Catholic priest who had known Lincoln in Illinois and claimed to have shared intimate discussions with him about the "the sinister influence of the Jesuits" in fomenting the entire war. Chiniquy described Booth as a "tool of the Jesuits" and charged that Pope Pius IX's support of Jefferson Davis and France's Grand Design for a Catholic monarchy in Mexico were part of a concerted conspiracy to destroy America's republican example to the world.[25]

THE UNION'S VICTORY ALSO FORCED CHANGE ON ITS NORTHERN border. The Civil War had served as a sharp reminder to Britain of the vulnerability of Canada. Confederates had launched terrorist raids from Canada into New England late in the war, and the Irish Fenian Brotherhood, made up of Union veterans, had conducted raids in the opposite direction after the war. Both were designed to drag Britain into war with the United States. Britain decided its imperial priorities lay in Europe and Asia, not Canada, and during the Civil War began transforming British North America into a semiautonomous nation that would defend itself.[26]

What was commonly referred to as "Canada" was a constellation of colonial provinces, each subject to British rule but with little political connection to one another. A series of conventions laid the groundwork for a new confederation, and in 1867 the "Dominion of Canada" was born. Officials prudently decided not to call it the "Kingdom of Canada" for fear of provoking its republican neighbors. When William Seward arranged for the US purchase of Alaska from Russia, also in 1867, Canada annexed provinces below Alaska to form one contiguous confederation, extending along the entire US border.[27]

Russia's sale of Alaska was yet another sign of the withdrawal of European empires from the Western Hemisphere. During the Civil War Russia had maintained a benign neutrality toward the Union by rejecting British and French entreaties to join their multilateral scheme for intervention in 1862 and again in 1863. A visit by Russian fleets to New York City and San Francisco in the fall of 1863 was widely interpreted as a gesture of support for the Union. US ships festooned with flags, full-dress banquets, lengthy toasts, and laudatory speeches had welcomed the Russian visitors. Seward's peaceful purchase of Alaska was also interpreted as a sign of good relations between the two countries, but it signified as well America's new capacity to enforce the Monroe Doctrine.[28]

THE REPUBLICAN RESURGENCE OF THE LATE 1860S ALSO SHOOK THE thrones of Europe. Lord Palmerston, the embodiment of the British ruling classes, died in October 1865, and Gladstone inherited a Liberal Party badly split over the vexing issue of democratization. The Reform League, a new grassroots movement, sponsored huge meetings across Britain in the summer of 1866. Brandishing red flags and wearing liberty caps, crowds of men and women poured into London's Trafalgar Square in tremendous displays of support for the expansion of voting rights. In May 1867 the government turned out thousands of police and armed troops to suppress reform "riots" in Hyde Park, but the Radicals refused to be intimidated. Facing what amounted to revolutionary defiance, the British governing classes caved in. Parliament passed the Reform Act of 1867, which vastly expanded voting rights for adult males and brought John Bright's dream of transatlantic Anglo-American republicanism that much closer.[29]

In France the opposition to Napoleon III's imperial regime was also emboldened by the American example. In a widely noted essay published in May 1865, the Comte de Montalembert, one of France's leading liberal Catholic intellectuals, eulogized Lincoln and heralded the Union's victory as a harbinger of democracy's triumph. "Every thing which has occurred in America, from all which is to follow in the future, grave teachings will result for us," Montalembert prophesied, "for, in spite of ourselves, we belong to a society irrevocably democratic."[30]

Napoleon III's reign came to its disastrous end three years after Maximilian's denouement in Mexico. Overreaching as always, the French emperor provoked war with Prussia in 1870. He was ignominiously captured while leading the French army at the Battle of Sedan and was thrown into prison. The opposition seized control of the French government and proclaimed the Third Republic in early September 1870. Following a brutal siege, starving Parisians, who had been reduced to eating rats, dogs, cats, even zoo animals, surrendered to Prussian forces in February 1871, and Bismarck led his victorious army through the streets of a city draped in black. The deposed emperor Napoleon III was later released by the Prussians and, with his wife, Eugénie, fled to exile in Chislehurst, England, where he died in 1873. The radical Paris Commune took command of the city, and for several weeks in the spring of 1871 the revolutionary Communards wreaked havoc on the symbols of aristocratic privilege in Haussmann's glittering city, leaving Napoleon III's Tuileries Palace in smoldering ruins. Thus, amid revolutionary violence and insoluble political divisions, France resumed its troubled experiment with republicanism.[31]

Whereas France was famed for the excesses of republicanism, Germany became known for the new authoritarian state that Otto von Bismarck, the "Iron Chancellor" of Prussia, was building. His vast, centralized German state had annexed large portions of Austria following its quick victory in the Austro-Prussian War of 1866. At the conclusion of the Franco-Prussian War in 1871, Germany took over the former French province of Alsace and parts of Lorraine. Bismarck was changing the map of Europe in other ways, too. The 1866 war had forced Austria to surrender Venice to the Italians. Then the Franco-Prussian war forced Napoleon III to abandon Rome and on September 20, 1870, Italian forces stormed the gates of Rome and drove Pope Pius IX into virtual imprisonment within the Vatican. The Italian Risorgimento was complete and with Rome about to become the capital of united Italy. The destiny of united Germany still lay ahead.[32]

Bismarck never had much patience for democracy. "The great questions of the day," he once famously said, "are not decided by speeches and majority votes . . . but by blood and iron." In 1863, during a tedious round of debate among politicians in the Diet over what he described as some petty "German squabble," Bismarck sat at his desk and feigned taking notes, but he was penning a letter to his old American friend John Lothrop Motley, the US minister to Austria. "My Dear Motley . . . I hate politics, but, as you say truly, like the grocer hating figs, I am none the less obliged to keep my thoughts increasingly occupied with those figs. . . . I am obliged to listen to particularly tasteless speeches out of the mouths of uncommonly childish and excited politicians." Moving from German to English and back again, even throwing in a bit of Italian, Bismarck then took a jab at his idealistic American friend. "You Anglo Saxon Yankees have something of the same kind also. *Do you all know exactly why you are waging such furious war with each other?* All certainly do not know, but they kill each other *con amore* [with love], that's the way the business comes to them. Your battles are bloody, ours wordy."[33]

The unlikely friendship between these men went back thirty years to their days together at the University of Göttingen, where the earnest young American distinguished himself as a scholar and Bismarck made his mark as a bon vivant notorious for drinking, dueling, and eccentric dress. Motley became an eminent historian, and his eloquent advocacy of the Union cause in Europe had earned him an appointment from President Lincoln as US minister to Austria. His friendship with Bismarck had endured vast and growing differences in political ideology. "He is as sincere and resolute a monarchist and absolutist as I am a Republican," Motley once told his daughter. "But that does not interfere with our friendship."[34]

It seemed to this time. Motley did not reply to Bismarck for a full year, and finally the Prussian leader reached out again, employing an unmistakable tone of jocular reconciliation, if not apology, to soothe his old friend "Jack" and implore him to come visit in Berlin. "Let politics be hanged, and come to see me," Bismarck fairly begged. "I promise that the Union jack shall wave over our house, and conversation and the best old hock shall pour damnation upon the rebels."

Motley's pique seemed calmed by his old friend's amiable plea, but he could not resist taking up the question that had gnawed at him for more than a year: "You asked me in the last letter before the present one 'if we knew what we were fighting for.' I can't let the question go unanswered. We are fighting to preserve the existence of a magnificent commonwealth which traitors are trying to destroy, and to annihilate the loathsome institution of negro slavery, to perpetuate and extend which was the sole cause of the Treason. If men can't fight for *such* a cause they had better stop fighting forevermore."[35]

Bismarck's question echoed the one Garibaldi had raised with US diplomats at the beginning of the war: was this no more than an American quarrel, just another petty local boundary dispute of no great consequence to the larger world? On this occasion Motley—and the Union—had an answer.

IN PARIS ONE EVENING IN APRIL 1865, AT A GATHERING AT PROFESSOR Laboulaye's home, friends began discussing the idea of a monument to the friendship between France and America. The discussion seemed to grow out of the same spirit as the "two sous" campaign for Mrs. Lincoln's medal. Censorship still made it risky for Laboulaye and his friends to take action, but five years later the idea was resurrected during another evening gathering of friends at Laboulaye's country home. Among them was Frédéric-Auguste Bartholdi, a young artist from Alsace, which had recently been lost to the Germans. Bartholdi was on his way to America, and the group commissioned him to solicit cooperation during his visit and come up with a design for the monument. After days at sea Bartholdi arrived in New York Harbor and was seized by the idea for a colossal allegorical figure of *La Liberté éclairant le monde* (Liberty enlightening the world), which would stand at the gateway to America.[36]

"She is not liberty with a red cap on her head and a pike in her hand, stepping over corpses," Laboulaye explained to French donors a few years later. Liberty "in one hand holds the torch—no, not the torch that sets afire but the *flambeau,* the candle-flame that enlightens." In her other hand, "she holds the tablets of law." Bartholdi had already begun work on the statue, and as the American centennial approached the unfinished Liberty could be seen looming over the streets of suburban Paris. He was able to send the head and torch-bearing arm to the Philadelphia Centennial in 1876, but another ten years would pass before the entire statue was ready to cross the Atlantic.[37]

39. *La Liberté éclairant le monde* (**Liberty enlightening the world**), under construction at the workshop of Frédéric-Auguste Bartholdi in Paris before it was erected in New York Harbor in 1886. (AUTHOR'S PRIVATE COLLECTION)

By 1886 when *Liberty Enlightening the World* was erected in New York Harbor, the resurgent republican spirit of 1865 was giving way to a conscious campaign of reconciliation that asked Americans to lay aside, if not forget, the disturbing legacy of slavery and secession that had torn the nation apart twenty-five years earlier. Americans were beginning to settle on the idea of the Civil War as a senseless and unnecessary interruption of national progress. Thanks to Emma Lazarus's moving poem "The New Colossus," written in 1883, the monument would be interpreted as America's welcome to the "huddled masses yearning to breathe free" and escaping the Old World to find refuge in a uniquely American asylum of liberty. In time the Statue of Liberty, as it came to be known, became the symbol of America as a sanctuary of freedom for refugees rather than *Liberty Enlightening the World,* the monument to the perseverance of republicanism throughout the world. As a national icon the Statue of Liberty would play a central role in the story of exceptionalism that Americans tell themselves about themselves.

But Laboulaye and Bartholdi had something else in mind. With her gaze fixed across the Atlantic, Liberty faces Europe and is striding toward it while at her feet lay the broken chains of slavery. In one hand she holds a tablet marked "July 4, 1776," and in the other the raised flambeau "radiant upon the two worlds," as Bartholdi described it.

Liberty Enlightening the World remains the greatest monument to America's Civil War as the cause of all nations. It honors the international struggle that in the 1860s shook the Atlantic world and decided the fate of slavery and democracy for the vast future that lay ahead.[38]

ACKNOWLEDGMENTS

MY PASSION FOR HISTORY BEGAN FIFTY YEARS AGO WHEN MY MOTHER, Barbara Ferron Doyle, brought home a shoe box full of letters my great-great-grandfather had sent home while serving as a drummer boy in the 3rd Vermont Infantry. I helped her organize and transcribe the letters, and, without quite knowing it yet, I became a historian that summer. Later I discovered that another ancestor, Frederick Salomon, a German immigrant from Wisconsin, had served as a Union general, and yet another ancestor was a Maryland slaveholder during the Civil War. After more than forty years of teaching and writing, the excitement of learning about the past that my mother ignited that summer has never died.

The inspiration for this book came from my wonderful wife and fellow historian, Marjorie Spruill. During the fall of 2008 I was honored to serve as the Douglas Southall Freeman Professor at the University of Richmond, and one of my duties was to deliver two public lectures. I was trying to launch a completely different project, but it kept stalling. As a bow to my patron, an eminent Civil War historian, I decided to present two lectures, "The South in the Age of Nationalism" and "Internationalizing America's Civil War." The seeds for the present book sprouted in Richmond. "*That's* the book you need to write," Marjorie told me. She has taken time from her own writing to listen to my good ideas with enthusiasm, and to my not-so-good ones with her knitted brow that always told me when I was off course. She understood what I was trying to say better than anyone. Our shared passion for the past has made this book much better, and my life much happier. "It's the wanting to know that makes us matter."

Thanks to the University of Richmond, and to Hugh West and his colleagues, who were genial hosts, and to Spencer Dicks, who gave able assistance as my research assistant that fall.

In the fall of 2010 the book finally got started during a superb sabbatical year in Washington, DC, the mother lode for Civil War historians. We found ourselves living in the Clara Barton apartments high above the allegedly haunted Office for Missing Soldiers Barton operated during the Civil War. Marjorie had won a fellowship at the Woodrow Wilson International Center for Scholars, and thanks to Sonya Michel of the US Studies program there, I was welcomed as an affiliate. The Wilson Center provided excellent library services, brilliant research assistants (David Endicott and Meagan Jeffries), and stimulating colleagues from all parts of the world. I am grateful to Janet Spikes, Lindsay Collins, and all the Wilson Center staff for making my stay so pleasant and productive.

I profited from presenting early stages of my work during my year in Washington. Sincere thanks to Adam Rothman and Chandra Manning and their Nineteenth-Century History seminar at Georgetown University; Aaron Mars and his stimulating colleagues in the Office of the Historian at the US State Department; and Christian Ostermann and Roger Louis of the Washington History Seminar that convened at the Wilson Center.

Thanks are due also to the staff at the National Archives II in College Park, Maryland, and the unusually helpful people at the Library of Congress Manuscript Reading Room. Special thanks to Michelle Krowl of the Abraham Lincoln Papers at the Library of Congress, who allowed me to hold in my hands the gold medal that French liberals had given to Mrs. Lincoln and the velvet box one of them said contained the heart of France.

As my year in Washington came to an end, I received an unforgettable telephone call from Kent Mullikin of the National Humanities Center in North Carolina, telling me that I was awarded the Archie K. Davis fellowship for the coming year. My time at the National Humanities Center was a magic combination of splendid isolation, stimulating fellows, and extraordinary support from staff who are as friendly as they are competent. Geoffrey Harpham and Kent Mullikin invited me to deliver an evening lecture at the center, the perfect test audience for the book I was writing. I owe special thanks to the center's librarians Brooke Andrade, Eliza Robertson, and Jean Houston for keeping the books flowing into my office. Karen Caroll went beyond the call of duty to copyedit early drafts of my chapters. Center fellows Erik Redling, Ezra Greenspan, and Karen Hagemann listened to me working out my ideas and provided many valuable suggestions. Thanks also to Amanda Brickell Bellows for her able research assistance during my time in North Carolina.

The helpful staffs of the Boston Athenaeum, the New York Public Library, and the Sanford Museum in Florida made my visits there both productive and pleasant.

I owe special thanks to the University of South Carolina and to Dean Mary Anne Fitzpatrick and my department chairs, Lacy Ford and Larry Glickman, who generously supported my research endeavors. The University of South Carolina has provided a wonderful venue for my career this past decade. I owe special thanks to the generous philanthropy of Peter and Bonnie McCausland. I could never have completed this book without the efficient services and vast collections of South Carolina's magnificent libraries. The helpful staff of the Thomas Cooper Library delivered a steady stream of books and scanned articles. Special Collections made the Anthony P. Campanella Collection available for my research on Garibaldi. The South Caroliniana Library's deep collection of manuscript materials on Confederate leaders was also invaluable. A generous award from the university's Provost Humanities grants program facilitated travel to several archival sites. Thanks also to several very able research assistants in the History Department at South Carolina: Ann Tucker, Michael Woods, Mitchell Oxford, and Caroline Peyton all helped expedite my research on this book. My colleague Matt Childs and the graduate students of the Atlantic History Group gave me helpful reactions to one chapter. Not least, thanks to the graduate students in my seminar who were the first audience for this book in its final stages.

So many people have shared their time and expertise helping me along the way that I cannot thank them all. Lucy Riall helped me better understand the Garibaldi story. David and Mary Alice Lowenthal graciously shared portions of their typescript of Caroline Marsh's diary. Allan T. Kohl, of the Minneapolis College of Art and Design, provided digital images of *Punch* cartoons. David Hacker helped me understand Dan

Smith's work on Union soldiers. Marco Pizzo at the Museo Centrale del Risorgimento in Rome provided a rare image of Pio Nono. Brian P. Fahey of the archives of the Catholic Diocese of Charleston provided the English version of Bishop Lynch's essay on slavery. Michael Sobiech shared his vast knowledge of Catholic history. Hugh Dubrulle was especially helpful to my understanding of British politics during this period. Brian Schoen shared his remarkable knowledge of Southern secessionists in Europe. Jörg Nagler and Marcus Gräser included me in two pioneering conferences on the international dimensions of the Civil War, in Jena, Germany, and the German Historical Institute in Washington, DC, which proved valuable to my understanding of the subject.

I am especially indebted to Susan-Mary Grant, Aaron Sheehan-Dean, Patrick Kelly, and Robert Bonner for their very helpful comments on earlier versions of the manuscript. In the grand tradition of Franco-American friendship, Stève Sainlaude read another version of the book and generously shared his unparalleled knowledge of French foreign policy. These and many other colleagues saved me from countless sins of omission and commission, but those remaining are due to my own failings.

I have been very fortunate to work with David Miller and Lisa Adams of the Garamond Agency, who helped me shape the proposal for the book and get it placed with Lara Heimert at Basic Books. Lara once admonished me not to cheapen the use of exclamation marks, but I must exclaim that she and all those at Basic Books who helped bring this book to life (Leah Stecher, Roger Labrie, Annette Wenda, Melissa Veronesi, and the entire Basic team) are the very best!

My main discovery in writing this book was that America's Civil War really mattered to the world. All the time I worked on it, I was haunted by Abraham Lincoln's remark that "the struggle of today, is not altogether for today—it is for a vast future also." It is in that spirit that I dedicate this book to my grandchildren—Jackson, Charlie, and Caroline—and their vast future ahead.

ABBREVIATIONS

ALPLC   Abraham Lincoln Papers, Library of Congress, http://memory.loc.gov /ammem/alhtml/malhome.html

AP   The Avalon Project, Yale Law School, http://avalon.law.yale.edu/

CA   Chronicling America, Historic American Newspapers, Library of Congress, http://www.chroniclingamerica.loc.gov

CSAA   Confederate States of America Archives, Library of Congress; previously known as the Pickett Papers

CWAL   *The Collected Works of Abraham Lincoln*, edited by Roy P. Basler, 8 vols., Abraham Lincoln Association, online at http://quod.lib.umich.edu/l /lincoln/

FRUS   Foreign Relations of the United States, 1861–65, University of Wisconsin Digital Collections, http://uwdc.library.wisc.edu/collections/FRUS

LoC   Library of Congress

NYPL   New York Public Library

NYT   *New York Times:* all references are to online archives, http://query.ny times.com/search/sitesearch/

OR   *The War of the Rebellion: A Compilation of the Official Records of the Union and Confederate Armies* (Washington, DC: GPO, 1880–1901), DVD (Guild Press of Indiana, 2002)

ORN   *Official Records of the Union and Confederate Navies in the War of the Rebellion* (Washington, DC: GPO, 1922), DVD (Guild Press of Indiana, 2002)

RG 59   Record Group 59: diplomatic and consular correspondence, microfilm collection, National Archives and Records Administration, NARA II, College Park, MD; foreign country names indicate US ministries; foreign city names indicate US consulates

SP   Henry S. Sanford Papers, Sanford Public Library, Sanford, FL

NOTES

INTRODUCTION:
AMERICAN CRISIS, GLOBAL STRUGGLE

1. Malakoff, "Important from Paris," *NYT*, March 29, 1861; "Foreign Intervention in American Affairs," *NYT*, April 1, 1861.

2. Malakoff, "Interesting from Paris," *NYT*, July 19, 1861.

3. John Bigelow, *Retrospections of an Active Life, 1865–1866* (New York: Baker and Taylor, 1909), 547.

4. Malakoff, "Interesting from Paris," *NYT*, May 16, 1865; William Edward Johnston, *Memoirs of "Malakoff,"* edited by R. M. Johnston (London: Hutchinson, 1907), 2:430–435.

5. Malakoff, "Interesting from Paris," May 16, 1865; Johnston, *Memoirs of "Malakoff,"* 2:431.

6. Allan Nevins, *The War for the Union* (New York: Scribner, 1959), 2:242.

7. Henry Sanford to William Seward, Paris, August 6, 1861, Belgium, RG 59. The US Civil War and public diplomacy are treated in Stephen Knott, *Secret and Sanctioned: Covert Operations and the American Presidency* (New York: Oxford University Press, 1996), 139–159; *Propaganda and Mass Persuasion: A Historical Encyclopedia, 1500 to the Present,* edited by Nicholas John Cull, David Holbrook Culbert, and David Welch (Santa Barbara, CA: ABC-CLIO, 2003), 88–89; Nicholas Cull, "'Public Diplomacy' Before Gullion: The Evolution of a Phrase," in *Routledge Handbook of Public Diplomacy,* edited by Nancy Snow and Philip M. Taylor (New York: Routledge, 2009), 19–23; and Henry M. Wriston, *Executive Agents in American Foreign Relations* (Baltimore: Johns Hopkins University Press, 1929), 779–780.

8. Joseph S. Nye, *Soft Power: The Means to Success in World Politics* (New York: Public Affairs, 2004); Kevin Peraino, *Lincoln in the World: The Making of a Statesman and the Dawn of American Power* (New York: Crown, 2013).

9. James Henry Hammond, *Selections from the Letters and Speeches of the Hon. James H. Hammond: Of South Carolina* (New York: J. F. Trow, 1866), 316–317;

David Christy et al., *Cotton Is King, and Pro-Slavery Arguments* . . . (Augusta, GA: Pritchard, Abbott, and Loomis, 1860).

10. The varied meanings of the word *experiment* are traced in the *Oxford English Dictionary Online,* http://www.oed.com/.

11. Walt Whitman, *Specimen Days and Collect* (Philadelphia: D. McKay, 1883), 64.

12. Alfred J. Hanna and Kathryn A. Hanna, *Napoleon III and Mexico: American Triumph over Monarchy* (Chapel Hill: University of North Carolina Press, 1971).

13. Robert E. May, *Manifest Destiny's Underworld Filibustering in Antebellum America* (Chapel Hill: University of North Carolina Press, 2002). Robert E. May, "Bury the Purple Dream: Confederate Visions of Empire," unpublished paper for conference on American Civil Wars, University of South Carolina, March 19–21, 2014, addresses expansionist ideas during the Confederacy.

14. Lincoln, "Gettysburg Address," AP.

15. *Courrier du Dimanche,* January 1, 1865, quoted in George McCoy Blackburn, *French Newspaper Opinion on the American Civil War* (Westport, CT: Greenwood, 1997), 127; Eugène Pelletan, *Adresse au Roi Coton* (Paris: Pagnerre, 1863), 11; Eugène Pelletan, *An Address to King Cotton,* translated by Leander Starr (New York: H. de Mareil, 1863), 5; Judith F. Stone, *Sons of the Revolution: Radical Democrats in France, 1862–1914* (Baton Rouge: Louisiana State University Press, 1996), 19–20.

16. Hermann Rauschning, *The Voice of Destruction* (New York: G. B. Putnam, 1940), 68–70.

17. David M. Potter, "The Civil War in the History of the Modern World: A Comparative View," in *The South and the Sectional Conflict* (Baton Rouge: Louisiana State University Press, 1968), 287.

18. Lincoln, "Annual Message to Congress," December 3, 1861, CWAL, 5:53.

CHAPTER 1: GARIBALDI'S QUESTION

1. Lucy Riall, *Garibaldi: Invention of a Hero* (New Haven, CT: Yale University Press, 2007); Jasper Ridley, *Garibaldi* (London: Phoenix Press, 2001); George Macaulay Trevelyan, *Garibaldi's Defence of the Roman Republic, 1848–9* (London: Longmans, Green, 1914), 35.

2. Riall, *Garibaldi,* 294–297; George Perkins Marsh to Seward, Turin, September 14, 1861, Italy, RG 59.

3. H. Nelson Gay, "Lincoln's Offer of a Command to Garibaldi: Light on a Disputed Point of History," *Century,* November 1907, 63–74; Charles Francis Adams Sr., "Lincoln's Offer to Garibaldi," *Proceedings of the Massachusetts Historical Society,* 3rd ser., 1 (1907): 319–325; Mary Philip Trauth, *Italo-American Diplomatic Relations, 1861–1882: The Mission of George Perkins Marsh, First American Minister to the Kingdom of Italy* (Westport, CT: Greenwood Press, 1980); David Lowenthal, *George Perkins Marsh, Prophet of Conservation* (Seattle: University of Washington Press, 2000), 239–241; Joseph A. Fry, *Henry S. Sanford: Diplomacy and Business in Nineteenth-Century America* (Reno: University of Nevada Press, 1982), 59–65; Jo-

seph A. Fry, "Eyewitness by Proxy: Nelson M. Beckwith's Evaluation of Garibaldi," *Civil War History* 28, no. 1 (1982): 65–70; Howard R. Marraro, "Lincoln's Offer of a Command to Garibaldi: Further Light on a Disputed Point of History," *Journal of the Illinois State Historical Society* 36, no. 3 (1943): 237–270.

4. "Garibaldi on Italy and America," *NYT,* May 27, 1861; "Garibaldi's Reply," *New York Daily Tribune,* August 13, 1861.

5. "Letters of Application and Recommendation During the Administrations of Franklin Pierce and James Buchanan, 1853–1861," M967, roll 36, RG 59; Quiggle to Seward, Antwerp, July 5, 1861, Antwerp, RG 59.

6. Quiggle to Garibaldi, Antwerp, June 8, 1861, enclosed with Quiggle to Seward, Antwerp, July 5, 1861, in Antwerp, RG 59.

7. Garibaldi to Quiggle, Caprera, June 27, 1861, in *La guerra civile Americana vista dall'Europa,* edited by Tiziano Bonazzi and Carlo Galli (Bologna: Mulino, 2004), 234 (author's translation).

8. Quiggle to Garibaldi, Antwerp, July 4, 1861, Antwerp, RG 59.

9. Howard Jones, *Blue and Gray Diplomacy: A History of Union and Confederate Foreign Relations* (Chapel Hill: University of North Carolina Press, 2010); Stephen C. Neff, *Justice in Blue and Gray: A Legal History of the Civil War* (Cambridge, MA: Harvard University Press, 2010); *Encyclopedia of American Foreign Policy: Studies of the Principal Movements and Ideas,* edited by Alexander DeConde (New York: Scribner, 1978), s.v. "Recognition Policy."

10. Gay, "Lincoln's Offer," 67.

11. Sanford to Seward, London, August 10, 1861; Sanford to Seward, Brussels, August 16, 1861, Belgium, RG 59; Sanford to Seward, Brussels, August 16, 1861, box 139, SP.

12. "The War for Union," *New York Daily Tribune,* August 11, 1861, CA.

13. Fry, *Henry S. Sanford,* 60.

14. Joseph Artoni to Sanford, Turin, September 3, 1861, box 39, SP; Sanford to Garibaldi, August 20, 1861, enclosed with Sanford to Seward, Turin, August 29, 1861, Belgium, RG 59.

15. Quiggle to Garibaldi, August 15, 1861, enclosed with Quiggle to Seward, Antwerp, August 15, 1861, Antwerp, RG 59.

16. Garibaldi to Sanford, Caprera, August 31, 1861, Belgium, RG 59; Caroline Marsh, Diary, September 3, 1861, George Perkins Marsh Collection, Special Collections, Bailey Library, University of Vermont. I am grateful to David and Mary Alice Lowenthal, who provided excerpts from this diary. See also Trauth, *Italo-American Diplomatic Relations,* 13–14n46.

17. Caroline Marsh, Diary, September 5, 1861; Trecchi to Sanford, Turin, September 7, 1861, Belgium, RG 59.

18. Sanford to Seward, Genoa, September 7, 1861, Belgium, RG 59.

19. Sanford to Seward, Turin, September 12, 1861, Belgium, RG 59; Sanford to Seward, Brussels, September 18, 1861, Belgium, RG 59.

20. Sanford to Seward, Brussels, September 18, 1861, Belgium, RG 59.

21. Ibid.

22. Ibid.; Sanford to Seward, Turin, September 12, 1861, Belgium, RG 59; Sanford to Seward, Brussels, September 18, 1861, Belgium, RG 59.

23. Fry, "Eyewitness by Proxy," 65–70; Beckwith to Sanford, Paris, September 9, [16], 17, 27, 1861, box 115, SP; Marsh to Sanford, Turin, September 23, 1861, box 128, SP; Sanford to Seward, Turin, September 4, 12, 1861, Belgium, RG 59; Sanford to Seward, Brussels, September 18, 27, 1861, Belgium, RG 59; Marraro, "Lincoln's Offer," 249, quoting Marsh to Seward, Turin, September 16, 1861.

24. Ridley, *Garibaldi,* 523, quoting John McAdam to Garibaldi, September 28, and Garibaldi reply, December 3, 1861.

25. Candido Augusto Vecchi, *Garibaldi e Caprera* (Naples: Fibreno, 1862), 68–70, punctuation modified; Candido Augusto Vecchi, *Garibaldi at Caprera,* translated by Lucy Ellis and Mary Ellis (London: Macmillan, 1862), 65–66. The passage on Garibaldi's plans for emancipation was strangely omitted in the English edition.

26. Garibaldi to Quiggle, Caprera, September [10], 1861, enclosed with Quiggle to Seward, Antwerp, September 30, 1861, Antwerp, RG 59.

27. Quiggle to Seward, Antwerp, August 15, September 30, 1861, Antwerp, RG 59.

28. John Franklin Meginness, *History of Lycoming County, Pennsylvania* (Chicago: Brown, Runk, 1892), 295.

CHAPTER 2: WE ARE A NATION

1. "Declaration of Independence, July 4, 1776," AP.

2. James Morton Callahan, *The Diplomatic History of the Southern Confederacy* (Baltimore: Johns Hopkins University Press, 1901), 96.

3. *Encyclopedia of American Foreign Policy: Studies of the Principal Movements and Ideas,* edited by Alexander DeConde (New York: Scribner, 1978), s.v. "Recognition Policy."

4. David Armitage, *The Declaration of Independence: A Global History* (Cambridge, MA: Harvard University Press, 2007), 105–107; David Armitage, "Secession and Civil War," in *Secession as an International Phenomenon: From America's Civil War to Contemporary Separatist Movements,* edited by Don H. Doyle (Athens: University of Georgia Press, 2010), 37; Don H. Doyle, "Introduction: Union and Secession in the Family of Nations," in *Secession as an International Phenomenon,* 1–16.

5. Malcolm Gladwell, *David and Goliath: Underdogs, Misfits, and the Art of Battling Giants* (New York: Little, Brown, 2013).

6. Andre M. Fleche, *The Revolution of 1861: The American Civil War in the Age of Nationalist Conflict* (Chapel Hill: University of North Carolina Press, 2012); Ann L. Tucker, "'Newest Born of Nations': Southern Thought on European Nationalisms and the Creation of the Confederacy, 1820–1865" (PhD diss., University of South Carolina, 2014).

7. Charles B. Dew, *Apostles of Disunion: Southern Secession Commissioners and the Causes of the Civil War* (Charlottesville: University Press of Virginia, 2001).

8. Charles H. Lesser, *Relic of the Lost Cause: The Story of South Carolina's Ordinance of Secession* ([Columbia]: South Carolina Department of Archives and History, 1990). "A Declaration of the Immediate Causes Which Induce and Justify the Secession of South Carolina from the Federal Union," AP.

9. Charles Edward Cauthen, *South Carolina Goes to War, 1860–1865* (Chapel Hill: University of North Carolina Press, 1950), 73–74.

10. "A Declaration of the Immediate Causes Which Induce and Justify the Secession of the State of Mississippi from the Federal Union," AP.

11. Preamble, "Constitution of the Confederate States, March 11, 1861," AP.

12. Edward B. Rugemer, *The Problem of Emancipation: The Caribbean Roots of the American Civil War* (Baton Rouge: Louisiana State University Press, 2008); Dew, *Apostles of Disunion.*

13. William C. Davis, *"A Government of Our Own": The Making of the Confederacy* (New York: Simon and Schuster, 1994), 83–89, 103, 224–225, 236–241, 244–256; "Constitution of the Confederate States, March 11, 1861," AP.

14. Ellis Merton Coulter, *The Confederate States of America, 1861–1865* (Baton Rouge: Louisiana State University Press, 1950), 58–59. Tennessee and Virginia also held plebiscites on secession.

15. William J. Cooper, *Jefferson Davis, American* (New York: Vintage, 2000), 353–354; Coulter, *Confederate States,* 26; Emory M. Thomas, *The Confederate Nation, 1861–1865* (New York: Harper and Row, 1979), 61–62.

16. "President J. Davis's Inauguration at Montgomery," *Harper's Weekly,* March 9, 1861, 156; William Howard Russell, *My Diary North and South* (Boston: Burnham, 1863), 173.

17. Cooper, *Jefferson Davis, American,* 232–234, 309–312, 347, 353–355; Russell, *My Diary,* 173; "President J. Davis's Inauguration at Montgomery," 156.

18. *Harper's Weekly,* February 23, 1861, 125; Thomas, *Confederate Nation,* 62; Jefferson Davis, "Confederate States of America, Inaugural Address of the President of the Provisional Government," February 18, 1861, AP.

19. Henry Cleveland, *Alexander H. Stephens in Public and Private: With Letters and Speeches Before, During, and Since the War* (Philadelphia: National Publishing, 1866), 96.

20. Ibid., 717–729; "Constitution of the Confederate States, March 11, 1861," Article 1, Section 9, Clause 4, AP.

21. Ibid., 637–651, 729–744; Alexander Hamilton Stephens, *Recollections of Alexander H. Stephens* (New York: Doubleday, Page, 1910), 172–174; Michael Kinsley, *New Republic,* June 18, 1984.

22. Cauthen, *South Carolina,* 44; Robert E. Bonner, "Slavery, Confederate Diplomacy, and the Racialist Mission of Henry Hotze," *Civil War History* 51, no. 3 (2005): 288–316; Robert E. Bonner, *Mastering America: Southern Slaveholders and the Crisis of American Nationhood* (Cambridge: Cambridge University Press, 2009); Michael T. Bernath, *Confederate Minds: The Struggle for Intellectual Independence in the Civil War South* (Chapel Hill: University of North Carolina Press, 2010);

Manisha Sinha, *The Counterrevolution of Slavery: Politics and Ideology in Antebellum South Carolina* (Chapel Hill: University of North Carolina Press, 2000); Arthur Gobineau, *Essai sur l'inégalité des races humaines* (Paris: Firmin-Didot, 1853); Arthur Gobineau, *The Moral and Intellectual Diversity of Races: With Particular Reference to Their Respective Influence in the Civil and Political History of Mankind*, edited by Josiah Clark Nott and Henry Hotze (Philadelphia: J. B. Lippincott, 1856); Michael D. Biddiss, *Father of Racist Ideology: The Social and Political Thought of Count Gobineau* (New York: Weybright and Talley, 1970).

23. Harry V. Jaffa, *A New Birth of Freedom: Abraham Lincoln and the Coming of the Civil War* (Lanham, MD: Rowman and Littlefield, 2000), 216; Agénor de Gasparin, *The Uprising of a Great People: The United States in 1861, Abridged* (London: S. Low, 1861), 75–78, appendix with full text of Stephens's Cornerstone Speech; Jay Monaghan, *Diplomat in Carpet Slippers: Abraham Lincoln Deals with Foreign Affairs* (Indianapolis: Bobbs-Merrill, 1962), 92–93; Serge Gavronsky, *The French Liberal Opposition and the American Civil War* (New York: Humanities Press, 1968), 90–91.

24. Davis, *"Government of Our Own,"* 137.

25. James D. Richardson, *A Compilation of the Messages and Papers of the Confederacy: Including the Diplomatic Correspondence, 1861–1865* (Nashville: United States Publishing, 1904), 1:55–56.

26. Samuel Wylie Crawford, *The Genesis of the Civil War: The Story of Sumter, 1860–1861* (New York: C. L. Webster, 1887), 325–330; Ludwell H. Johnson, "Fort Sumter and Confederate Diplomacy," *Journal of Southern History* 26, no. 4 (1960): 456–459; Glyndon G. Van Deusen, *William Henry Seward* (New York: Oxford University Press, 1967), 178–179; Davis, *"Government of Our Own,"* 209; Doris Kearns Goodwin, *Team of Rivals: The Political Genius of Abraham Lincoln* (New York: Simon and Schuster, 2005), 336, 341.

27. Davis, *"Government of Our Own,"* 203; Callahan, *Diplomatic History,* 84; Robert Barnwell Rhett and William C. Davis, *A Fire-Eater Remembers: The Confederate Memoir of Robert Barnwell Rhett* (Columbia: University of South Carolina Press, 2000), 33–38.

28. Frank Lawrence Owsley, *King Cotton Diplomacy: Foreign Relations of the Confederate States of America*, 2nd ed. (1931; reprint, Chicago: University of Chicago Press, 1959), 24–50; Eugène Pelletan, *An Address to King Cotton*, translated by Leander Starr (New York: H. de Mareil, 1863).

29. Owsley, *King Cotton Diplomacy,* 51–52.

30. Eric H. Walther, *William Lowndes Yancey and the Coming of the Civil War* (Chapel Hill: University of North Carolina Press, 2006), 299–300; Davis, *"Government of Our Own,"* 203–204.

31. Walther, *Yancey and the Coming of the Civil War,* 297–299; Owsley, *King Cotton Diplomacy,* 51–52; Edwin De Leon, *Secret History of Confederate Diplomacy Abroad*, edited by William C. Davis (Lawrence: University Press of Kansas, 2005), 50.

32. Paul Pecquet du Bellet, *The Diplomacy of the Confederate Cabinet of Richmond and Its Agents Abroad*, edited by William Stanley Hoole (Tuscaloosa, AL: Confederate Publishing, 1963), 30–32; Burton Jesse Hendrick, *Statesmen of the Lost Cause:*

Jefferson Davis and His Cabinet (New York: Literary Guild of America, 1939), 140; *Encyclopedia of the American Civil War: A Political, Social, and Military History,* edited by David Stephen Heidler and Jeanne T. Heidler (New York: W. W. Norton, 2002), s.v. "Rost, Pierre Adolphe."

33. A. Dudley Mann, *"My Ever Dearest Friend": The Letters of A. Dudley Mann to Jefferson Davis, 1869–1889* (Tuscaloosa, AL: Confederate Publishing, 1960), 11–16; *Encyclopedia of the American Civil War,* s.v. "Mann, Ambrose Dudley"; Hendrick, *Statesmen of the Lost Cause,* 141; Owsley, *King Cotton Diplomacy,* 52; De Leon, *Secret History,* 52.

34. Charles M. Hubbard, *The Burden of Confederate Diplomacy* (Knoxville: University of Tennessee Press, 1998), 33–34; J. Preston Moore, "Lincoln and the Escape of the Confederate Commissioner," *Journal of the Illinois State Historical Society* 57, no. 1 (1964): 23–29.

35. William Stanley Hoole, ed., "Notes and Documents: William L. Yancey's European Diary, March–June 1861," *Alabama Review* 25, no. 2 (1972): 134–142; Walther, *Yancey and the Coming of the Civil War,* 304–305; Hubbard, *Burden of Confederate Diplomacy,* 33–34; Yancey and Mann to Toombs, London, May 21, 1861, ORN, ser. 2, 3:214–216.

36. Jasper Godwin Ridley, *Lord Palmerston* (New York: Dutton, 1971), 548, 6–8.

37. Palmerston to Russell, London, October 28, 1862, in Hugh Dubrulle, "'We Are Threatened with . . . Anarchy and Ruin': Fear of Americanization and the Emergence of an Anglo-Saxon Confederacy in England During the American Civil War," *Albion* 33, no. 4 (2001): 586.

38. Ridley, *Lord Palmerston,* 427–428, 489; Eugenio F. Biagini, *Liberty, Retrenchment and Reform: Popular Liberalism in the Age of Gladstone, 1860–1880* (Cambridge: Cambridge University Press, 2004), 67–83; Ephraim Douglass Adams, *Great Britain and the American Civil War* (1924; reprint, New York: Russell and Russell, 1958), 1:24, 28–31, 2:276–289.

39. Adams, *Great Britain,* 90; E. D. Steele, *Palmerston and Liberalism, 1855–1865* (Cambridge: Cambridge University Press, 1991), 292–305.

40. David Urquhart, *Public Opinion and Its Organs* (London: Trübner, 1855), 24–25.

41. Yancey and Mann to Toombs, London, May 21, 1861, ORN, ser. 2, 3:214–216.

42. Francis Deák and Philip C. Jessup, eds., *A Collection of Neutrality Laws, Regulations and Treaties of Various Countries* (Washington, DC: Carnegie Endowment for International Peace, 1939), 1:57, 100, 161, 590, 688, 2:814–815, 903, 939; Yancey and Mann to Toombs, London, May 21, 1861, ORN, ser. 2, 3:214–216; Dean B. Mahin, *One War at a Time: The International Dimensions of the American Civil War* (Washington, DC: Brassey's, 1999), 197–207.

43. Lynn Marshall Case and Warren F. Spencer, *The United States and France: Civil War Diplomacy* (Philadelphia: University of Pennsylvania Press, 1970), 60–61; Yancey and Mann to Toombs, London, May 21, ORN, ser. 2, 3:214–216; Stève Sainlaude, *Le gouvernement impérial et la guerre de sécession (1861–1865): L'action diplomatique* (Paris: Harmattan, 2011).

44. Yancey and Mann to Toombs, London, May 21, 1861; Yancey, Rost, and Mann to Toombs, London, June 1, 1861; Yancey and Mann to Toombs, London, July 15, 1861; Yancey and Mann to Hunter, London, August 1, 1861, all in ORN, ser. 2, 3:214–216, 3:219–220, 3:221–226, 3:229–230.

45. Henry Harrison Simms, *Life of Robert M. T. Hunter: A Study in Sectionalism and Secession* (Richmond, VA: William Byrd Press, 1935), 187–201; Hunter to Yancey, Rost, and Mann, Richmond, July 29, 1861, ORN, ser. 2, 3:227–229.

46. Yancey, Rost, and Mann to Toombs, London, August 7, 1861, ORN, ser. 2, 3:235–237.

47. Ibid., August 14, 1861, 238–246.

48. Russell to Yancey, Rost, and Mann, London, August 24, 1861, ORN, ser. 2, 3:247–248.

49. Walther, *Yancey and the Coming of the Civil War*, 315.

50. Ibid., 226–231, 319, 321; Owsley, *King Cotton Diplomacy*, 76–77; De Leon, *Secret History*, 50–52.

51. Thomas Le Grand Harris, *The* Trent *Affair: Including a Review of English and American Relations at the Beginning of the Civil War* (Indianapolis: Bowen Merrill, 1896), 91–109.

52. Weed to Seward, London, December 4, 1861, ALPLC (two letters, same date); Malakoff, "Important from Paris, the Seizure of Mason and Slidell the Result of a Preconcerted Plan," *NYT,* January 4, 1862.

53. Harris, Trent *Affair,* 137–162.

54. "The Seizure of the *Trent,*" *Times* (London), November 28, 1861.

55. Brian Jenkins, *Britain and the War for the Union* (Montreal: McGill-Queen's University Press, 1974), 1:220; Norman B. Ferris, *The* Trent *Affair: A Diplomatic Crisis* (Knoxville: University of Tennessee Press, 1977), 179.

56. Ferris, Trent *Affair,* 54–68; Kenneth Bourne, *Britain and the Balance of Power in North America, 1815–1908* (Berkeley: University of California Press, 1967), 206–249; Phillip E. Myers, *Caution and Cooperation: The American Civil War in British-American Relations* (Kent, OH: Kent State University Press, 2008), 64–88; Amanda Foreman, *A World on Fire: Britain's Crucial Role in the American Civil War* (New York: Random House, 2011), 173–196.

57. Yancey, Rost, and Mann to Hunter, London, December 2, 1861, ORN, ser. 2, 3:304–306.

58. Mann to Hunter, London, December 2, 1861, ORN, ser. 2, 3:307.

59. Rost to Hunter, Paris, December 24, 1861, ORN, ser. 2, 3:311–312.

CHAPTER 3: WE WILL WRAP THE WORLD IN FLAMES

1. Lincoln, "First Inaugural Address," March 4, 1861, CWAL, 4:249–261, 262–271.

2. William Howard Russell, *My Diary North and South* (Boston: Burnham, 1863), 381, 387, July 4, December 16, 1861; Seward to Adams, Washington, July 28, 1862, FRUS, 1862, 154–158.

3. Michael Burlingame, *Abraham Lincoln: A Life* (Baltimore: Johns Hopkins University Press, 2008), 2:41.

4. "The Inauguration Ceremonies," *NYT*, March 5, 1861; Julia Taft Bayne, *Tad Lincoln's Father*, edited by Mary A. DeCredico (Lincoln: University of Nebraska Press, 2001), 18; Walt Whitman, *Specimen Days and Collect* (Philadelphia: D. McKay, 1883), 64.

5. "The New Administration," *NYT*, March 5, 1861.

6. Burlingame, *Abraham Lincoln: A Life*, 1:707; Marsh to Seward, Turin, June 28, 1861, Italy, RG 59.

7. Harold Holzer, *Lincoln President-Elect: Abraham Lincoln and the Great Secession Winter, 1860–1861* (New York: Simon and Schuster, 2008), 437–446; Walter Stahr, *Seward: Lincoln's Indispensable Man* (New York: Simon and Schuster, 2012), 239–241.

8. Burlingame, *Abraham Lincoln: A Life*, 2:45–51, 58.

9. "The Inauguration Ceremonies"; Burlingame, *Abraham Lincoln: A Life*, 2:61–62.

10. "The New Administration"; Samuel Wylie Crawford, *The Genesis of the Civil War: The Story of Sumter, 1860–1861* (New York: C. L. Webster, 1887), 304, 321.

11. Emer de Vattel, *The Law of Nations; or, Principles of the Law of Nature, Applied to the Conduct and Affairs of Nations and Sovereigns*, edited by Bela Kapossy and Richard Whatmore (1797; reprint, Indianapolis: Liberty Fund, 2008), 86–87; Lincoln, "First Inaugural Address, Final Text," March 4, 1861, CWAL, 4:264; Emory M. Thomas, *The Confederate Nation, 1861–1865* (New York: Harper and Row, 1979), 63.

12. Burlingame, *Abraham Lincoln: A Life*, 2:47; James M. McPherson, *Battle Cry of Freedom: The Civil War Era* (New York: Oxford University Press, 1988), 252–253.

13. Seward circular, Washington, March 9, 1861, FRUS, 1861, 32–33.

14. Benjamin Moran, *The Journal of Benjamin Moran, 1857–1865*, edited by Sarah Agnes Wallace and Frances Elma Gillespie (Chicago: University of Chicago Press, 1948), 1:806.

15. Sanford to Seward, Paris, April 19, 1861, Belgium, RG 59; "The Great Rebellion," *NYT*, August 13, 1861; *Biographical Directory of the US Congress*, s.v. "Faulkner, Charles James," http://bioguide.congress.gov.

16. Eduard Maco Hudson, *Der Zweite Unabhängigkeits-Krieg in Amerika* (Berlin: A. Charisius, 1862); Eduard Maco Hudson, *The Second War of Independence in America*, 2nd ed. (London: Longman, Green, 1863). On disloyal diplomats: Sanford to Seward, Paris, April 19, September 19, 1861 (on Faulkner); Sanford to Seward, London, April 27, 1861, Belgium, RG 59 (on Fair); Perry to Seward, Madrid, April 20, 1861, Spain, RG 59 (on Preston).

17. Margaret Antoinette Clapp, *Forgotten First Citizen: John Bigelow* (Boston: Little, Brown, 1947), 149.

18. Stahr, *Seward: Lincoln's Indispensable Man*, 253–254; Thurlow Weed, *Life of Thurlow Weed Including His Autobiography and a Memoir* (Boston: Houghton Mifflin, 1884), 1:600–601; Burlingame, *Abraham Lincoln: A Life*, 2:91–95.

19. Lincoln to Seward, Washington, March 11, 1861, CWAL, 4:281.

20. Burlingame, *Abraham Lincoln: A Life*, 2:108–113; Stahr, *Seward: Lincoln's Indispensable Man*, 254–255.

21. Russell, *My Diary*, 37–39.

22. John Taylor, *William Henry Seward: Lincoln's Right Hand* (New York: HarperCollins, 1991), 186–187; Norman B. Ferris, "Lincoln and Seward in Civil War Diplomacy: Their Relationship at the Outset Reexamined," in *For a Vast Future Also: Essays from the Journal of the Abraham Lincoln Association*, ed. Thomas F. Schwartz (New York: Fordham University Press, 1999), 170–189; Doris Kearns Goodwin, *Team of Rivals: The Political Genius of Abraham Lincoln* (New York: Simon and Schuster, 2005), 364–365, 386–388.

23. Glyndon G. Van Deusen, *William Henry Seward* (New York: Oxford University Press, 1967), 336; Taylor, *William Henry Seward*, 181.

24. William Henry Seward and Frederick William Seward, *Seward at Washington, 1846–1861* (New York: Derby and Miller, 1891), 511; Norman B. Ferris, *Desperate Diplomacy: William H. Seward's Foreign Policy, 1861* (Knoxville: University of Tennessee Press, 1976), 3; Frederick William Seward, *Reminiscences of a War-Time Statesman and Diplomat, 1830–1915* (New York: G. P. Putnam's Sons, 1916), 147.

25. Seward to Lincoln, "Some Thoughts for the President's Consideration," Washington, April 1, 1861, ALPLC.

26. Ibid.; "Astounding Intelligence: Aggressive Designs of Spain in the West Indies," *NYT*, March 30, 1861.

27. William Henry Seward, *The Works of William H. Seward*, edited by George E. Baker (Boston: Houghton, Mifflin, 1884), 648–649; Kinley J. Brauer, "Seward's 'Foreign War Panacea': An Interpretation," *New York History* 55, no. 136 (1974): 145–147; Patrick Sowle, "A Reappraisal of Seward's Memorandum of April 1, 1861, to Lincoln," *Journal of Southern History* 33 (May 1, 1967): 234–239; Ferris, "Lincoln and Seward"; Ferris, *Desperate Diplomacy*, 1012; Taylor, *William Henry Seward*, 150–153.

28. Daniel B. Carroll, *Henri Mercier and the American Civil War* (Princeton, NJ: Princeton University Press, 1971), 51–52; Howard Jones, *Blue and Gray Diplomacy: A History of Union and Confederate Foreign Relations* (Chapel Hill: University of North Carolina Press, 2010), 25.

29. Jones, *Blue and Gray Diplomacy*, 24, 27; Ferris, "Lincoln and Seward."

30. Lincoln to Seward, Washington, April 1, 1861, ALPLC; Taylor, *William Henry Seward*, 150–151; Burlingame, *Abraham Lincoln: A Life*, 2:118.

31. Ferris, *Desperate Diplomacy*; Ferris, "Lincoln and Seward"; Sowle, "Reappraisal of Seward's Memorandum"; Brauer, "Seward's 'Foreign War Panacea.'"

32. Sowle, "Reappraisal of Seward's Memorandum."

33. Ibid.

34. "Foreign Intervention in American Affairs," *NYT*, April 1, 1861.

35. Van Deusen, *William Henry Seward*, 292; James W. Cortada, "Spain and the American Civil War: Relations at Mid-Century, 1855–1868," *Transactions of the American Philosophical Society* 70, no. 4 (1980): 33–34.

36. Seward to Adams, Washington, April 10, 1861, FRUS, 1861, 71–80.

37. Seward to Dayton, Washington, April 22, 1861, FRUS, 1861, 195–201; Stahr, *Seward: Lincoln's Indispensable Man,* 179.

38. William Henry Seward and Frederick William Seward, *William H. Seward: An Autobiography, 1831–1846* (New York: Derby and Miller, 1877), 27–28; Stahr, *Seward: Lincoln's Indispensable Man,* 16.

39. Taylor, *William Henry Seward,* 73–74.

40. Stahr, *Seward: Lincoln's Indispensable Man,* 178–181, 189–190, 193.

41. Sanford to Seward, Paris, May 10, 1861, Belgium, RG 59.

42. Schurz to Seward, San Ildefonso, Spain, September 14, 1861, Spain, RG 59, reprinted in Carl Schurz, *Speeches, Correspondence and Political Papers of Carl Schurz,* edited by Frederic Bancroft (New York: G. P. Putnam's Sons, 1913), 185–193; Frederic Bancroft, *The Life of William H. Seward* (New York: Harper and Brothers, 1899), 323.

43. Schurz, *Speeches, Correspondence and Political Papers,* 1:191–193.

44. Henry M. Wriston, *Executive Agents in American Foreign Relations* (Baltimore: Johns Hopkins, 1929), 776–780; *Propaganda and Mass Persuasion: A Historical Encyclopedia, 1500 to the Present,* edited by Nicholas John Cull, David Holbrook Culbert, and David Welch (Santa Barbara, CA: ABC-CLIO, 2003), s.v. "Civil War, United States" and "Public Diplomacy"; Nicolas J. Cull, "'Public Diplomacy' Before Gullion: The Evolution of a Phrase," in *Routledge Handbook of Public Diplomacy,* edited by Nancy Snow and Philip M. Taylor (New York: Routledge, 2009), 19–23.

45. Benedict Anderson, *Imagined Communities: Reflections on the Origin and Spread of Nationalism,* 3rd ed. (New York: Verso Books, 2006); Lynn M. Case, ed., *French Opinion on the United States and Mexico, 1860–1867: Extracts from the Reports of the Procureurs Généraux* (New York: D. Appleton-Century, 1936), ix–x.

46. Sanford to Seward, Paris, April 19, 1861, Belgium, RG 59.

47. Harriet Chappell Owsley, "Henry Shelton Sanford and Federal Surveillance Abroad, 1861–1865," *Mississippi Valley Historical Review* 48, no. 2 (1961): 222; Malakoff, "From France: French Sentiment upon Secession," *NYT,* March 15, 1861; Charles Sumner and A. Malespine, *Les relations exteirieures des États-Unis* (Paris: E. Dentu, 1863); A. Malespine, *Solution de la question mexicaine* (Paris: E. Dentu, 1864); A. Malespine, *Les États-Unis en 1865* (Paris: E. Dentu, 1865).

48. John Bigelow, *Retrospections of an Active Life, 1817–1863* (New York: Baker and Taylor, 1909), 364–365; Clapp, *Forgotten First Citizen,* 165–182; Beckles Willson, *America's Ambassadors to France (1777–1927): A Narrative of Franco-American Diplomatic Relations* (London: J. Murray, 1928), 262–263, quoting Dayton to Seward, Paris, May 27, 1861.

49. Aaron W. Marrs, "The Civil War Origins of the FRUS Series, 1861–1868," chap. 2 of "Toward 'Thorough, Accurate, and Reliable': A History of the Foreign Relations of the United States Series," online at US Department of State, Office of the Historian, http://history.state.gov/historicaldocuments/frus-history/chapter-2; "Secret Diplomatic Service Abroad," *NYT,* February 5, 1868; Stephen F. Knott, *Secret and Sanctioned: Covert Operations and the American Presidency* (New York:

Oxford University Press, 1996), 140–144; Peter Bridges, "US Agents Give Special European Service," *Washington Times,* June 25, 2005; Wriston, *Executive Agents,* 779–780; Van Deusen, *William Henry Seward,* 306–307; Henry Adams, *The Education of Henry Adams: An Autobiography* (Boston: Houghton Mifflin, 1918), 126.

50. Weed, *Life of Thurlow Weed,* 2:351, 1:634–639; Stahr, *Seward: Lincoln's Indispensable Man,* 307.

51. Charles Francis Adams, "Charles Francis Adams Diaries, 1823–1880" (Massachusetts Historical Society, Boston, 1954), December 1, 9, 1861; H. Adams, *Education of Henry Adams,* 119.

52. Bigelow, *Retrospections of an Active Life, 1817–1863,* 384–392; Weed, *Life of Thurlow Weed,* 1:654–656, and see 2:350 for a different version.

53. John R. G. Hassard, *Life of the Most Reverend John Hughes* (New York: D. Appleton, 1866), 463–468.

54. Ibid., 456–482.

55. H. Adams, *Education of Henry Adams,* 147; Weed, *Life of Thurlow Weed,* 1:642–643.

56. Weed, *Life of Thurlow Weed,* 1:642–643.

57. Stahr, *Seward: Lincoln's Indispensable Man,* 316–317.

58. Weed, *Life of Thurlow Weed,* 2:352–353.

59. Amanda Foreman, *A World on Fire: Britain's Crucial Role in the American Civil War* (New York: Random House, 2011), 180–189.

60. C. Adams, "Charles Francis Adams Diaries," January 10, 1862.

61. John Stuart Mill, *The Contest in America* (Boston: Little, Brown, 1862), 3.

CHAPTER 4: THE REPUBLICAN EXPERIMENT

1. John Bigelow, *Retrospections of an Active Life, 1817–1863* (New York: Baker and Taylor, 1909), 346, quoting Russell to Bigelow, London, February 4, 1861; Daniel T. Rodgers, "Republicanism: The Career of a Concept," *Journal of American History* 79, no. 1 (1992): 11–38.

2. Capitani Regenti to Lincoln, San Marino, March 29, 1861, Archivo dal Stato, San Marino; Captain Regents to President Obama, San Marino, May 6, 2011 (punctuation modified; all spelling as in the original). I am grateful to the State Archives of San Marino for sending me copies of the 1861 letters and to Rakesh Surampudi at the Italian Desk of the US State Department for providing me with a copy of the 2011 letter from San Marino to President Obama.

3. Lincoln and Seward to the Regent Captains of the Republic of San Marino, Washington, May 7, 1861, CWAL, 4:360; John Taylor, *William Henry Seward: Lincoln's Right Hand* (New York: HarperCollins, 1991), 167; Don H. Doyle, "From San Marino, with Love," in *The "New York Times": Disunion—Modern Historians Revisit and Reconsider the Civil War from Lincoln's Election to the Emancipation Proclamation,* edited by Ted Widmer, Clay Risen, and George Kalogerakis (New York: Black Dog and Leventhal, 2013), 86–90.

4. Maurizio Viroli, *Republicanism,* translated by Antony Shugaar (New York: Hill and Wang, 2001); Jonathan I. Israel, *A Revolution of the Mind: Radical Enlightenment and the Intellectual Origins of Modern Democracy* (Princeton, NJ: Princeton University Press, 2010), vii–x; E. J. Hobsbawm, *The Age of Revolution, 1789–1848* (New York: Vintage Books, 1996); David Brion Davis, *Revolutions: Reflections on American Equality and Foreign Liberations* (Cambridge, MA: Harvard University Press, 1990); Harry V. Jaffa, *A New Birth of Freedom: Abraham Lincoln and the Coming of the Civil War* (Lanham, MD: Rowman and Littlefield, 2000), 12, 26.

5. Jaffa, *New Birth of Freedom,* 111, quoting Jefferson to Roger Wightman, June 24, 1826.

6. Ibid., 127–135.

7. Seymour Drescher, *Abolition: A History of Slavery and Antislavery* (New York: Cambridge University Press, 2009); Davis, *Revolutions,* 17–18; Lacy K. Ford, *Deliver Us from Evil: The Slavery Question in the Old South* (New York: Oxford University Press, 2009); James Oakes, *Freedom National: The Destruction of Slavery in the United States, 1861–1865* (New York: W. W. Norton, 2013).

8. George Bancroft, *Memorial Address on the Life and Character of Abraham Lincoln* (Washington, DC: GPO, 1866), 6; James M. McPherson, *Abraham Lincoln and the Second American Revolution* (New York: Oxford University Press, 1990).

9. Bancroft, *Memorial Address,* 5.

10. Jaffa, *New Birth of Freedom,* 121–135, 176.

11. Davis, *Revolutions;* Hobsbawm, *Age of Revolution.*

12. Henry Blumenthal, *A Reappraisal of Franco-American Relations, 1830–1871* (Chapel Hill: University of North Carolina Press, 1959), 5; Serge Gavronsky, *The French Liberal Opposition and the American Civil War* (New York: Humanities Press, 1968), 24–25; Fred R. Shapiro, *The Yale Book of Quotations* (New Haven, CT: Yale University Press, 2006), 327.

13. Jonathan Sperber, *The European Revolutions, 1848–1851,* 2nd ed. (Cambridge: Cambridge University Press, 2005), 56–59, 68.

14. Ibid., 80.

15. Ibid., 116.

16. Ibid., 82, 122.

17. J. A. S. Grenville, *Europe Reshaped, 1848–1878* (Oxford: Blackwell, 2000), 87–100, 141–153.

18. Sperber, *European Revolutions,* 234–235; Grenville, *Europe Reshaped, 1848–1878,* 59–68, 111–123; Karl-Heinz Bannasch, "Eduard Zimmermann, Spandaus Bürgermeister in der Revolutionszeit von 1848–49," in *Spandauer Forschungen,* edited by Joachim Pohl et al. (Berlin: Heimatkundliche Vereinigung Spandau, Fördererkreis Museum Spandau, 2012), 188–191; Mary Lou Salomon, "Salomon Family Genealogy," 2005, entry for "Frederick Salomon," author's personal library.

19. Sperber, *European Revolutions;* Grenville, *Europe Reshaped, 1848–1878,* 87–202.

20. Hilda Sabato, "The Republican Experiment: On People and Government in Nineteenth Century Spanish America" (presented at the Shelby Cullom Davis

Center for Historical Studies, Princeton University, 2012); Paul W. Drake, *Between Tyranny and Anarchy: A History of Democracy in Latin America, 1800–2006* (Stanford, CA: Stanford University Press, 2009), 52–56, 88–125.

21. Robert Kagan, *Dangerous Nation* (New York: Alfred A. Knopf, 2006), 157–180, quote on 177; Harold William Vazeille Temperley, *The Foreign Policy of Canning, 1822–1827: England, the Neo-Holy Alliance and the New World* (London: G. Bell, 1925), 158–159.

22. Jay Sexton, *The Monroe Doctrine: Empire and Nation in Nineteenth-Century America* (New York: Hill and Wang, 2011), 85–122.

23. Sexton, *Monroe Doctrine;* Drake, *Between Tyranny and Anarchy,* 55–56.

24. Alexis de Tocqueville, *Democracy in America* (London: Saunders and Otley, 1838), 1:xxix, xxxii, 12.

25. Ephraim Douglass Adams, *Great Britain and the American Civil War* (1924; reprint, New York: Russell and Russell, 1958), 275; Alexander Mackay, *The Western World; or, Travels in the United States in 1846–47,* 4th ed. (London: R. Bentley, 1850), 3:24.

26. "The Conservative Leaders on the War," *NYT,* November 17, 1861.

27. Hugh Dubrulle, "'We Are Threatened with . . . Anarchy and Ruin': Fear of Americanization and the Emergence of an Anglo-Saxon Confederacy in England During the American Civil War," *Albion* 33, no. 4 (2001): 583–613; Martin Crawford, ed., *William Howard Russell's Civil War: Private Diary and Letters, 1861–1862* (Athens: University of Georgia Press, 2008), 155, quoting Russell to Sumner, London, October 14, 1861.

28. A. J. B. Beresford Hope, *The American Disruption in Three Lectures* (London: James Ridgway, 1862); "Mr. Beresford Hope, M.P., on the Contest," *NYT,* December 9, 1861.

29. Hope, *American Disruption in Three Lectures.*

30. Malakoff, "Important from France," *NYT,* June 3, 1861.

31. *Hansard Parliamentary Debates,* 3rd ser., May 27, 30, 1861, 163:133–134, 276, 332, http://hansard.millbanksystems.com; Spencer Walpole, *The Life of Lord John Russell* (London: Longmans, Green, 1889), 338.

32. "Conservative Leaders on the War"; "A Leaden-Headed Lord on Democracy," *NYT,* November 19, 1861.

33. Monadnock, "From London: The English People and the American Troubles," *NYT,* September 24, 1861.

34. "Affairs in England," *NYT,* June 17, 1861; Walpole, *Lord John Russell,* 338; "English Feeling Towards America," *NYT,* June 19, 1861; "Anglican Political Quacks," *NYT,* October 27, 1861; "A Leaden-Headed Lord on Democracy"; Charles Francis Adams, "Charles Francis Adams Diaries, 1823–1880" (Massachusetts Historical Society, Boston, 1954), January 10, February 19, 1862.

35. "Secession Agents in Paris Appreciated," *NYT,* December 7, 1861; Matías Romero, *Proceedings of a Meeting of Citizens of New York, to Express Sympathy and Respect for the Mexican Republican Exiles* (New York: J. A. Gray and Green, 1865), 31, quoting Boissy.

36. George McCoy Blackburn, *French Newspaper Opinion on the American Civil War* (Westport, CT: Greenwood, 1997), 114, 30, quoting *Le Monde,* January 8, 1861.

37. Gavronsky, *French Liberal Opposition,* 27; Taxile Delord, *Histoire du Second Empire: 1848–1869* (Paris: G. Baillière, 1869), 3:17; Henri Soret, *Histoire du conflit Américain, de ses causes, de ses résultats* (Tarbes: Telmon, 1863), 7.

38. "Letter from Hamburg," *New York Evening Post,* February 16, 1861.

39. Donaldson Jordan and Edwin J. Pratt, *Europe and the American Civil War* (Boston: Houghton Mifflin, 1931), 251–252; Edwin Pratt, "Spanish Opinion of the North American Civil War," *Hispanic American Historical Review* 10, no. 1 (1930): 20, quoting *El Pensamiento Español,* September 6, 1862.

40. James Spence, *The American Union: Its Effect on National Character and Policy, with an Inquiry into Secession as a Constitutional Right, and the Causes of the Disruption* (London: R. Bentley, 1861), 39–42.

41. A. J. B. Beresford Hope, *A Popular View of the American Civil War,* 3rd ed. (London: J. Ridgway, 1861), 12–13.

42. Howell Cobb, "Letter . . . to the People of Georgia," in *Southern Pamphlets on Secession, November 1860–April 1861,* edited by Jon L. Wakelyn (Chapel Hill: University of North Carolina Press, 1996), 88–101.

43. William Howard Russell, *My Diary North and South* (Boston: Burnham, 1863), 148, 227; Sheldon Vanauken, *The Glittering Illusion: English Sympathy for the Southern Confederacy* (Washington, DC: Regnery Gateway, 1989). Russell's diary testifies to similar antidemocratic sentiments among New Yorkers.

44. Russell, *My Diary,* 134, 263–264; William Howard Russell, *Pictures of Southern Life, Social, Political, and Military* (New York: James G. Gregory, 1861), 3; Robert E. Bonner, *Mastering America: Southern Slaveholders and the Crisis of American Nationhood* (Cambridge: Cambridge University Press, 2009), 266.

45. Russell, *My Diary,* 263–264; Crawford, *Russell's Civil War,* 89–90; Russell, *Pictures of Southern Life.*

46. "The South to Be a Monarchy," *New York Tribune,* April 2, 1861.

47. "The Fixed Purposes of the People," *Commercial Advertiser,* July 12, 1861.

48. Malakoff, "France and Secession," *NYT,* February 5, 1861; Malakoff, "From France: French Sentiment upon Secession," *NYT,* March 15, 1861; "A Crown with a Cotton Lining," *NYT,* July 10, 1861; Brian Schoen, "Secessionist Plots and Foreign Powers: Diplomats and Rumor in the Coming of the Civil War," unpublished paper. Schoen raises doubts about some of these rumors.

49. Lincoln, "Annual Message to Congress," December 3, 1861, CWAL, 5:51.

50. Minetta Altgelt Goyne, *Lone Star and Double Eagle: Civil War Letters of a German-Texas Family* (Fort Worth: Texas Christian University Press, 1982), 47–48; Chandra Manning, *What This Cruel War Was Over: Soldiers, Slavery, and the Civil War* (New York: Alfred A. Knopf, 2007), 66; Patrick J. Kelly, "The North American Crisis of the 1860s," *Journal of the Civil War Era* 2, no. 3 (2012): 348–349; Bonner, *Mastering America,* 266.

51. James Morton Callahan, *The Diplomatic History of the Southern Confederacy* (Baltimore: Johns Hopkins University Press, 1901), 244; J. B. Jones, *A Rebel*

War Clerk's Diary at the Confederate States Capital (Philadelphia: Lippincott, 1866), 2:355, December 15, 1864; Jeff Sowers Kinard, "Lafayette of the South: Prince Camille de Polignac and the American Civil War" (PhD, Texas Christian University, 1997), 304–305; C. J. Polignac, "Polignac's Mission," *Southern Historical Society Papers* 35 (January–December 1907): 326–334.

52. Thurlow Weed, *Life of Thurlow Weed Including His Autobiography and a Memoir* (Boston: Houghton Mifflin, 1884), 2:313–314; "Benjamin" to Archibald, New York, August 11, 1860, and Archibald to Lord Lyons, Lebanon Springs, NY, August 14, 1860, box 204, NY Consul, Archibald, 1860, Lyons Papers, West Sussex County Record Office, Chichester, UK. I am grateful to Brian Schoen for sending me a copy of this fascinating correspondence.

53. Robert Douthat Meade, *Judah P. Benjamin: Confederate Statesman* (Baton Rouge: Louisiana State University Press, 2001), 140–141; Eugene H. Berwanger, *The British Foreign Service and the American Civil War* (Lexington: University Press of Kentucky, 1994), 14–15; "History of the Benjamin Letter," *NYT,* March 23, 1884; Eli N. Evans, *Judah P. Benjamin, the Jewish Confederate* (New York: Free Press, 1988), 237.

CHAPTER 5: THE EMPIRES RETURN

1. "Foreign Intervention in American Affairs," *NYT,* April 1, 1861.

2. Malakoff, "Important from Paris," *NYT,* March 29, 1861; "Foreign Intervention in American Affairs"; "Astounding Intelligence: Aggressive Designs of Spain in the West Indies," *NYT,* March 30, 1861; Malakoff, "Our Rebellion Abroad," *NYT,* May 5, 1861; "Our Washington Correspondence," *NYT,* April 2, 1861.

3. A. R. Tyrner-Tyrnauer, *Lincoln and the Emperors* (New York: Harcourt, Brace, and World, 1962), 3–12.

4. Jay Sexton, *The Monroe Doctrine: Empire and Nation in Nineteenth-Century America* (New York: Hill and Wang, 2011), 49–73.

5. James F. McMillan, *Napoleon III* (London: Longman, 1991), 143–152.

6. Alfred J. Hanna and Kathryn A. Hanna, *Napoleon III and Mexico: American Triumph over Monarchy* (Chapel Hill: University of North Carolina Press, 1971), 58–60, 183; Michel Chevalier, *Mexico Ancient and Modern,* translated by Thomas Alpass (London: J. Maxwell, 1864), 2:201; Walter Mignolo, *The Idea of Latin America* (Malden, MA: Wiley-Blackwell, 2005), 77–79; Michel Gobat, "The Invention of Latin America: A Transnational History of Anti-Imperialism, Democracy, and Race," *American Historical Review* 118, no. 5 (2013): 1345–1375.

7. Hanna and Hanna, *Napoleon III and Mexico,* 3–20; John Leddy Phelan, "Pan-Latinism, French Intervention in Mexico (1861–1867) and the Genesis of the Idea of Latin America," in *Conciencia y autenticidad históricas,* edited by Juan Antonio Ortega y Medina (Mexico City: UNAM, 1968), 279–298.

8. Phelan, "Pan-Latinism"; Gobat, "Invention of Latin America."

9. Michel Chevalier and Ernest Rasetti, *La France, le Mexique et les États Confédérés* (Paris: E. Dentu, 1863); "France, Mexico and the Confederate States," *NYT,*

September 25, 1863; Michel Chevalier, *France, Mexico, and the Confederate States,* translated by William Henry Hurlbert (New York: C. B. Richardson, 1863); Vine Wright Kingsley, *French Intervention in America; or, A Review of la France, le Mexique, et les États-Confédérés* (New York: C. B. Richardson, 1863); Hanna and Hanna, *Napoleon III and Mexico,* 60–65.

10. "The Mexican Question," *NYT,* February 28, 1862.

11. Nathan L. Ferris, "The Relations of the United States with South America During the American Civil War," *Hispanic American Historical Review* 21, no. 1 (1941): 65–66; Hanna and Hanna, *Napoleon III and Mexico,* 182–183; James Schofield Saeger, *Francisco Solano López and the Ruination of Paraguay: Honor and Egocentrism* (Lanham, MD: Rowman & Littlefield, 2007).

12. Frank Moya Pons, *The Dominican Republic: A National History* (Princeton, NJ: Markus Wiener, 1998), 91–192.

13. Nancy Nichols Barker, *Distaff Diplomacy: The Empress Eugénie and the Foreign Policy of the Second Empire* (Austin: University of Texas Press, 2011), 63–65.

14. Schurz to Seward, San Lorenzo (Escorial), September 27, Spain, 1861; James W. Cortada, "Spain and the American Civil War: Relations at Mid-Century, 1855–1868," *Transactions of the American Philosophical Society* 70, no. 4 (1980): 33; Edwin Pratt, "Spanish Opinion of the North American Civil War," *Hispanic American Historical Review* 10, no. 1 (1930): 14–25; Wayne H. Bowen, *Spain and the American Civil War* (Columbia: University of Missouri Press, 2011), 2–3, 6.

15. Cortada, "Spain and the American Civil War," 30–33; Moya Pons, *Dominican Republic,* 197–210; Bowen, *Spain and the American Civil War,* 84–90.

16. Cortada, "Spain and the American Civil War," 30, 33–36; Moya Pons, *Dominican Republic,* 204–205; Bowen, *Spain and the American Civil War,* 84–90; Kinley J. Brauer, "Gabriel García y Tassara and the American Civil War: A Spanish Perspective," *Civil War History* 21, no. 1 (1975): 5–27; William Moss Wilson, "The Foreign War Panacea," *NYT,* March 17, 2011, sec. "The Opinionator: Disunion," http://opinionator.blogs.nytimes.com; "Spain and San Domingo," *NYT,* May 10, 1861; "Will Spain Be Able to Retain Dominica?," *NYT,* June 3, 1861.

17. Brauer, "García y Tassara," 11–12; Cortada, "Spain and the American Civil War," 33.

18. Glyndon G. Van Deusen, *William Henry Seward* (New York: Oxford University Press, 1967), 281–282, 292; Patrick Sowle, "A Reappraisal of Seward's Memorandum of April 1, 1861, to Lincoln," *Journal of Southern History* 33 (May 1, 1967): 234–239.

19. "Protest of the Dominicans Against the Spanish Invasion Call to Arms," *NYT,* April 2, 1861; Anne Eller, "'Rise, Compatriots': Dominican Civil Wars, Slavery, and Spanish Annexation, 1844–1865" (paper presented at "American Civil Wars" conference, University of South Carolina, March 19–21, 2014) (Cabral quote); Anne Eller, "Let's Show the World We Are Brothers: The Dominican Guerra de Restauracion and the Nineteenth-Century Caribbean" (PhD diss., New York University, 2011).

20. "Important from St. Domingo," *NYT,* March 30, 1861; "Astounding Intelligence"; Wilson, "The Foreign War Panacea."

21. Perry to Seward, Madrid, May 8, 27, 1861, Spain, RG 59.

22. Ramón Gómez de la Serna, *Mi tía Carolina Coronado* (Buenos Aires: Emecé, 1942).

23. Perry to Seward, Madrid, May 8, 27, June 4, 1861, Spain, RG 59.

24. Perry to Seward, Madrid, April 20, May 27, 1861, Spain, RG 59.

25. Toombs to Crawford, Montgomery, April 2, 1861, reel 1, CSA; Hunter to Yancey, Rost, and Mann, Richmond, November 20, 1861; Helm to Hunter, Havana, October 22, November 8, 1861, ORN, ser. 2, 3:284, 296.

26. Toombs to Charles Helm, Richmond, July 22, 1861; Toombs to Yancey, Rost, and Mann, Richmond, August 24, 1861, ORN, ser. 2, 3:225–226, 249–252.

27. Frank Lawrence Owsley, *King Cotton Diplomacy: Foreign Relations of the Confederate States of America,* 2nd ed. (1931; reprint, Chicago: University of Chicago Press, 1959), 84; Rost to Hunter, Madrid, March 21, 1862, ORN, ser. 2, 3:367–370.

28. "Important from St. Domingo."

29. Eric Van Young, *The Other Rebellion: Popular Violence, Ideology, and the Mexican Struggle for Independence, 1810–1821* (Stanford, CA: Stanford University Press, 2001); Brian R. Hamnett, *A Concise History of Mexico* (New York: Cambridge University Press, 2006), 111–171; Brian R. Hamnett, *Juárez* (New York: Longman, 1994); Jasper Godwin Ridley, *Maximilian and Juárez* (New York: Ticknor and Fields, 1992).

30. Hamnett, *Juárez,* 89, 99.

31. Hamnett, *Juárez;* Ridley, *Maximilian and Juárez.*

32. Daniel Dawson, *The Mexican Adventure* (London: G. Bell and Sons, 1935), 80–91; Erika Pani, "Dreaming of a Mexican Empire: The Political Projects of the 'Imperialistas,'" *Hispanic American Historical Review* 82, no. 1 (2002): 1–31; Erika Pani, *El Segundo Imperio: Pasados de usos múltiples* (Mexico City: Centro de Investigación y Docencia Económicas: Fondo de Cultura Económica, 2004).

33. Dawson, *The Mexican Adventure,* 58–128.

34. Karl Marx, "The Intervention in Mexico," *New York Daily Tribune,* November 23, 1861, originally written November 8, 1861, Marxists Internet Archive, http://www.marxists.org/archive/marx/works/1861/11/23.htm.

35. Dawson, *The Mexican Adventure,* 73–78, 116–119, 120–121; Carl H. Bock, *Prelude to Tragedy: The Negotiation and Breakdown of the Tripartite Convention of London, October 31, 1861* (Philadelphia: University of Pennsylvania Press, 1966).

36. Hanna and Hanna, *Napoleon III and Mexico,* 40.

37. "The Expedition to Mexico," *NYT,* January 3, 1862; Bock, *Prelude to Tragedy,* 275.

38. Hanna and Hanna, *Napoleon III and Mexico,* 40.

39. "Colonization of Discrowned Heads in America," *NYT,* March 5, 1862.

40. Ronnie C. Tyler, *Santiago Vidaurri and the Southern Confederacy* ([Austin]: Texas State Historical Association, 1973), 30–31, 34, 52–53, 56–59.

41. Darryl E. Brock, "José Agustín Quintero: Cuban Patriot in Confederate Diplomatic Service," in *Cubans in the Confederacy: José Agustín Quintero, Ambro-*

sio José Gonzales, and Loreta Janeta Velazquez (Jefferson, NC: McFarland, 2002), 9–142; Tyler, *Santiago Vidaurri;* Patrick J. Kelly, "The North American Crisis of the 1860s," *Journal of the Civil War Era* 2, no. 3 (2012); Toombs to Vidaurri, Montgomery, May 21, 22, 1861; William M. Brown to Quintero, Richmond, September 3, December 9, 1861, ORN, ser. 2, 3:101, 116, 217–218, 253–255.

42. Thomas D. Schoonover, *Dollars over Dominion: The Triumph of Liberalism in Mexican–United States Relations, 1861–1867* (Baton Rouge: Louisiana State University Press, 1978), 19–21.

43. Owsley, *King Cotton Diplomacy,* 91–92; US Department of State, *The Present Condition of Mexico* (Washington, DC: GPO, 1863), 16, 24, quoting Corwin to Seward, Mexico City, July 29, September 7, 1861.

44. Lester D. Langley, *Struggle for the American Mediterranean: United States–European Rivalry in the Gulf-Caribbean, 1776–1904* (Athens: University of Georgia Press, 1976), 116–121.

45. Forsyth to Davis, Washington, March 20, 1861, vol. 1, John T. Pickett Papers, LoC; Owsley, *King Cotton Diplomacy,* 89–91; Mary Wilhelmine Williams, "Letter from Colonel John T. Pickett, of the Southern Confederacy, to Senor Don Manuel De Zamacona, Minister of Foreign Affairs, Mexico," *Hispanic American Historical Review* 2, no. 4 (1919): 611–617; "Important from Mexico," *NYT,* December 18, 1861.

46. Schoonover, *Dollars over Dominion,* 25–29; John T. Pickett to John Forsyth, Washington, March 13, 1861, John T. Pickett Papers, LoC.

47. Owsley, *King Cotton Diplomacy,* 90–91, suggests Pickett added the advice on bribery; Toombs to Pickett, Montgomery, May 17, 1861, ORN, ser. 2, 3:202–205.

48. Ibid., 92–103; US Department of State, *Present Condition of Mexico,* 20, quoting Corwin to Seward, Mexico City, August 28, 1861; Pickett to Martin J. Crawford, Veracruz, February 2, 1862, letterbook 1:118, John T. Pickett Papers, LoC.

49. Owsley, *King Cotton Diplomacy,* 95–97.

50. Ibid., 93–95, 101–102; US Department of State, *Present Condition of Mexico,* 31–32, quoting Corwin to Seward, Mexico City, October 21, 1861.

51. Schoonover, *Dollars over Dominion,* 42–43; Owsley, *King Cotton Diplomacy,* 98, quoting Pickett to Toombs, Mexico City, November 29, 1861.

52. Schoonover, *Dollars over Dominion,* 43.

53. John T. Pickett to Martin J. Crawford, Veracruz, February 2, 1862; Pickett to Jefferson Davis, Veracruz, February 22, 1862, John T. Pickett Papers, LoC.

54. Schurz to Seward, Madrid, November 16, 1861, Spain, RG 59; Sara Yorke Stevenson, *Maximilian in Mexico: A Woman's Reminiscences of the French Intervention, 1862–1867* (New York: Century, 1899), 28n2.

55. "Proclamation of the Allied Commissioners to the People of Mexico, Vera Cruz, January 10, 1862," *House Divided,* n.d., http://hd.housedivided.dickinson.edu/node/38607; Dawson, *The Mexican Adventure,* 158–182, 235–243; Hanna and Hanna, *Napoleon III and Mexico,* 42–44.

56. Hanna and Hanna, *Napoleon III and Mexico,* 45–46, 69; Dawson, *The Mexican Adventure,* 244–245.

57. Dawson, *The Mexican Adventure,* 244–246.

58. Stevenson, *Maximilian in Mexico,* 68; Hamnett, *Juárez,* 171.

59. Hanna and Hanna, *Napoleon III and Mexico,* 77–81, 89, quoting Napoleon III to Forey, July 3, 1862, February 14, 1863.

60. Ibid., 78–80; Ridley, *Maximilian and Juárez,* 78, 134; Pani, "Dreaming of a Mexican Empire"; Michel Chevalier, *L'expédition du Mexique* (Paris: E. Dentu, 1862); Chevalier and Rasetti, *La France, le Mexique et les États Confédérés;* Chevalier, *France, Mexico, and the Confederate States.*

61. Hanna and Hanna, *Napoleon III and Mexico,* 87–92.

62. Dawson, *The Mexican Adventure,* 118–119.

63. Robert Ryal Miller, "Arms Across the Border: United States Aid to Juárez During the French Intervention in Mexico," *Transactions of the American Philosophical Society* 63, no. 6 (1973): 1–68; Robert Ryal Miller, "Matías Romero: Mexican Minister to the United States During the Juarez-Maximilian Era," *Hispanic American Historical Review* 45, no. 2 (1965): 236; *Correspondencia de la Legacion Mexicana en Washington durante la intervencion extranjera, 1860–1868,* edited by Matías Romero, 10 vols. (Mexico: Imprenta del Gobierno, 1870).

64. Miller, "Matías Romero," 232–233.

65. Matías Romero, *A Mexican View of America in the 1860s: A Foreign Diplomat Describes the Civil War and Reconstruction,* edited by Thomas David Schoonover (Teaneck, NJ: Fairleigh Dickinson University Press, 1991); Schoonover, *Dollars over Dominion;* Thomas D. Schoonover, *Mexican Lobby: Matías Romero in Washington, 1861–67* (Lexington: University Press of Kentucky, 1986); Matías Romero, *Proceedings of a Meeting of Citizens of New York, to Express Sympathy and Respect for the Mexican Republican Exiles* (New York: J. A. Gray and Green, 1865), 7–8, speech by Leavitt; Robert E. May, ed., *The Union, the Confederacy, and the Atlantic Rim,* rev. ed. (Gainesville: University Press of Florida, 2013).

66. Egon Caesar Corti, *Maximilian and Charlotte of Mexico,* translated by Catherine Alison Phillips (New York: Alfred A. Knopf, 1928), 435; Dawson, *The Mexican Adventure,* 318, 343–344; Ridley, *Maximilian and Juárez,* 156–157.

67. Ridley, *Maximilian and Juárez,* 47–48, 1–5.

68. John Lothrop Motley, *The Correspondence of John Lothrop Motley* (New York: Harper and Brothers, 1889), 2:143.

69. William Edward Johnston, *Memoirs of "Malakoff,"* edited by R. M. Johnston (London: Hutchinson, 1907), 2:437.

70. Ridley, *Maximilian and Juárez,* 165–166.

CHAPTER 6: FOREIGN TRANSLATIONS

1. Marsh to Seward, Turin, September 3, 1861, Italy, RG 59; Marsh to Seward, Turin, July 6, 1861, FRUS, 1861, 322–323 (emphasis added).

2. Agénor Gasparin, *Un grand peuple qui se relève* (Paris: Michel Levy, 1861); Agénor Gasparin, *The Uprising of a Great People,* translated by Mary L. Booth (New York: C. Scribner, 1861); Malakoff, "The American Crisis in France," *NYT,* May

15, 1861; Serge Gavronsky, *The French Liberal Opposition and the American Civil War* (New York: Humanities Press, 1968), iv, 59–60.

3. Gavronsky, *French Liberal Opposition*, 59, 60, 254; Théodore Borel, *The Count Agénor de Gasparin* (New York: A. D. F. Randolph, 1879); "The Distinguished Strangers," *NYT*, September 14, 1861; Monadnock, "Renewed Rumors of Intervention," *NYT*, June 6, 1862; "Louis Napoleon's Designs and Dangers," *NYT*, December 7, 1862.

4. Gasparin, *Uprising of a Great People*, ix–x.

5. Ibid., 10, 11, 259.

6. Édouard Laboulaye, *Why the North Cannot Accept of Separation* (New York: C. B. Richardson, 1863), 3, from introduction by M. L. A.

7. Harriet P. Spofford, "Mary Louise Booth," in *Our Famous Women* (Hartford, CT: A. D. Worthington, 1883), 117–133; Madeline B. Stern, "Mary Louise Booth," in *Notable American Women*, edited by Edward T. James, Janet Wilson James, and Paul Boyer (Cambridge, MA: Belknap Press, 1971), 1:207–208.

8. Mary L. Booth, *History of the City of New York* (New York: W. R. C. Clark, 1859).

9. Spofford, "Mary Louise Booth"; Stern, "Mary Louise Booth."

10. Malakoff, "The American Crisis in France"; "A Remarkable French Book," *NYT*, May 27, 1861; "Mary Louise Booth," *Student* 11, no. 1 (1890): 341–343; Stern, "Mary Louise Booth."

11. Spofford, "Mary Louise Booth," 27; "The Uprising of a Great People: The United States in 1861; From the French of Count Agénor de Gasparin, by Mary L. Booth," *North American Review* 93, no. 193 (1861): 583–585.

12. Agénor de Gasparin, *The Uprising of a Great People: The United States in 1861, Abridged* (London: S. Low, 1861); Agénor Gasparin, *A Word of Peace on the American Question* (London: S. Low, 1862); Jay Monaghan, *Diplomat in Carpet Slippers: Abraham Lincoln Deals with Foreign Affairs* (Indianapolis: Bobbs-Merrill, 1962), 92–93; Agénor Gasparin, *Een Groot Volk Dat Zich Verheft: De Vereenigde Staten in 1861* (Utrecht: L. E. Bosch en Zoon, 1861); "A Word from Count Gasparin," *NYT*, December 29, 1861.

13. Agénor de Gasparin, *L'Amérique devant l'Europe* (Paris: M. Lévy Frères, 1862); Agénor Gasparin, *America Before Europe: Principles and Interests*, translated by Mary L. Booth (New York: C. Scribner, 1862).

14. Lincoln to Booth, August 1, 1862, CWAL, 5:352.

15. Gasparin, *America Before Europe*, 302, 345.

16. John Bigelow, *Some Recollections of the Late Edouard Laboulaye* (New York: G. P. Putnam Sons, 1889), 1–2.

17. Édouard Laboulaye, "La guerre civile aux États-Unis," *Journal des Débats* (October 2, 1861): second part in October 3 issue; Bigelow, *Some Recollections of Laboulaye*, 1–4; Walter Dennis Gray, *Interpreting American Democracy in France: The Career of Édouard Laboulaye, 1811–1883* (Newark: University of Delaware Press, 1994), 77–78; Tim Verhoeven, "Shadow and Light: Louis-Xavier Eyma (1816–76)

and French Opinion of the United States During the Second Empire," *International History Review* 35, no. 1 (2013): 143–161.

18. Malakoff, "A French Writer on the American Crisis," *NYT,* October 27, 1861.

19. Ibid.; Édouard Laboulaye, *The United States and France* (Boston: Boston Daily Advertiser, 1862).

20. Bigelow, *Some Recollections of Laboulaye,* 1–4; Gray, *Interpreting American Democracy,* 77–84.

21. Bigelow, Diary, October 5, 1861, August 30, 1862, box 103, Bigelow Family Papers, NYPL; Bigelow, *Some Recollections of Laboulaye,* 3–4; John Bigelow, *Retrospections of an Active Life, 1817–1863* (New York: Baker and Taylor, 1909), 532–533; David Hackett Fischer, *Liberty and Freedom* (New York: Oxford University Press, 2005), 368; Édouard Laboulaye, *Les États-Unis et la France* (Paris: E. Dentu, 1862).

22. Gray, *Interpreting American Democracy;* Philip G. Nord, *The Republican Moment: Struggles for Democracy in Nineteenth-Century France* (Cambridge, MA: Harvard University Press, 1998), 34; George McCoy Blackburn, *French Newspaper Opinion on the American Civil War* (Westport, CT: Greenwood, 1997), 12, 14, 65.

23. Bigelow, *Some Recollections of Laboulaye;* Blackburn, *French Newspaper Opinion,* 16–17, 105; Gray, *Interpreting American Democracy,* 76.

24. Gray, *Interpreting American Democracy,* 29–30.

25. Bigelow, *Some Recollections of Laboulaye,* 4.

26. Ibid., 5.

27. Ibid., 4–7; Laboulaye, *United States and France;* Gray, *Interpreting American Democracy,* 79, quoting Sumner to Laboulaye, November 14, 1863.

28. Édouard Laboulaye, *Paris en Amérique* (Paris: Charpentier, 1863); Édouard Laboulaye, *Paris in America,* translated by Mary L. Booth (New York: Charles Scribner, 1863); Gray, *Interpreting American Democracy,* 65–67.

29. Among Laboulaye's other writings on behalf of the Union were *Pourquoi le Nord ne peut accepter la séparation* (New York: Messager Franco-Américain, 1863); *Upon Whom Rests the Guilt of the War?; Separation: War Without End* (New York: W. C. Bryant, 1863); *Why the North Cannot Accept of Separation; Separation: War Without End* (New York: W. C. Bryant, 1864); and *The Election of the President of the United States* (Washington, DC: Union Congressional Committee, 1864).

30. James Spence, *The American Union: Its Effect on National Character and Policy, with an Inquiry into Secession as a Constitutional Right, and the Causes of the Disruption* (London: R. Bentley, 1861), xi; Donaldson Jordan and Edwin J. Pratt, *Europe and the American Civil War* (Boston: Houghton Mifflin, 1931), 75; Brian Jenkins, *Britain and the War for the Union* (Montreal: McGill-Queen's University Press, 1974), 2:35–37. For other details on Spence, see Mason to Benjamin, London, May 2, 1862; and Spence to Mason, Liverpool, April 28, 1862, ORN, ser. 2, 3:401–405.

31. Mason to Benjamin, London, February 7, 1862, ORN, ser. 2, 3:331.

32. Spence, *American Union,* 39–41, 57–58, 103, 110, 317; Frank Lawrence Owsley, *King Cotton Diplomacy: Foreign Relations of the Confederate States of America,* 2nd ed. (1931; reprint, Chicago: University of Chicago Press, 1959), 172–173.

33. Spence, *American Union*, 122–123.

34. Hotze to Hunter, London, February 28, March 18, 1862, ORN, ser. 2, 3:353–354, 362–363.

35. Mason to Benjamin, London, May 2, 1862, ORN, ser. 2, 3:401–402.

36. James Spence, *L'union Américaine: Ses effets sur le caractère national et la politique causes de la dissolution et étude du droit constitutionnel de séparation* (Paris: Michel Lévy Frères, 1862); James Spence, *Die Amerikanische Union*, translated by August P. Wetter (Barmen: W. Langewiesche, 1863); James Spence, *The American Union: Its Effect on National Character and Policy, with an Inquiry into Secession as a Constitutional Right, and the Causes of the Disruption* (Richmond: West and Johnston, 1863); Hotze to Hunter, London, February 28, March 18, 1862; Hotze to Benjamin, London, April 25, May 2, 1862, ORN, ser. 2, 3:353–354, 362, 400–402.

37. Spence, *American Union*, 131–132, 158–165.

38. George Macaulay Trevelyan, *The Life of John Bright* (Boston: Houghton Mifflin, 1913), 1–3.

39. Ibid., 2–3, 302, 303; Keith Robbins, *John Bright* (London: Routledge, 1979), 197.

40. John Bright, *Speeches of John Bright, M.P., on the American Question* (Boston: Little, Brown, 1865), 1–7.

41. Trevelyan, *Life of John Bright*, 301–302.

42. John Bright, *A Liberal Voice from England: Mr. John Bright's Speech at Rochdale, December 4, 1861, on the American Crisis* (New York: G. P. Putnam, 1862), 1.

43. Bright, *Speeches of John Bright*, 10–11; Trevelyan, *Life of John Bright*, 1.

44. Bright, *Speeches of John Bright*, 8–67, quotes on 14, 17.

45. Ibid., 66–67.

46. Trevelyan, *Life of John Bright*, 313; Bright, *Liberal Voice*.

47. Trevelyan, *Life of John Bright*, 313, 304.

48. Ibid., 314–315.

49. Burton Jesse Hendrick, *Lincoln's War Cabinet* (Boston: Little, Brown, 1946), 206–208; Michael Burlingame, *Abraham Lincoln: A Life* (Baltimore: Johns Hopkins University Press, 2008), 2:226, 250.

50. Ephraim Douglass Adams, *Great Britain and the American Civil War* (1924; reprint, New York: Russell and Russell, 1958), 2:1–32, esp. 6–7; Eugenio F. Biagini, *Liberty, Retrenchment and Reform: Popular Liberalism in the Age of Gladstone, 1860–1880* (Cambridge: Cambridge University Press, 2004), 69–78, esp. 70, 73n259; Jenkins, *Britain and the War for the Union*, 2:163–164; R. J. M. Blackett, *Divided Hearts: Britain and the American Civil War* (Baton Rouge: Louisiana State University Press, 2001).

51. Trevelyan, *Life of John Bright*, 297.

52. August H. Nimtz, *Marx, Tocqueville, and Race in America: The "Absolute Democracy" or "Defiled Republic"* (Lanham, MD: Lexington Books, 2003), 64, 84n57; Robert Chadwell Williams, *Horace Greeley: Champion of American Freedom* (New York: New York University Press, 2006), 133–137; *Encyclopedia of the American Civil War: A Political, Social, and Military History*, edited by David Stephen

Heidler and Jeanne T. Heidler (New York: W. W. Norton, 2002), s.v. "New York Tribune."

53. Williams, *Horace Greeley*, 135.

54. Francis Wheen, *Karl Marx: A Life* (New York: W. W. Norton, 2001); Kevin Peraino, *Lincoln in the World: The Making of a Statesman and the Dawn of American Power* (New York: Crown, 2013), 170–223.

55. Asa Briggs, *Marx in London: An Illustrated Guide* (London: BBC, 1982), 37–58; Williams, *Horace Greeley*, 133–136; Marx to Engels, London, May 13, 1865, Marxists Internet Archive, http://www.marxists.org/archive/marx/works/1865/letters/65_05_13.htm.

56. Karl Marx and Frederick Engels, *The Civil War in the United States* (New York: International, 1969); Wheen, *Karl Marx: A Life*, 84–85, 186–187, 218–219, 223–224, 224–227.

57. Marx and Engels, *Civil War*; Gerald Runkle, "Karl Marx and the American Civil War," *Comparative Studies in Society and History* 6 (January 1964): 117–141; Wheen, *Karl Marx: A Life*, 223–224; Karl Obermann, *Joseph Weydemeyer: Pioneer of American Socialism* (New York: International, 1947); Karl Marx, *Karl Marx and Frederick Engels: Letters to Americans, 1848–1895, a Selection* (New York: International, 1953), 3–5, 304.

58. Karl Marx, "The North American Civil War," *Die Presse*, no. 293 (1861), Marxists Internet Archive, http://www.marxists.org/archive/marx/works/1861/10/25.htm; Barrington Moore, *Social Origins of Dictatorship and Democracy: Lord and Peasant in the Making of the Modern World* (Boston: Beacon Press, 1966), 111–158; Nimtz, *Marx, Tocqueville, and Race*, 95–96.

59. Marx and Engels, *Civil War*, 23–24.

60. Ibid., 25.

61. Ibid., 45, 51.

62. Ibid., 43–44.

63. Ibid., 40, 47–54.

64. Ibid., 49, 48.

65. Ibid., 57–220.

66. "Address of the International Working Men's Association to Abraham Lincoln, President of the United States of America, Presented to U.S. Ambassador Charles Francis Adams, January 28, 1865, Marxists Internet Archive, http://www.marxists.org/archive/marx/iwma/documents/1864/lincoln-letter.htm.

67. Maria Diedrich, *Love Across Color Lines: Ottilie Assing and Frederick Douglass* (New York: Hill and Wang, 1999), chaps. 2–3; Ottilie Assing, *Radical Passion: Ottilie Assing's Reports from America and Letters to Frederick Douglass*, edited by Christoph K. Lohmann (New York: Peter Lang, 1999), xiv–xvi.

68. Frederick Douglass, *Sclaverei und Freiheit autobiographie*, translated by Ottilie Assing (Hamburg: Hoffmann und Campe, 1860); Diedrich, *Love Across Color Lines*, 237.

69. Diedrich, *Love Across Color Lines*, 234–237.

70. Ibid., 237.

71. Assing, *Radical Passion,* 215.

72. Diedrich, *Love Across Color Lines,* 237, 254–256, 371–375, 377–379.

CHAPTER 7: FOREIGN LEGIONS

1. Dillon to Seward, Turin, June 10, 1861, FRUS, 1861, 319–320; George C. D. Nanglo to Sanford, Turin, August 23, 1861, box 94, folder 18, SP.

2. Campbell J. Gibson and Emily Lennon, "Historical Census Statistics on the Foreign-Born Population of the United States: 1850 to 1990," 1999, table 13, "Nativity of the Population, for Regions, Divisions, and States: 1850 to 1990," http://www.census.gov/population/www/documentation/twps0029/twps0029.html.

3. "China at Gettysburg," *NYT,* July 12, 1863; "A Chinaman from Rebeldom," *NYT,* March 12, 1864; Benjamin Apthorp Gould, *Investigations in the Military and Anthropological Statistics of American Soldiers* (New York: Hurd and Houghton, 1869), 27–28, 574; Daniel Scott Smith, "Who Fought for the Union Army?" (presented at the annual meeting of the American Historical Association, Chicago, 2000). Thanks to David Hacker for sending me a copy of Smith's paper, following the author's untimely death, and for taking time to help me understand his methods and findings.

4. Martin Öfele, *True Sons of the Republic: European Immigrants in the Union Army* (Westport, CT: Praeger, 2008), 55; George Brinton McClellan, *The Armies of Europe* (Philadelphia: J. B. Lippincott, 1861).

5. Gould, *Investigations in the Military and Anthropological Statistics,* 15–16, 28–29.

6. Ibid., 4.

7. "Civil War Treasures from the New York Historical Society (American Memory, Library of Congress)," http://memory.loc.gov/ammem/ndlpcoop/nhihtml/cwnyhsarcpp.html#pos.

8. Maurizio Viroli, *For Love of Country: An Essay on Patriotism and Nationalism* (Oxford: Oxford University Press, 1995); "Adopted Citizens and the War," *NYT,* August 12, 1861.

9. James Epstein, *Radical Expression: Political Language, Ritual, and Symbol in England, 1790–1850* (New York: Oxford University Press, 1994), 70–99.

10. Philip G. Nord, *The Republican Moment: Struggles for Democracy in Nineteenth-Century France* (Cambridge, MA: Harvard University Press, 1998), 202; Lloyd S. Kramer, *Nationalism in Europe and America: Politics, Cultures, and Identities Since 1775* (Chapel Hill: University of North Carolina Press, 2011), 8, 27–28, 46, 99.

11. David Hackett Fischer, *Liberty and Freedom* (New York: Oxford University Press, 2005), 298–300; Ellen L. Berg, "Hail, Columbia!," *NYT,* July 2, 2011, sec. "The Opinionator: Disunion," http://opinionator.blogs.nytimes.com/2011/07/02/hail-columbia/; Jeannene M. Przyblyski, "Between Seeing and Believing . . . ," in *Making the News: Modernity and the Mass Press in Nineteenth-Century France,* edited by Dean De la Motte (Amherst: University of Massachusetts Press, 1999), 323–324.

12. Fischer, *Liberty and Freedom*, 298–300, 368–374; Guy Gugliotta, *Freedom's Cap: The United States Capitol and the Coming of the Civil War* (New York: Hill and Wang, 2012).

13. Peter Welsh, *Irish Green and Union Blue: The Civil War Letters of Peter Welsh, Color Sergeant, 28th Regiment, Massachusetts Volunteers* (New York: Fordham University Press, 1986), 100–103 (all spelling and punctuation as in original).

14. Walter D. Kamphoefner and Wolfgang Johannes Helbich, eds., *Germans in the Civil War: The Letters They Wrote Home* (Chapel Hill: University of North Carolina Press, 2006), 122, 124, 128 (punctuation modified).

15. Ibid., 267–268.

16. Ibid., 317, 350.

17. Elizabeth Cady Stanton et al., *History of Woman Suffrage* (New York: Fowler and Wells, 1881), 2:59.

18. J. David Hacker, "A Census-Based Count of the Civil War Dead," *Civil War History* 57, no. 4 (2011): 307–348.

19. William Osborn Stoddard, *Inside the White House in War Times* (New York: C. L. Webster, 1890), 278–279; E. B. Long and Barbara Long, *The Civil War Day by Day: An Almanac, 1861–1865* (Garden City, NY: Doubleday, 1971), 705, summarizing and citing earlier estimates; Aaron Sheehan-Dean, "'Awful Arithmetic': Regular and Irregular Violence in the U.S. Civil War," unpublished paper.

20. *Encyclopedia of the American Civil War: A Political, Social, and Military History*, edited by David Stephen Heidler and Jeanne T. Heidler (New York: W. W. Norton, 2002), s.v. "Conscription, C.S.A."

21. Gould, *Investigations in the Military and Anthropological Statistics*, chap. 2.

22. Long and Long, *Civil War Day by Day*, 704.

23. Gould, *Investigations in the Military and Anthropological Statistics*, 24.

24. Seth C. Chandler, "Benjamin Apthorp Gould," *Proceedings of the American Academy of Arts and Sciences* 32, no. 17 (1897): 355–360; George C. Comstock, "Biographical Memoir Benjamin Apthorp Gould," *National Academy of Science* 7 (1922); Andrew McFarland Davis, *Benjamin Apthorp Gould* (Worcester, MA: American Antiquarian Society, 1897).

25. *Times* (London), June 19, 1862, quoted in dispatch from A. Dudley Mann to Charles Rogier, Brussels, May 29, 1862, ORN, ser. 2, 3:430–431.

26. Slidell to Benjamin, Paris, July 25, 1862, ORN, ser. 2, 3:481–483; Dean B. Mahin, *The Blessed Place of Freedom: Europeans in Civil War America* (Washington, DC: Brassey's, 2002), 10.

27. Gould, *Investigations in the Military and Anthropological Statistics*, 15–16, 28–29; Susannah Ural Bruce, *The Harp and the Eagle: Irish-American Volunteers and the Union Army, 1861–1865* (New York: New York University Press, 2006), 146–147.

28. Wilhelm Kaufmann, *Die Deutschen im amerikanischen bürgerkriege* (Munich: R. Oldenbourg, 1911); Wilhelm Kaufmann, *The Germans in the American Civil War: With a Biographical Directory*, edited by Don Heinrich Tolzmann, translated by Steven W. Rowan (Carlisle, PA: John Kallmann, 1999), 70–76.

29. Gould, *Investigations in the Military and Anthropological Statistics*, 24, 25, 27, 574. Ella Lonn, *Foreigners in the Union Army and Navy* (New York: Greenwood Press, 1969), 582, revises Gould's estimate of foreign enlistees to 518,000; Smith, "Who Fought?," raises it to 543,000. All three confirm that immigrants enlisted at higher rates than native-born Americans.

30. "Ay—down to the dust with them, slaves as they are, / From this hour, let the blood in their dastardly veins, / That shrunk at the first touch of Liberty's war, / Be wasted for tyrants, or stagnate in chains," from Thomas Moore, *The Poetical Works of Thomas Moore* (London: Longman, Orme, 1841), 392; Catherine C. Catalfamo, "The Thorny Rose: The Americanization of an Urban, Immigrant, Working Class Regiment in the Civil War; A Social History of the Garibaldi Guard, 1861–1864" (PhD diss., University of Texas, Austin, 1990), viii.

31. George E. Waring, "The Garibaldi Guard," in *Liber Scriptorum: The First Book of the Authors Club* (New York: Authors Club, 1893), 570–571; Frank W. Alduino and David J. Coles, *Sons of Garibaldi in Blue and Gray: Italians in the American Civil War* (Youngstown, NY: Cambria Press, 2007), 55–56; Michael Bacarella, *Lincoln's Foreign Legion: The 39th New York Infantry, the Garibaldi Guard* (Shippensburg, PA: White Mane, 1996), 31.

32. Bacarella, *Lincoln's Foreign Legion*, 35, quoting George E. Waring.

33. Mann to Benjamin, Brussels, July 5, 1862, ORN, ser. 2, 3:453–455; James Shields to Brigadier-General Carroll, Columbia Bridge, VA, June 7, 1862, OR, ser. 1, 12:352–353.

34. Smith, "Who Fought?"; Gould, *Investigations in the Military and Anthropological Statistics*, 27, 574; Kaufmann, *Germans in the American Civil War*, 70–76; James M. McPherson, *Battle Cry of Freedom: The Civil War Era* (New York: Oxford University Press, 1988), 606–607; Long and Long, *Civil War Day by Day*, 704, 705, 708. Joseph C. G. Kennedy, *Population of the United States in 1860* (Washington, DC: GPO, 1864), xvii, estimates the military population in 1860.

35. Ute Frevert, *A Nation in Barracks: Modern Germany, Military Conscription and Civil Society* (Oxford: Berg, 2004), chap. 2; Karen Hagemann, "Revisiting Prussia's Wars Against Napoleon: War, Political Culture and Memory," private correspondence with the author on her work in progress, March 8, 2012; Mary Lou Salomon, "Salomon Family Genealogy," 2005, author's personal library.

36. Ray Allen Billington, *The Protestant Crusade, 1800–1860: A Study of the Origins of American Nativism* (1938; reprint, Chicago: Quadrangle Books, 1964); Dale T. Knobel, *Paddy and the Republic: Ethnicity and Nationality in Antebellum America* (Middletown, CT: Wesleyan University Press, 1986); Bruce, *Harp and Eagle*, 10–12.

37. Christian G. Samito, *Becoming American Under Fire: Irish Americans, African Americans, and the Politics of Citizenship During the Civil War Era* (Ithaca, NY: Cornell University Press, 2009); Bruce, *Harp and Eagle*.

38. Michael Cavanagh, *Memoirs of Gen. Thomas Francis Meagher* (Worcester, MA: Messenger, 1892), 368–369.

39. Paul R. Wylie, *The Irish General: Thomas Francis Meagher* (Norman: University of Oklahoma Press, 2007); Thomas S. Lonergan, "General Thomas Francis Meagher," *Journal of the American-Irish Historical Society* 12 (1913): 111–128; John M. Hearne and Rory T. Cornish, eds., *Thomas Francis Meagher: The Making of an Irish American* (Dublin: Irish Academic Press, 2006); Bruce, *Harp and Eagle*, 55–58.

40. Bruce, *Harp and Eagle*, 1, 3, 63.

41. Gould, *Investigations in the Military and Anthropological Statistics*, 27, 574.

42. US Bureau of the Census, *Historical Statistics of the United States, Colonial Times to 1970* (Washington, DC: Bureau of the Census, 1975), 106; Gould, *Investigations in the Military and Anthropological Statistics*, 8; Mahin, *Blessed Place of Freedom*, 51–58.

43. Wright to Seward, Berlin, May 26, 1861; Dayton to Seward, Paris, May 22, 1861, FRUS, 1861, 39–40, 319–320; Lonn, *Foreigners in the Union Army and Navy*, 409, quoting Bornstein to Seward, September 12, 1862, Hamburg, Bremen, RG 59.

44. Stephen C. Neff, *Justice in Blue and Gray: A Legal History of the Civil War* (Cambridge, MA: Harvard University Press, 2010), 169–170; Ephraim Douglass Adams, *Great Britain and the American Civil War* (1924; reprint, New York: Russell and Russell, 1958), 1:94–95, 2:200–201.

45. Paul W. Gates, *Free Homesteads for All Americans: The Homestead Act of 1862* (Washington, DC: Civil War Centennial Commission, 1963).

46. Seward, Circular 19, August 8, 1862, FRUS, 1862, 172.

47. John Bigelow, *Retrospections of an Active Life, 1817–1863* (New York: Baker and Taylor, 1909), 563.

48. John Taylor, *William Henry Seward: Lincoln's Right Hand* (New York: HarperCollins, 1991), 201; Bigelow to Seward, Paris, September 19, 1862, Paris, RG 59; Bigelow, *Retrospections of an Active Life, 1817–1863*, 562, quoting Seward to Bigelow, October 27, 1862.

49. Malakoff, "American Matters in France," *NYT*, August 23, 1862; Dayton to Seward, Paris, September 9, 1862, FRUS, 1862, 387.

50. John Bigelow, *Les États-Unis d'Amerique en 1863* (Paris: Hachette, 1863); Bigelow, *Gli Stati Uniti d'America nel 1863* (Milan: Corona e Caimi, 1863); John Bigelow, Diary, April 1, 1863, box 103, Bigelow Family Papers, NYPL; Bigelow to Seward, Paris, November 21, 1862, Paris, RG 59.

51. Gould, *Investigations in the Military and Anthropological Statistics*, 2, 4, 28; *Historical Statistics of the United States: Millennial Edition* (New York: Cambridge University Press, 2006), online edition, table Ad1–2.

52. Charles P. Cullop, *Confederate Propaganda in Europe, 1861–1865* (Coral Gables, FL: University of Miami Press, 1969), 100–116; Adams, *Great Britain*, 200–202; Frank Lawrence Owsley, *King Cotton Diplomacy: Foreign Relations of the Confederate States of America*, 2nd ed. (1931; reprint, Chicago: University of Chicago Press, 1959), 495–499.

53. Lincoln, Annual Message to Congress, December 6, 1864, CWAL, 8:141. What we may call the "Barbier Affair," after the principal litigant, was detailed in multiple documents: FRUS, 1865, 173–194.

54. Ibid., 192.

55. Ibid., 174–175.

56. Adams, *Great Britain,* 2:200–201; Bigelow, *Retrospections of an Active Life, 1817–1863,* 562–564.

CHAPTER 8: THE LATIN STRATEGY

1. Hotze to M, London, August 23, 1863, ORN, ser. 2, 3:868.

2. George C. Rable, *The Confederate Republic: A Revolution Against Politics* (Chapel Hill: University of North Carolina Press, 1994), 88–92; James D. Richardson, *A Compilation of the Messages and Papers of the Confederacy: Including the Diplomatic Correspondence, 1861–1865* (Nashville: United States Publishing, 1904), 1:183–188.

3. Richardson, *Compilation of the Messages and Papers of the Confederacy,* 1:183–188.

4. Eric H. Walther, *William Lowndes Yancey and the Coming of the Civil War* (Chapel Hill: University of North Carolina Press, 2006), 334–335; Edwin De Leon, *Secret History of Confederate Diplomacy Abroad,* edited by William C. Davis (Lawrence: University Press of Kansas, 2005), 99–101.

5. Rable, *Confederate Republic,* 2–5, 21–22, 30, 210–213, 214–254.

6. Eli N. Evans, *Judah P. Benjamin, the Jewish Confederate* (New York: Free Press, 1988), 3–48; Robert Douthat Meade, *Judah P. Benjamin: Confederate Statesman* (Baton Rouge: Louisiana State University Press, 2001), 3–138.

7. Evans, *Judah P. Benjamin;* Meade, *Judah P. Benjamin;* Robert N. Rosen, *The Jewish Confederates* (Columbia: University of South Carolina Press, 2000).

8. Benjamin to Mason, Richmond, September 20, 1864, ORN, ser. 2, 3:1256.

9. Stève Sainlaude, *Le gouvernement impérial et la guerre de sécession (1861–1865): L'action diplomatique* (Paris: Harmattan, 2011); Phillip E. Myers, *Caution and Cooperation: The American Civil War in British-American Relations* (Kent, OH: Kent State University Press, 2008), 24–27, 35–63; Ephraim Douglass Adams, *Great Britain and the American Civil War* (1924; reprint, New York: Russell and Russell, 1958), 1:76–78.

10. Stève Sainlaude, *La France et la Confédération sudiste, 1861–1865: La question de la reconnaissance diplomatique pendant la guerre de sécession* (Paris: Harmattan, 2011), 67–104.

11. Lonnie Alexander Burnett, ed., *Henry Hotze, Confederate Propagandist: Selected Writings on Revolution, Recognition, and Race* (Tuscaloosa: University of Alabama Press, 2008); Robert E. Bonner, "Slavery, Confederate Diplomacy, and the Racialist Mission of Henry Hotze," *Civil War History* 51, no. 3 (2005): 288–316; Joseph V. Trahan, "Henry Hotze: Propaganda Voice of the Confederacy," in *Knights of the Quill: Confederate Correspondents and Their Civil War Reporting* (West Lafayette, IN: Purdue University Press, 2010).

12. Hunter to Hotze, November 14, 1861, ORN, ser. 2, 3:293–294.

13. Charles L. Dufour, *Nine Men in Gray* (Garden City, NY: Doubleday, 1963), 267–298; Burnett, *Henry Hotze.*

14. Arthur Gobineau, *The Moral and Intellectual Diversity of Races: With Particular Reference to Their Respective Influence in the Civil and Political History of Mankind*, edited by Josiah Clark Nott and Henry Hotze (Philadelphia: J. B. Lippincott, 1856); Bonner, "Slavery, Confederate Diplomacy"; Burnett, *Henry Hotze*, 5; Michael D. Biddiss, *Father of Racist Ideology: The Social and Political Thought of Count Gobineau* (New York: Weybright and Talley, 1970).

15. Frank Lawrence Owsley, *King Cotton Diplomacy: Foreign Relations of the Confederate States of America*, 2nd ed. (1931; reprint, Chicago: University of Chicago Press, 1959), 157.

16. Hotze to Benjamin, London, April 25, 1862, ORN, ser. 2, 3:400–401.

17. Charles P. Cullop, *Confederate Propaganda in Europe, 1861–1865* (Coral Gables, FL: University of Miami Press, 1969), 54.

18. Hotze to unnamed correspondent in Manchester, London, August 21, 1863; Hotze to Benjamin, London, January 17, 1863, ORN, ser. 2, 3:865–866, 661–663. See also Paul Pecquet du Bellet, *The Diplomacy of the Confederate Cabinet of Richmond and Its Agents Abroad*, edited by William Stanley Hoole (Tuscaloosa, AL: Confederate Publishing, 1963), 43.

19. De Leon, *Secret History*, xi–xxxi; Charles P. Cullop, "Edwin De Leon, Jefferson Davis' Propagandist," *Civil War History* 8, no. 4 (1962): 386–400; Cullop, *Confederate Propaganda*, 67–84; Edwin De Leon Papers, South Caroliniana Library, University of South Carolina, Columbia; Helen Kohn Hennig, "Edwin DeLeon" (master's thesis, University of South Carolina, 1928).

20. Davis to De Leon, Washington, January 8, 1861; De Leon to Davis, London, October 24, 1861, in *The Papers of Jefferson Davis*, edited by Mary Seaton Dix and Lynda Lasswell Crist (Baton Rouge: Louisiana State University Press, 1992), 7:6–7, 374–378.

21. Pecquet du Bellet, *Diplomacy of the Confederate Cabinet*, 65.

22. De Leon, *Secret History*, 90, 94–95.

23. Ibid., 102–104.

24. Edwin De Leon and Ellie De Leon, *Thirty Years of My Life on Three Continents* (London: Ward and Downey, 1890), 68–69; De Leon, *Secret History*, 102–104.

25. De Leon, *Secret History*, 104.

26. Ibid., xvi–xvii.

27. Benjamin to Mason, Richmond, April 12, 1862, ORN, ser. 2, 3:384–385.

28. Ibid.

29. Hotze to Hunter, London, February 1, 1862, ORN, ser. 2, 3:325.

30. Benjamin Moran, *The Journal of Benjamin Moran, 1857–1865*, edited by Sarah Agnes Wallace and Frances Elma Gillespie (Chicago: University of Chicago Press, 1948), 2:1040, 1212.

31. Mason to Hunter, London, February 22, 1862; Benjamin to Mason, Richmond, April 14, July 18, 1862, ORN, ser. 2, 3:343–344, 740.

32. Beckles Willson, *John Slidell and the Confederates in Paris (1862–65)* (New York: Minton, Balch, 1932), 43.

33. Thomas Wiltberger Evans, *Memoirs of Dr. Thomas W. Evans: The Second French Empire,* edited by Edward A. Crane (New York: D. Appleton, 1905), 118, 119.

34. Ibid., 72–74.

35. Ibid., 74–75; Charles Priestly, "Death in Paris: The Mysterious Case of William L. Dayton" (Confederate Historical Association of Belgium, 2014). Priestly questions but does not dismiss Willson's account. I am grateful to Gerald Hawkins for sending me this excellent article.

36. Louis Martin Sears, *John Slidell* (Durham, NC: Duke University Press, 1925).

37. Owsley, *King Cotton Diplomacy,* 214, 273, 277, 325, 326–329, 422.

38. Ibid., 326, 442, 447–449; Sainlaude, *Le gouvernement impérial,* 98n30. See also Slidell to Benjamin, Paris, April 29, 1863, ORN, ser. 2, 3:756, for an enclosed translated letter from his "friend" and informant that is signed "Cintrat." My thanks to Stève Sainlaude for bringing this to my attention.

39. Slidell to [Hunter], Paris, February 11, 1862, ORN, ser. 2, 3:336.

40. Mason to Hunter, London, February 7, 1862, ORN, ser. 2, 3:330–331; Slidell to Mason, Paris, February 12, 1862, J. M. Mason Papers, LoC; Louis Martin Sears, "A Confederate Diplomat at the Court of Napoleon III," *American Historical Review* 26, no. 2 (1921): 257.

41. Michel Chevalier and Ernest Rasetti, *La France, le Mexique et les États Confédérés* (Paris: E. Dentu, 1863); Michel Chevalier, *France, Mexico, and the Confederate States,* translated by William Henry Hurlbert (New York: C. B. Richardson, 1863).

42. Benjamin to Slidell, Richmond, April 12, 1862, ORN, ser. 2, 3:386–390.

43. Slidell to Benjamin, Paris, July 25, 1862, ORN, ser. 2, 3:481–487.

44. As explained in his earlier memorandum to Thouvenel, Slidell to Thouvenel, Paris, July 21, 1862, ORN, ser. 2, 3:475.

45. Slidell to Benjamin, Paris, July 25, 1862, ORN, ser. 2, 3:481–487; Sears, "Confederate Diplomat."

46. Slidell to Benjamin, Paris, July 25, 1862, ORN, ser. 2, 3:479.

47. De Leon to Benjamin, Vichy, July 30, 1862, OR, ser. 4, 2:23–26; Cullop, "Edwin De Leon," 391.

48. De Leon, *Secret History,* xxi, 28–30, 40–46, 135–138, 151–152; Owsley, *King Cotton Diplomacy,* 164; George McCoy Blackburn, *French Newspaper Opinion on the American Civil War* (Westport, CT: Greenwood, 1997), 11–12; Cullop, *Confederate Propaganda,* 67–84, esp. 74.

49. Edwin De Leon, *La vérité sur les États Confédérés d'Amérique* (Paris: E. Dentu, 1862); De Leon, *Secret History,* app. 3, includes the first English translation of De Leon's pamphlet *The Truth About the Confederate States of America,* 209–219.

50. De Leon, *La vérité,* 14; De Leon, *Secret History,* 211, 212.

51. De Leon, *La vérité,* 24–25; De Leon, *Secret History,* 216–217.

52. De Leon, *La vérité,* frontispiece; Pecquet du Bellet, *Diplomacy of the Confederate Cabinet,* 68.

53. De Leon, *La vérité,* 29–30; De Leon, *Secret History,* 218–219; Robert E. Bonner, "Roundheaded Cavaliers? The Context and Limits of a Confederate Racial Project," *Civil War History* 48, no. 1 (2002): 34–59.

54. De Leon, *La vérité*, 29–31; De Leon, *Secret History*, 218–219.

55. David G. McCullough, *The Greater Journey: Americans in Paris* (New York: Simon and Schuster, 2011), 131; John Bigelow, "A Breakfast with Alexandre Dumas," *Scribner's Monthly* 1, no. 6 (1871): 597–600.

56. De Leon, *Secret History*, 141–143. For the full dispatch, see De Leon to Judah P. Benjamin, Paris, September 30, 1862, OR, ser. 4, 2:99–105.

57. Pecquet du Bellet, *Diplomacy of the Confederate Cabinet*, 65–74; Malakoff, "Affairs in Europe," *NYT*, September 12, 1862; Paul Pecquet du Bellet, *La Révolution Américaine dévoilée* (Paris: E. Dentu, 1861); Paul Pecquet du Bellet, *Lettre sur la guerre Américaine* (Paris: Imprimerie de Schiller Aîné, 1862); Paul Pecquet du Bellet, *Lettre a l'empereur: De la reconnaissance des États Confédérés d'Amérique* (Paris: Schiller Aîné, 1862); Salwa Nacouzi, "Les créoles louisianais défendent la cause du Sud à Paris (1861–1865)," *Transatlantica: Revue d'études américaines*, no. 1 (October 1, 2002), http://transatlantica.revues.org/.

58. Pecquet du Bellet, *Diplomacy of the Confederate Cabinet*, 67, 72–73.

59. Ibid., 65–66, 72, 28–29; Nacouzi, "Les créoles louisianais."

60. Hotze to Benjamin, London, April 25, 1862, September 26, 1863, ORN, ser. 2, 3:399, 914–917.

CHAPTER 9: GARIBALDI'S ANSWER

1. Howard Jones, *Abraham Lincoln and a New Birth of Freedom: The Union and Slavery in the Diplomacy of the Civil War* (Lincoln: University of Nebraska Press, 1999); Howard Jones, *Union in Peril: The Crisis over British Intervention in the Civil War* (Chapel Hill: University of North Carolina Press, 1992).

2. Walter Stahr, *Seward: Lincoln's Indispensable Man* (New York: Simon and Schuster, 2012), 338–339.

3. Carl Schurz, Frederic Bancroft, and William Archibald Dunning, *The Reminiscences of Carl Schurz* (New York: McClure, 1907), 2:281–282.

4. Hans Louis Trefousse, *Carl Schurz: A Biography* (New York: Fordham University Press, 1998), 3–79.

5. Schurz to Seward, Madrid, November 14, 1861, Spain, RG 59; Schurz to Lincoln, Madrid, November 11, 1861, in *Speeches, Correspondence and Political Papers of Carl Schurz*, edited by Frederic Bancroft (New York: G. P. Putnam's Sons, 1913), 2:193.

6. Schurz, Bancroft, and Dunning, *Reminiscences of Carl Schurz*, 2:309.

7. Ibid.

8. Ibid., 310.

9. Ibid.

10. Ibid., 306–317.

11. George McCoy Blackburn, *French Newspaper Opinion on the American Civil War* (Westport, CT: Greenwood, 1997), 6.

12. Gary W. Gallagher, *The Union War* (Cambridge, MA: Harvard University Press, 2011).

13. Abraham Lincoln, Message to Congress in Special Session, July 4, 1861, CWAL, 4:438.

14. H. Nelson Gay, "Lincoln's Offer of a Command to Garibaldi: Light on a Disputed Point of History," *Century*, November 1907, 67.

15. Lincoln, "Speech at Peoria, Illinois, October 16, 1854," CWAL, 2:255.

16. Michael Vorenberg, *Final Freedom: The Civil War, the Abolition of Slavery, and the Thirteenth Amendment* (New York: Cambridge University Press, 2001); Allen C. Guelzo, *Lincoln's Emancipation Proclamation: The End of Slavery in America* (New York: Simon and Schuster, 2006); James Oakes, *Freedom National: The Destruction of Slavery in the United States, 1861–1865* (New York: W. W. Norton, 2013).

17. Michael Burlingame, *Abraham Lincoln: A Life* (Baltimore: Johns Hopkins University Press, 2008), 2:333.

18. Kate Masur, *An Example for All the Land: Emancipation and the Struggle over Equality in Washington, D.C.* (Chapel Hill: University of North Carolina Press, 2010); Oakes, *Freedom National*; Chandra Manning, *What This Cruel War Was Over: Soldiers, Slavery, and the Civil War* (New York: Alfred A. Knopf, 2007), 81–111.

19. Gideon Welles, *Diary of Gideon Welles* (Boston: Houghton Mifflin, 1911), 1:70–71; Burlingame, *Abraham Lincoln: A Life*, 2:360–361. For examples of Seward's emphasis on the specter of servile war, see Seward to Adams, Washington, February 17, May 28, July 5, 1862, FRUS, 1862, 37–38, 101–105, 124.

20. Stahr, *Seward: Lincoln's Indispensable Man*, 341–345.

21. Ibid.; Burlingame, *Abraham Lincoln: A Life*, 2:363.

22. Doris Kearns Goodwin, *Team of Rivals: The Political Genius of Abraham Lincoln* (New York: Simon and Schuster, 2005), 468; Stahr, *Seward: Lincoln's Indispensable Man*, 342–345.

23. Salmon P. Chase, *Inside Lincoln's Cabinet: The Civil War Diaries of Salmon P. Chase*, edited by David Herbert Donald (New York: Longmans, Green, 1954), 99–100; Guelzo, *Lincoln's Emancipation Proclamation*, 112–113, 122–124, 156; Burlingame, *Abraham Lincoln: A Life*, 2:363–364; Goodwin, *Team of Rivals*, 467–468.

24. James M. McPherson, *Crossroads of Freedom: Antietam* (New York: Oxford University Press, 2002).

25. Stahr, *Seward: Lincoln's Indispensable Man*, 346–347; Seward to Adams, Washington, September 22, 1862, FRUS, 1862, 195.

26. Seward to Adams, Washington, July 28, 1862, FRUS, 1862, 154–158.

27. Emer de Vattel, *The Law of Nations; or, Principles of the Law of Nature, Applied to the Conduct and Affairs of Nations and Sovereigns*, edited by Bela Kapossy and Richard Whatmore (1797; reprint, Indianapolis: Liberty Fund, 2008), 648; *Encyclopedia of American Foreign Policy: Studies of the Principal Movements and Ideas*, edited by Alexander DeConde (New York: Scribner, 1978), s.v. "Recognition Policy"; Henry Wheaton, *Elements of International Law*, edited by William Beach Lawrence, 6th ed. (1836; reprint, Boston: Little, Brown, 1855), 106.

28. Ephraim Douglass Adams, *Great Britain and the American Civil War* (1924; reprint, New York: Russell and Russell, 1958), 1:302–305; Henry Adams, *The Education of Henry Adams: An Autobiography* (Boston: Houghton Mifflin, 1918), 136;

D. P. Crook, *The North, the South, and the Powers, 1861–1865* (New York: Wiley, 1974), 218–219.

29. Slidell to Mason, October 2, 1862, J. M. Mason Papers, LoC.

30. E. Adams, *Great Britain,* 2:118–135.

31. Benjamin Moran, *The Journal of Benjamin Moran, 1857–1865,* edited by Sarah Agnes Wallace and Frances Elma Gillespie (Chicago: University of Chicago Press, 1948), 2:1040, 1212; Amanda Foreman, *A World on Fire: Britain's Crucial Role in the American Civil War* (New York: Random House, 2011), 278–280.

32. Martin B. Duberman, *Charles Francis Adams, 1807–1886* (Boston: Houghton Mifflin, 1961), 292–298; Crook, *North, South, and Powers,* 215–225; Charles Francis Adams, "Charles Francis Adams Diaries, 1823–1880" (Massachusetts Historical Society, Boston, 1954), July 17, September 21, 24, 1862; Worthington Chauncey Ford, ed., *A Cycle of Adams Letters, 1861–1865* (Boston: Houghton Mifflin, 1920), 1:161–162.

33. Spencer Walpole, *The Life of Lord John Russell* (London: Longmans, Green, 1889), 2:349–350; E. Adams, *Great Britain,* 2:39.

34. E. Adams, *Great Britain,* 2:38.

35. Charles Francis Adams, *Trans-Atlantic Historical Solidarity* (Oxford: Clarendon Press, 1913), 99; Walpole, *Lord John Russell,* 2:350–352; E. Adams, *Great Britain,* 2:40–41.

36. C. Adams, *Trans-Atlantic Historical Solidarity,* 99; Walpole, *Lord John Russell,* 2:350–352; E. Adams, *Great Britain,* 2:40–41; Lynn Marshall Case and Warren F. Spencer, *The United States and France: Civil War Diplomacy* (Philadelphia: University of Pennsylvania Press, 1970), 339.

37. Guelzo, *Lincoln's Emancipation Proclamation,* 153–156; *Belfast Morning News,* October 6, 1862; *London Standard,* October 6, 1862; *Times* (London), October 6, 1862.

38. Walpole, *Lord John Russell,* 2:351.

39. Ibid.; E. Adams, *Great Britain,* 2:40.

40. Case and Spencer, *United States and France,* 307.

41. Ibid., 333, quoting Bigelow to Seward, Paris, August 22, 1862, Paris, RG 59.

42. Ibid., 313–314, 336, 340; Stève Sainlaude, *La France et la Confédération sudiste, 1861–1865: La question de la reconnaissance diplomatique pendant la guerre de sécession* (Paris: Harmattan, 2011), 64–65.

43. Case and Spencer, *United States and France,* 336, 340.

44. Ibid., 336–341.

45. Ibid., 341–342.

46. Ibid., 342–343.

47. David Urquhart, *Public Opinion and Its Organs* (London: Trübner, 1855), 24–25.

48. Jasper Ridley, *Garibaldi* (London: Phoenix Press, 2001), 534–536. Ridley finds no evidence of collusion.

49. Ibid., 525–535.

50. Ibid., 535; Nancy Nichols Barker, *Distaff Diplomacy: The Empress Eugénie and the Foreign Policy of the Second Empire* (Austin: University of Texas Press, 2011), 94–106.

51. Ridley, *Garibaldi*, 536–543.

52. Lucy Riall, "Hero, Saint or Revolutionary? Nineteenth-Century Politics and the Cult of Garibaldi," *Modern Italy* 3, no. 2 (1998): 200; Lucy Riall, *Garibaldi: Invention of a Hero* (New Haven, CT: Yale University Press, 2007), 324–328; Ridley, *Garibaldi*, 542–543; Malakoff, "Affairs in France," *NYT*, December 20, 1862.

53. Marsh to Seward, Turin, September 2, 1862, enclosure Marsh to Baron, August 31, 1862, Italy, RG 59.

54. Garibaldi to Marsh, Varignano, October 7, 1862, enclosed with Marsh to Seward, Turin, October 8, 1862, Italy, RG 59; Gay, "Lincoln's Offer," 72n3, quoting an earlier draft of the same letter. Garibaldi was apparently referring to his public letter "To the English Nation," dated September 28.

55. Lincoln to Seward, Washington, June 29, 1861, CWAL, 4:418; Burlingame, *Abraham Lincoln: A Life*, 1: 563–564, 2:83; Herbert Mitgang, "Garibaldi and Lincoln," *American Heritage* 26, no. 6 (1975): 34; Gay, "Lincoln's Offer"; "Allendorf to America: Canisius Family," http://www.kinfolks.info/allendorf/other/canisius.htm#Theodor.

56. Canisius to Garibaldi, Vienna, September 1, 1862, Vienna, RG 59 (spelling as in the original).

57. Garibaldi to Canisius, Varignano, September 14, 1862, Vienna, RG 59; Giuseppe Garibaldi and Domenico Ciampoli, *Scritti politici e militari: Ricordi e pensieri inediti* (Rome: E. Voghera, 1907), 91 (original Italian version).

58. "Foreign Intelligence, Austria," *Times* (London), September 24, 1862, 8; Canisius to Seward, Vienna, September 14, 1862, Vienna, RG 59; "Garibaldi Desires to Fight for the North," *NYT*, October 4, 1862.

59. Seward to Canisius, Washington, October 10, 1862, Vienna, RG 59; "Garibaldi and the American War," *NYT*, October 9, 1862; Gay, "Lincoln's Offer"; Mary Philip Trauth, *Italo-American Diplomatic Relations, 1861–1882: The Mission of George Perkins Marsh, First American Minister to the Kingdom of Italy* (Westport, CT: Greenwood Press, 1980), 22–28.

60. Caroline Marsh, Diary, September 1, 1862, George Perkins Marsh Collection, Special Collections, Bailey Library, University of Vermont, Burlington, notes from David and Mary Alice Lowenthal.

61. Sheridan Gilley, "The Garibaldi Riots of 1862," *Historical Journal* 16, no. 4 (1973): 697–732.

62. Garibaldi, "Alla Nazione Inglese," in *Scritti politici e militari*, by Garibaldi, 292–293; "Garibaldi to the English People," *Times* (London), October 3, 1862; "Garibaldi on America," *NYT*, October 18, 1862.

63. "The Public Opinion of Great Britain," *Dundee Advertiser*, September 29, 1861; "Riotous Proceedings in Hyde Park," *Morning Post*, October 6, 1862; "Another Great Riot in Hyde Park," *London Standard*, October 6, 1862; "Garibaldian

Riots in Hyde Park," *NYT,* October 22, 1862; "A London Sunday Shindy," *NYT,* October 23, 1862; Gilley, "Garibaldi Riots."

64. Adams to Seward, London, October 3, 1862, FRUS, 1862, 205.

65. Malakoff, "From Paris," *NYT,* November 14, 1862; Malakoff, "Affairs in France," *NYT,* December 20, 1862.

66. Case and Spencer, *United States and France,* 330, 347–351; Malakoff, "Affairs in Europe," *NYT,* September 12, 1862; "Louis Napoleon's Designs and Dangers," *NYT,* December 7, 1862; Malakoff, "From Paris"; Barker, *Distaff Diplomacy,* 103–105.

67. De Leon to Benjamin, Paris, September 30, 1862, OR, ser. 4, 2:99–105; Edwin De Leon, *Secret History of Confederate Diplomacy Abroad,* edited by William C. Davis (Lawrence: University Press of Kansas, 2005), 105; Louis Martin Sears, "A Confederate Diplomat at the Court of Napoleon III," *American Historical Review* 26, no. 2 (1921): 265–266; Case and Spencer, *United States and France,* 350–351.

68. Benjamin to Slidell, Richmond, October 17, 1862, ORN, ser. 2, 3:556–558; Alfred J. Hanna and Kathryn A. Hanna, *Napoleon III and Mexico: American Triumph over Monarchy* (Chapel Hill: University of North Carolina Press, 1971), 118–119.

69. Adams to Seward, London, September 4, 1862, FRUS, 1862, 184.

70. Albert A. Woldman, *Lincoln and the Russians* (Cleveland: World, 1952).

71. Jones, *Union in Peril,* 177, 190–191; Adams to Seward, London, September 25, 1862, FRUS, 1862, 199.

72. "Mr. Gladstone in the North," *Times* (London), October 9, 1862, 7–8; Walter R. Fisher, "Gladstone's Speech at Newcastle-on-Tyne," *Speech Monographs* 26, no. 4 (1959): 255–262.

73. Ibid.; Monadnock, "From Great Britain," *NYT,* October 26, 1862; C. Adams, "Diaries," October 9, 1862.

74. C. Adams, *Trans-Atlantic Historical Solidarity,* 105–107; Duncan Andrew Campbell, *English Public Opinion and the American Civil War* (Woodbridge, Suffolk: Royal Historical Society, Boydell Press, 2003), 177–179.

75. After the war there would be accusations that Gladstone was invested in Confederate bonds and betting on Southern victory. See John Morley, *The Life of William Ewart Gladstone* (London: Macmillan, 1911), 753; John Bigelow, *Lest We Forget: Gladstone, Morley and the Confederate Loan of 1863, a Rectification* (New York: DeVinne, 1905); "American Topics: The Confederate Loan, Mr. Gladstone's Alleged Connection with the Matter," *NYT,* October 19, 1865; "Mr. Gladstone Bought No Confederate Bonds," *NYT,* July 4, 1915.

76. Jones, *Lincoln and a New Birth of Freedom,* 119–120, 126–127, 128–129; Sir George Cornewall Lewis, "Recognition of the Independence of the Southern States of the North American Union," November 7, 1862. I am grateful to Howard Jones for sending me a copy of Lewis's paper.

77. Jones, *Union in Peril,* 186–197; Ridley, *Garibaldi,* 542–545; Hugh Dubrulle, "'We Are Threatened with . . . Anarchy and Ruin': Fear of Americanization and the

Emergence of an Anglo-Saxon Confederacy in England During the American Civil War," *Albion* 33, no. 4 (2001): 586, quoting Palmerston to Russell, October 28, 1862; Jasper Godwin Ridley, *Lord Palmerston* (New York: Dutton, 1971), 559.

78. Stève Sainlaude, *Le gouvernement impérial et la guerre de sécession (1861–1865): L'action diplomatique* (Paris: Harmattan, 2011), 77–84, 347–397; Case and Spencer, *United States and France*, 347–400; Howard Jones, *Blue and Gray Diplomacy: A History of Union and Confederate Foreign Relations* (Chapel Hill: University of North Carolina Press, 2010), 293–294; "The Uprising in Poland," *NYT*, February 17, 1863; "France and the Polish Rebellion," *NYT*, March 13, 1863.

79. Trauth, *Italo-American Diplomatic Relations*, 27–28; "Allendorf to America: Canisius Family." Canisius went on to a career with the State Department that took him to several posts around the world.

80. "Garibaldi and His Braves," *NYT*, October 5, 1862.

81. Gay, "Lincoln's Offer," 73, quoting Marsh to Garibaldi, October 22, 1862.

82. Giuseppe Garibaldi, Menotti Garibaldi, and Ricciotti Garibaldi to Lincoln, Thursday, August 6, 1863, ALPLC.

CHAPTER 10: UNION AND LIBERTY

1. M. E. Grant Duff, *Notes from a Diary, 1851–1872* (London: J. Murray, 1897), 203–204, Carlyle comment recorded July 30, 1862.

2. Monadnock, "From Great Britain," *NYT*, October 26, 1862.

3. *Times* (London), October 7, 1862.

4. Hotze to Benjamin, London, October 24, 1862; Mason to Benjamin, London, November 7, 1862, ORN, ser. 2, 3:565–567, 3:600.

5. Howard Jones, *Union in Peril: The Crisis over British Intervention in the Civil War* (Chapel Hill: University of North Carolina Press, 1992), 176; Duncan Andrew Campbell, *English Public Opinion and the American Civil War* (Woodbridge, Suffolk: Royal Historical Society, Boydell Press, 2003), 130–133. Campbell points out the press response was mixed in Britain.

6. "Comments on the North American Events," October 7, 1862, published in *Die Presse* (Vienna), October 12, 1862, in *Karl Marx, Frederick Engels: Collected Works*, by Karl Marx (New York: International, 1975), 19:248–251.

7. Malakoff, "American Affairs in France: Reception of the President's Emancipation Proclamation," *NYT*, October 25, 1862; Malakoff, "American Affairs in France: The Parisian Press on the President's Emancipation Proclamation," *NYT*, November 10, 1862.

8. Malakoff, "Reception of the President's Emancipation Proclamation"; Lynn Marshall Case and Warren F. Spencer, *The United States and France: Civil War Diplomacy* (Philadelphia: University of Pennsylvania Press, 1970), 330, quoting Sanford to Seward, October 10, 1862.

9. Seward to Sanford, Washington, May 23, 1862; Seward to Adams, Washington, July 28, 1862, FRUS, 1862, 556–558.

10. Seward to Adams, Washington, September 26, 1862; Seward to Dayton, Washington, October 20, 1862, FRUS, 1862, 202, 398; Case and Spencer, *United States and France,* 368.

11. Ephraim Douglass Adams, *Great Britain and the American Civil War* (1924; reprint, New York: Russell and Russell, 1958), 2:106; Jefferson Davis, General Orders no. 111, December 24, 1862, ORN, ser. 2, 3:140–142.

12. Malakoff, "American Topics at Paris," *NYT,* January 13, 1863; *Address of the French Protestant Pastors to Ministers and Pastors of All Denominations in Great Britain, on American Slavery . . .* (Manchester: J. F. Wilkinson, 1863), reprinted in FRUS, 1863, 720–721.

13. George Macaulay Trevelyan, *The Life of John Bright* (Boston: Houghton Mifflin, 1913), 321.

14. Lincoln to the Workingmen of Manchester, Washington, January 19, 1863, CWAL, 6:63–65; Adams to Seward, London, February 12, 1863, FRUS, 1863, 128.

15. Trevelyan, *Life of John Bright,* 113.

16. Charles Francis Adams, "Charles Francis Adams Diaries, 1823–1880" (Massachusetts Historical Society, Boston, 1954), January 16, 1863.

17. Adams to Seward, January 16, 1863, FRUS, 1863, 59–60; E. Adams, *Great Britain,* 110, 224n3; Goldwin Smith, *The Civil War in America* (London: Simpkin, Marshall, 1866); Francis William Newman, *Character of the Southern States of America: Letter to a Friend Who Had Joined the Southern Independence Association* (Manchester: Union and Emancipation Society, 1863); Union and Emancipation Society and Manchester, *Earl Russell and the Slave Power* (Manchester: Union and Emancipation Society, 1863); Union and Emancipation Society and Manchester, *War Ships for the Southern Confederacy: Report of Public Meeting in the Free-Trade Hall, Manchester; with Letter from Professor Goldwin Smith to the "Daily News"* (Manchester: Union and Emancipation Society, 1863); Thomas Bayley Potter, *Building of Vessels of War for the "So-Styled" Confederate States: To the Chambers of Commerce of Great Britain and Ireland* (Manchester: Union and Emancipation Society, 1863); "Important Documents," *NYT,* January 18, 1863; "The Protest from the Manchester Emancipation Society," *NYT,* April 12, 1863.

18. C. Adams, "Diaries," January 16, 17, 1863; Adams to Seward, London, January 16, February 19, 1863, FRUS 1863, 62–66, 136. The Adams Collection, Boston Athenaeum Library, includes a vast number of publications the US minister received during the war.

19. Adams to Seward, London, January 22, 1863, FRUS, 1863, 93.

20. Seward to Adams, Washington, March 2, 1863, FRUS, 1863, 151.

21. John Bright, *Speeches of John Bright, M.P., on the American Question* (Boston: Little, Brown, 1865), 150–151, 159.

22. Trevelyan, *Life of John Bright,* 307–308.

23. Hotze to Benjamin, London, February 14, 1863, ORN, ser. 2, 3:693; E. Adams, *Great Britain,* 108, quoting Adams to Seward, January 22, 1863.

24. The Civil War, Charles Francis Adams Jr. later remarked in a historical address in England, was decided not "at Washington, or at Gettysburg, nor indeed in America at all; it was here in England—here in your Lancashire cotton spinning district and in Downing Street." Charles Francis Adams, *Trans-Atlantic Historical Solidarity* (Oxford: Clarendon Press, 1913), 52.

25. Hotze to Benjamin, London, January 17, 1863, ORN, ser. 2, 3:663.

26. James Spence, *The American Union: Its Effect on National Character and Policy, with an Inquiry into Secession as a Constitutional Right, and the Causes of the Disruption* (London: R. Bentley, 1861), 131–132.

27. Hotze to Benjamin, London, October 24, 1862, ORN, ser. 2, 3:566–567.

28. Frank Lawrence Owsley, *King Cotton Diplomacy: Foreign Relations of the Confederate States of America*, 2nd ed. (1931; reprint, Chicago: University of Chicago Press, 1959), 362–382; Judith Fenner Gentry, "A Confederate Success in Europe: The Erlanger Loan," *Journal of Southern History* 36, no. 2 (1970): 157–188; Marc D. Weidenmier, "The Market for Confederate Cotton Bonds," *Explorations in Economic History* 37, no. 1 (2000): 76–97.

29. Spence's expectations are revealed in Spence to Benjamin, Liverpool, April 28, 1862, ORN, ser. 2, 3:402–405. On Erlanger, Slidell, and CSA finance, see Gentry, "Confederate Success in Europe"; Owsley, *King Cotton Diplomacy*, 369–376, 165; Malakoff, "Our Paris Correspondent," *NYT*, January 13, 1863; "Our Paris Correspondence," *NYT*, August 12, 1863; "General News," *NYT*, September 19, 1864; and "The Marriage of Miss Slidell," *NYT*, October 19, 1864.

30. "Important Documents"; Benjamin Moran, *The Journal of Benjamin Moran, 1857–1865*, edited by Sarah Agnes Wallace and Frances Elma Gillespie (Chicago: University of Chicago Press, 1948), 2:1117; Owsley, *King Cotton Diplomacy*, 173–176.

31. Review of *The American Union*, *Richmond Enquirer*, March 4, May 7, 1863; Hotze to Benjamin, London, November 21, 1863; James Spence, *Southern Independence: An Address Delivered at a Public Meeting, in the City Hall, Glasgow, 16th November, 1863* (London: R. Bently, 1863); Benjamin to Hotze, Richmond, January 9, 1864, and Hotze to Benjamin, London, March 12, 1864, ORN, ser. 2, 3:759–762, 993–994, 1060; Benjamin to Spence, Richmond, January 11, 1864, quoted in Owsley, *King Cotton Diplomacy*, 383–384.

32. Hotze to Benjamin, London, June 6, 1863, ORN, ser. 2, 3:783–785; Mason to Benjamin, London, July 2, 1862, 3:824.

33. Slidell to Benjamin, Paris, June 19, 1863, ORN, ser. 2, 3:810–814.

34. Case and Spencer, *United States and France*, 398–426; Hansard Parliamentary Debates, 3rd ser., House of Commons, June 30, 1863, 171:1771–1780, http://hansard.millbanksystems.com; Hotze to Benjamin, London, July 11, 1863, ORN, ser. 2, 3:839–841.

35. Benjamin to Mason, Richmond, August 4, October 8, 1863, ORN, ser. 2, 3:852, 3:922–928; Owsley, *King Cotton Diplomacy*, 492–494.

36. William Graham Swan, *Foreign Relations: Speech of Hon. W. G. Swan, of Tennessee, Delivered in the House of Representatives of the Confederate States, February 5,*

1863 (Richmond: Smith, Bailey, 1863); James Morton Callahan, *The Diplomatic History of the Southern Confederacy* (Baltimore: Johns Hopkins University Press, 1901), 94–97; Edwin De Leon, *Secret History of Confederate Diplomacy Abroad,* edited by William C. Davis (Lawrence: University Press of Kansas, 2005), xx; Benjamin to De Leon, Richmond, August 17, 1863, De Leon Papers, SCL; Benjamin to Lamar, Richmond, June 11, 1863; Benjamin to Slidell, Richmond, October 8, 1863, ORN, ser. 2, 3:796, 922-927.

37. Slidell to Mason, Paris, July 17, 1863, Mason Papers, LoC.

38. Louis Martin Sears, "A Confederate Diplomat at the Court of Napoleon III," *American Historical Review* 26, no. 2 (1921): 273.

39. Owsley, *King Cotton Diplomacy,* 164–165; De Leon, *Secret History,* xxii–xxiv; "Intercepted Rebel Correspondence," *NYT,* November 16, 1863.

40. "Intercepted Rebel Correspondence."

41. S. P. Lee to Gideon Welles, *Newport News,* November 11, 1863, ORN, ser. 1, 9:276; "Rebel Operations in Europe, the Intercepted Correspondence," *NYT,* November 16, 1863; "Intercepted Rebel Correspondence"; "Rebel Diplomatists," *NYT,* April 7, 1864; Charles P. Cullop, "Edwin De Leon, Jefferson Davis' Propagandist," *Civil War History* 8, no. 4 (1962): 398–399; Benjamin to Slidell, Richmond, December 9, 1863, ORN, ser. 2, 3:973.

42. De Leon to Benjamin, Paris, February 13, 1864, folder 18, De Leon Papers, South Caroliniana Library, University of South Carolina, Columbia.

43. Cullop, "Edwin De Leon," 399; De Leon, *Secret History,* xxii–xxiii.

CHAPTER 11: THE UNSPEAKABLE DILEMMA

1. Hotze to Benjamin, London, July 23, 1863, ORN, ser. 2, 3:849–851; Frank Lawrence Owsley, *King Cotton Diplomacy: Foreign Relations of the Confederate States of America,* 2nd ed. (1931; reprint, Chicago: University of Chicago Press, 1959), 376; Judith Fenner Gentry, "A Confederate Success in Europe: The Erlanger Loan," *Journal of Southern History* 36, no. 2 (1970): 157–188; Marc D. Weidenmier, "The Market for Confederate Cotton Bonds," *Explorations in Economic History* 37, no. 1 (2000): 76–97.

2. Mason to Russell, London, September 21; Hotze to Benjamin, London, December 26, 1863, ORN, ser. 2, 3:904, 984.

3. Owsley, *King Cotton Diplomacy,* 376; Gentry, "Confederate Success in Europe"; Weidenmier, "Market for Confederate Cotton Bonds."

4. Slidell to Benjamin, Paris, March 24, 1864, ORN, ser. 2, 3:1077–1079; Malakoff, "Affairs in France: The Results of the Elections," *NYT,* June 20, 1863; Malakoff, "Affairs in France," *NYT,* July 3, 1863; Malakoff, "Affairs in France," *NYT,* July 10, 1863.

5. John Bigelow, *Retrospections of an Active Life, 1863–1865* (New York: Baker and Taylor, 1909), 120–121; Beckles Willson, *John Slidell and the Confederates in Paris (1862–65)* (New York: Minton, Balch, 1932), 150–153. Bigelow took un-

usual delight in telling this story to Sanford and others, but there is no evidence that he or other Union agents played any role in planning this affray. Willson questions Bigelow's story based on Slidell's own account, but it was a humiliating episode in either telling.

6. George Bancroft, *Memorial Address on the Life and Character of Abraham Lincoln* (Washington, DC: GPO, 1866), 34; David J. Alvarez, "The Papacy in the Diplomacy of the American Civil War," *Catholic Historical Review* 69, no. 2 (1983): 237n30.

7. Bancroft, *Memorial Address,* 34; Alvarez, "Papacy in the Civil War," 237n30.

8. Pope Pius IX to Venerable Brother John [Hughes], October 18, 1862, ORN, ser. 2, 3:559–560; "A Letter from Pope Pius IX, to the Catholics of Chicago," *NYT,* November 28, 1862; Leo Francis Stock, "Catholic Participation in the Diplomacy of the Southern Confederacy," *Catholic Historical Review* 16 (April 1930): 16; Alvarez, "Papacy in the Civil War," 237–238.

9. Morehead to Slidell, Rome, March 17, 1863, enclosed with Slidell to Benjamin, Paris, April 11, 1863, ORN, ser. 2, 3:738–740.

10. Benjamin to Slidell, Richmond, June 22, 1863, ORN, ser. 2, 3:816–817.

11. "A Catholic View of Our Troubles," *NYT,* August 3, 1863.

12. Benjamin to Mann, Richmond, September 23, 1863; Mann to Benjamin, Brussels, June 30, 1862, ORN, ser. 2, 3:910; 3:449–451.

13. David I. Kertzer, *Prisoner of the Vatican: The Pope's Secret Plot to Capture Rome from the New Italian State* (Boston: Houghton Mifflin, 2004), 9, 22–23, 107, 164; "The Pope's Encyclical," *NYT,* January 29, 1865.

14. John Bigelow, "The Southern Confederacy and the Pope," *North American Review* 157 (October 1893): 462–475; Owsley, *King Cotton Diplomacy,* 495–506.

15. Mann to Benjamin, Rome, November 14, 1863, ORN, ser. 2, 3:952–955.

16. Mann to Benjamin, Rome, December 9, 1863; Pope Pius IX to Davis, Vatican, December 3, 1863, ORN, ser. 2, 3:973–975. The original letter in Latin is found in the Department of State, Diplomatic Missions, Belgium, reel 4, CSAA. I am grateful to the anonymous Latin experts on the Lingua Latina forum of Word reference.com who helped me translate key elements of the pope's letter.

17. Benjamin to Mann, Richmond, February 1, 1864, ORN, ser. 2, 3:1014–1017.

18. Joseph O. Baylen and William W. White, "A. Dudley Mann's Mission in Europe, 1863–1864: An Unpublished Letter to Jefferson Davis," *Virginia Magazine of History and Biography* 69, no. 3 (1961): 324–328.

19. Mann to Davis, Brussels, May 9, 1864, OR, ser. 4, 3:401; Bigelow, "Southern Confederacy and the Pope."

20. Mann to Benjamin, Paris, December 28, 1863, ORN, ser. 2, 3:385–386.

21. De Leon to Benjamin, Vichy, July 30, 1862, OR, ser. 4, 2:25; Benjamin to Capston, Richmond, July 3, 1863, ORN, ser. 2, 3:828–829; Charles P. Cullop, *Confederate Propaganda in Europe, 1861–1865* (Coral Gables, FL: University of Miami Press, 1969), 108–109.

22. Benjamin to Bannon, Richmond, September 4, 1863, ORN, ser. 2, 3:893–895.

23. Cullop, *Confederate Propaganda*, 101, 110–113; Phillip Thomas Tucker, *The Confederacy's Fighting Chaplain Father: John B. Bannon* (Tuscaloosa: University of Alabama Press, 1992); William Barnaby Faherty, *Exile in Erin: A Confederate Chaplain's Story; The Life of Father John B. Bannon* (St. Louis: Missouri Historical Society Press, 2002); Patrick N. Lynch, "Reports of Bishop Lynch of Charleston, South Carolina, Commissioner of the Confederate States to the Holy See," *American Catholic Historical Researches* (July 1905): 50–59, includes an informative letter on Irish emigration, Lynch to Benjamin, Paris, June 20, 1864.

24. Cullop, *Confederate Propaganda*, 100–116; Stock, "Catholic Participation," 8; "Irishmen and the American War," *NYT,* March 27, 1864; "Our London Correspondence," *NYT,* May 31, 1865.

25. Mann to Benjamin, Brussels, March 11, 1864, ORN, ser. 2, 3:1057–1058; Stock, "Catholic Participation," 8–9.

26. David C. R. Heisser, "Bishop Lynch's Civil War Pamphlet on Slavery," *Catholic Historical Review* 84, no. 4 (1998): 681–696.

27. Ibid.; [Bishop Patrick N. Lynch], *Lettera di un missionario sulla schiavitù domestica degli stati confederati di america* (Rome: G. Cesaretti, 1864); [Bishop Patrick N. Lynch], *L'esclavage dans les États Confédérés* (Paris: E. Dentu, 1865); [Bishop Patrick N. Lynch], *Die sclaverei in den südstaaten Nord-Amerika's: Dargestellt von einem katholischen missionär* (Frankfurt: Verlag für Kunst und Wissenschaft, 1865); Bishop Patrick N. Lynch, "A Few Words on the Domestic Slavery in the Confederate States of America," edited by David C. R. Heisser, pts. 1 and 2, *Avery Review* 2, no. 1 (Spring 1999): 64–103; 3, no. 1 (Spring 2000): 93–123. Thanks to Brian P. Fahey at the Catholic Diocese of Charleston for help finding the English version.

28. Heisser, "Bishop Lynch's Civil War Pamphlet"; Lynch, "Domestic Slavery," pt. 1.

29. Heisser, "Bishop Lynch's Civil War Pamphlet."

30. Full accounts of the CSA debates on this are found in Robert Franklin Durden, *The Gray and the Black: The Confederate Debate on Emancipation* (Baton Rouge: Louisiana State University Press, 1972); and Bruce Levine, *Confederate Emancipation: Southern Plans to Free and Arm Slaves During the Civil War* (New York: Oxford University Press, 2006).

31. Cleburne et al. memo on arming slaves, January 2, 1864, OR, ser. 1, 52:586–592.

32. Levine, *Confederate Emancipation*, 2–3; Eli N. Evans, *Judah P. Benjamin, the Jewish Confederate* (New York: Free Press, 1988), 248–249.

33. Levine, *Confederate Emancipation*, 32–35; Benjamin to Frederick A. Porcher, Richmond, December 21, 1864, OR, ser. 4, 3:959–960.

34. See *Index,* November 10, 1864, 709; December 8, 1864, 778; and Mason to Benjamin, London, December 16, 1864, January 21, 1865, ORN, ser. 2, 3:1251, 1258–1259.

35. Durden, *Gray and the Black,* 204–207; Owsley, *King Cotton Diplomacy,* 535–536; Gregory Mattson, "Pariah Diplomacy: The Slavery Issue in Confeder-

ate Foreign Relations" (PhD diss., University of Southern Mississippi, 1999), 285, 420–421; "Recognition," *New York Tribune,* December 23, 1864.

36. Cobb to J. A. Seddon, Macon, GA, January 8, 1865, OR, ser. 4, 3:1009–1010; N. W. Stephenson, "The Question of Arming the Slaves," *American Historical Review* 18, no. 2 (1913): 295–308.

37. Durden, *Gray and the Black,* 191–192, quoting *Richmond Examiner,* February 10, 1865; Levine, *Confederate Emancipation,* 4, 10–13, 16–17, 29–36, 89–92; J. B. Jones, *A Rebel War Clerk's Diary at the Confederate States Capital* (Philadelphia: Lippincott, 1866), 2:437, 444.

38. Jefferson Davis, *The Rise and Fall of the Confederate Government* (New York: D. Appleton, 1881), 1:518; Levine, *Confederate Emancipation,* 4–5; Cobb to J. A. Seddon, Macon, GA, January 8, 1865, OR, ser. 4, 3:1009–1010.

39. "Davis's Ultimatum," *New York Tribune,* January 5, 1865; James Morton Callahan, *The Diplomatic History of the Southern Confederacy* (Baltimore: Johns Hopkins University Press, 1901), 248; Craig A. Bauer, "The Last Effort: The Secret Mission of the Confederate Diplomat, Duncan F. Kenner," *Louisiana History: The Journal of the Louisiana Historical Association* 22, no. 1 (1981): 75–76; Durden, *Gray and the Black,* 151–153, quoting *Richmond Sentinel,* December 28, 1864; William J. Cooper, *Jefferson Davis, American* (New York: Vintage, 2000), 552–558; Jones, *Rebel War Clerk's Diary,* 2:355.

40. Jeff Sowers Kinard, "Lafayette of the South: Prince Camille de Polignac and the American Civil War" (Ph.D. diss., Texas Christian University, 1997), 304–305; C. J. Polignac, "Polignac's Mission," *Southern Historical Society Papers* 35 (January–December 1907): 328–331.

41. Kinard, "Lafayette of the South," 304–305; Polignac, "Polignac's Mission," 333–334.

42. William Wirt Henry, "Kenner's Mission to Europe," *William and Mary Quarterly* 25, no. 1 (1916): 9–10.

43. Benjamin to Slidell, Richmond, December 27, 1864, ORN, ser. 2, 3:1253–1256.

44. "Letter from New York," *New Orleans Times-Picayune,* March 2, 1865; Bauer, "Last Effort"; Owsley, *King Cotton Diplomacy,* 530–541; Bigelow, *Retrospections of an Active Life, 1865–1866,* 77–81.

45. Craig A. Bauer, *A Leader Among Peers: The Life and Times of Duncan Farrar Kenner* (Lafayette: Center for Louisiana Studies, University of Southwestern Louisiana, 1993), 230; Bigelow to Seward, Paris, January 27, March 14, 21, 1865, France, RG 59.

46. Bauer, "Last Effort," 87–88.

47. Owsley, *King Cotton Diplomacy,* 538; Bauer, *Leader Among Peers,* 230–232; Bauer, "Last Effort," 90.

48. Levine, *Confederate Emancipation,* 111; Owsley, *King Cotton Diplomacy,* 530–541; Henry, "Kenner's Mission to Europe"; Callahan, *Diplomatic History,* 246–267; Benjamin to Slidell and Mason, Richmond, December 27, 1864; Mason to Benjamin,

London, March 31, 1865, ORN, ser. 2, 3:1253–1256, 1270–1277; Virginia Mason, *The Public Life and Diplomatic Correspondence of James M. Mason* (Roanoke, VA: Stone, 1903), 552–561.

49. Bauer, *Leader Among Peers*, 233–236; Owsley, *King Cotton Diplomacy*, 538–541; Mason to Benjamin, London, March 31, 1865, with enclosures: "Minutes of a conversation held with Lord Palmerston, at Cambridge House," March 14, 1865, and "Minutes of a conversation held with the Earl of Donoughmore, Sunday, March 26, 1865, ORN, ser. 2, 3:1270–1277.

50. Kinard, "Lafayette of the South," 308–309.

51. John Bigelow, "The Confederate Diplomatists and Their Shirt of Nessus: A Chapter of Secret History," *Century* 42 (1891): 126n1.

CHAPTER 12: SHALL NOT PERISH

1. For typical examples of Lincoln's universalizing language, see CWAL, 4:195, 8:254–255, 4:426, 5:53.

2. Lincoln, "Address Delivered at the Dedication of the Cemetery at Gettysburg," November 19, 1863, CWAL, 7:23.

3. Joseph Rossi, *The Image of America in Mazzini's Writings* (Madison: University of Wisconsin Press, 1954), 134–136; Denis Mack Smith, *Mazzini* (New Haven, CT: Yale University Press, 1996), 84; John L. Haney, "Of the People, by the People, for the People," *Proceedings of the American Philosophical Society* 88, no. 5 (1944): 359–367; Eugenio F. Biagini, "'The Principle of Humanity': Lincoln in Germany and Italy, 1859," in *The Global Lincoln* (New York: Oxford University Press, 2011), 76–94.

4. Charles Sumner, *Charles Sumner: His Complete Works* (Boston: Lee and Shepard, 1900), 272.

5. Osborn H. Oldroyd, ed., *Words of Lincoln* (Washington, DC: O. H. Oldroyd, 1895), 84. Goldwin Smith, "President Lincoln," *Macmillan's* 11 (June 1865): 302, expresses this slightly differently.

6. Kirk Harold Porter and Donald Bruce Johnson, *National Party Platforms, 1840–1972* (Urbana: University of Illinois Press, 1978), 1:35–36.

7. Édouard Laboulaye, *Professor Laboulaye, the Great Friend of America, on the Presidential Election: The Election of the President of the United States* (Washington, DC: Union Congressional Committee, 1864); "Our Election Abroad," *NYT*, October 25, 1864.

8. "We Are Coming, Father Abraham," http://www.civilwarpoetry.org/union /songs/comingex.html.

9. Elizabeth Cady Stanton et al., *History of Woman Suffrage* (New York: Fowler and Wells, 1881), 2:50–81.

10. This episode is interpreted in the film *Lincoln* (Dreamworks Pictures, 2012), with screenplay by Tony Kushner. See also Michael Vorenberg, *Final Freedom: The Civil War, the Abolition of Slavery, and the Thirteenth Amendment* (New York: Cambridge University Press, 2001).

11. Francis P. Blair Sr. to Jefferson Davis, Friday, December 30, 1864; Blair, "Suggestions Submitted to Jefferson Davis, President," January 12, 1865; Blair, Memorandum of Conversation with Jefferson Davis, January 12, 1865; Blair to Lincoln, February 8, 1865, ALPLC.

12. William C. Harris, "The Hampton Roads Peace Conference: A Final Test of Lincoln's Presidential Leadership," *Journal of the Abraham Lincoln Association* 21, no. 1 (2000): 30–61.

13. Ibid.; Michael Burlingame, *Abraham Lincoln: A Life* (Baltimore: Johns Hopkins University Press, 2008), 2:752; Clement A. Evans, ed., *Confederate Military History: A Library of Confederate States History* (Atlanta: Confederate Publishing, 1899), 543–559.

14. John Archibald Campbell, *Reminiscences and Documents Relating to the Civil War During the Year 1865* (Baltimore: J. Murphy, 1887); Harris, "Hampton Roads Peace Conference."

15. Burlingame, *Abraham Lincoln: A Life*, 2:756–758; Harris, "Hampton Roads Peace Conference."

16. Harris, "Hampton Roads Peace Conference"; Alexander Hamilton Stephens, *A Constitutional View of the Late War Between the States: Its Causes, Character, Conduct and Results, Presented in a Series of Colloquies at Liberty Hall* (Philadelphia: National Publishing, 1868), 598–619; Campbell, *Reminiscences and Documents*.

17. Abraham Lincoln, "Second Inaugural Address of Abraham Lincoln," March 4, 1865, AP.

18. James L. Swanson, *Bloody Crimes: The Chase for Jefferson Davis and the Death Pageant for Lincoln's Corpse* (New York: William Morrow, 2010), 28–30.

19. Burlingame, *Abraham Lincoln: A Life*, 2:788–792.

20. Charles Adolphe Pineton Chambrun, *Personal Recollections of Mr. Lincoln* (New York: Charles Scribner's Sons, 1893), 29.

21. Cooper, *Jefferson Davis, American*, 565–568; Swanson, *Bloody Crimes*, 90–92.

22. Edward Steers, *Blood on the Moon: The Assassination of Abraham Lincoln* (Lexington: University Press of Kentucky, 2001); Michael W. Kauffman, *American Brutus: John Wilkes Booth and the Lincoln Conspiracies* (New York: Random House, 2004).

23. Burlingame, *Abraham Lincoln: A Life*, 2:810–817.

24. Swanson, *Bloody Crimes*, 195–196.

25. Hampton to Davis, Hillsborough, NC, April 19, 1865; Hampton to Davis, Greensboro, NC, April 22, 1865, OR, ser. 1, 47:813–814, 829–830.

26. Swanson, *Bloody Crimes*, 224; Kauffman, *American Brutus*, 297, 306.

27. Pierce Butler, *Judah P. Benjamin* (Philadelphia: G. W. Jacobs, 1907), 363; Cooper, *Jefferson Davis, American*, 657–679; Felicity Allen, *Jefferson Davis, Unconquerable Heart* (Columbia: University of Missouri Press, 2000), 441–442.

28. "Is President Lincoln a Martyr?," *NYT*, April 26, 1865; David B. Chesebrough, *No Sorrow Like Our Sorrow: Northern Protestant Ministers and the Assassination of Lincoln* (Kent, OH: Kent State University Press, 1994); Thomas Reed Turner, *Beware the People Weeping: Public Opinion and the Assassination of Abraham Lincoln*

(Baton Rouge: Louisiana State University Press, 1982); "The Martyred President: Sermons Given on the Occasion of the Assassination of Abraham Lincoln," Pitts Theological Library, Emory University, http://beck.library.emory.edu/lincoln/index .html; Merrill D. Peterson, *Lincoln in American Memory* (New York: Oxford University Press, 1994), 1–35.

29. Peterson, *Lincoln in American Memory,* 20.

30. Originally published in 1865, reprinted: Walt Whitman, "When Lilacs Last in the Dooryard Bloom'd," *Leaves of Grass* (Boston: Small, Maynard, 1904), 256.

31. "Messages of Condolence," 5 boxes, E-177, RG 59, NARA II.

32. Bigelow to Weed, Paris, May 12, 1865, in Margaret Antoinette Clapp, *Forgotten First Citizen: John Bigelow* (Boston: Little, Brown, 1947), 237.

33. US Department of State, *The Assassination of Abraham Lincoln . . . Expressions of Condolence and Sympathy Inspired by These Events* (Washington, DC: GPO, 1866), 111. An expanded edition was published under the same title in 1867.

34. Ibid., 434, 85, 560, 433.

35. Ibid., 56; Philip G. Nord, *The Republican Moment: Struggles for Democracy in Nineteenth-Century France* (Cambridge, MA: Harvard University Press, 1998), 15–31.

36. US Department of State, *Assassination,* 71, 76; Nord, *Republican Moment,* 15–31.

37. John Bigelow, *Retrospections of an Active Life, 1865–1866* (New York: Baker and Taylor, 1909), 53–54, 57.

38. Benjamin Gastineau, *Histoire de la souscription populaire à la médaille Lincoln* (Paris: A. Lacroix Verbœckoven, 1865); Jason Emerson, "A Medal for Mrs. Lincoln," *Register of the Kentucky Historical Society* 109, no. 2 (2011): 187–205; Malakoff, "European News," *NYT,* June 2, 1865.

39. Bigelow, *Retrospections of an Active Life, 1863–1865,* 596–597; Jean Jules Jusserand, *With Americans of Past and Present Days* (New York: Charles Scribner's Sons, 1916), 299. The medal, velvet box, and accompanying notes are at the Library of Congress, cont. 1, ser. 4, ALPLC. I am grateful to Michele Krowl for making it possible for me to see, and hold, this extraordinary medal.

40. Bigelow, *Retrospections of an Active Life, 1863–1865,* 596–597; Jusserand, *Past and Present Days,* 299.

41. Seward to Bigelow, Washington, January 1, 1865; Bigelow to Seward, Paris, January 27, 1865, Bigelow Papers, NYPL; Charles Priestly, "Death in Paris: The Mysterious Case of William L. Dayton" (Confederate Historical Association of Belgium, 2014); L[izzie] St. John Eckel, *Maria Monk's Daughter: An Autobiography* (New York: United States Publishing, 1874), 108–118; Bigelow, *Retrospections of an Active Life, 1863–1865,* 234–238, 329; Beckles Willson, *John Slidell and the Confederates in Paris (1862–65)* (New York: Minton, Balch, 1932), 232–252. Willson's story that Mrs. Eckel performed onstage as Sophie Bricard is not reliable, as Priestly warns. See also John Louis Bonn, *And Down the Days* (New York: Macmillan, 1942).

42. Bigelow, *Retrospections of an Active Life, 1865–1866,* 90–107.

CODA: REPUBLICAN RISORGIMENTO

1. H. C. Allen, "Civil War, Reconstruction, and Great Britain," in *Heard Round the World: The Impact Abroad of the Civil War,* edited by Harold Hyman (New York: Alfred A. Knopf, 1969), 73, quoting Edward Beesly; David M. Potter, "Civil War," in *The Comparative Approach to American History,* edited by C. Vann Woodward (New York: Basic Books, 1968), 135–145..

2. Joseph Rossi, *The Image of America in Mazzini's Writings* (Madison: University of Wisconsin Press, 1954), 137–148; Stefano Recchia and Nadia Urbinati, eds., *A Cosmopolitanism of Nations: Giuseppe Mazzini's Writings on Democracy, Nation Building, and International Relations* (Princeton, NJ: Princeton University Press, 2009), 219–223; C. A. Bayly and Eugenio F. Biagini, eds., *Giuseppe Mazzini and the Globalisation of Democratic Nationalism, 1830–1920* (Oxford: Oxford University Press for the British Academy, 2008).

3. Anne Eller, "Let's Show the World We Are Brothers: The Dominican Guerra de Restauracion and the Nineteenth-Century Caribbean" (PhD diss., New York University, 2011); Wayne H. Bowen, *Spain and the American Civil War* (Columbia: University of Missouri Press, 2011), 92–106; James W. Cortada, "Spain and the American Civil War: Relations at Mid-Century, 1855–1868," *Transactions of the American Philosophical Society* 70, no. 4 (1980): 37–40; Frank Moya Pons, *The Dominican Republic: A National History* (Princeton, NJ: Markus Wiener, 1998), 210–218; "From Mexico: Advices from Santo Domingo and Hayti," *NYT,* July 4, 1865.

4. Cortada, "Spain and the American Civil War," 92–101; Nathan L. Ferris, "The Relations of the United States with South America During the American Civil War," *Hispanic American Historical Review* 21, no. 1 (1941): 69–71; William Columbus Davis, *The Last Conquistadores: The Spanish Intervention in Peru and Chile, 1863–1866* (Athens: University of Georgia Press, 1950).

5. Cortada, "Spain and the American Civil War," 87–88; John Bigelow, *Retrospections of an Active Life, 1865–1866* (New York: Baker and Taylor, 1909), 510; "The Spanish Revolt," *NYT,* February 6, 1866; "New Life for Old Spain," *NYT,* October 28, 1868.

6. Dale T. Graden, *Disease, Resistance, and Lies: The Demise of the Transatlantic Slave Trade* (Baton Rouge, LA: Louisiana State University Press, 2014), 209, quoting Robert Schufeldt to Seward, Havana, January 14, 1862, Havana, RG 59; Christopher Schmidt-Nowara, *Empire and Antislavery: Spain, Cuba, and Puerto Rico, 1833–1874* (Pittsburgh: University of Pittsburgh Press, 1999), 125–138.

7. Rafael de Bivar Marquese, "The Civil War in the United States and the Crisis of Slavery in Brazil" (paper presented at "American Civil Wars" conference, University of South Carolina, March 19, 2014).

8. Jasper Godwin Ridley, *Maximilian and Juárez* (New York: Ticknor and Fields, 1992), 205; A. R. Tyrner-Tyrnauer, *Lincoln and the Emperors* (New York: Harcourt, Brace, and World, 1962), 129–133; D. P. Crook, *The North, the South, and the Powers, 1861–1865* (New York: Wiley, 1974), 365.

9. Alfred J. Hanna and Kathryn A. Hanna, *Napoleon III and Mexico: American Triumph over Monarchy* (Chapel Hill: University of North Carolina Press, 1971), 124.

10. Grant to Johnson, Washington, June 19, 1865, OR, ser. 1, 48:923–924; Andrew F. Rolle, *The Lost Cause: The Confederate Exodus to Mexico* (Norman: University of Oklahoma Press, 1965); Hanna and Hanna, *Napoleon III and Mexico,* 221–235; Ridley, *Maximilian and Juárez,* 215–217; Sara Yorke Stevenson, *Maximilian in Mexico: A Woman's Reminiscences of the French Intervention, 1862–1867* (New York: Century, 1899), 169–174; Elizabeth Boatwright Coker, *The Grasshopper King: A Story of Two Confederate Exiles in Mexico During the Reign of Maximilian and Carlota* (New York: Dutton, 1981); Matthew Pratt Guterl, *American Mediterranean: Southern Slaveholders in the Age of Emancipation* (Cambridge, MA: Harvard University Press, 2008).

11. Thomas D. Schoonover, *Dollars over Dominion: The Triumph of Liberalism in Mexican–United States Relations, 1861–1867* (Baton Rouge: Louisiana State University Press, 1978), 193–211; Philip Henry Sheridan, *Personal Memoirs of P. H. Sheridan, General United States Army* (New York: C. L. Webster, 1888), 2:105–106; Ulysses S. Grant, *Personal Memoirs of U. S. Grant* (New York: C. L. Webster, 1885), 2:181; Joseph Wheelan, *Terrible Swift Sword: The Life of General Philip H. Sheridan* (Cambridge, MA: Da Capo Press, 2012), 213–214; Matías Romero, *Proceedings of a Meeting of Citizens of New York, to Express Sympathy and Respect for the Mexican Republican Exiles* (New York: J. A. Gray and Green, 1865), 26, 33.

12. Stevenson, *Maximilian in Mexico,* 169; Hanna and Hanna, *Napoleon III and Mexico,* 153.

13. Ridley, *Maximilian and Juárez,* 217–220; Erika Pani, *Para mexicanizar el segundo imperio: El imaginario político de los imperialistas* (Mexico City: Colegio de México, 2001).

14. John Bigelow, "The Heir-Presumptive to the Imperial Crown of Mexico," *Harper's Monthly,* April 1883, 735–748; Bigelow, *Retrospections of an Active Life, 1865–1866,* 269–276; "Maximilian Charged with Kidnapping an American Child," *NYT,* January 9, 1866; Malakoff, "Foreign Affairs," *NYT,* December 8, 1865; C. M. Mayo, *The Last Prince of the Mexican Empire: A Novel Based on the True Story* (Denver: Unbridled Books, 2009).

15. Ridley, *Maximilian and Juárez,* 228–240; Stevenson, *Maximilian in Mexico,* 309–314.

16. Bigelow, *Retrospections of an Active Life, 1863–1865,* 535–539.

17. Hanna and Hanna, *Napoleon III and Mexico,* 271–272.

18. José Ortiz Monasterio, *"Patria," tu ronca voz me repetía: Biografía de Vicente Riva Palacio y Guerrero* (Mexico City: UNAM, 1999), 93–95. Gracias to Erika Pani for advising me on this tricky translation.

19. Ridley, *Maximilian and Juárez,* 247–249; Hanna and Hanna, *Napoleon III and Mexico,* 270–278; Egon Caesar Corti, *Maximilian and Charlotte of Mexico,* translated by Catherine Alison Phillips (New York: Alfred A. Knopf, 1928), 2:659–716.

20. "Mexican Intelligence: The Trial of Maximilian," *NYT,* July 16, 1867; "Mexican Intelligence: Maximilian's Crimes," *NYT,* August 1, 1867; Bigelow, "Heir-Presumptive to the Imperial Crown"; Ridley, *Maximilian and Juárez,* 242–243, 255–256, 257–269.

21. "Mexican Intelligence: Particulars of the Execution of Maximilian," *NYT,* July 3, 1867; Ridley, *Maximilian and Juárez,* 277; Felix Salm-Salm, *My Diary in Mexico in 1867* (London: R. Bently, 1868), 307–308; Samuel Basch, *Memories of Mexico: A History of the Last Ten Months of the Empire* (San Antonio: Trinity University Press, 1973), 221; Corti, *Maximilian and Charlotte,* 2:822–823n51.

22. Ridley, *Maximilian and Juárez,* 282–290; Mayo, *Last Prince of the Mexican Empire.*

23. William J. Cooper, *Jefferson Davis, American* (New York: Vintage, 2000), 657–679; Felicity Allen, *Jefferson Davis, Unconquerable Heart* (Columbia: University of Missouri Press, 2000), 441–442; US Department of State, *The Assassination of Abraham Lincoln . . . Expressions of Condolence and Sympathy Inspired by These Events* (Washington, DC: GPO, 1866), 528.

24. "City Religious Press," *New York Evangelist,* May 11, 1865; "The Anti-Catholic War," *Clearfield Republican,* June 7, 1865; Merrill D. Peterson, *Lincoln in American Memory* (New York: Oxford University Press, 1994), 92–93; William Hanchett, *The Lincoln Murder Conspiracies* (Urbana: University of Illinois Press, 1983), 233–240; Howard Rosario Marraro, "Canadian and American Zouaves in the Papal Army, 1868–1870," *Canadian Catholic Historical Association Report* 12 (1944–1945): 83–102.

25. Charles Paschal Telesphore Chiniquy, *Fifty Years in the Church of Rome* (New York: Fleming H. Revell, 1886), 699–700. See also T. M. Harris, *Assassination of Lincoln: A History of the Great Conspiracy; Trial of the Conspirators by a Military Commission and a Review of the Trial of John H. Surratt* (Boston: American Citizen, 1892); Hanchett, *The Lincoln Murder Conspiracies,* 233–240. I am grateful to Michael Sobiech for sharing this material and his vast knowledge of Charles Chiniquy and the Catholic conspiracy theory.

26. Robin W. Winks, *The Civil War Years: Canada and the United States,* 4th ed. (Montreal: McGill-Queen's University Press, 1998), 376–377.

27. Ibid., 322–326, 370–371, 374–381; Phillip A. Buckner, ed., *Canada and the British Empire* (Oxford and New York: Oxford University Press, 2008), 66–86.

28. "Our Russian Guests," *NYT,* October 2, 1863; "The Russian Banquet," *NYT,* October 20, 1863; Albert A. Woldman, *Lincoln and the Russians* (Cleveland, OH: World, 1952); Tyrner-Tyrnauer, *Lincoln and the Emperors,* 83–84; Howard Jones, *Blue and Gray Diplomacy: A History of Union and Confederate Foreign Relations* (Chapel Hill: University of North Carolina Press, 2010), 293–294.

29. Brent E. Kinser, *The American Civil War in the Shaping of British Democracy* (Farnham, UK: Ashgate, 2011).

30. Charles Forbes Montalembert, *La victoire du Nord aux États-Unis* (Paris: E. Dentu, 1865); Count de Montalembert, *The Victory of the North in the United*

States (Boston: Littell and Gay, 1866), quote on 22; Bigelow, *Retrospections of an Active Life, 1865–1866,* 3–4.

31. Philip Mark Katz, *From Appomattox to Montmartre: Americans and the Paris Commune* (Cambridge, MA: Harvard University Press, 1998); David G. McCullough, *The Greater Journey: Americans in Paris* (New York: Simon and Schuster, 2011), 295–330.

32. J. A. S. Grenville, *Europe Reshaped, 1848–1878* (Oxford: Blackwell, 2000), 205–250.

33. John Lothrop Motley, *The Correspondence of John Lothrop Motley* (New York: Harper and Brothers, 1889), 3:125, quoting Bismarck to Motley, Berlin, April 17, 1863; James Pemberton Grund, "Bismarck and Motley with Correspondence till Now Unpublished," *North American Review* 167, no. 502 (1898): 360–376.

34. Motley, *Correspondence of Motley,* 2:167.

35. Ibid., 3:17, 23, quoting Bismarck to Motley, Berlin, May 23, 1864; Motley to Bismarck, Vienna, May 28, 1864.

36. Frédéric-Auguste Bartholdi, *The Statue of Liberty Enlightening the World,* translated by Allen Thorndike Rice (New York: North American Review, 1885), 16–20; David Hackett Fischer, *Liberty and Freedom* (New York: Oxford University Press, 2005), 369–370.

37. Fischer, *Liberty and Freedom,* 370, quoting Laboulaye, "Speech at the Opera of Paris, 25 April, 1876."

38. Adam Gopnik, "Memorials," *New Yorker,* May 9, 2011.

INDEX

Adams, Charles Francis
  British labor supporting the
    Union, 232, 245–247
  British threat of intervention,
    81, 220–222, 225, 234
  Emancipation Proclamation,
    243–244, 246, 248–249
  London appointment, 59
  Palmerston's retreat from
    intervention, 235
  Seward's instructions on
    slavery, 65–66
  Weed, Hughes and
    McIlvaine's mission to
    London, 76–77
Adams, Henry, 75, 78–79,
  252
Adams, W. E., 149
African American experience,
  Assing's writings on the,
  155–157
Age of Revolution, 85–93
Alabama, CSS, 221
Alaska, Russian sale of, 308
Alexander II, 234
Allen, George, 104, 274
Allen, Julian, 179–180
America Before Europe: Principles
  and Interests (Gasparin),
  137–138, 141
American Union (Spence),
  143–145, 251
Anthony, Susan B., 135,
  285
Anti-Corn Law League, 146
Antietam, Battle of (1862),
  218–219
Antonelli, Giacomo (cardinal),
  261–262, 263(fig.), 264

Archibald, Edward, 104–105
Artoni, Giuseppe, 22–24
Aspromonte, Garibaldi's debacle
  at, 227
Assing, Ottilie, 72, 155–157

Bancroft, George, 1(quote), 89
Bannon, John B., 267
Bartholdi, Frédéric-Auguste,
  311, 313
Beckwith, Nelson M., 25
Benjamin, Judah P., 189(fig.)
  background, 187–188
  Confederate emancipation,
    278–279
  De Leon promoting the
    Confederate cause in
    Europe, 195–197
  De Leon's indiscretion in
    France, 255–256
  English exile after the war,
    291
  European trade plan, 38
  French separation from the
    Confederacy, 233–234
  French strategy, 203–205
  mission to the Vatican, 262,
    264–266, 269
  sacrificing slavery for
    recognition, 272–273,
    275–276
  severing diplomatic relations
    with Britain, 253–254,
    258
  Spence's views on slavery,
    145, 249–250, 251
  Union enlistments in Ireland,
    267
Bertinatti, Giuseppe, 59–60

Bigelow, John, 58, 74(fig.)
  American Homestead Act
    and Circular 19, 177–178
  appointment to Paris, 73
  British-French plan for
    intervention, 224
  Confederate emancipation
    plan, 277, 280
  Dayton's controversial death,
    297–298
  France's shift in public
    opinion towards the
    South, 138
  French concerns over British
    war, 76
  Laboulaye, 139–142
  Lincoln assassination,
    294–295
  republican resurgence, 299
  Spanish republican
    revolution, 301
  student demonstration in
    Paris, 1–2
  threat of US-British war,
    76–77
Bismarck, Otto von, 92,
  309–311
Black Decree (1865, Mexico),
  304, 305
Blair, Francis Preston, Sr.,
  286–288
Blockade, 38–39, 187, 189,
  203–206, 250
Bolívar, Simón, 94
Bonaparte, Jerome Napoleon,
  103
Bonds, Confederate, 250,
  258–259, 259(fig.),
  271–272

Booth, John Wilkes, 290, 307
Booth, Mary Louise, 135–137, 136(fig.), 140, 142
Brazil, 284
  Garibaldi in, 16
  Napoleon III's Grand Design, 107–109
  neutrality, 43
  path to independence, 88
  restoration of imperial rule in Latin America, 109–110
  slavery and abolition, 89, 248, 301
Bribery, 72–73, 190, 203
Bricard, Sophie, 200
Bright, John, 145–149, 157, 236, 245, 247–248, 252
Britain
  backing away from intervention, 234–237
  Bigelow-Scott letter of conciliation, 77
  British and French plan for intervention, 219–225, 234–237
  Confederate emancipation promise, 277–279
  Confederate European commission, 42–46
  Confederate foreign policy objectives, 5–6
  Confederate partisanship, 100–101
  Confederates cultivating support from, 5–6, 42–46, 142–145
  Garibaldi's support of Union cause, 231–232
  Garibaldi's march on Rome upsetting plans for European intervention, 225–229
  Lincoln and Seward's diplomatic appointments, 58–59
  Lincoln and Seward's response to Spanish aggression in the New World, 65
  Lincoln assassination, 293(fig.)
  Marx's criticism of, 154
  Marx's flight to, 151
  Mason and Slidell, 197–198
  Napoleon III's Grand Design, 9
  nurturing Latin American monarchies, 94
  preservation of imperial rule in Americas, 106–107
  press attach on the Union, 76
  race theory as support for the Confederate position, 192–193
  recognition of the Confederacy, 251–253
  Reform Act of 1867, 308
  response to the Emancipation Proclamation, 241–242, 244–245
  Russell and Palmerston's distrust of democracy, 41–42
  spread of republicanism, 90–91, 95–98
  stance on slavery, 209
  Trent affair, 47–49, 76, 78–81, 114, 117, 137, 145, 147–148, 154, 190, 197–198
  Tripartite Alliance, 117–118, 122, 202
  Union defenders, 145–150
  Weed's mission of conciliation, 78–81
Brucker, Magnus, 166
Buchanan, James, 52–53, 53(fig.), 73
Bull Run, Battle of (1861), 20–21, 34(fig.), 44–45, 73
Bull Run, Second Battle of (1862), 218, 222
Butler, Benjamin, 206–207, 220, 244

Cabral, José-Maria, 111–112
Campbell, Robert, 287
Canada, 42, 48, 62, 79, 94, 96, 107, 159, 178, 190, 276, 307–308
Canisius, Heinrich Theodore, 229–230, 237–238
Canning, George, 94
Capston, J. L., 267
Carlists (Spain), 110
Carlyle, Thomas, 240
Castilla, Ramón, 109
Casualty figures, 167
Catholic Church
  anti-Irish feeling in America, 174–175
  Confederate alignment with Mexico's party, 122
  Congress of Vienna's restoration of, 90
European response to the Emancipation Proclamation, 247–248
French invasion of Mexico, 125–126
Grand Design of Napoleon III, 8–9, 107–108, 186, 190, 202, 252, 304
  influencing America's peace movement, 261–262
  Lincoln assassination, 307
  Mexico's Reforma, 114–115
Céspedes, Carlos Manuel de, 301
Chambrun, Marquis de, 290
Charlotte of Belgium, 129–130, 130(fig.), 303–306
Chartist movement, 91, 149
Chevalier, Michel, 108–109
Chiniquy, Charles, 307
Cinco de Mayo, 124, 125(fig.), 190
Cintrat, Pierre, 202, 220, 255
Circular 19, 177–178, 180–181, 267–268
Citizenship for immigrants in military service, 160
Clay, Cassius, 58
Cleburne, Patrick, 270–271
Cobb, Howell, 32, 257(quote), 272–273
Cobden, Richard, 146, 147, 149, 242
Colonial uprisings, 217–218
Columbia, iconography of, 164, 293(fig.)
Communist Manifesto (Marx and Engels), 152–153
Confederacy
  arming Southern slaves, 270–271, 272–273
  Benjamin's foreign policy, 38, 105, 188–191, 275–276
  Britain, severing diplomatic relations with, 253–254, 258
  British partisanship, 99–105
  British-French plan for intervention, 219–223k
  casualties, 167
  cotton bonds, 250, 258, 259(fig.), 271
  cultivating British support, 142–145, 191, 193
  cultivating Spanish support, 112–114, 122

Davis's inaugural addresses, 32–35, 33(fig.), 186–187
De Leon's public diplomacy campaign for the South, 195–197, 205–209
diplomatic efforts in Europe, 38–44, 56–57, 74, 112–114, 142–145, 199–205
emancipation proposal, 257–260, 274–280
European commission, 38–44
European invasion of Mexico, 118–120
European response to the Emancipation Proclamation, 249–251
European view of the "holy war," 9, 261, 266
European antislavery views, 6, 9, 20, 25, 29, 37, 44, 45, 46, 70, 144–145, 192, 202, 249–250, 251, 273
Garibaldi's march on Rome upsetting plans for European intervention, 225–229, 233–234
Grand Design reliance on Southern success, 202–203
insults to the Mexican government, 121–122
Lincoln's assassination, 290–291
Lincoln's first inaugural address, 45, 53–54
Mexican foreign policy, 118–122, 202, 204, 252, 302
monarchist leanings, 100–105
motives for secession and war, 27–32, 35–37
Napoleon III's Grand Design, 29–32, 109, 202–203
Palmerston accused of secret collaboration with, 246–247
perpetuation of slavery, 10, 30–31, 35
Pius IX's plea for peace, 261–265
pursuit of international recognition, 44–46, 188–191, 204–205, 219–225, 251–252

race theory as support for, 36, 144, 191–192
secession of states from, 54–55
secession from Union, 30–32
surrender, 289–290
the *Trent* affair, 47–49, 76, 78–81, 114, 117, 137, 145, 147–148, 154, 190, 197–198
Union recruitment of immigrants, 178–180
Washington "peace commission," 37–38
See also Benjamin, Judah P.; Cotton; Davis, Jefferson; De Leon, Edwin; Mason, James M.; Slavery; Slidell, John
Congress of Vienna, 90
Constitution, Confederate, 35–37, 168
Constitution, US, 100, 216
Constitutional monarchy, 90–91
Copperheads, 211
Cornerstone Speech, 35–37, 137
Corwin, Thomas, 58–59, 119, 121
Cotton
Bright championing the Union cause, 146
Confederate cotton bribe to France, 203–204
Confederate-European trade plan, 38–39
cotton bond prices, 258–259, 259(fig.)
cotton famine, 39, 146, 149, 188
economic justification of slavery, 45
impact of emancipation, 217–218
King Cotton diplomacy, 5, 39, 188
Crawford, Martin, 37–38, 113
Cuba, 58, 89, 106–107, 110, 113–114, 119, 248, 300–301

Dallas, George, 56
Davis, Jefferson, 34(fig.), 53(fig.)
Blair's designs on Mexico, 286–287
Cleburne Memorial, 270–271

Confederate emancipation, 273
Confederate policy in Mexico, 120–121, 286–287
Davis's decrees of execution, 244
De Leon's connection to, 195–197
De Leon's portrayal to the French, 207
desire for formal recognition of the Confederacy, 28, 271–274
European commission, 39
expanding diplomatic efforts in Europe, 46–49
flight, capture, and trial, 289–291
inaugurations, 32–35, 33(fig.), 186–187
liberty symbol, 165
Lincoln assassination, 290–291
peace talks, 286
Pius IX's plea for peace, 264–266
provisional government, 32
refusal to surrender, 290
release from prison, 306–307
sacrificing slavery for recognition, 271–274
severing diplomatic relations with Britain, 253
Washington "peace commission," 37–38
See also Confederacy
Dayton, William
Bigelow's appointment to Paris, 73–74
British-French plan for intervention in the war, 223–225
controversial death, 297–298
French partisanship for the South, 200
immigrant volunteers, 176
London appointment, 58
response to the Emancipation Proclamation, 243
Seward's instructions on slavery, 66–67
De Leon, Edwin, 194(fig.)
appealing to the Catholic Church, 269–270
appointment as Confederate agent, 195–197
background of, 193–195

De Leon, Edwin (*continued*)
calls for withdrawal of
Confederate envoys in
Europe, 254
dismissal, 258
European public diplomacy,
205–209
Garibaldi swaying public
opinion towards the
Union, 233
Slidell's hostility towards,
254–256
Union enlistments in Ireland,
266–267
Declaration of Independence,
29–30, 34, 104
Delacroix, Eugène, 164–165
Delord, Taxile, 99
Democracy
Bright's support for Union
ideals, 147–148
Confederacy's antidemocratic
appeal abroad, 9, 95–97,
100, 105, 198
European perception of the
Confederacy, 6
French criticism of American
republicanism, 98–99
Lincoln framing the Union
cause, 51, 211
Queen Victoria's dislike of, 81
Russell and Palmerston's
distrust of, 41–42
secession as rebellion against,
101–104
See also Republicanism;
Self-government
Democracy in America
(Tocqueville), 95
Dillon, Romaine, 158
Diplomacy
Benjamin and Confederate
foreign policy, 188–191
British sentiment toward
Mason and Slidell,
197–198
British-French plan for
intervention, 219–225
Confederate European
commission, 38–46
Confederate "peace
commission" to
Washington, 37–38
Confederates severing
diplomatic relations with
Britain, 253–254
Davis's expansion of efforts
in Europe, 46–49

De Leon promoting the
Confederate cause abroad,
193–197
Garibaldi's debacle at
Aspromonte, 228–229
Lincoln's engagement with
British labor, 245
Lincoln's relationship with
Seward, 60–65
shaping diplomacy by
influencing public
opinion, 70–73
Slidell's efforts in France,
199–205
Union-Confederate
competition for European
favor, 73–78
See also Recognition of the
Confederacy
Donoughmore, Richard John
Hely-Hutchinson, Earl
of, 279
Douglas, Stephen, 54
Douglass, Frederick, 155–157
Draft, military (Confederacy),
167–168, 189–190
Drouyn de Lhuys, Édouard,
233, 237
Dubois de Saligny, Alphonso,
124
D'Utassy, Frederick George,
172

Eckel, Lizzie St. John, 297
Emancipation
America as global model for
republicanism, 10
British movement, 245–247
Garibaldi's commitment to,
20, 24–26
Emancipation policy,
Confederate, 271–280
Emancipation Proclamation
British response to, 149–150,
235, 245–249
British-French plan for
intervention in the war,
223
Confederation reaction to,
241, 248, 249–251
European reaction to,
240–244
Garibaldi's support of Union
coinciding with, 231–232
growing favor in Europe,
247–249, 260
intervention as potential
result of, 210–211

legitimizing the Union cause,
211–216
Lincoln on international
republicanism, 282–284
Lincoln's plans and strategies,
216–218
Marx's response to, 155,
157
Pius IX's understanding of,
269–270
popular response to in
Union, 285–286
women's rights and, 285
Embargo policy, Davis's, 39
Engels, Friedrich, 151
Enlightenment ideals, 87
Erlanger, Frédéric Emile d',
250–251, 254, 258–259
Espionage and intelligence
gathering, 72, 202
Eugénie, Empress of France,
116, 201, 226, 260,
305, 309
European states
allied invasion of Mexico,
122–126
American Homestead Act
and Circular 19,
176–178
America's republican
experiment, 8–10, 85–88,
95–96, 99
Benjamin's foreign policy,
189–191
Confederate commission,
38–41
Confederate defense of
slavery's economic role,
45–46
Confederate emancipation,
273–280
Confederate states' need for
support from, 30
De Leon promoting the
Confederate cause,
193–197
debate over Confederate
secession, 138
declining support for the
South, 257–260
Emancipation Proclamation,
210–216, 240–244
Garibaldi's march on Rome
upsetting plans for
European intervention in
America, 225–229
immigrant soldiers in the
Union, 159–160

international legal stance on supporting a domestic insurrection, 55–56

lack of sympathy for the South, 187

Lincoln and Seward's response to Spanish aggression in the New World, 65

Lincoln assassination, 292–295

Lincoln's diplomatic appointments, 57–60

Lincoln's framing of the war, 281–284

Lincoln's threats over intervention, 65–67

motive for American civil war, 131–132

neutrality declarations, 43

perception of abolition as cause of war, 69–70

race theory as support for the Confederate position, 191–193

republican resurgence, 308–311

response to 'extreme democracy,' 100–101

response to Union victory, 300–306

restoration of imperialism, 106–109, 114–116

Seward's diplomatic missions to court favor in, 73–78

Seward's foreign policy, 62–63

Seward's overtures to Garibaldi, 73

Seward's threat of global war, 50–51

Seward's tour of the Middle East and, 68

shaping diplomacy by influencing public opinion, 70–73

Southern monarchism, 101–105

spread of republican ideals, 89–93

Tripartite Alliance, 117–118, 122

Union and Confederate diplomatic strategies, 5–7

voluntary enlistment with the Union, 238

See also individual states

Evans, Thomas, 199–200

Extreme democracy, 11, 31–32, 96–97, 100, 187, 198

Farroupilhas, War of the, 16

Faulkner, Charles, 56–57

Favre, Jules, 138

Feudalism: Marx's view of America, 155

Fire-Eaters, 30, 32–33

Fogg, George, 18

Foote, Henry S., 273

Forbes, John Murray, 131(quote)

Foreign debt, Mexico's, 119–120

Foreign policy, Confederate
Benjamin's diplomatic efforts and, 188–191
rightward shift, 185–186
See also Benjamin, Judah P.

Foreign policy, Union
European response to the Emancipation Proclamation, 210–216
leftward maneuvering, 185–186
Seward's clash with Lincoln, 61–63
See also Seward, William Henry

Forey, Elie Frédéric, 124–126

Forsyth, John, 37–38, 120, 191

Forty-Eighters, 92, 93(fig.), 173, 229

Fould, Achille, 98

France
admiration for American republicanism, 132–135
American Homestead Act and Circular 19, 177–178
America's republican experiment, 9–10
Bigelow-Scott letter of conciliation, 77–78
British and French plan for intervention, 219–225
Confederate emancipation promise, 277, 279–280
Confederate foreign policy objectives, 5–6
Confederate mission to Europe, 43–44
Confederates' hope for support from, 190
Confederates severing diplomatic relations with Britain, 254

De Leon's frustration with, 255–256

De Leon's public diplomacy campaign for the South, 206–209

declining support for the Confederacy, 233–234, 259

defending the Republic of Rome against, 16

distancing itself from the Confederacy, 233–234

Garibaldi's support of Union cause, 231

Garibaldi's march on Rome upsetting plans for European intervention, 225–229

invasion of Mexico, 123–126, 128–130

Lincoln and Seward's response to Spanish aggression in the New World, 65

Lincoln assassination, 294–297

Marx's criticism of, 154

Napoleon III's Grand Design, 8–9

press censorship, 72

public opinion on the American experiment, 138–141

rejoicing over American civil war, 98–99

republican resurgence, 308–309

response to the Emancipation Proclamation, 237, 242–244

restoration of imperial rule in Latin America, 106–109

Slidell's diplomatic efforts, 199–205

spread of republican ideals, 89–92

Statue of Liberty, 311–313

Tripartite Alliance, 117–118, 122, 202

Union alliance with French republicanism, 209

Union-Confederate competition for favor, 76

withdrawal from Mexico, 304–305

Zouave forces, 163

Franklin, Benjamin, 71

Free trade, 5, 146, 149

Frémont, John C., 58
French Revolution, 89–90
Friedrich Wilhelm IV, 92
Fugitive Slave Act (1850), 198
Fugitive slaves, 217

Garibaldi, Giuseppe, 15(quote),
19(fig.), 210(quote),
228(fig.), 299(quote)
    arrival in America, 17–20
    Canisius's invitation to
        join the Union cause,
        222–233, 237–238
    Emancipation Proclamation,
        215
    immigrant soldiers in the
        Union forces, 159
    Louis-Napoleon's coup, 92
    march on Rome upsetting
        plans for European
        intervention in America,
        211, 225–229
    Mexico's *Reforma,* 114
    popularity in America,
        20–21
    praise of Lincoln, 238–239
    Quiggle's scheme for, 19–24,
        26, 159, 229
    Risorgimento, 15–17,
        260–261
    Seward's secret service
        operations, 75
    Union alliance, 22–25
Garibaldi Guard, 160–164,
    170–173, 172(fig.)
Garnier-Pages, Louis-Antoine,
    76
Gasparin, Agénor de, 132–133,
    133(fig.), 134–138,
    140–141, 157
Gasset y Mercader, Manuel,
    117–118
German immigrant soldiers,
    162, 165–167, 173
Germany
    Lincoln and Seward's
        diplomatic appointments,
        59
    Ottilie Assing, 155–157
    rejoicing over American civil
        conflict, 99
    republican hopes, 92
    republican resurgence,
        309–310
    See also Prussia
Gettysburg, Battle of, 249, 262
Gettysburg Address (1863), 9,
    281–284, 281(quote)

Gladstone, William, 223,
    234–236
Glorious Revolution (1868,
    Spain), 301
Gobineau, Arthur, 36–37, 144,
    191–192
Gould, Benjamin Apthorp,
    168–170, 173, 178
Grand Design of Napoleon III,
    8–9, 107–108, 186, 190,
    202, 252, 304
Grant, Ulysses S., 302
Grassroots activism: Anti-Corn
    Law League, 146
Greek nationalist independence
    movements, 29
Greeley, Horace, 150
Guizot, François, 90–91
Gutiérrez de Estrada, José
    María, 115–116,
    126–127

Hampton Roads conference,
    276–277, 287–288
Hard-power diplomacy, 4, 6,
    65, 81–82, 219
Hidalgo, José, 115–116,
    126–127
Hitler, Adolf, 10–11, 192
Homestead Act (1862),
    177–178, 180–181.
    See also, Circular 19
Hope, Alexander James
    Beresford Beresford,
    96–97
Horstmann, August, 165–166
Hotze, Henry, 185(quote)
    Benjamin's effort to
        "enlighten" Europe,
        190–193
    British failure to recognize
        the Confederacy, 252
    British sentiment toward
        Mason and Slidell,
        197–198
    British debate on recognition
        of the Confederacy,
        251–252
    Confederate mission to the
        Vatican, 269–270
    Confederate reaction
        to the Emancipation
        Proclamation, 249
    De Leon promoting the
        Confederate cause
        in Europe, 196–197,
        205–206
    emancipation debate, 272

European response to
    the Emancipation
    Proclamation, 241
    expanding diplomatic duties,
        258
    French stance on slavery, 209
    sacrificing slavery for
        recognition, 277
    Spence's views on slavery,
        145, 249–250, 251
    Spence's Confederate
        propaganda, 144–145
Hudson, Eduard Maco, 57
Hughes, John, 73, 77–78,
    261–262, 266–269
Hugo, Victor, 295
Hunter, Robert Mercer
    Taliaferro, 44, 46,
    113–114, 187, 191,
    273, 287
Hyde Park demonstrations,
    231–232, 236, 308

Immigrants
    Confederate accusations
        of Union profiteering,
        178–180
    De Leon's denigration of
        Union forces, 207–208
    enlistment in Garibaldi
        Guards, 170–173
    Homestead Act and Circular
        19, 176–178, 180–181
    recruitment posters,
        160–164, 161(fig.),
        162(fig.), 164(fig.)
    Union soldiers, 158–160,
        165–176
    statistics, 159, 170
Index, A Weekly Journal of
    Politics, Literature, and
    News, 192–193, 196–197,
    206
Inequality, racial, 36–37
International law, 51, 54–56,
    189, 220
Ireland and Irish immigrants,
    165–166, 171, 173–176,
    232, 266–269, 268(fig.)
Irish Brigade, 174–175
Isabella II, 110–112, 300–301
Italy
    Garibaldi's march on Rome
        upsetting plans for
        European intervention in
        America, 225–229
    Garibaldi's pressure on Victor
        Emmanuel, 22–24

Lincoln assassination, 294–295
Lincoln's diplomatic reception, 59–60
Risorgimento, 16, 22, 29, 126, 260–261, 309
Iturbide, Agustín de, 88, 94
Iturbide, Agustín de (prince), 303–304, 306

Jackson, Thomas Jonathan "Stonewall," 252
Jefferson, Thomas, 34, 36, 87–88, 282
Johnson, Andrew, 290, 301–302
Johnston, William E. *See* Malakoff
Juárez, Benito, 58, 115, 116(fig.), 119–121, 126

Kenner, Duncan F., 275, 277, 286, 289
King, Rufus, 307
Know-Nothings, 174, 186, 270

La Marseillaise, 91, 163, 172, 290
Laboulaye, Édouard René Lefèbvre de, 138–140, 139(fig.), 140–142, 157, 283, 311, 313
Lamar, L. Q. C., 253
Language, 159–165, 171–172, 209
Latin America
 Marx on slavery, 155
 restoration of imperial rule, 106–112
 revolutionary movements, 16
 Spanish and French withdrawal from, 300–306
 spread of republicanism, 88–89, 93–94
 See also Mexico; *individual states*
Latin Catholic empire, European scheme for. *See* Grand Design
Latrille de Lorencez, Charles, 123–124
Lazarus, Emma, 313
Lee, Robert E., 173, 218, 289–290
Les États-*Unis et la France* (pamphlet), 141–142

Lewis, George Cornewall, 236
Liberty Enlightening the World, 311–313
Liberty Leading the People (Delacroix), 164–165
Lincoln, Abraham, 53(fig.), 66(fig.)
 abhorrence of slavery, 216
 appeal for French youth, 2–3
 assassination of, 290–294, 296–297, 306–307
 British support for Union ideals, 149
 Canisius and, 229, 238
 Confederate "peace commission" to Washington, 38
 Confederate surrender, 290
 culmination of 'extreme democracy,' 100–101
 diplomatic appointments, 56–57
 Emancipation Proclamation, 211–218, 219, 285–286
 encouraging immigration, 179
 European diplomatic appointments, 57–60
 Garibaldi's popularity in America, 17–18
 Gettysburg Address, 9, 281–284, 281(quote)
 inaugural addresses, 51–55, 288–289
 international campaign for republicanism, 281–284
 Juárez and, 115, 116(fig.)
 Marx's response to, 155
 national and international legal stance on foreign policy, 51
 public response to the Emancipation Proclamation, 213
 reelection, 271–272
 relationship with Seward, 60–63
 response to Southern monarchism, 103–104
 reunion and reconstruction, 287–288
 San Marino's desired alliance with American republicans, 86–87
 Schurz and, 59, 213–214,

Seward's first acquaintance with, 68
 slaveowners' rights, 6
 See also Emancipation Proclamation
Lincoln, Mary Todd, 295–297
Lindsay, William, 221, 252
London Emancipation Society, 246
Louis Philippe, 90–91
Louisiana, 31, 40, 64, 101, 103, 104, 107, 141, 186, 195, 199, 200, 205, 262, 267
 seeks French aid, 274–275, 270–280
Louis-Napoleon. *See* Napoleon III
Lubbock, Francis, 233–234
Lynch, Patrick, 261, 269–270

Mackay, Charles, 48
Malakoff (*New York Times* reporter)
 American Homestead Act and Circular 19, 178
 De Leon's pamphlet on slavery, 208–209
 European reaction to the Emancipation Proclamation, 242–243
 foreign intervention in the Americas, 64
 Garibaldi's support of Union cause, 232–233
 Gasparin's republican stance, 132–133, 135–136
 international press, 72
 Laboulaye's essay, 138
 Palmerston's hatred of the Union, 97
 restoration of imperial rule in Americas, 107
 Southern monarchist leanings, 103
 student protest in Paris, 2
 the *Trent* affair, 47–48
Malespine, A., 72–73
Mann, Ambrose Dudley, 39–46, 48–49, 173, 262–266, 268–269, 277–278
Mann, Grayson, 262–264
Marsh, George Perkins, 22–23, 25, 132, 228–229, 238
Martens, Friedrich, 166
Marx, Karl, 72, 150–155, 152(fig.), 157, 242, 248

Mason, James M., 199(fig.)
British and French plan for
intervention, 221
British views on, 197–198,
253
Confederate emancipation
proposal, 272, 275–278
Hotze's *Index* finding
favor, 193
replacing Yancey in
London, 46
sacrificing slavery for
recognition, 277–279,
289
severing diplomatic relations
with Britain, 253–254,
258
Seward's public diplomacy
efforts to counter, 74
Spence's Confederate
propaganda, 144–145
the *Trent* affair, 47, 81, 114
Maximilian, 166, 286, 291
adopts heir, 303–304
chosen as emperor of Mexico,
117, 125, 126–130,
130(fig.)
execution, 305, 306(fig.)
relations with US, 301–306,
306(fig.)
welcomes Confederate
colonization, 302
Mazzini, Giuseppe, 114, 172,
175, 194, 262, 283,
294–295, 299–300
McClellan, George, 134,
159–160, 203, 211,
221, 237
McIlvaine, Charles, 75, 82
Meagher, Thomas Francis,
174–175
Mercier, Henri, 62, 65,
224–225
Mexico
allied invasion plan, 117–118,
122–126, 153–154
Blair's designs for invasion of,
286–288
Confederate alliance with
Vidaurri, 118–119
Confederate insults against,
121–122
Confederate-French alliance
strategy, 190–191,
203–205
European rule, 128–130
French invasion of, 8,
124–128

Grand Design reliance
on Southern success,
202–203
Lincoln and Seward's
diplomatic appointments,
58–59
Maximilian's dynastic
ambitions, 303–304
Napoleon's fear of Union
action, 204–205
Reform War, 114–116
response to Union victory,
303
Spanish zeal for reconquest
of, 114–115
spread of republicanism,
88–89
Union and Confederate
foreign policy,
118–120
Michelet, Jules, 108, 140
Migration
during war, 176–178. *See
also* Homestead Act;
Circular 19
European exodus after the
Napoleonic Wars, 8
Military forces
Garibaldi Guard, 170–173
immigrant soldiers, 158–160,
165–176
potential for Northern
military population
expansion, 168–169
Military population, 168,
Mill, John Stuart, 81
Miltenberger, Ernest, 274–275,
280
Mississippi, secession
declaration, 30–31
Monadnock (*New York Times*
reporter), 72, 97–98,
235, 241
Monarchy
British attempt to limit
republicanism in Latin
America, 94–95
Confederate monarchist
leanings, 101–105
Confederate sympathies
with Latin America's
restoration of, 9, 94–95
European perception of the
Union, 6
Gettysburg Address,
283–284
Mexican monarchist
experiment, 126, 301–302

Monroe Doctrine, 94–95, 107,
111, 113, 122, 127, 186,
204, 288, 302, 308
*The Moral and Intellectual
Diversity of Races*
(Gobineau), 191–192
Moran, Benjamin, 56
Morehead, Charles S.,
261–262
Morny, Charles Morny, Duc de,
117, 201–202, 279–280
Morrill Tariff (1861), 42–43,
146
Motives for secession and
war, 35–37, 131–132.
See also Republicanism;
Self-government; Slavery
Motley, John Lothrop, 129,
148, 310–311

Nanglo, George, 158–159
Napoleon I, 90, 92, 141
Napoleon III
allied invasion of Mexico,
124–130, 304
Bigelow-Scott letter of
conciliation, 77–78
Blair's designs on Mexico,
286
Confederate emancipation,
278
coup d'état (1851), 92
European republican
resurgence, 309
French rejoicing over
American civil conflict, 99
French support for the
South, 200
Garibaldi's support of
Union, 233
Garibaldi's march on
Rome, 226
Grand Design, 8–9,
107–109, 126–128, 186,
190, 202, 252, 304
Maximilian's execution,
305–306
Maximilian's withdrawal
from Mexico, 304–305
Pius IX, 16, 92, 226, 260,
262, 263, 309
response to Union victory,
303
Risorgimento, 260
Slidell's meeting with,
203–204
Southern monarchism, 104
Spanish connection, 116

Nationalist independence movements, 28–32, 34–35

Naval forces, 38, 47, 106–107, 170, 203–204, 220–221, 225, 235–236, 255, 300

Nélaton, Auguste, 227, 228(fig.), 233

Neutrality, 43, 220–221, 234–237, 246

New Orleans, 159, 199, 200, 206, 261

Nicholls, George. See Monadnock

Nott, Josiah, 191–192

Obama, Barack, 87

O'Donnell, Leopoldo, 111

Orléanists, 133–134

Pakington, John, 95–96

Palmerston, Henry John Temple, Lord
backing away from intervention, 234–236
British and French plan for intervention, 219–223
Confederate plan to sacrifice slavery for recognition, 279
death of, 308
distrust of democracy, 41–42
Emancipation Proclamation, 246
motives for neutrality, 190
rejoicing over Union losses, 96–97
threat of British war, 76
Trent affair, 49

Pecquet du Bellet, Paul, 208–209

Pelletan, Eugène, 9–10, 296

Perry, Horatio J., 112–113

Persigny, Jean Gilbert Victor Fialin, duc de, 201–203

Phrygian cap (liberty cap), 91, 109, 163, 164, 183, 308

Pickett, John T., 120–122

Pierce, Franklin, 194

Pius IX, 263(fig.)
antipathy to Garibaldi, 17, 114
Confederate effort to win recognition from, 257–270
Davis and, 306
Garibaldi's support of Union cause, 231–232

Garibaldi's march on Rome, 226
imprisonment, 309
letter to Jefferson Davis, 265–266, 268–269
Mann's meeting with, 163–165
Mexico's Reforma, 114–115
Napoleon III's coup d'état, 92
Napoleon III's Grand Design, 9
plea for peace, 261–266
Risorgimento, 260–261
slavery concerns, 257–258, 264, 269

Polignac, Camille de, 274–275, 279–280, 289

Polish uprising, 237

Polygenesis, theory of, 36–37, 191–192

Popular government, See Republicanism; Democracy; Self-government

Press
Assing and Douglass's antislavery writings, 156–157
British denunciation of American republicanism, 96–97
British pro-South factions, 143
British retreat from intervention, 235–236
Confederate emancipation, 272–274
De Leon promoting the Confederate cause abroad, 193–197, 205–209
Emancipation Proclamation, 241–243, 245
European invasion of Mexico, 118
European opinion on the American republican experiment, 99, 138–139, 141–142
foreign correspondents, 72, 150, 156
Garibaldi-Union relations, 26
Hotze's Confederate propaganda abroad, 192–193
influencing public opinion among European readers, 3–4

Marx and, 151–155
Napoleon III's Grand Design, 109
Pius IX's plea for peace, 262
response to Gasparin's book, 136–137
revealing Spence's Confederate connection, 251
shaping diplomacy by influencing public opinion, 72–73
Southern monarchism, 102–103
Spain's imperial designs on Latin America, 112
See also Malakoff; Marx; Monadnock; Russell, William Howard

Preston, William, 57, 112–113

Prim, Juan, 122–123, 300–301

Provisional government, 31–32

Prussia, 92, 173, 212, 303, 309–310

Public diplomacy, 3–5, 17, 24, 37, 58–59, 69, 82, 127, 177, 188
Benjamin launches Confederate program, 186, 191. See also, Hotze, Henry; De Leon, Edwin
Seward launches Union program, 70–77. See also, Bigelow, John; Sanford, Henry
Weed, Hughes, McIlvaine mission, 78–81

Public opinion
Benjamin's European "enlightenment" about the South, 190–191
British shift towards emancipation, 245–249
De Leon's French campaign for the South, 205–209
declining European support for the South, 259–260
emancipation as the goal of the war, 69–71, 213–214
European sympathy with secessionists, 138
French admiration for republicanism, 132–135
French opinion of the American experiment, 138–142
Garibaldi's support of Union cause, 230–231

Public opinion (*continued*)
Palmerston on, 42, 226
tension between slavery and
emancipation, 132

Quakers, 146–147, 245
Quiggle, James W., 19–24, 26,
159, 229
Quintero, Agustín, 119

Race
black soldiers in the Union
army, 168
Stephens's Cornerstone
Speech on racial
inequality, 36
Race theory, 36, 144, 191–192
Race war, threats of, 6, 30, 31,
217, 211, 241
Ramsden, John, 97–98
Rattazzi, Urbano, 227
Raymond, Henry J., 63–64
Recognition of the
Confederacy, 44–46,
188–191, 204–205,
219–225, 251–252
Reconstruction, 300
Recruitment of immigrant
soldiers, 160–164,
177–178
Red republicans, 91, 163, 207,
209, 228–229
Red Shirts, 16, 92, 211,
225–229
Reform Act (1832; Britain),
41–42
Reform League (Britain), 308
Reform War (1858–1861,
Mexico), 114–116
La Reforma, 114–115
Republicanism
British opposition to Latin
America, 94–95
Cuba's independence
movement, 301
European experiments with,
86–93
European perception of the
Union and Confederacy,
6–7
France and, 89–90, 91–92,
163, 309
Latin America, 88, 93–94
origins and spread of,
87–93
slavery and, 88–89
threat of US-British war, 77
Union triumph, 299–300

United States as model for,
9–10, 95–97
Universal Republican
Alliance, 299–300
Reunion and reconstruction,
287–288, 300
Revolution, Age of, 85–93
Revolution of 1848, 91–93,
93(fig.), 128, 150, 156,
173, 175, 212, 215, 229
Rhett, Robert Barnwell, 30,
38–40
Risorgimento (Italy), 16, 22,
29, 126, 309
Roebuck, John Arthur, 252–253
Roman, Andre, 37–38
Romero, Matías, 127, 128(fig.),
129–130, 302
Rost, Pierre, 39–45, 49, 113
Russell, John, Earl Russell
backing away from
intervention, 234
British and French plan for
intervention, 219–223
Confederate bid for British
recognition, 43, 45–46
Confederates severing
diplomatic ties with
Britain, 258
diplomatic coolness towards
the South, 253
distrust of democracy, 41–42
Hotze's *Index* finding favor,
193
Mason, 198
prolonging the war, 97
threat of US-British war, 42,
79–81
Russell, William Howard,
59–60, 72, 85(quote), 86,
96, 100–101, 101(fig.),
102, 136–137
Russia
British-French plan for
intervention, 220,
222–223, 234
sale of Alaska, 308

Salomon, Frederick, 92, 93(fig.),
173
San Marino, Most Serene
Republic of, 86–87
Sanders, George, 246
Sanford, Henry Shelton, 18(fig.)
antislavery crusade in
England, 69–70
Bigelow-Scott letter of
conciliation, 77–78

countering pro-Confederacy
diplomatic appointments,
57
Garibaldi and, 15–16,
20–24, 233
immigrant soldiers, 158–159
public diplomacy, 3, 69,
72–73
Quiggle's invitation to
Garibaldi, 21–22
secret service operations,
72–73
Santana, Pedro, 110–111
Santo Domingo, 109–112, 300
Schurz, Carl, 69–70, 110, 123,
212–214, 218, 244
Scott, Winfield, 73–74, 76–77
Secession
British-French plan for
intervention, 219–223
legal arguments, 6, 29, 50,
54–55, 65, 211
Lincoln and Seward's foreign
policy strategy, 65
Lincoln's inaugural address,
54–55
Second Confiscation Act
(1862), 217
Self-government
Confederate motives for
war, 29
Confederate soft-power
diplomacy, 5–6
resilience of, 1–3
the republican experiment,
7–8
Separatist rebellions,
justification for, 27–29
Seward, William Henry,
50(quote), 66(fig.)
Alaska purchase, 308
background influencing
foreign policy, 67–69
British and French plan for
intervention, 219–223
British working people's
support for the Union,
247
Canisius's invitation to
Garibaldi, 230–233, 238
Confederate cultivation
of Spanish sympathy,
112–113
Confederate "peace
commission" to
Washington, 38
Dayton's controversial death,
297–298

diplomatic missions to
  Europe, 56–59, 73–78
Emancipation Proclamation,
  211–219, 243–244
European experiment in
  Mexico, 304
European perception
  of abolition as cause of
  war, 70
European restoration of
  imperial rule, 107
foreign policy, 55–57,
  61–65, 67–69
Garibaldi's connection,
  17–18, 20–21, 23–24, 26
Homestead Act and Circular
  19, 177–178, 180–181
ideological motives for war,
  131–132
Lincoln assassination, 290
Lincoln's ideological clash
  with, 281–282
Lincoln's inaugural address,
  53–54
Mann's arrival in
  Washington, 40
North-South peace
  negotiation, 286
preserving slavery, 6
recruitment of foreign
  soldiers, 161–162
response to Confederate
  claims and justifications,
  50–51
reunion and reconstruction,
  287–288
San Marino's American
  alliance, 87
slavery, 67–69, 217–218
the Trent affair, 47–48
Union alliance with French
  red republicans, 209
Union-Mexican alliance, 302
working relationship with
  Lincoln, 60–63
See also, Democracy;
  Republicanism
Sheridan, Philip, 302
Slavery
arming Southern slaves,
  270–271
Brazil's abolition, 301
Britain's role in introducing,
  45
British anti-slavery faction,
  147–148
British pro-South faction,
  144–145

Catholic clergy and, 270
Confederate dreams of
  eternal perpetuation, 10
Confederate emancipation,
  271–280
Confederate hopes of a
  Spanish alliance, 113–114
Confederate states' secession
  declarations, 30–31
Cuba's emancipation, 301
De Leon's efforts to educate
  the French, 207–209
Emancipation Proclamation
  legitimizing the Union
  cause, 211–216
European public opinion,
  4–5, 187, 189–191, 202
expansion abroad, 10
former slaves as Union
  soldiers, 168
French opinion on the
  American experiment,
  138–139
Garibaldi's questions about
  Union policies, 20,
  24–26
incompatibility with
  republicanism, 88–89
increasing support for the
  Union cause abroad,
  210–211
Lincoln and Seward's foreign
  policy, 61–62, 65–67
Lincoln's inaugural addresses,
  55, 288–289
Marx's view of, 155
North-South distinctions
  over, 240–241
Pius IX's concerns over,
  269–270
Seward's background
  influencing foreign policy,
  67–69
South Carolina's Declaration
  of Immediate Causes, 30
Spence's views, 145,
  249–250, 251
Statue of Liberty, 313
Stephens's Cornerstone
  Speech, 36
Thirteenth Amendment, 288
See also Emancipation
  Proclamation
Slidell, John, 201 (fig.)
British sentiment towards,
  197–198
Confederate emancipation
  proposal, 275–278, 289

Confederate mission to the
  Vatican, 261–262
cotton bribe to France,
  250–251
De Leon's resentment of, 195
diplomatic efforts in France,
  46, 186, 199–205
emancipation proposal,
  276–277
foreign-born Union soldiers,
  169–170
hostility towards De Leon,
  254–256
Napoleon III meetings, 200,
  203–205, 223, 252,
  254, 278
sacrificing slavery for
  recognition, 277–278, 289
Seward's public diplomacy
  efforts to counter, 74
the Trent affair, 47, 114
threat of US-British war, 81
waning popularity of the
  South in Europe,
  258–260
Smart power, 4
Smith, Goldwin, 283
Smolinski, Joseph, 162–163
Socialism, 91, 100, 157
Soft-power diplomacy, 4
Soret, Henri, 99
South Carolina, 30, 101–102
Sovereignty
Britain's Proclamation of
  Neutrality, 43
Confederates' desire for
  recognition, 28
international debate over the
  American question, 77
Jefferson's Enlightenment
  ideals, 87–88
Spain
as potential Confederate ally,
  112–114, 122–128
Confederate trade relations,
  38–39
Davis's expansion of
  diplomatic efforts in
  Europe, 46–47
Lincoln and Seward's
  diplomatic appointments,
  58
Lincoln and Seward's
  response to Spanish
  aggression in the New
  World, 65
rejoicing over American civil
  conflict, 99

Spain (*continued*)
restoration of imperial rule in Latin America, 106–107, 109–112
Schurz in, 59, 69–70, 110, 123, 212–213
Tripartite Alliance, 117–118, 122, 202
withdrawal from Latin America, 300–301
Spanish American republics, 29
Spence, James, 100, 143–145, 157, 206, 249–251
Spurgeon, Charles, 247
Stanton, Elizabeth Cady, 285
Statue of Liberty, 311–313
Stephens, Alexander, 35–37, 89, 137, 287–288
Stevens, Thaddeus, 285
Stevenson, Sarah Yorke, 303
Stoeckl, Eduard, 62
Suffrage, 90–91, 103–104, 145–146
Sumner, Charles, 137, 148–149, 283
Surratt, John, 307
Surratt, Mary, 307
Swain, James, 64
Swann, William G., 253

Tariff. *See* Morrill Tariff; Free trade
Ten Years' War (Cuba), 301
Tennent, James Emerson, 79
Thirteenth Amendment proposal, 55, 285, 287, 288
Thouvenel, Édouard, 78, 202, 223–225, 233
Tocqueville, Alexis de, 95, 144
Toombs, Robert, 27(quote), 38, 44, 113, 119, 187, 280

Trade relations
Confederate bribe to France, 203–204
Confederate mission to Europe, 38–41
Confederate view of the beneficial effects of slavery, 45–46
Trent affair, 47–48, 76, 78–81, 114, 117, 137, 145, 147–148, 154, 190, 197–198
Tripartite Alliance, 117–118, 122–124, 153–154, 202
Tuckerman, Henry, 17–18
Two sous' subscription, 295–296

Union
British support for, 145–150
Canada and, 307–308
casualties, 167
enlistment of black soldiers, 168, 217–218
European republican resurgence, 308–309
Homestead Act and Circular 19, 176–178, 180–181
immigrant soldiers, 158–160, 165–167, 170–176
Marx's advocacy for, 150–155
Mexican foreign policy, 120–121
military victory, 218–219
public diplomacy, 3–4, 69, 72–76
response to French rule in Mexico, 129–130
the *Trent* affair, 47–49, 76
See also Adams, Charles Francis; Bigelow, John; Dayton, William;

Emancipation Proclamation; Garibaldi, Giuseppe; Lincoln, Abraham; Marsh, George Perkins; Sanford, Henry; Seward, William Henry; Slavery
The Uprising of a Great People (Gasparin), 135–137

Vichy meeting, 203–205, 207, 223–224
Victor Emmanuel II, 22–23
Vidaurri Valdez, José Santiago, 118–120
Voting rights, 90–91, 103–104, 145–146

Weed, Thurlow, 47–48, 63, 68, 73, 76–81, 79(fig.), 198
Weld, Angelina Grimké, 285
Welles, Gideon, 217
Welsh, Peter, 165
Weydemeyer, Joseph, 151–152
Whitman, Walt, 8, 52, 292
Wilkes, Charles, 47
Women
Butler's "woman's order," 206, 220
Garibaldi Guard, 171
suffrage, 90, 156, 285
Thirteenth Amendment, 285
Women's National Loyal League, 166, 285

Yancey, William, 39–48, 113, 154, 187
Young Italy movement, 194, 283
Young Ireland movement, 175

Zaragoza, Ignacio, 124
Zouave forces, 163